This is my body

Luther's Contention for the Real Presence in the Sacrament of the Altar

BY HERMANN SASSE

Chi Rho
Lutheran Publishing House,
205 Halifax Street, Adelaide, S.A.

Revised Australian edition published March 1977.

ISBN 0 85910 034 0

Preface

The first draft of this book was finished in 1954 and offered to Augsburg Publishing House, Minneapolis, Minnesota, which had adopted and taken care of the author's orphaned *Here We Stand* at a time when communication between Germany and the U.S.A. was not yet possible. In 1955 the Publication Board of the Evangelical Lutheran Church accepted the manuscript. However, the desire was expressed for the insertion of material from previous publications on the same subject in German,* which were out of print and could not be printed again under conditions prevailing in the post-war years. This suggestion was agreed upon, though it meant not only an enlargement of the size of the book, but also structural changes that might interfere with the laws of literary architecture. As it now appears, the book represents not only studies made for more than twenty years, but in its inadequacies and deficiencies (of which no one is more aware than the author) it reveals something of the destiny of a generation in many a Lutheran church whose theological work was interrupted and disturbed by ten years of wars, to say nothing of what followed or preceded these wars.

At first sight, it might have seemed easier for the author, and most certainly more pleasant for the reader, if this book could have been written in German and then put into good English by an able translator, such as I always had the good fortune to find in America and England. For several reasons this was not possible. In the first place, the Marburg Colloquy needed reconstruction in English. W. Koehler's masterly German reconstruction, with its attempt to render the original mode of speech, cannot be simply translated. Nor could it be used for theological discussion without constant reference to the sources. Thus a new version had to be made, the first draft of which I tried out at seminars held with my students at Immanuel Theological Seminary, North Adelaide. On the basis of these experiences, and continuous re-examinations of the sources and earlier

*Mainly *Kirche und Herrenmahl* (1938) and *Vom Sakrament des Altars* (1941).

reconstructions from Hospinian to Rade and Koehler, and especially an evaluation of Koehler's results, I have tried to improve the text until it has reached the present form.

For permission to make such use of Koehler's publications I desire to express gratitude to Professor Heinrich Bornkamm at Heidelberg, the faithful literary executor of his great predecessor's theological life-work. Documents and other texts of the time of the Reformation have been quoted from translations already available (*Concordia Triglotta, Luther's Correspondence* by Smith-Jacobs, S. M. Jackson's work on Zwingli). Some very important texts are contained in M. Reu's book on the Augsburg Confession. My source is acknowledged in each case. I want to thank particularly Professor J. Bodensieck, Dubuque, for the kind permission to make use of his translations in the book by M. Reu.

If, then, a major part of the present book had to be written in English to begin with, then it seemed advisable to think and to write all of it in this language, even at the risk of linguistic deficiencies. That these have been limited to an inevitable minimum, as I hope, is due to the assistance given by Professor Walter Engelhardt of Concordia College, St Paul, Minn. He deserves the thanks not only of the author, but also of the readers, for the unselfish, painstaking service of going over the entire manuscript and improving its style. My very special thanks are naturally due to those who have made possible this publication, to the Publication Board of the Evangelical Lutheran Church, as well as to the Augsburg Publishing House, Minneapolis, and its General Manager, Dr R. E. Haugan. They did not eschew the venture of bringing out a monograph that presented some particularly difficult editorial problems. These difficulties were overcome by the experienced and efficient staff of the Publishing House.

A very special tribute is due to the Manuscript Editor, Mr Paul T. Martinsen, who with never-failing patience carried the burdens created by the fact that publisher and author were separated by thousands of miles. Without mentioning names I want to thank also my friends in America, Germany and Australia who have been helping me in many ways to finish this book.

The long distance separating (even in this age of a shrinking globe) Australia from America and Europe presented difficulties also to the author. They were not so much in the field of sources and literature, for the great Australian libraries are well equipped, and they provide a friendly and even generous service. Practically all the great collections of sources are available with the exception of the old (Schuler-Schulthess) and the new edition of Zwingli's works (*Corpus Reformatorum*). Thus I had to rely on the older editions (*St Louis Edition of Luther's Works,* R. Christoffel) and translations (S.M. Jackson) of individual writings of the Swiss Reformer, on my own collections, and, in very few cases, on quotations from Koehler. The beautiful volumes of the *Hauptschriften* (Zwingli Verlag, Zurich) arrived when the manuscript was finished; as did also some other books, like the second edition of Hans Grass, *Die Abendmahlslehre bei Luther und Calvin.* This valuable book is quoted here from the first edition, which creates no difficulties as the text of the passages referred to has remained unaltered. The greatest problem was posed by the fact that I could read only one set of proofs. All quotations have been verified several times by the author. We did our best to fight that strange devil who can be fought only with the ink-well, but who has such an infamous way of retaliating with the same weapon. If some misprints should have crept in, as they probably have, they may be pardoned, as also some discrepancies in the form of quotations and in the spelling of names with the German *Umlaut*.

Scope and nature of this book are described in the Introduction. As some years have elapsed since this was written, a word may be in place as to the discussions on the Lord's Supper that have been going on during these years. It seems that we are experiencing a resumption of the eucharistic discussions of the 16th century on a world-wide ecumenical scale. Two significant documents deserve our special attention. The first is the statement agreed upon by the Lutheran and the Reformed *(Hervormde)* Churches in Holland, intended to serve as the theological basis of the intercommunion that has already been practised for a long time. It has grown out of the theological discussions on the Continent, especially in Germany (see below p 9), and may be destined to play a role also in other countries. It should not be regarded as a doctrinal agreement in the proper sense, for the passage which deals with the decisive difference reads as follows: 'Both churches confess that Christ in and by the Sacrament is truly present. The Lutherans ask the Calvinists whether and in what measure they can vindicate . . . answer 47 of the *Heidelberg Catechism* ("Christ is true Man and true God; according to His human nature He is now not on earth, but according to His Godhead, majesty, grace and Spirit He is at no time absent from us"). The Calvinists ask the Lutherans whether an omnipresence of the human nature of Christ does not actually mean the annulment of the incarnation. Both churches, therefore, believe that the doctrine of the Lord's Supper must once more be thought through theologically' (quoted from the text given in *Concordia Theological Monthly,* January 1957, 65, 66). This leaves the question open. For the conservative Reformed (*Gereformeerde*) Church in the Netherlands, Professor G. C. Berkouwer, perhaps the greatest living scholar in the field of the theology of the sacraments in the Reformed world (see his new book *Dogmatische Studien. De Sacramenten,* 1954) has replied to the question addressed to the Calvinists in the negative.

The other document is the statement, 'The Table of the Lord', Report of Section IV at the Oberlin Conference of the Commission on Faith and Order of the World Council of Churches, the decisive passage of which reads: 'Jesus Christ on the night in which He was betrayed chose bread and wine as the elements for the first Eucharist at the Last Supper. Rejecting any one-sided preoccupation with the elements in isolation, we agree that in the entire eucharistic action the whole Christ is personally present as both subject and object, i.e., as the One who is at the same time the Giver of the Gift.' What does 'one-sided preoccupation with the elements in isolation' mean? Who is guilty of such 'preoccupation'? Luther most certainly not. Neither could it be said of Aquinas, the author of *Adoro te devote* and *Lauda Sion,* which render his eucharistic doctrine most faithfully. Would the authors of the statement of Oberlin find such 'preoccupation' in the Eastern liturgy or in the Roman mass, in *Gott sei gelobet und gebenedeiet* or in the *Ave verum* ? If so, then they must find it also with St Paul, and even with our Lord himself. For it was he who first spoke of eating his flesh and drinking his blood, and who said: 'Take, eat, this is my body'. Most certainly he is present in the entire eucharistic action. However, it is not enough to say 'that this action is our participation in His risen life', if Paul speaks clearly of the bread and the cup being the communion or partaking of Christ's body and blood.

This statement, too, avoids answering the crucial question as to how the eucharistic words of the New Testament are to be understood. We are fully aware of the necessity of a thorough theological discussion of the Lord's Supper in the light of a sound exegesis of the New Testament after modern scholarship has opened new horizons to all churches. Every church is today confronted with the problem of the Sacrament. It is most significant that even Pope Pius XII had to take issue with Roman Catholic theologians who argued 'that the doctrine of transubstantiation ought to be revised depending as it does on a conception of substance which is now out of date' (*Humani Generis,* 1950, quoted from the translation by R. Knox, see below p 34).

With gratitude we take cognizance of the remarkable fact that even the Ecumenical Movement begins to give up the modern Anglican view that it is enough to celebrate the Sacrament, leaving its doctrinal understanding to the private judgment of the individual minister or member of the church. Every Lutheran theologian will be prepared to make his contribution to a serious discussion, knowing that also his church needs a rethinking of its doctrine. But what we need is a **serious** discussion, based on solid knowledge of the problems.

In writing this book I have been thinking of former students, colleagues, and friends in the English-speaking world, in the United States of America, in Canada, South Africa, and Australia. I am mindful of the entire Church of the Augsburg Confession in these countries, which still confesses, with heart and mouth, in word and deed, the faith of the Fathers, not because it is our Fathers' faith, but because it is the faith of the New Testament.

HERMANN SASSE

Adelaide, South Australia,
on the Day of St Augustine
August 28, 1958

ABBREVIATIONS

Bek. Schr.	*Die Bekenntnisschriften der evangelisch-lutherischen Kirche, herausgegeben im Gedenkjahr der Augsburgischen Konfession 1930, 3. Auflage* (1956)
CR	*Corpus Reformatorum*
CSEL	*Corpus Scriptorum Ecclesiasticorum Latinorum* (Vienna)
Denz	*Denzinger-Umberg, Enchiridion Symbolorum, Definitionum et Declarationum, Editio 27* (1951)
EA	*Luthers sämmtliche Werke, Erlanger Ausgabe*
Enders	*Luthers Briefwechsel*
GCS	*Die Griechischen Christlichen Schriftsteller der ersten drei Jahrhunderte* (Berlin)
MPG	*Migne, Patrologiae Cursus Completus, Series Graeca*
MPL	*Migne, Patrologiae Cursus Completus, Series Latina*
Philad.	*Works of Martin Luther* (Philadelphia: Holman, 1915-31)
PRE	*Realenzyklopädie für protestantische Theologie und Kirche, 3. Auflage*
RGG	*Die Religion in Geschichte und Gegenwart, 2. Auflage*
St. Louis	*Dr Martin Luthers sämmtliche Schriften, hrsg. von Walch, Revidierte Neuausgabe* (St Louis: Concordia Publishing House 1880-1910)
Trigl.	*Concordia Triglotta* (St Louis: Concordia Publishing House 1921)
WA	*Luthers Werke, Weimarer Ausgabe*
WA BR	*Weimarer Ausgabe, Briefe*
WA TR	*Weimarer Ausgabe, Tischreden*

PREFACE TO THE REVISED EDITION

The original edition of *This Is My Body* has been out of print for a considerable number of years, and many conservative Lutheran pastors, seminary students, and others have urged its reprinting. In the current ecumenical climate, such a venture may be considered rather courageous. However, Lutheran Publishing House agreed to provide this service for the Christian world, and negotiated with Augsburg Publishing House for the necessary publication rights. We are grateful for Augsburg's immediate goodwill and warm interest, and for their generous agreement and cooperation with our proposals.

This is a revised edition of the work first published in 1958, not a mere reprint. In addition to evident changes in layout, the original manuscript was improved in wording here and there, and various necessary corrections have been made. It was also the author's plan to amplify this by a second preface and by an epilogue after Chapter 7, in which he wished to comment on trends and developments in the area of the Eucharist since he penned the original manuscript in 1954. However, on August 9, 1976, God in his unsearchable wisdom suddenly called Hermann Sasse from his life before these additions had been put to paper.

In place of the planned epilogue, we have reprinted two appropriate, fairly-recent articles which appeared in the *Lutheran Theological Journal.*

We gratefully dedicate this edition to the memory of the late author, widely-known scholar, and also confessor of the truth as it is in Christ Jesus.

THE PUBLISHERS

Contents

Introduction

'As often as ye eat this bread and drink this cup, ye do shew the Lord's death till he come.' These words, added to our oldest written report of an event in the life of Jesus (his Last Supper), and of words spoken by him (the Words of Institution), are the first commentary on the Sacrament of the Altar. Whether this commentary (1 Cor. 11:26) was framed by St Paul himself, or whether it belongs to the oral tradition which he 'received' and faithfully 'delivered' to the church of Corinth (v 23) when he founded it in AD50, makes no difference.[1] In either case, the New Testament testifies to the close connection between the Lord's Supper and the Gospel. The Gospel is the glad tidings of the incarnation of the Son of God, his atoning death for us, his resurrection from the dead, his ascension into heaven, his session at the right hand of God the Father Almighty, from whence he shall come to judge the living and the dead. It was Christ's will that this Gospel should be preached to all nations until the end of the world. But the Gospel was to be not only a message of what had happened in the past and what was going to happen in the future; the proclamation of the message was to be accompanied by the celebration of that Sacrament, which in itself was a showing of the Lord's death till he come. Without this Sacrament the Gospel might be understood as one of the many religious messages in the world. Without the proclamation of the Gospel this Sacrament might be understood as one of the many religious rites in the world. But the Gospel is more than a religious message, and the Sacrament more than a religious ceremony. Both the Gospel and the Sacrament contain one and the same gift, forgiveness of sins — not only a message that there is forgiveness, and not only a ceremony which would illustrate that message, but rather the forgiveness itself, which no one can give except him who died as the Lamb of God for the sins of the world, who will come again in glory, and who is present in his Gospel and his Sacrament.

[1] See the discussion of the New Testament questions in chapter VII.

This close connection between the proclamation of the Gospel and the Sacrament of the Altar explains the fact that at all times the Eucharist has been the centre of the church's worship and life. At the Lord's Table the church has been gathering since the days of the apostles. There, at Holy Communion, it experiences the 'communion of saints'. There it is one in the unity of the one body and one Spirit in the bond of peace, each member partaking of the one bread which is the body of Christ. Church-fellowship has been altar-fellowship from the beginning of the church, no unbaptized person being admitted to the solemn assembly where the people of God meet their Saviour and Lord. Even the outward organization and the external activities of the church have been connected with this Sacrament. The officers of the earliest congregations, bishops and deacons, were the persons officiating at the Eucharist. The Christians laid their gifts on the Lord's Table, and the deacons brought the gifts of love from the altar to the sick and poor. Thus, this Sacrament was in every respect the life of the church. It was never to be separated from the Gospel. The church of the first centuries was the church of the Eucharist. A Sunday, a Lord's Day, was unthinkable without the Lord's Supper. But if ever the church was a preaching church, the church of the apostles and the Church Fathers was. The same is true of all great periods of the church. The Sacrament and the sermon belong together, and it is always a sign of the decay of the church if one is emphasized at the expense of the other.

If the Sacrament of the Altar occupies such a central position in the church, it is easily understood why it has become, time and again, the subject of dissension and controversy. Every disease of the church becomes manifest at the Lord's Table. The schisms and heresies, for instance, against which Paul had to fight in the church of Corinth seem to have become noticeable first in the celebration of the Lord's Supper.[2] It is noteworthy that these schisms, and the decay of the Sacrament connected with them, caused the apostle to speak on this subject (which he does not discuss in any other epistle, though he silently presupposes it wherever he speaks of the unity or the disunity of the church). Thus, the controversies over the Lord's Supper, which so often provoked the criticism of Christians and non-Christians—Holy Communion having become the cause of unholy **dis**union — go back to the time of the New Testament. Thé reason for such controversies may be found in a lack of love, as seems to have been

[2] 1 Cor. 11:17-22; see also 1:10-17.

the case at Corinth.[3] But it may be found also in the fact that every dissension concerning the Gospel necessarily expresses itself in a dissension over the Lord's Supper. Just as Christ's Church becomes conscious of its own nature as it gathers around the Lord's Table, so its weaknesses, errors, and sins also become manifest on that occasion. Each misunderstanding of the Gospel must needs lead to a misunderstanding of the Sacrament; each misunderstanding of the Sacrament is bound to lead to a wrong concept of the Gospel. If this rule applies to the church even in the apostolic age, we shall not be surprised to see the controversies over the Lord's Supper, like the controversies over the Gospel, accompany the entire history of the church.

It is not within the purpose of this book to relate even briefly the whole history of these controversies, or to discuss all doctrinal problems which have arisen in connection with this Sacrament. Our purpose is rather to describe and to make understandable, against the background of the preceding history and of the history of the whole Reformation, Luther's fight for the Real Presence. To understand this fight means to understand the origin and the meaning of the Lutheran doctrine on the Sacrament of the Altar.

It was to be expected that a reformation of the church, as it was longed for by all serious Christians at the end of the Middle Ages, would lead to grave controversies not only over the Gospel, but also over the Sacrament, especially since the Lord's Supper had been the object of controversies, and even the cause of splits, in Western Christendom for a hundred years before Luther's Reformation began. Regret has often been expressed that such controversies broke out even among those who had been excommunicated from the Roman church, and thus were compelled to build up their own churches. We shall later see why this was inevitable. Whatever one may think of the controversy out of which the Lutheran and the Reformed churches have grown, with whichever side one may sympathize (for to be quite neutral has been impossible even for the great historians), everybody will admit that the controversy between Luther and Zwingli is one of the greatest events in the history of Christendom, an event the results of which have deeply influenced even the political and cultural development of Europe. This controversy, therefore, with the Marburg Colloquy as its climax, will form the main part of this book. It was this colloquy that decided the

---

[3] Compare these passages on the schisms with 1 Cor. 13 and 16:22.

history of Protestantism for centuries, for the controversies and colloquies that followed Marburg in the 16th and 17th centuries (after Calvin and Calvinism had taken up and developed the heritage of Zwingli, and Melanchthon and his school had tried to pave the way for a union that could not be attained during Martin Luther's lifetime) were not able to alter the decision of Marburg. The attempts of 18th century Pietism and Rationalism, and of the unions of the 19th century, to declare the old antagonism obsolete and no longer touching the real life of the church, also failed.

Even the modern ecumenical movement, which in many parts of Christendom has more or less wiped out the borderlines between the old confessional churches, has not been able to overcome the old antagonisms concerning the Lord's Supper and the Real Presence. On the contrary, modern biblical scholarship as well as the great Liturgical Movement, which in our time is penetrating all churches from Rome to the most outspoken Protestant denominations, is confronting all Christendom again with the problem of the Sacraments. What is a sacrament, especially the Sacrament of the Altar, according to the New Testament? What has the church since the days of the apostles meant when speaking of the Real Presence of the body and blood of Christ? These are questions that each church has to answer again today. Their discussion should not and, obviously, cannot be a mere repetition of the debates of 16th and 17th centuries. Nor can we discuss those questions as if they had never been discussed before us. We could, of course, make the New Testament the starting-point of our discussions. But we would soon find out that no living Christian can read the New Testament without remembering the catechism in which he has been brought up. The Scriptures must be the final authority for our acceptance or non-acceptance of this or that understanding of the Sacrament; our final doctrine on the Lord's Supper will be taken from and based on them. But we cannot forget that this Sacrament has been celebrated for 1,900 years, and that the greatest thinkers of Christendom have meditated on the words which our Lord spoke at his Last Supper. A really new and profitable discussion of the mystery of this Sacrament must be based, not on dark reminiscences or even denominational prejudices, but on a real knowledge of what was said, and why it was said, at the time of the Reformation. This knowledge must comprise not only the understanding of the various Protestant doctrines and attitudes, but also an understanding of what the Roman church actually teaches on this Sacrament. Irreconcilable as the various ideas of Roman Catholics, Anglicans, Lutherans, Reformed, and other Christians may be, they all have the same background, namely, the history of more than a thousand years which the Sacrament of the Altar had in Western Christendom before the Reformation, a thousand years which again were preceded by a five-hundred-year history of this Sacrament in the Ancient Church, Eastern and Western.

To write a history of the Sacrament of the Altar in its various aspects—doctrinal, liturgical, ecclesiastical—from the New Testament time till today, would be an enterprise transcending the abilities of any individual church historian.[4] We shall be satisfied here to give an outline of the common medieval background, before we speak of Luther, Zwingli, and the controversy that led to the Marburg Colloquy. This colloquy we shall present in an English translation, based on the texts contained in the *Weimar Edition of Luther's Works* (WA XXX, part 3), and on the masterly attempt by Walther Koehler to combine the sources and to reconstruct the colloquy.[5] Although our text is not a translation of Koehler's German version, and although in some points we deviate from his order, it may be said from the outset that the present book does not claim to compete with the works of Koehler, to whose life-long research on Zwingli and his relation to Luther our generation owes the detailed knowledge of the Marburg Colloquy and the controversies and negotiations which preceded and followed that great debate. We can only gratefully acknowledge what present-day church history has learned, and still has to learn, from the amazing

---

[4] The most complete work on the doctrinal side is the excellent book by Darwell Stone, *A History of the Doctrine of the Holy Eucharist* (two volumes, London, 1909). The most interesting work on the liturgical aspect is *The Shape of the Liturgy* by Gregory Dix (1945).

[5] Walther Koehler, *Zwingli und Luther. Ihr Streit über das Abendmahl nach seinen politischen und religiösen Beziehungen.* Vol.I: *Die religiöse und politische Entwicklung bis zum Marburger Religionsgespräch* 1529 (1924); Vol. II: *Vom Beginn der Marburger Verhandlungen 1929 bis zum Abschluss der Wittenberger Konkordie 1536* (1953)—Idem, *Das Marburger Religionsgespräch 1529, Versuch einer Rekonstruktion* (1929). Idem, *Huldrych Zwingli* (1943), especially 191-219. G. J. Beto, 'The Marburg Colloquy of 1929. Textual Study', *Concordia Theological Monthly* (Feb. 1945) gives a good survey of the sources and the events, and enumerates the English literature. His text of the *Marburg Articles* is taken from the St Louis edition of Luther (Walch), and is therefore antiquated. Beto states: 'At the present time there is no English monograph on the Marburg Colloquy available'. See also E.G. Schwiebert, *Luther and His Times*, 695-714.

life-work of the great scholar who died in 1946 before he could see in print the second volume of his *magnum opus* which he had finished three years before. Our book is not concerned with all details of the history of the church at that time. We must even omit important characters and events of that history. For these details the reader should turn to the work by Koehler. This book wants, rather, to be nothing but a modest contribution to the history of doctrine *(Dogmengeschichte).* This is true also of the chapter that follows the presentation and evaluation of Marburg. It tries to show the attempts to revise or revoke the decision of Marburg, until the *Formula of Concord* definitely established the separation between the Lutheran and the Reformed churches.

No book on a subject like this has ever been written, and can ever be written, with absolute impartiality. Great historians of the Christian dogma cease to be quite objective when it comes to the doctrine of Luther, and especially Luther's doctrine on the Sacrament. What famous and otherwise-excellent works on the history of the 16th century say about Marburg and the controversies on the Lord's Supper shows that even great historians are able to write on things which they do not understand. One can only express the hope that works like that of Walther Koehler may help historians to understand that very serious questions were at stake in these colloquies, and that the theologians of the 16th century did not indulge in mere logomachies. The attitude of Koehler himself, the great disciple of Troeltsch, toward the issues under discussion is that of a modern scholar who would take sides with neither party, looking with sympathy to both, and trying to pass an impartial judgment where a judgment has to be passed. But it is evident that he stands beyond what must seem to him a tragedy which was historically necessary, but not touching what he himself calls *das Wesen des Christentums,* the essence of Christianity. He would be nearer to Bucer (who, as he states, was the first to coin the phrase *ratio Christianismi*) than to Zwingli or Luther, if he had to take his place among the dramatis personae. But he would not do that, and prefers to remain a spectator. His is the tragedy of the great historic theology of the last hundred years. No one should dare to despise it, or to neglect the true results of this theology. The question, however, which troubles our generation is whether we can afford to be neutral in one of the greatest spiritual conflicts of Christendom. There can be no doubt that the arguments about the Real Presence, the controversies on the Lord's Supper, belong to the greatest issues, not only of the past, but also of the present age of the church, and of the future, too. Who would believe that the conflict, for that which for almost 2,000 years has been the centre of the worship and life of the church, was an argument over words, a useless dispute?

Here lies the reason why all books written on the Sacrament of the Altar in the course of the centuries bear the character of personal confessions and have a practical tendency. The rediscovery of the theology of the Reformers in Europe, and especially in Germany, after World War I has led to a new examination of their doctrines on the Sacrament. But it was not a merely academic interest that caused the theologians to return to the study of the old doctrines, but rather the longing for the divine truth by which the Church lives. After 1933, when the churches had to fight for their very existence against the claims of the totalitarian state, the theological issues became still more momentous. If it is true that the Church lives by the Word and by the Sacrament, if Word and Sacrament are the weapons which we have to use against the old evil foe who appears again and again in new disguises — what, then, is the Word? What is the Sacrament? Nobody can look through the numerous books and essays written from 1923 to 1941 (when the printing of theological books in Germany was stopped) without being touched by the seriousness with which the question of the Sacrament was discussed by theologians of Reformed and Lutheran persuasion and by definite adherents of a union. Solid theological scholarship was employed in the service of the church.[6] A similar rediscovery of the sacramental life of the church was noticeable in the Catholic church, mainly under the influence of the Liturgical Movement. What surprises most is the fact that the new interest in the Sacrament was by no means limited to theologians and to some congregations. On the contrary, men of

---

[6] We mention here the most important and significant publications in German: ***Karl Barth,*** *Ansatz und Absicht in Luthers Abendmahlslehre* (1923), reprinted in the 2nd volume of Barth's collected lectures: *Die Theologie und die Kirche* (1928). The most important monograph from the Lutheran side at that time is ***Ernst Sommerlath,*** *Der Sinn des Abendmahls nach Luthers Gedanken 1527-29* (1930). ***W. Elert,*** *Morphologie des Luthertums, I* (1931), deals extensively with the Lutheran doctrine on the Sacraments and its far-reaching consequences. Barth's suggestion that the doctrine of Calvin could help to overcome the old antagonism and pave the way for a better union than those of the 19th century was taken up by his disciple ***Wilhelm Niesel,*** an outstanding Reformed theologian and churchman, in *Calvins Lehre vom Abendmahl* (2nd edition, 1935). Another disciple of Barth of Lutheran background tried to show the possibilities of a rapprochement of the two confessions in two scholarly publications: ***Helmut Gollwitzer*** (now incumbent of Barth's former chair in Bonn), *Die Abendmahlsfrage als Aufgabe kirchlicher Lehre* in the symposium *Theologische*

whom no one had expected that the old questions of the 16th century could ever become living issues began to ask for the Sacrament, for the Real Presence; philosophers, mathematicians, scientists, men of high education and real scholarship became interested, and very seriously interested, in these problems. This is true not only of the Roman church (among whose practising members there are astronomers, physicists, and other scientists of high rank, who obviously have no difficulty in accepting even the doctrine of transubstantiation, as their frequent, if not daily, communion shows); it is also true of certain sections of Protestantism, mainly such as are influenced by the Liturgical Movement. There is a longing for the Sacrament even in circles where theologians do not expect it. Do we hear this question? And are we able to give an answer? We must frankly confess that, despite all endeavours on the part of modern theology to regain a real understanding of the doctrine of the Reformers concerning the Sacraments, and particularly of Luther's doctrine of the Lord's Supper, our positive answers have been very weak. Nothing is more significant of the weakness of our theology in this respect than the fact that books on the theology of Luther have been written which say nothing or almost nothing on Luther's doctrine on the Sacrament.[7] What great new insights have been given

---

Aufsätze dedicated to Barth on the occasion of his 50th birthday, and *Coena Domini, Die altlutherische Abendmahlslehre in ihrer Auseinandersetzung mit dem Calvinismus* (1937). A 'Confessional Synod' of the Church of the Prussian Union, initiated by the book *Abendmahlsgemeinschaft* (***Wolf, Niesel, Asmussen,*** a.o.) declared that intercommunion between Lutherans and Reformed was possible. The answer from the Lutheran side was given by the author of this book in *Kirche und Herrenmahl* (1938), and in a symposium by Lutheran theologians (***Frölich, Hopf, Knolle, Preuss, Procksch, Sasse, Strasser***), *Vom Sakrament des Altars* (1941). Also ***W. Elert***, *Der christliche Glaube* (1941) must be mentioned in this connection. In 1940 two important monographs had appeared: ***Hans Grass***, *Die Abendmahlslehre bei Luther und Calvin,* and ***Ernst Bizer,*** *Studien zur Geschichte des Abendmahlsstreits im 16.Jahrhundert* (a really scholarly work on the Wittenberg Concord with the view of a future solution of the sacramental question along the lines of this Concord). The discussion went on after World War II, however without the result of a settlement which was hoped for by many, as is shown by ***J. Schniewind*** and ***E. Sommerlath,*** *Abendmahlsgespräch,* ed. by ***E. Schlink,*** and ***Peter Brunner,*** *Grundlegung des Abendmahlsgesprächs* (1954). For later discussions see Preface.

[7] Joh. v. Walter, *Die Theologie Luthers* (1940, Lectures printed after his death), an otherwise-excellent book, does not mention the Sacraments. The older standard work by Theodosius Harnack, *Luthers Theologie* (2 vols., 1862 and 1886), shows the same shortcoming, due to the fact that it was not completed. Similar observations may be made with respect to modern Swedish Luther research and its American offshoots, notwithstanding the merits of this literature.

to our generation concerning Luther's *theologia crucis* and his doctrine on justification! Much of this knowledge of Luther, however, has remained mere theory. Why is that so? Is, perhaps, one of the reasons to be found in the fact that we have not attained the proper understanding of his doctrine on the Sacrament? The Lutheran Church has become what it is by the twofold struggle of Luther against Rome and against the 'sacramentarians', by his fight for the *sola fide* and the Real Presence, for the Gospel and the Sacrament. No one can understand Luther unless he has understood his fight for the Real Presence. Here lies the reason why so many modern Lutheran theologians no longer accept the Lutheran doctrine on the Sacrament, but rather look for a new one which would not be far from the doctrines of Bucer and Calvin.

Thus, the Lutheran church today is confronted again with the problem which she had to face in the beginning. The life or death of our church depends on the question whether she will be able to regain Luther's deep understanding of the Sacrament and to proclaim this understanding to the men and women of our age who are longing for the Sacrament. It is no use closing our eyes to the fact that a vast number of Lutherans, pastors as well as laymen, have lost the old understanding of the Lord's Supper which even in the first half of the 19th century caused thousands of Lutheran Christians to sever their old church-connections, and even to leave their homeland and all their earthly possessions, in order to attain the freedom to re-establish the Lutheran altar. On the other hand, we must be clear about the fact that a doctrine like the precious doctrine of our church on the Real Presence cannot be preserved simply by being handed on from one generation to the next one. If it is, as we believe, the true biblical doctrine, it is our duty to proclaim it to the world and to all Christendom, because Christ's Church lives by the Sacrament, as Christ instituted it. But only if we are deeply convinced that our doctrine is the true biblical one, are we allowed, and will we be able, to maintain it. Faith cannot be inherited like other possessions. It must be given to each generation anew, and it will be given through the means of grace — *ubi et quando visum est Deo.* Thus, the belief in the Real Presence, the true understanding of the Lord's Supper, can be regained only if the Holy Spirit opens Holy Scripture to us again. For not by any human authority, not even by the authority of Luther, can we accept it, but solely on the authority of God's Word. This was the way which led Luther to the understanding of the Sacrament. There is no other way for us.

CHAPTER I

The Medieval Background

1. The Medieval Origin of the Eucharistic Dogma

Christendom had celebrated the Sacrament of the Altar as the centre and climax of all Christian worship for almost 1,500 years before this Sacrament, together with the quest for the Gospel, became one of the foremost issues of the Reformation. The old rule was reaffirmed that the quest for the Gospel was the quest for the Sacrament, and vice versa. Those 1,500 years, however, were by no means occupied with doctrinal strife on the Lord's Supper. On the contrary, it took a very long time before this Sacrament became a subject of doctrinal strife and dogmatic definitions. If the principle holds good anywhere, which is being quoted so often in modern theological discussions, that 'the law of prayer is the law of belief',[1] then it holds good for the sacramental life and belief of the church. No one can understand the Sacraments and the controversies about them, unless he keeps in mind that the Sacrament is primarily something to be celebrated, not to be speculated on. Baptism, for example, is an object of faith, as the Nicene Creed shows, but what Baptism is was not defined doctrinally by the church before the Reformation. It was only the decay and the corruption of the Sacraments which time and again compelled the church to formulate dogmas on the Sacraments in view of error and misuse (which, of course, does not mean that all such doctrinal definitions are correct

[1] *Lex orandi lex credendi.* This famous principle was established by Celestine I (422-32): '. . . *ut legem credendi lex statuat supplicandi*'. Each dogma actually occurs in the liturgy before it is defined — e.g., the Trinitarian formula is older than the definition of the dogma on the Trinity. However, this is true also of false doctrines (such as Mariolatry and Mariology). Thus, even Pius XII in the Encyclical of 1947 on the sacred liturgy, *Mediator Dei*, asserted that the principle, *lex orandi lex credendi* (Denz, 139 and 2200), must also be inverted: 'It is perfectly correct to say: "*Lex credendi legem statuat supplicandi*" — let the rule of belief determine the rule of prayer' (English text, section 48). How much more careful should Lutherans be in applying that maxim which plays a great role in modern Protestantism!

from the point of view of a scriptural theology). Thus, we shall not be surprised to find that the first dogma on the Sacrament of the Altar was formulated as late as the Middle Ages.

This does not, of course, mean that the Early Church did not possess very definite views on the Sacraments, and especially on the Lord's Supper. Almost all the Church Fathers have written on them, partly because no Christian theology can pass by the Sacraments as vital facts of the faith and life of the church, and partly because the catechumens had to be instructed on the Eucharist shortly before or after baptism.[2] There were various opinions and differing views on the interpretation of the Sacrament, but, in spite of this great variety, there was no doubt about the doctrinal content of the Sacrament. To take the most elucidating example, no theologian of the Early Church ever doubted that, according to the Words of Institution, the consecrated bread ***is*** the body, and the consecrated wine ***is*** the blood of Christ; the differences referred only to the theological theories about the right understanding of the doctrine on which all were agreed. Had there been any dissension as to the fact of the Real Presence, the church would have been compelled to formulate a dogma. The one and only case when an ecumenical council had to deal with the Eucharist is a decision of the Synod of 787 (Nicaea II) which, when recognizing the veneration of images (icons), incidentally rejected a resolution of the Synod of 754 which had declared that in the church there could not be any image of Christ other than the elements in the Eucharist. That decision of 787 implied the doctrine, and so it was understood everywhere, that the consecrated bread and wine are not images, figures, or symbols, but the true body and blood of Christ. An explicit dogma regarding this truth was unnecessary since it was safeguarded in the liturgy.

That this understanding of the Sacrament was generally accepted in the Eastern church is shown by the recognition of the great dogmatic work which John of Damascus wrote in the same century.[3]

---

[2] The Fourth of the *Mystagogical Catecheses* by Cyril of Jerusalem, 'On the body and blood of Christ' (MPG 33, 1097), was given after the new Christians had received baptism and first communion. See also Ambrose, *De mysteriis* (MPL 16).

[3] *De fide orthodoxa 4,13* (MPG 94, 1144). John summarizes the most important thoughts of the earlier Greek Fathers. He compares the Words of Institution with the powerful words of God spoken at creation. According to the Eastern rite of the invocation of the Holy Spirit he compares the eucharistic miracle with the miracle brought about by the Holy Spirit in the conception of Jesus. The body of Christ in the Eucharist is identical with the body born of the Virgin. Not as if the body of Christ came down from heaven; rather, the bread and wine are transformed into the body and

His doctrine on the Real Presence corresponds exactly to the Eastern liturgy, in which the prayer of consecration entreats God:

> Make this bread the precious body of Thy Christ . . . and the content of this chalice the precious blood of Thy Christ, changing (*metabalōn*) them through Thy Holy Spirit.

This is the doctrine which the Eastern church has retained. After the Council of Lyons in 1274, when the ideas of Western Scholasticism (such as transubstantiation, or the view on the number of sacraments—not less and not more than seven) were taken over by Eastern theologians, this did not mean a change in the doctrine of the church. Apart from theological textbooks, catechisms, and local confessions with a very limited authority, the Eastern churches have to this day no explicit dogma on the Eucharist, but only a liturgy which is binding on the whole Eastern church as to its dogmatic content.

The same applies to the Western church up to the High Middle Ages. Here, too, the dogma on the Sacraments was hidden in the liturgy. What the theologians wrote on the Eucharist remained a private interpretation of the content of the mass. In contradistinction to the East, however, the West soon was no longer satisfied with the mere traditional practice of the Sacraments. A new interest in the individual Sacraments is to be observed, which led to the development of a theology of the Sacraments, and, after the end of the 11th century, to important dogmatic decisions. These are the beginning of an elaborate dogma on the Sacraments which distinguishes the Western Catholic church from the church of the East and from the Early Church. Apart from the fact that Western Christendom has always been more intellectual than the Christians of the East, the deeper reason for this process is a very living interest in the Sacraments as means of grace. As grace (justifying and sanctifying grace), according to all Catholic churches, is always being given through the Sacraments, a theology of grace, growing out of the Augustinian heritage of the Latin church, was bound to be

---

blood of the Lord. If we ask how this could be, then it ought to be sufficient to know that it is a miracle wrought by the Holy Spirit. 'We know nothing more than that the Word of God is true, effective and almighty, but the *how* is past finding out.' In spite of this correct theological insight, he produces an old simile: The transformation of bread and wine in the Eucharist is compared with the transformation of food and drink into our bodies. It is not necessary to trace the sources of these ideas, some of which go back to the second century (Justin, Irenaeus), nor to attempt to systematize them, as the historians of Christian doctrine have tried to do. They belong to the sphere of theological speculation, and have never been dogmatized.

closely connected with a theology of the Sacraments. It is noteworthy that this characteristic feature of the Western church is by no means limited to medieval Catholicism. The 16th century, which brought to consummation the Roman doctrine on the Sacrament of the Altar at the Council of Trent, also produced the sacramental doctrines of the various churches of the Reformation, just as the doctrines on sin and grace, justification, and sanctification put forward by Catholics, Lutherans, and the various types of Reformed Protestants are, each in its way, the answer to the great question which for more than a thousand years since Augustine had dominated Western theology: What do we mean by confessing in the Creed that the Son of God came down from heaven and was made man **for us men and for our salvation**? As the 16th century cannot be separated from the Middle Ages with regard to the doctrine of grace, so the age of the Reformation is in many respects the time when the medieval quest for the Sacrament found its final answers.

This connection between the Middle Ages and the Reformation becomes evident if we look at two sacraments that attained special importance for medieval Christendom. The first is the sacrament of penance, which in the Early Middle Ages grew out of the remnants of the church discipline of the first centuries and of the practice of regular confession in the monasteries. No medieval Christian could live without receiving sacramental absolution; failure to receive it could mean for a king or an emperor the loss of his crown. It is certainly not accidental that the Reformation started with a controversy on the misuse of this very sacrament. The second sacrament that occupied the souls and minds of all medieval Christians, because it was the very centre of all worship of the church, was the Sacrament of the Altar. The 11th century, which gave to the priest the power to pronounce absolution in the exhibitive, declarative form, instead of a mere intercession for the sinner (with which the first 1,000 years had been satisfied), established the dogma of the Real Presence formally and firmly in 1079. The Council of 1215, which declared the Real Presence to be understood as transubstantiation, made Easter confession compulsory for all Christians. Again, it was not by accident that the Reformation, which had begun as a controversy on the sacrament of penance, later became to a larger degree a controversy about the Sacrament of the Altar. History of doctrine reveals the remarkable fact that for about 500 years — strictly speaking, from the declaration *Ego Berengarius* of 1079 to the *Formula of Concord* of 1577 — Western Christendom was occupied with the quest for the Sacrament as never before, and never after. Perhaps no modern Christian is able to understand the vital interest which Christendom took during those 500 years, before and during the Reformation, in these sacraments, and especially in the *sacramentum sacramentorum*, or **the** Sacrament, as Luther simply called the Lord's Supper.

Apart from some incidental papal decisions on Baptism, confirmation, and some questions connected with the sacrament of penance that do not really constitute a dogma, the Eucharist is the only subject on which the medieval church made dogmatic decisions of great importance for the future. One may say that the doctrine on the Lord's Supper is the only dogma that the medieval church produced. This dogma is contained in three short decisions: (a) in *Ego Berengarius* of 1079;[4] (b) in the *Caput Firmiter*, the Creed of 1215;[5] (c) in the decision on the *communio sub una* of the Council of Constance in 1415.[6] These three documents belong together. They are the fruit of an amazing work done by scholastic theology for centuries, as well as the preparatory work for the final definition of the Roman Catholic doctrine on the Sacrament which was to be rendered by the Council of Trent. At the same time these medieval decisions are the presupposition for the theological work and the doctrinal decisions of all churches of the Reformation. We shall try to understand these documents in their significance for the Reformation by discussing the individual doctrines which together make up the medieval dogma on the Sacrament of the Altar.

2. The Eucharistic Sacrifice

We begin with the doctrine on the sacrifice of the mass, which became such a great issue between Rome and all churches of the Reformation. It is noteworthy that, during the Middle Ages, only the sects that rejected the whole sacramental system of the church (because they regarded the church as completely apostasized) rejected the Roman mass, and with it the sacrifice. But as far as we can ascertain, the ideas of priesthood and sacrifice as such were never attacked by Christians who wanted to be faithful members of the Catholic church. Thus, the only statements on the mass as a sacrifice are found in the 'profession of faith' demanded from the Waldensians

[4] Denz, 355.
[5] Denz, 430.
[6] Denz, 626.

in 1208, and in the Creed of 1215 directed against the Albingensians and other heretics. Here we read:

> There is one universal church of the faithful, outside of which no one is saved. In this church Jesus Christ Himself is priest (*sacerdos*) and sacrifice, whose body and blood are truly contained in the Sacrament of the Altar under the species of bread and wine, the bread having been transubstantiated into the body, and the wine into the blood by divine power . . .

This is, of course, no elaborate doctrine on the sacrifice of the mass, but it is a sufficient statement that the Eucharist is a *sacrificium* that can be made by the lawfully-ordained *sacerdos* only, as later indicated. Nothing more was required at that time, since all Christendom, Eastern and Western, regarded the Eucharist as a sacrifice, and the minister as a priest. No medieval Christian ever doubted that, for the idea that the mass is a sacrifice was deeply rooted in all liturgies.

The understanding of the Sacrament of the Altar is perhaps the greatest example of what tradition, as a source of doctrine, means to the Catholic churches. This understanding goes back to the Early Church. Traces of it may be found as early as the first century when in *1 Clem.* 40 f, the Christian liturgy is compared with the sacrificial cult of the Old Testament, and the ministers of the church, who together with the people perform that liturgy, are likened to the high priest, priests, and Levites. It is easily understood that the early Christians who came either from Judaism or from the pagan religions of the ancient world, could not think of a divine service without sacrifice. Just as the Jews after the destruction of the Temple looked for a substitute for the sacrifices which were no longer possible, and found them in the study of the Law and other spiritual exercises, so the Christians had their spiritual sacrifices. The Old Testament also refers to such spiritual sacrifices as the prayers of the faithful or the repentance of a contrite heart (see Psalm 50:14; 51:17). In the New Testament the Church as the priestly people of God (1 Peter 2:5-9; Rev. 1:6; 5:10) offers its spiritual sacrifices. Such offerings are the bodies of the Christians, that is, their whole lives (Rom. 12:1); prayers and confession (Heb. 13:15; Rev. 5:8; 8:3); and the gifts of brotherly love (Heb. 13:16) which have always been connected with Holy Communion (*koinōnia).* Such gifts were put on the Lord's Table and administered by the deacons to the least of Christ's brethren (who represent Christ himself, Matt. 25:40). If the church had been satisfied with such metaphorical use of the word 'sacrifice' for the Eucharist as the most solemn and sacred prayer and the most excellent act of worship, no objection could have been raised, as

Martin Chemnitz rightly points out in his *Examen Concilii Tridentini* (Pars II, Locus VI, Sectio 1, Art. 1, 2) ed. Preuss, 383 f.

Unfortunately, the Early Church did not stop at this point. While for the Fathers of the second century the sacrifice is the prayer, or the whole celebration, or the gifts of bread and wine put on the altar, the idea arises in the third century that the body and blood of the Lord are the sacrifice. In the Early Church the people of God as a whole offer the sacrifice, the bishop acting in behalf of the people in saying the Eucharist; but in the middle of the third century Cyprian presents the idea of a special priesthood, a real *sacerdos* who offers in behalf of the people. Bishops and presbyters became priests in a special sense. The idea of a universal priesthood of all believers in the sense that the whole Church is a priestly people, as Israel was God's priestly people in the Old Testament times, was never given up. According to the *Canon Missae*, 'we Thy servants, but also Thy holy people' still offer the sacrifice of the mass today.[7] The modern Liturgical Movement in the Roman church likes to emphasize the fact that all believers, all the people of God, have a share in this sacrifice. And yet, it is impossible to trace the idea of the sacrifice of the mass back to the New Testament. In passages like 1 Cor. 10:18-21 and Heb. 13:10 — if the latter should refer to the Lord's Supper, which is possible — nothing more can be found than the understanding of the Sacrament of the Altar as a sacrificial meal in which we receive that which has been sacrificed at Calvary once for all. Nowhere in the New Testament do we find the idea of the modern Liturgical Movement that the Church as the Body of Christ offers the sacrifice together with Christ, the Head. There is no other atoning sacrifice than the sacrifice which Christ made quite alone. There is no priesthood in the New Testament besides the High Priesthood of Christ and the universal priesthood of his people. There is not the slightest indication that apostles, prophets, doctors, bishops, and other office-holders in the New Testament churches have a special dignity or office as priests beyond that which all Christians have. Thus, the Catholic churches have never succeeded in discovering the institution of a special priesthood, except in the words at the Last Supper, 'This do in remembrance of me'. This poor and untenable exegesis proves that the whole idea of a special priesthood whose duty and privilege it is to offer the sacrifice of the mass has no scriptural basis at all.

---

[7] '*Nos servi tui, sed et plebs tua sancta*' in the *Unde et memores*. Cf '*Hanc . . . oblationem servitutis nostrae, sed et cunctae familiae tuae*' in the *Hanc igitur*.

If we ask how it was possible that the 'tradition' of the sacrifice of the mass could arise, and gain such an authority that up to the Reformation practically no theologian and no Christian, except a few Waldensians, had any doubts about it, our answer can only be this: The whole idea is another expression of that synergism which entered the church so early, and which became the most characteristic feature of Catholicism, Eastern and Western. Just as the *sola gratia* and *sola fide* of the New Testament were abandoned in favour of the theory that in the process of salvation God and man, divine grace and human freedom, must cooperate; just as Mary's *fiat* (Luke 1:38) was regarded as the necessary human answer to God's redeeming will,[8] so the mass became a sacrifice in which Christ the High Priest and the human priesthood work together. Against this background one must see the dogma of the sacrificial character of the mass, in order to understand the unquestioned tenacity with which it was held by all Catholic churches, until in the Reformation the question was raised whether this synergism was to be reconciled with the Gospel of Christ in the New Testament.

3. The Real Presence as Conversion

While the doctrine on the sacrifice of the mass was practically extra-controversial during the Middle Ages, and therefore mentioned very briefly only in a few documents, the real problem which was under discussion for some centuries was the dogma of the Real Presence. It seems that no other mystery of the Christian faith has to such a degree occupied not only the minds of theologians, but also the imagination of lay people. Moreover, the whole piety of medieval Christendom finds its centre more and more in the miracle of the Real Presence. Popular superstition, which expresses itself in legends about miraculous hosts; profound speculation by the schoolmen, for whom the Real Presence becomes more and more

---

[8]This synergistic character of the cult of Mary has become more and more evident, especially since the titles of co-redeemer and mediatrix of all graces have been given to her. Since Benedict XV, a feast and mass of *Maria mediatrix omnium gratiarum* (May 31) have been granted to many dioceses, and the proclamation of the corresponding dogma is demanded by a growing number of Catholics. The title occurs, by the way, in the ancient church of the East, e.g., in the Coptic liturgy. Pope Pius XII in his encyclical *Mystici Corporis* (1943), concluding chapter, says of Mary: 'As another Eve she offered Him (sc. Christ) on Golgotha to the Eternal Father for all the children of Adam sin-stained by his fall, and her mother's rights and her mother's love were included in the holocaust'.

one of the foremost subjects of theology; the beautiful eucharistic hymns, the churches, altars, and tabernacles built as dwelling places of the eucharistic Christ; the new forms of eucharistic worship which grew out of the belief in the Real Presence after about AD 1200, as we shall see: all testify to the growing importance of this doctrine for the medieval church, and explain why the new dogma was regarded as necessary.

The beginnings of a new interest in the theology of the Sacrament of the Altar may be observed in the ninth century when Paschasius Radbertus wrote the first medieval book on the Sacrament,[9] and thus inaugurated a discussion among the theologians of his time in which Rabanus Maurus and Ratramnus were the most important disputants. It was not a controversy like those of later times. There was no actual strife, no condemnation. Radbertus was a representative of sacramental realism. He believed in the miracle of the consecration by which bread and wine are changed into the body and blood of Christ, the body being that which was born of the Virgin, crucified, and raised from the dead. His opponents, especially Ratramnus, did not deny that the consecrated bread and wine are the body and blood of Christ, but Ratramnus distinguished the body in the Sacrament from the body of the historic Christ. The elements are not changed; they remain bread and wine. Only virtually are they the body and blood of the Lord. They are, after the consecration, the 'image' of the body and blood, signs with which the faithful receive the '*res*', the celestial blessing of the spiritual communion with Christ. At first sight, it seems that here we have our earliest contact with the two views on the Sacrament which have played such a role in later controversies. But this is only partly true. For the realism of Radbertus does not prevent him from denying what later was called the *manducatio impiorum.* He held that only the faithful receive the body and blood of Christ. On the other hand, Ratramnus does not hesitate to use such words as 'change' (*mutatio*) to denote the spiritual character of the consecrated elements. The deeper reason for this lack of clarity is to be found in the fact that all disputants were bound to the ecclesiastical terminology. They wanted to interpret the doctrinal content of the liturgy. Thus, it is not permissible to argue: If the question of the Lord's Supper was not divisive for the church in the ninth century, why should it have been

[9] *De corpore et sanguine Christi,* written in 831, published in 844. Ratramnus wrote his criticism under the same title at the request of Charles the Bold in 844. (Note the interest of the laity.) See MPL 120, 1267 ff and 121, 125 ff.

in the 16th or in the later centuries? The peaceful discussion of the Carolingian age was a first attempt on the part of the Early Medieval church to solve a problem which had been left to the Middle Ages by the Early Church.

Not from the Later Middle Ages or from the Reformation can this first discussion on the Sacrament of the Altar be understood, but, like all theology of the Early Middle Ages, from the church of the Fathers. Two great authorities stand behind the disputants of the ninth century, as behind all discussions of the Sacrament in the Middle Ages: Ambrose and Augustine. Ambrose is the great authority for the sacramental realism which prevailed more and more in the following centuries. Augustine is the father of that spiritualistic understanding of the Sacrament which we find not only among outspoken spiritualists — like Berengar, Wyclif, Zwingli and Calvin — but also, at least to a certain degree, among representatives of a realistic doctrine, like Thomas and the young Luther. One must never forget that the Middle Ages were unable to discover the antagonism that existed between the two great Fathers who were regarded as incarnations of patristic authority, and that even the Reformation was so much under the spell of the authority of Augustine that even Luther followed him where he should have tried to get rid of the Augustinian heritage (for example, the definition of the Sacrament as a sign, which could open the door to a symbolic understanding, and which has no basis in Holy Scripture).[10]

---

[10]In Gen. 17:11 circumcision is called '*signum foederis inter me et vos*', which the Authorized Version correctly renders 'a token of the covenant betwixt me and you'. Paul places Baptism and the Lord's Supper side by side in 1 Cor. 10:1 ff, but nowhere in the New Testament are they called 'signs'. In Col. 2:11 ff where Old Testament circumcision is contrasted with Baptism as *circumcisio Christi*, the difference between these two rites is clearly pointed out. Such passages, however, could lead to the idea of 'Old Testament sacraments'. Since the idea of a sacrament is merely a theological one — Jesus did not institute 'sacraments', but, rather, Baptism, his Supper, and the Office of the Keys — it is a question of terminology as to what one likes to call a sacrament and what not. Besides, it should not be forgotten that *sacramentum* in Latin is a term which the Eastern church does not know. She uses the word *mystērion* instead; and even in the West the word *sacramentum* is still used in the Middle Ages in the sense of 'mystery' — as in *De sacramentis* by Hugo of St Victor (died 1141), a book on the mysteries of the Christian faith, including such mysteries as the Trinity or the Incarnation. The Lutheran church, like the church of the first 1,100 years, has preserved the freedom of terminology. The *Apology of the Augsburg Confession*, like Luther, recognizes three sacraments. Whether absolution is a sacrament or not, depends solely on our understanding of a sacrament. If an element is required, then absolution is not a sacrament, but rather a special form of proclaiming the Gospel. Hence the Lutheran church has the freedom to apply the term 'sacrament' also to Old

The difference between the Ambrosian and the Augustinian understanding of the Sacrament seems to go back to different liturgical traditions. Ambrose, who has left us the first eucharistic liturgies in Latin in his *De mysteriis* and in *De sacramentis* (which modern scholarship again ascribes to him), recognized a liturgy in which a change (*transformatio, transfiguratio, mutatio*) of the elements was expressed. His doctrine, which he shares with his contemporary John Chrysostom, is that the Words of Institution as words of Christ effect a change of the bread into the body, the wine into the blood of Christ. His liturgy corresponds in this respect to the Eastern liturgies in which in the eucharistic prayer — be it in the invocation of the Logos or the Holy Spirit, or be it through the whole prayer, and especially the Words of Institution — God is asked to make the bread the precious body, the content of the chalice

———

Testament rites. If this is done, it must be made clear from the outset, as it is done Col. 2:11 ff, that the New Testament sacrament is infinitely more than what would be called a sacrament in the Old Testament. 'Old Testament sacraments', like circumcision or the Passover, would be 'types' (*typoi*, cf 1 Cor. 10:6) of the sacraments instituted by the Word Incarnate, whatever they might mean in themselves. The great mistake made by Augustine was that he tried to formulate a concept of the sacrament that would cover sacred actions or signs, not only of the old people of God or of the Church, but of every religion. 'Never can men be united in a religion, be it true or false, except by common participation in some visible signs or sacraments (*nisi aliquo signaculorum, seu sacramentorum visibilium consortio*)', *Contra Faustum* 19, 11 (MPL 42, 355). Thus the great Father of the West arrives at an understanding of the sacrament as something that belongs to any religion, even to pagan ones. A sacrament is a sacred sign (*sacrum signum*, as in *De civ. Dei X. cap. 5*) that unites the adherents of a certain religion. This is, of course, not all that Augustine has to say in that respect. However, in view of the authority which the great *doctor ecclesiae* exercised throughout the Middle Ages and the age of the Reformation up to this very day, this definition could not fail to do the greatest damage to the understanding of the Sacraments of Christ. Thomas tried to improve it by introducing the idea of a *signum efficax*. In his early years, Luther was still under the spell of Augustine, and unable to see that the *doctor gratiae* could not be regarded also as *doctor eucharistiae*, until the fight against the enthusiasts and Zwingli opened his eyes. To Zwingli, Calvin, and the Reformed churches the sacraments are 'signs', Augustine being their great authority. Melanchthon deals with the Sacraments in the first edition of his *Loci* under the title *'De signis'*, while the word *signum* does not occur in the definition of the Sacraments in the last edition. After Luther's new emphasis on the efficacy of the Sacrament, a tendency may be observed within Lutheran theology to overcome the dangerous definition of Augustine. Thus, Johann Gerhard (*Loci XVIII, 25*: ed. Preuss IV, 147, 8) finds the nature of the sacrament no longer *in genere signi*, but rather *in genere actionis*. The sacrament is a divine action, performed by man at the command of Christ.

The root of Augustine's understanding of the sacrament as a sign is not the Bible but his neo-Platonism. The sacrament is a visible sign of the invisible *res* or *virtus*. The distinction was easily applicable to Baptism, where the visible sign of water points to

the precious blood of Christ, changing (*metabolōn*) them through his Holy Spirit. The formula of distribution, too, leaves no doubt as to the transformation which has taken place. This is the reason why the Eastern churches never had any doubt about the Real Presence. After the consecration the bread is the body, the wine is the blood in a realistic sense, even if the question as to how that might be possible is not answered. This realism of the East is to be observed with Ambrose and with all Western liturgies that have been influenced by the Eastern tradition, such as the Gallican and the Spanish (Mozarabic) rites.

On the other hand, there was a liturgical tradition in the West which did not mention any *metabolē* in the eucharistic prayer. It is a most remarkable fact that the Roman mass, and especially the *Canon Missae,* which otherwise is closely related to the eucharistic

---

the invisible grace. But what about the other sacraments? What about the Sacrament of the Altar? If bread and wine, corresponding to the element of water in Baptism, are the *signum*, what then is the *res,* that aim of the Sacrament which God's grace is going to give us? It is the communion of the spiritual body of Christ, the bond of love existing in the true church. One can understand that Zwingli and all his successors appealed to Augustine as their authority. Augustine was not yet able to describe the *proprium* of this Sacrament, as the schoolmen did when they distinguished three strata in this Sacrament: that which is sign only (*sacramentum tantum*); the *res*, i.e. the invisible grace; and in between these two, that which is sign and *res* (*sacramentum et res*). The *sacramentum tantum* (mere sign) is bread and wine. The *res tantum* is the bond of love between the members of Christ's mystical body; the *sacramentum et res* is the body and blood of Christ, which is *res* in relationship to the elements, but still sign in relationship to the real *res*. This is an attempt on the part of medieval theology to overcome the weakness of Augustine's theory. It is still taught today in Roman theology. Actually this complicated distinction proves that Augustine's distinction of *signum* and *res* cannot be applied to the Sacrament of the Altar. Augustine himself, as shown later, was unable to understand the Eucharist in that way, which would abolish the Real Presence. His attempts to apply this theory to the Lord's Supper were bound to fail. This explains the lack of clarity in his doctrine of the Eucharist — if he ever had a real doctrine in that respect. The overwhelming authority which he still exercises today over Catholics, Calvinists, and even Lutherans, has proved disastrous, at least with regard to the doctrine on the Sacraments. It is noteworthy that the Reformed confessions used to have an article on the Sacraments before dealing with the individual sacraments. The Lutheran church has no dogma *de sacramentis*. In the *Augsburg Confession* an article on the use (or purpose) of the Sacraments follows the articles on Baptism, the Lord's Supper, Confession, and Penance. At any rate, the attempts to understand the Sacrament of the Altar from the general concept of a sacrament should be abandoned; they have no biblical foundation. It is really astonishing that the churches which claim the *sola Scriptura* so emphatically, as e.g. the Calvinistic churches, have accepted so much from Augustine without asking whether or not these doctrines are truly scriptural. How amazing is the power of tradition in the church!

prayer of Ambrose and to the Gallican rite, does not speak of anything which might indicate a transformation,[11] let alone a transubstantiation. This does not, of course, mean that the Roman mass does not recognize the Real Presence. But there is no prayer for a transformation. The Roman *Canon Missae* is a prayer of sacrifice in which God is asked to accept the offering:

> Which oblation do Thou, O God, vouchsafe in all things to bless, approve, ratify, make worthy and acceptable, that it may become for us the Body and Blood of Thy most beloved Son, our Lord Jesus Christ.

The original meaning of this old text, which goes back to the fifth or sixth century, is obviously that, not the Words of Institution but, the acceptance of the offering makes the elements the body and blood of Christ. What if God does not accept the oblation as he was pleased to accept the gifts of Abel, Abraham, and Melchizedek? The current interpretation of the Roman mass is an attempt to read into the old text a doctrine that was developed in the Middle Ages on the basis of the realistic metabolism of Ambrose. That the original form of the Roman mass must be very old is proved by the fact that, in contra-distinction to the Eastern masses, it contains no invocation to the Mother of God.

If we ask where else this type of eucharistic prayer without the idea of a *metabolē* has existed, we are led to Africa, the cradle of the Latin church. This would account for the fact that the African Fathers, Tertullian, Cyprian, and Augustine, differ so much in their sacramental theology from most of their contemporaries. Africa, together with Alexandria, seems to be the home of what we would call sacramental spiritualism.[12] In the Eucharist the bread and wine

---

[11]This is done in the Gallican liturgy after the Words of Institution, in the prayer: 'remembering, therefore, and following the command of Thine only begotten Son, we pray Thee, Almighty Father, that Thou wouldst pour into the created things laid upon Thine altar the spirit of sanctification that through the pouring in of the celestial and invisible sacrament this bread, changed into the flesh, and this chalice, transformed into the blood (*per transfusionem caelestis et invisibilis sacramenti panis hic mutatus in carnem et calix translatus in sanguinem*), may mean grace to all and medicine to them who partake of it. Through Jesus Christ . . .' (from Lietzmann's edition in *Kleine Texte* No. 19, 27).

[12]Fragments only of the African liturgy are preserved in the writings of Augustine and Fulgentius. They prove that in the centre of the *prex mystica,* as Augustine calls the prayer of consecration, there was the narrative of the institution. An *epiclēsis* or invocation to the Holy Spirit followed, the content of which was a prayer for the communicant church and a worthy reception of the body and blood of the Lord. (This beautiful prayer has been partly translated from Fulgentius by Gregory Dix, *Shape of*

are not changed, but they receive a new quality which makes them, as Tertullian puts it, the 'figure' of the body and blood of Christ. They represent, as it were, Christ's body and blood. However, one must take care not to understand words like 'figure' or 'symbol' in a modern sense, as Zwingli and his followers did. For the ancients, 'figure' or 'symbol' is not a mere sign, but a sign filled with reality. Thus, the African Fathers can use also traditional ecclesiastical terminology. For Tertullian the bread, as the *figura corporis*, is at the same time the body. The consecrated bread is no longer common bread; it is carefully reserved; it must be eaten before any other food is taken; the Christian partakes of it every morning. All this is not a concession to the usage of the church. It is rather an undeveloped idea of the Real Presence. In the case of Augustine, it is obvious that his understanding of the Sacrament is determined by his neo-Platonism. The distinction between *signum* and *res*; the fact that he places all the emphasis on the invisible reality which underlies the visible sign; his idea that not outward signs, but solely the Spirit of God in his direct influence on man, can bring salvation: all these belong to his neo-Platonic convictions. Also of great importance for the future is his idea that the body of Christ is in heaven until his Second Advent, and, therefore, cannot be on the altar.

However, this is not the whole of Augustine's doctrine. There is another aspect of his eucharistic theology. As a Catholic he uses ecclesiastical terminology, so that the later medieval theologians could quote him as an authority for their understanding of the Real Presence. And this was by no means an accommodation to the belief of his people and to the language of the church. In the later period of

---

the Liturgy, 297.) It does not contain a petition for transformation and the like. The Real Presence was effected, according to this view, by the Words of Institution, not by the *epiclēsis*. The belief in the Real Presence is shown by the formula of distribution which (see MPL 46, 386) was simply, as in the Eastern church: *'Corpus Christi'*, *'Sanguis Christi'*. The communicants answered: *'Amen'*. For further information, see the excellent description of the Church of Africa by Friedrich Heiler, *Altkirchliche Autonomie und Päpstlicher Zentralismus* (1941), the Second Part of Heiler's *magnum opus, Die Katholische Kirche des Ostens und Westens*. There cannot be any doubt that the Church of Africa, the highest authority of which was St Augustine, believed in the Real Presence, even if it did not speak of a 'mutation' or 'transformation'. Whatever we may think of Augustine's theories, it is quite unthinkable that he wanted to give to his communicants anything else than he said in the formula of distribution: the body and blood of Christ which were to be received orally by all participants, even by the unworthy (see next footnote). Here lies the difference between Augustine and the Reformed churches.

his life, when he had to fight Pelagianism and Donatism, we find a new emphasis on the objective side of the Sacraments, including the Sacrament of the Altar. As Baptism is necessary for salvation, so, according to his understanding of John 6:51-53, is Holy Communion. Just as children cannot be saved unless they have been baptized, so the flesh of Christ gives life to them as to adults.[13] The medieval custom of giving Communion to newly-baptized children cannot be completely explained by such utterances of Augustine. But his authority justified that custom which actually goes back to the church of the first centuries when Baptism was followed by the first Holy Communion. Augustine was never able to reconcile his older spiritual views of the Sacraments with his Catholic practice, and with the corresponding utterances of his later years. His thinking on the Sacraments, and especially on the Eucharist, lacks that clarity which we often miss in the theological thought of that great thinker. One must distinguish various strata in the theological thinking of this Father who became the greatest authority for the Middle Ages, and who was still an authority for the Reformers. Western Catholicism as well as Protestantism, Lutheranism as well as Calvinism, can appeal to him, for example, in the doctrine of grace, but also in the doctrine on the Sacraments. If the Middle Ages could not see the incompatibility between Augustine and the great Bishop of Milan, how can we expect that Ambrose and Augustine themselves and their contemporaries noticed that actually two different ideas of the Eucharist appeared in the writings of these two Fathers? The two types of understanding of the Sacraments existed side by side. The Real Presence of the body and blood of Christ could be understood in a more realistic or in a more spiritualistic way. The difference could be tolerated because the question as to the actual relationship between the body of the crucified and risen Lord, on the one hand,

---

[13] *De peccatorum meritis et remissione I, 26* (MPL 44, 123) and other passages. The biblical basis is John 6:53,54 which later was applied to spiritual eating. Other examples of a more realistic understanding are the view that Jesus at the Last Supper carried his body in his hands (e.g. *Enarratio in Psalm 33*; MPL38, 303); the idea that Judas received the body and blood of the Lord like the other disciples (e.g. *Sermo 71;* MPL 38, 453); furthermore, the idea that the Jews who had become Christians drank the blood which they had shed (*Sermo 77;* MPL 38, 485). Each of these passages can be understood spiritually. Taken together they show that Augustine's understanding of the Eucharist had still another side. Such utterances would be impossible in the mouth of Zwingli and Calvin. The famous words, 'believe and thou hast eaten (*crede et manducasti*)' (MPL 35, 1904), occur in the explanation of John 6:27-29 and have no direct bearing on the Eucharist.

and the body of Christ in the Sacrament, on the other, had not yet become a theological problem.

Modern Christians might regard this as a very happy state of affairs. Would it not be the best solution to the problem of this Sacrament if the Real Presence of Christ could be confessed, and the question as to how this Real Presence should be understood were left open? The Reformed churches have held this view since the 16th century. They used to say: There is general agreement, at least between the Lutheran and the Reformed churches concerning the presence (which is an impermissible simplification, since it is not the **presence of Christ**, but rather the **presence of his body and blood** that is at stake). There is disagreement, they say, only concerning the **mode** of the presence; such disagreement can and must be tolerated as it refers to a minor point only. The modern union churches have acted accordingly. 'We cannot be one in the doctrine of this Sacrament, but we can unite in celebrating it', so we are told by ecumenically-minded Anglicans. And their view seems to be corroborated by the modern Liturgical Movement and its guiding principle, *Lex orandi lex credendi:* 'Let us celebrate the Lord's Supper and not speculate on it. For Jesus gave it to his Church as a rite to be performed, not to be speculated on'.

We shall find the answer to that problem if we ask when and why the medieval church for the first time felt the necessity for defining a doctrine on the Real Presence. This was the case in the 11th century when Berengar became the protagonist for a spiritualistic view which the church felt to be unbearable. Much of what he said had been taught either by Augustine or by later Augustinians like Ratramnus.[14] Berengar could appeal to these authorities when he pointed out that the body of Christ, as it was born of the Virgin, crucified, and raised from the dead, was now in heaven and would remain there until the Second Advent; consequently, this body could not be on the altar. Similarly, he remained within the Augustinian tradition when he distinguished between the outward sacrament (*signum, figura, pignus*), which could be taken orally, and the spiritual blessing which only believers receive (*res*). He did not deny that the consecration was effective insofar as by it the element became a sacrament in the sense of a holy sign. Thus far, his doctrine did not differ much from what other theologians before him had

[14]Berengar ascribed the book by Ratramnus to John Scotus Erigena.

taught on the authority of Augustine. Why, then, was this doctrine condemned as heresy? It was not only, as he believed, because 'the foolish multitude' could no longer bear it.[15] Nor can his fate, his trials, condemnations, and enforced revocations be explained by the intrigues of the church politicians of his time. The deeper reason was, first, the fact that during the 200 years after Radbertus and Ratramnus the Sacrament of the Altar had become, for the laity as well as for the theologians, the great mystery of the Christian faith (in the sense of the *mystērion* of the Greeks). It seems, furthermore, that the general trend of this period toward liturgical uniformity had extinguished not only the liturgical, but also the theological, varieties that were tolerated in Carolingian times. It was not superstition only that had grown, but also a real sacramental piety characterized by a deep reverence for the mystery of the Real Presence.

It was this piety that clashed with the rationalism of Berengar. The mysterious, miraculous character of the Sacrament, which was the very centre of Christian worship, was attacked by a man who was the protagonist of the new 'dialectics' or, as we would say, rationalism. Berengar, like all medieval thinkers, recognized, of course, the authority of the Bible and of the Fathers. But, more than he knew, his real authority was reason. *Confugere ad rationem* was one of his watchwords. The strongest reason for his rejection of the Real Presence, as it was held by the majority of the theologians of his time, was that their doctrine was logically impossible (*vecordia*). Here lies the basic difference between him and Augustine. In this respect he is the forerunner of Wyclif, Zwingli, and all who later rejected the Real Presence as a logical absurdity, as something contrary to what Berengar understood by the 'reasonable service (*logikē latreia*)' of Rom. 12:1. He could have used Zwingli's words at Marburg: '*Deus non proponit nobis incomprehensibilia* (God does not propose to us incomprehensible things)'. Berengar was, as far as we know, the first to interpret the Words of Institution merely tropically, the *est* as meaning *significat*. In this respect he went far beyond Augustine, whose neo-Platonic mysticism cannot be put on the same level as Berengar's rationalism. Another reason why the church could not tolerate his doctrine lies in the fact that he, one of the leading theologians of his generation, had followers, and that even people who did not accept his views were impressed by his arguments.

---

[15] '*multitudo ineptorum*'. See R. Seeberg, *Lehrbuch der Dogmengeschichte, III*, 209.

Guitmund (Widmund) of Aversa who wrote between 1073 and 1079 was evidently shocked by Berengar's influence. He classifies the adversaries of what he regards as the correct doctrine into four groups: (a) those who, like Berengar, deny the Real Presence completely; (b) those whom Guitmund calls *impanatores*; (c) those who teach a partial conversion of the elements only; and (d) those who deny the *manducatio indignorum*.[16] In order to understand the seriousness with which the Berengarian controversy was carried on, we must remember that the question of the Sacrament of the Altar played an important role also in the schism between Rome and Byzantium, which occurred in the very same years that the controversy with Berengar started. Was it by accident that the question of the *azyma*, the unleavened bread which the Western church used, became the great doctrinal issue between the churches, though it actually is no dogmatic question at all, and had never played a role before?[17] Somehow, 11th century Christendom, Eastern and Western, must have been occupied in a special way with the Sacrament of the Altar. Error concerning this Sacrament was regarded as the most dangerous heresy. On the other hand, it was assumed that a person who breaks the unity of the church cannot have the true Sacrament of the Altar, which is the *sacramentum unitatis*.

The most important result of the Berengarian controversy was a dogmatic decision which, for the Roman church, definitely settled the disputes on the Real Presence that had arisen time and again out of the heritages of Ambrose and Augustine. As early as 1059 Berengar had been forced to accept a very crass formula in which the conversion was understood as implying that the body of Christ 'is crushed by the teeth of the faithful'. Since this view was considered as dogmatically wrong even by scholastic theologians, as we shall see later, it was replaced in 1079 by the declaration *Ego Berengarius,*

---

[16]*Libri tres de corporis et sanguinis Domini veritate* (MPL 149, 1430 ff; see the entire Liber I).

[17]The question was not mentioned in the Photian schism. This proves that unleavened bread was introduced into the Roman church not earlier than in the ninth century. The leavened bread corresponds to the tradition of the East which follows the Gospel of St John which does not regard the Last Supper as a Passover meal (John 18:28). One of the most terrifying scenes in the history of this Sacrament took place when the Chancellor of the Patriarch Caerularius broke open the tabernacles of the Latin churches in Constantinople and trampled upon the consecrated hosts as being nothing but 'Jewish bread'.

which has become a dogma of the Roman church, the first dogmatical definition of the Real Presence. Here it is stated:

> that bread and wine . . . through the mystery of the sacred prayer and by the words of the Redeemer,[18] are substantially converted (*substantialiter converti*) into the proper and life-giving flesh and blood of our Lord Jesus Christ, and that, after consecration,they are the true body of Christ which was born of the Virgin Mary and hung on the cross for the salvation of the world and which now sitteth on the right hand of the Father, and the true blood of Christ which was shed from his side, not only as a sign and by virtue of the sacrament, but in their proper nature and true substance.[19]

Even if this declaration settled the controversy, it did not answer all questions which Berengar had put to the church of his time. It was easy to condemn his views and to compel him to revoke his errors; it was difficult to refute the objections he had raised against the traditional realistic conception of the conversion of the elements. Such questions were: What is the relationship between Christ's body in heaven and Christ's body in the Sacrament? If this body is supposed to be in heaven and on earth at the same time, how can it be on many altars simultaneously? If these questions are answered by referring to the inexplicable miracle of sacramental conversion, another question arises. How is it to be explained that a conversion of the substance leaves all the accidents of bread and wine unchanged? What is changed, and what not? Berengar seems to have been the first to apply the terms 'substance' and 'accidents' in this connection (though he did not yet understand them in the sense of strict Aristotelianism, which did not enter the church until the turn of the 12th and 13th centuries). By these questions Berengar forced his critics to develop a theory which finally became the doctrine of transubstantiation.

4. The Real Presence as Transubstantiation and Concomitance

Up to the time of Berengar, the Western church, like that of the East, had been satisfied with the simple belief that the eucharistic conversion was an inscrutable mystery. This belief, a real, living Christian faith in the Real Presence of the Saviour in the Sacrament of the Altar, remained the very heart of the endeavours of medieval theologians who tried to answer the questions put by Berengar and the new 'dialectics'. This is especially true of men like Anselm of

---

[18]It is noteworthy that according to this view the consecration is effected not only by the words of Christ, but by the whole eucharistic prayer which contains these words. The doctrine of consecration was not yet fully developed at that time.

[19]Denz, 355.

Canterbury, Guitmund of Aversa, Alger of Lüttich and Hugo of St Victor. Their attempts to penetrate into the mystery of the Real Presence are today overshadowed by the mature work of Thomas Aquinas.

One must not forget, however, the refreshing morning which preceded the noontide of High Scholasticism. These early schoolmen, though still unable to build up a system, are real theologians insofar as their thinking is dominated by a deep piety (Anselm wrote his famous 'ontological' proof of the existence of God in the form of a prayer), and by a profound reverence for the Word of God. The seriousness with which Guitmund calls Berengar back to Scripture reminds the reader of Luther. And yet, one question never occurred to these defenders of the Real Presence, namely, whether the understanding of the Real Presence as a conversion is correct. The New Testament does not teach a change of the elements. It does not say anything which could be understood as *conversio, mutatio,* or *transformatio.* It even calls the consecrated elements bread and wine (1 Cor. 10:16, 17; 11:26-28). The medieval theologians were so much under the spell of tradition that they could not get rid of the idea that bread and wine can be the true body and blood of Christ only if they are changed. We have seen that this idea had its roots in the Eastern liturgies, and in those rites of the West that were influenced by the East. The Real Presence seemed to be better safeguarded by this theory than by the formulas of the African-Augustinian tradition. Even the *Apology of the Augsburg Confession* still quotes, as testimonies of the Real Presence, passages from the Greek mass and from Theophylact which speak of a conversion of the elements.[20] If the Lutheran church, even at that time, did not yet realize, as she did after the Council of Trent, how dangerous it is to speak of a conversion of the elements, we shall bear with the Fathers around AD 1100.

---

[20] 'Id enim testatur *canon missae* apud illos, in quo aperte orat sacerdos, ut ***mutato pane*** ipsum corpus Christi ***fiat***. Et Vulgarius (Theophylact) scriptor ***ut nobis videtur non stultus***, diserte inquit, *panem non tantum figuram esse, sed* ***vere in carnem mutari***' (Trigl. 246, 55, *emphasis mine*). See the entire Article 10 of the *Apology*. The Greek word *metaballein* is here translated as *mutare*. It is interesting that in a quotation from Chrysostom in the *Formula of Concord* (*Sol. Decl. VII, 76*, Trigl. 998) the corresponding *metarythmizein* was translated *consecrare*. The Greek terminology is very rich. Besides *metaballein* and *metarythmizein*, we find *metapoiein*, *methistanai*, *metaskeuazein*, *metastoicheioun*. This variety indicates the freedom of the Eastern theologians, as well as what Western theology would call a lack of precision.

The danger does not lie so much in the use of the words *conversio, mutatio,* and the like, which for many might not mean anything more than an attempt to express in human language the incomprehensible mystery that the elements after consecration really are the body and blood of Christ. The danger is, rather, that such words are understood as a sort of explanation of what happens in that miracle, an explanation which requires more explanations. The Eastern church has remained by the simple statement of the liturgy that a *metabolē* takes place. The Roman church has yielded to the temptation to supplement the dogma of the conversion by another dogma about the nature of this conversion. She has defined this conversion as transubstantiation. The development of this new doctrine took place between 1079 and the Council of 1215. It was the work of those theologians that defended the Real Presence. Their writings, like the corresponding books of Eastern theologians on the Sacrament of the Altar, were private writings. However, while the eucharistic theories in the Eastern church remained in the sphere of private speculation, the Western church developed out of the theories of her theologians the new dogma which Eastern Christendom has never accepted (though it has been held as a private opinion by quite a number of theologians since 1274 when, at the second Council of Lyons, it became known to the East).

The doctrine on transubstantiation grew slowly, but with logical consequence, out of the theological work of the adversaries of Berengar, the most important of whom seems to have been Guitmund of Aversa. Almost all elements of the later dogma, except the word 'transubstantiation', originated with him. His definite rejection of 'impanation' (the theory that Christ assumed the bread, as he assumed flesh in the Incarnation) as well as of any other theory that would contradict the real conversion, paved the way for the new dogma. Bread and wine are changed into that body and that blood of Christ which he once had on earth, and which are now glorified in heaven. The question as to how the body can be in heaven and simultaneously on earth is answered by Guitmund, as by Alger, by assuming a sort of 'ubiquity' (as it was called at the time of the Reformation). The human nature, Christ's flesh, shares the omnipresence of Christ's divinity, and thus can be present, without leaving heaven, wherever Christ wants it to be.[21]

[21]'He can be present in heaven and on earth even in a bodily way wherever it may please Him, *ubique unum corpus Christi est',* Alger (MPL 180, 785). For similar utterances of other authors, see R. Seeberg, *op. cit.,* 212.

If Guitmund there reminds us of Luther, he also anticipates Thomas Aquinas, on the other hand, by teaching the illocal presence and the indivisibility of the body of Christ:

> Of this bread, if it is taken, the individual partaker receives not less than all partakers: *Totum unus, totum duo, totum plures sine diminutione percipiunt, quia benedictio huius sacramenti scit distribui, nescit distributione consumi. Idem quoque dicimus, etsi mille missae eodem tempore celebrentur.* (If there is one communicant, he receives the whole body; if there is two, they receive the whole body; if there are more, they receive the whole body without diminution. For the consecration of this Sacrament makes it possible for the body to be distributed. However, it is impossible for it to be consumed by the distribution. The same we must say even if a thousand masses were celebrated at the same time.)[22]

This idea has been taken from a passage of Gregory the Great which at that time was regarded as Augustinian.[23] But it was probably Guitmund that inspired the famous lines of Thomas Aquinas in his '*Lauda Sion salvatorem*' which so frequently have been quoted by Luther and the early Lutherans:

> *Sumit unus, sumunt mille / Quantum isti, tantum ille / nec sumptus consumitur.* (They, too, who of him partake / Sever not, nor rend nor break / But entire their Lord receive / Whether one or thousands eat / All receive the selfsame meat / Nor the less for others leave.)[24]

If the Real Presence is to be accepted in this sense as an unspeakable miracle, more questions must arise. Who receives the body and blood of our Lord? It was Lanfranc who at the very beginning of the Berengarian controversy established the doctrine of the *manducatio impiorum* for the future. The older theologians had been doubtful about it. But now, Augustine's view (based on the fact that Judas, too, had received the consecrated Sacrament with the other disciples[25]), that infidels receive the Lord's body 'according to

———

[22] MPL 149, 1435, 1436.

[23] '*Singuli accipiunt Christum Dominum, et in singulis portionibus totus est, nec per singulas minuitur, sed integrum se praebet in singulis'*, Gregorius M., *Liber sacramentorum, dom. 5 post Epiph.* (MPL 78, 48).

[24] In Luther's *Short Confession* of 1544-45, (WA 54, 146, 3f). There is another example: '*Grund reiner Lehre von dem hochwürdigen Sakrament des wahren Leibes und Blutes Christi, etc., von den Predigern der Grafschaft Mansfeld (1571) fol D 3.* The whole sequence, '*Lauda Sion*', which Thomas wrote for the office of the Feast of Corpus Christi, was sung in Latin (with the lines on transubstantiation slightly changed) in Lutheran churches, as Lucas Lossius's (Lueneburg) *Psalmodia* (Nuremberg, 1553) shows. The hymn is still echoed in German hymns like '*Schmücke dich, o liebe Seele*'.

[25] '*Numquid et Judas magistri venditor et traditor impius, quamvis primum ipsum manibus eius confectum* [the same word is used by Ambrose, *De myst. 9, 53,* to denote

its essence, but not according to its salutary effects',[26] was definitely accepted. Other questions, which the *Formula of Concord, Sol. Decl. VII, 128* (Trigl. 1015) later rejected as 'presumptuous, frivolous, blasphemous', were asked throughout the Middle Ages and even in the 16th century, such as: What happens if an animal, a mouse or a dog, eats a consecrated host, or if such a host is destroyed by fire or otherwise desecrated? It was not only scholastic curiosity which asked such borderline questions, but also the desire to clarify the nature of the Real Presence, and to distinguish the sacramental eating from a materialistic, Capernaitic manducation. There was a general conviction that in such cases a violation of the body of Christ did not take place. Some schoolmen thought that the body of Christ was miraculously removed by angels, or otherwise, and the species only remained. They were not yet ready to teach with Aquinas: As the substance of the body remains as long as the species exist, a violation of the species involves an indirect violation of the body. An animal would eat, with the species, the body, though not as a sacrament (III, 80, 4 ad 3). Otherwise, the doctrine of the Real Presence presented by Thomas was almost completed at the turn of the 11th and 12th centuries. Even the doctrine of concomitance, according to which the whole Christ is present under either species, may be found in the teachings of Anselm of Canterbury.[27] These terms later became popular with the critics of Berengar.

Thus, we are not surprised that during the 12th century the expression 'transubstantiation' appears as another word for 'conversion'. We do not know exactly who was the first to use the new term; perhaps it was Stephen of Autun before 1139.[28] Nor is it known precisely what the theologians who introduced it meant by it, since the classic philosophy of Aristotle did not conquer the church until about the year 1200. The necessity of distinguishing between that which is converted by the consecration and that which evidently remains unchanged (colour, taste, etc. of the elements) had led to the

---

the conversion of the bread which is effected by the consecration] *sacramentum carnis et sanguinis eius cum ceteris discipulis . . . manducaret et biberet, mansit in Christo aut Christus in eo? Sermo 71, 11, 17* (MPL 38, 453).

[26]Lanfranc, *De corpore et sanguine Domini, cap. 20* (MPL 150, 436). See also Alger 1, 21 (MPL 180, 798). The unworthy receive the body '*quantum ad substantiam et non vere quantum ad effectum gratiae*'.

[27]*Ep. 107 (De corpore et sanguine Domini),* (MPL 159, 255).

[28]There is a possibility that another Stephen of Autun, some decades later, is referred to in this tradition.

new theory. Peter Lombard, who died in 1160, still speaks of *conversio* in his *Sentences,* which remained the standard textbook of dogmatics up to the time of the Reformation. But, soon after Lombard, transubstantiation became the technical term for conversion. It was finally dogmatized in that passage of the *Caput Firmiter* of 1215, which we have already quoted in connection with the doctrine of the eucharistic sacrifice.[29] Henceforth, this dogma was the answer to the question as to how the doctrine on the Real Presence, as established by *Ego Berengarius*, was to be understood. It is noteworthy that no further explanation of what transubstantiation means was given by the Council of 1215. The dogma speaks of 'substance' and 'species'. It avoids the term 'accidents', as does also the Council of Trent. The official explanation by the Council of Trent states:

> By the consecration of bread and wine a conversion is brought about of the entire substance of the bread into the body of our Lord Jesus Christ, and of the entire substance of the wine into His blood. This conversion is conveniently and properly called by the Holy Catholic Church 'transubstantiation'.[30]

The corresponding canon, too, avoids speaking of 'accidents'. It condemns those who deny that a transubstantiation takes place in which 'the species of bread and wine only remain'.[31] Also the *Professio Fidei Tridentina,* the summary of the doctrine of Trent, which every Catholic priest must solemnly confess, speaks of 'substance' and 'species'.[32] However, that 'species' here is the same as 'accidents' is shown by the *Catechismus Romanus (Pars II, Cap. 4, Q. 23)* which, though not dogma in itself, is nevertheless an important interpretation of the dogma. Although modern Roman theologians try to minimize the philosophical content of the doctrine of transubstantiation, they must admit that the distinction between 'substance' and 'accidents' is an integral part of the dogma, and as such cannot be neglected or discarded.[33] There is at least one

---

[29] Denz, 430. See above, 15.

[30] *Sessio XIII, Cap. 4* (Denz, 877).

[31] Denz, 884.

[32] Denz, 997.

[33] Dogmaticians like Michael Schmaus (*Kath. Dogmatik, Vol. III, Part 2, 181 ff*) and the commentators in *Deutsche Thomas-Ausgabe* (Vol. 30, 511 f) interpret 'substance' and 'accidents' as not identical with what Thomas, following Aristotle, understood by these terms. They interpret 'substance' as the innermost nature, the core of a thing, while 'species' or 'accidents' then would mean the outward appearance, that which can be perceived by our senses. But even this would not remove the difficulty, as for example, the innermost nature of bread is inseparable from the appearance of bread.

dogmatical decision of the Roman church in which the word 'accidents' is used, namely, the condemnation by the Council of Constance in 1415 of the errors of John Wyclif, one of them being the opinion that 'the accidents of the bread do not remain without subject in this sacrament'.[34]

The implications of the decision of 1215 did not become obvious until the great thinkers of the 13th century embarked upon the great task of interpreting the sacramental system of the church, and especially the Eucharist, in terms of the newly-discovered Aristotelian philosophy. Thomas Aquinas will always remain the classical theologian in the field of Catholic eucharistic doctrine even to those who personally prefer the pious simplicity of Guitmund of Aversa and Hugo of St Victor to the versatility of *doctor angelicus,* who is never at a loss to answer a question. Of the spiritual side of the theology of Thomas we shall speak later. Here we need only state that it was he who gave to the Roman church that understanding of transubstantiation which substantially became the dogma of Trent, and is, therefore, binding on all Catholic theologians, notwithstanding the possibility of deviating in some minor points.

In all this, Luther was not so wrong as his critics (especially Denifle[35]) believed him to be, when he regarded Thomas as the real author of that doctrine. By understanding the words 'substance', 'accidents', and 'transubstantiation', which had been in use for some generations, in the strict sense of Aristotelian philosophy, Aquinas gave to the dogma of 1215 that clarity which is characteristic of the dogma of the Roman church. In some respects Roman dogmatics reached its highest perfection in the final form which Thomas Aquinas gave to the doctrine of transubstantiation.

Before we briefly sketch his views, two remarks may be made in view of popular Protestant prejudices which Lutherans should not share.

First, the Catholic doctrine of transubstantiation should not be denounced as materialistic, otherwise the Lutheran conception of the Sacrament would come under the same verdict. For it is not less realistic in its assumption that Christ's body and blood are *substantialiter* present. The word *substantialiter* means in the

---

[34]Denz, 582. Compare also the condemnation by Pius VI (1794) of the Synod of Pistoia which had tried to understand the Real Presence '*remotis quaestionibus scholasticis*' (Denz, 1529). For a similar warning by Pius XII, see Preface, viii.

[35]H. Denifle, *Luther und Luthertum, I* (1904), 237 ff.

Lutheran doctrine nothing else than *essentialiter* (*wesentlich*),[36] as we speak of the *essentia divina* which is the same as the *substantia divina* (in Greek, *ousia*).[37] 'Substance' is neither in the Lutheran nor in the Catholic dogmatics the same as *materia* (matter), although it may include the material side of a thing. At any rate, 'substance' in this connection is not what the physicist calls substance. For Thomas, *substantia* is a metaphysical concept (as Aristotle understood it): the innermost essence of an individual thing which remains if we take away all qualities attached to it, the 'accidents'. A wall may be white and have a certain height. Being white and having a certain height, however, do not belong to the substance of the wall; they are 'accidents', something which is added to the substance. The 'substance' is the bearer of the 'accidents'. We may leave open the question whether this metaphysical distinction is correct. Aristotle, by the way, did not think of a separation between substance and accidents, but only of a distinction. At any rate, it is not permissible to call transubstantiation, that is, the alleged conversion of one substance into another substance, 'materialistic'. The whole idea belongs to the sphere of metaphysics. What we as Lutheran theologians object to in the doctrine of transubstantiation is that it is a wrong philosophical explanation or description of a miracle which defies all human attempts to explain or describe it.

Secondly, we should never speak of the 'magic' of the Roman mass, as if the words of consecration which effect the Real Presence were a sort of magical incantation. 'Magic' is the attempt of man to compel the deity to do something. A magical formula must always be the same, while the words of consecration may be spoken in different languages and even in various forms, as happens to be the case in the Western and Eastern church. According to Thomas, the words are effective as the words of Christ. He refers to utterances of the Fathers in which the power of consecration is solely attributed to the

[36] *Form. Conc., Epitome VII* (Trigl. 808, 2 and 6), the Latin '*vere et substantialiter*' is equivalent to '*wahrhaftig und wesentlich*'. The German here, of course, is the original text. In his suggestion of a union formula at Marburg (below, 214, 215), Luther explained '*wahrhaftiglich*' (truly) by '*hoc est substantialiter et essentialiter*'. This shows what Lutheran theology means when speaking of the substance of the body and blood: the real, true body and blood. The Latin words no longer have a philosophical meaning.

[37] In AC Article 1 '*una essentia . . . tres personae*' corresponds to the original Latin formula: '*una substantia . . . tres personae*'.

almighty words of Christ, and insists on the minister's being only the instrument of Christ in this case.[38] Theoretically, for Thomas as for the Lutheran church, Christ is the real consecrator. What we criticize, together with the Lutheran church of all times, is that Thomas and the Roman church did not stick to this conviction, but rather made the priest a partner of Christ in this most solemn act of the mass. As the consecration is at the same time the act of offering, the priest not only acts *ex persona Christi*, but exercises the power, given to him in ordination, 'to offer sacrifice to God for the living and the dead'. If the Roman church had taken quite seriously the idea that Christ is the real consecrator, she could not have tolerated or even encouraged the popular glorification of the priest's power to 'make' (*conficere*) the body of Christ.

What, then, is transubstantiation according to Thomas? It is the great miracle of the conversion of bread and wine into the true body and blood of Christ which takes place as soon as the priest has spoken the words in the prayer *Qui pridie* of the *Canon Missae:* 'This is my body' and 'This is the chalice of my blood'. With the last sound of 'This is my body', the entire substance of the bread is changed into the entire substance of the body of Christ. The same miraculous change of the substance of the wine into the substance of the blood takes place in the very moment when the words on the chalice have been uttered. The Thomistic doctrine, thus, has fixed what is called 'the moment of consecration', the moment when bread and wine cease to be what they were before, and become the body and blood of Christ. It may be stated that this doctrine specifies also the end of the Real Presence. It is the moment in which the species of bread and wine are destroyed, be it by the process of digestion or by another event. The consequences of this view we shall discuss later.

What is the difference between the old *conversio* and transubstantiation as Thomas understood it? The theory of Thomas is an attempt to describe the miracle of conversion which had privately been called 'transubstantiation' in terms of Aristotelian philosophy

---

[38] *Summa theol. III, Q. 78, Art. 1,* Thomas in the *'Sed contra'* quotes Ambrose, *De sacramentis, 4, 4: 'Consecratio fit verbis et sermonibus Domini Jesu Christi'.* In the body of the Article, Thomas says expressly of the minister that his only function is to recite the words of Christ. The priest acts *'ex persona Christi loquentis'.* Very often the theologians of the Middle Ages quote the famous passage of Chrysostom, *De prod. Judae 1, 6* (MPG 45, 380) which is also used by the *Form. Conc.* (*Sol. Decl. VII, 75, 6;* Trigl. 998 ff) to show that the almighty words of Christ spoken at the Last Supper are effective for all times, like the words of the Creator in Gen. 1:28.

as early as the 12th century, and officially since 1215. The distinction between 'substance' and 'accidents' in the strict sense of Aristotelian metaphysics, which had already been applied to the doctrine of the Eucharist by Albertus Magnus,[39] made it possible to give an accurate answer to the question as to what is changed by the consecration and what not. It was now possible to explain how a complete conversion took place while no change in the elements was noticeable, and the 'species' remained to the human senses what they had been before. The great advantage of this interpretation of the dogma was that the miracle of transubstantiation remained in the sphere of metaphysics and spirituality, and that the physical qualities of bread and wine as 'accidents', which are not affected by the change, could be fully recognized even after consecration. The great disadvantage of this theory is the necessity to explain how 'accidents' can exist without their proper 'substance', as H.B. Workman puts it:

> How can appearances exist without anything that appears — how can the *noumenon* alone be changed while all the *phenomena* or accidents remain, e.g. the *panitas* and *vinitas*, to use the jargon of the schools.[40]

Thomas knows that such things cannot happen except by a special miracle of almighty God which takes place in the Eucharist only. The assumption of such a miracle is for him a necessary conclusion from the fact that, on the one hand, there is a complete conversion of the elements and that, on the other hand, the species remain what they have been. The miracle of conversion is proved, as Thomas thinks, by the Words of Institution.[41] *'Hoc est corpus meum'* can mean nothing else but that what Jesus held in his hands and gave to his disciples was his body; otherwise he would have said, ***'Hic est corpus meum (Here is my body)',*** namely, where the bread is. Besides, the veneration of the Sacrament would be impossible if bread, a created substance, were present. We shall have to speak later of the relationship between the dogma of transubstantiation and the veneration of the

———

[39]The influence which the *doctor universalis* had on Thomas's doctrine on the Eucharist cannot be exaggerated. Thus, for instance, even the hymn '*Adoro te devote / Latens Deitas / Qui sub his figuris / Vere latitas . . .*' was inspired by a treatise of Albert on the hidden deity. Albert compares the deception of Isaac by Jacob with the deception of the senses in the Eucharist: '*Ibi fallitur visus . . . gustus . . . sensus*'. Hearing only is not deceived. Nothing is more true than the words of Christ: 'This is my body'. This is the source of Thomas's stanza: '*Visus, tactus, gustus in te fallitur / Sed auditu solo tuto creditur / Credo quidquid dixit Dei filius / Nil hoc verbo veritatis verius*'.

[40]H.B. Workman, *John Wyclif, II* (Oxford, 1926), 31.

[41]*Summa theol. III, Q. 75, Art. 2.*

Sacrament. Here we need only state that Thomas tries to base his doctrine on Christ's words alone. Transubstantiation is for him, therefore, an article of 'faith alone', to be believed on the authority of the Word of God.[42] But the conclusion which he draws, that in this unique case accidents can exist without substance, was a mere philosophical sentence which was bound to lead to further philosophical assumptions. Each accident must have a *subjectum,* something of which it is an accident. If the unique miracle takes place that the accidents of bread and wine exist without their proper substance, then a substitute for this substance must be found. Following Albert, Thomas assumes that the *quantitas dimensiva* becomes the *subjectum* of the accidents of bread and wine. It is not necessary to explain in detail what Thomas meant when he assumed that 'quantity' (the second of the categories of Aristotle) stepped into the place of 'substance' (the first of the categories). Suffice it to say that the miracle of the Real Presence here becomes a metaphysical miracle. We have here the most outstanding example of the great synthesis of Christian faith and Aristotelian philosophy which is the characteristic feature of Thomism. Not only the Reformation (which had to reject the confusing of the Gospel with a more-or-less pagan philosophy) asked the question whether the assumption of such a 'miracle' of accidents existing without their substance belonged in the realm of the Christian faith; the schoolmen who succeeded Thomas in the building up of scholastic theology were already aware of the insuperable difficulties of this doctrine of transubstantiation and tried to improve it, as far as this was possible.

The theory of Thomas definitely established the doctrine, which had already been held by the earlier theologians, that the presence of Christ's body and blood is not to be understood as a local one. The body is present, not locally, but substantially.[43] What, then, is the relationship of the body of Christ to space? Must we not say that the body is at a certain place? Christ's body is in heaven, and Thomas, like most of the schoolmen, understands that to mean that there is a

---

[42]*Sola fide* (in the sense of obedient assent to the revealed doctrine) do we know that body and blood are present, not by the perception of the senses or by our intellect: *Summa theol. III, Q. 75, Art. 1;* compare the lines from Thomas's '*Pange lingua*': '*Et si sensus deficit / Ad firmandum cor sincerum / Sola fides sufficit* (Hymn for the Vespers of Corpus Christi).

[43]*Summa theol. III, Q. 76, Art. 5: 'Corpus Christi non est in hoc sacramento sicut in loco* (localiter), *sed per modum substantiae'.*

certain place in heaven where Christ is sitting on the right hand of the Father. The body of Christ, however, is at the same time, according to its substance, on all altars where the Eucharist is celebrated. It is obviously not on the whole altar, but just where the species are. What is this *ubi eucharisticum,* as theologians later formulated the problem? If Christ's body is where the consecrated species are, is not this a sort of local presence? Thomas answers this question by referring to the two modes of presence which the philosophers attribute to a body.[44] The first is the local or *circumscriptive* presence that belongs to a physical body. There the boundaries of the body coincide with the boundary of the space that it fills. This is not the mode of the presence of Christ's body; otherwise, it could not be at more than one place at one time. The second is what Thomas calls the definite presence, the *esse definitive* (*definitive* here to be understood in its original Latin meaning: 'setting a boundary'). An angel, for instance, may be in a house, but does not fill it. These two modes of presence cannot be attributed to the body of Christ, though the *definitive* comes nearer to that presence than the *circumscriptive.* His final answer is that the presence of the eucharistic body is something unique, owing to the uniqueness of the conversion of the substance.[45] Here Thomas left a problem to subsequent scholastic schools.

The doctrine of transubstantiation, as Thomas formulated it, contains the doctrine of concomitance, which had already been suggested by Anselm. According to this theory, the blood of Christ is *per concomitantiam* together with the body after the consecration of the bread and, accordingly, the body with the blood after the wine has been consecrated. Body and blood, furthermore, are accompanied by the soul of Christ and by his divine nature.[46] The presence of Christ in this Sacrament is, then, always the presence of the whole Christ, his human and his divine nature. This theory was

---

[44] *Summa theol. III, Q. 76, Art. 5.* The illocal presence had been accepted for several centuries as we have shown. See Luther's *Short Confession* (of 1544) about Marburg: '*Und der Zwingel hatte ein lang ungereimt Geschwätz mit mir de locali inclusione, dass im Brot nicht sein könnte der Leib Christi, wie im Raum oder Gefässe, gerade als lehrten wir, dass Christus' Leib im Brot wäre wie Stroh im Sacke oder Wein im Fass. Demnach ihrer etliche entschuldigten sich, sie hätten's nicht anders verstanden, wir und die Papisten lehrten also, dass Christus' Leib wäre im Sakrament localiter, wie Stroh im Sacke. O das war eine faule, kalte, lahme Entschuldigung. Denn sie wussten sehr wohl, dass weder die Papisten noch wir so hatten gelehrt*' (WA 54, 153, 10ff).

[45] *Comm. Sent., Liber 4, Dist. 10, Art. 3, Q. 1, ad. 1.*

[46] *Summa theol. III, Q. 76, Art. 1.*

dogmatized exactly two hundred years after the dogma of transubstantiation, when the Council of Constance in 1415 definitely imposed upon the Roman church the communion under one species, with the statement that

> the whole body and blood of Christ are truly contained under the species of the bread as well as under the species of the wine.[47]

The Council of Trent accepted and confirmed the whole doctrine of Thomas concerning this matter by expressly including the soul and the divinity of Christ in the concomitance.[48]

The doctrine of concomitance had a compelling practical meaning, not only with respect to the *communio sub una,* but also as an important presupposition for the veneration of the Sacrament, of which we have to speak later. Since the consecrated host is transubstantiated into the body of Christ, the veneration of this host is a veneration of the whole Christ. This presence of Christ is, according to Thomas, not limited to the celebration of the Eucharist, as some older historians like Fr. Loofs understand the earlier schoolmen.[49] The passages quoted in support of that view do not refer at all to the question whether a consecrated host remains the body of Christ. The question was never debated by the medieval theologians, because it had never been a problem for the Catholic churches since the second century, if not earlier. It is the presupposition for the custom to send the Eucharist (that is, the consecrated bread) to others (to the sick, to other churches as a token of communion, and the like). Even Luther makes a distinction between the consecrated and unconsecrated host. Thomas gives a theoretical answer to the question as to the duration of the presence. The body of Christ remains as long as the species remain. Only when

[47]Denz, 626.

[48]*Sessio XIII;* Denz, 876.

[49]Fr. Loofs, *Leitfaden der Dogmengeschichte,* (4th ed., 1906), 579, 580. The passages quoted, however, refer to what happens to the host after the *sumptio,* not after the *usus* (the celebration). In this sense only is Hugo, *De sacramentis II, 8, 13* (MPL 176, 471) to be understood: '*Postquam sensus corporalis in percipiendo deficit, deinceps praesentia quaerenda non est',* which means that we should not ask what becomes of the host after its reception. In this connection the answer to the question as to what happens to the consecrated host if a mouse or a dog eats it, must be understood as given by Innocent III (on the basis of former discussions of that problem which was still debated in the Reformation). *De sacro altaris mysterio 4, 11* (MPL 217, 863): A mouse cannot eat the body of Christ because the Real Presence, as it begins miraculously, in such a case ends miraculously. The answer of Thomas we have mentioned on p 32. There has always been a tendency in the Roman church to 'burn such questions in the fire of faith'.

they are destroyed, either by the process of digestion, or by an accident like fire, the Real Presence ceases.[50] This solution of a much-debated problem includes, by the way, another miracle. How can accidents without a real substance be dissolved into another substance, which happens, for example, when the consecrated bread (or rather, to put it in terms of Thomistic theology, the species of bread) is assimilated by the human body? It is true, Thomas denies that there is a second miracle.[51] He does not deny that the species can be used as food. But it is not bread and wine that nourishes him who partakes of the species. It is rather the *quantitas dimensiva* of bread and wine, from which the new substance arises in the process of the destruction of the species.

One last problem of Thomas's doctrine on the Sacrament of the Altar has to be mentioned because it played a great role in the Late Middle Ages as well as in the Reformation. That is the question whether or not this Sacrament is necessary for salvation. This question was answered in the affirmative by most of the Ancient Fathers,[52] and by practically the whole church in the West up to the end of the 12th century, and by the church in the East until today. This explains the old custom of giving the Eucharist not only to adults but also to children, at least under the species of the wine, immediately after Baptism and confirmation. The biblical basis for this view was John 6:53: 'Except ye eat the flesh of the Son of man, and drink his blood, ye have no life in you'. The decision which Thomas gives is based on Augustine.[53]

While the great Latin Father in the later period of his life, following the tradition of his church, gave Holy Communion to newly-baptized children as a means of grace necessary for salvation, his classical writings contain a spiritual understanding of John 6, according to which belief in Christ constitutes that eating and drinking.[54] Besides, not the mere Sacrament, the *signum,* but the *res*

———

[50] *Summa theol. III, Q.77, Art. 4-6.*

[51] He regards it as a consequence of the former miracle which makes accidents exist without their substance: *Summa theol. III, Q. 77, Art. 5.*

[52] For instance, Cyril of Alexandria, like many Eastern theologians, teaches the bodily effect of the Sacrament (resurrection, John 6:54); in the West, Isidore of Seville, the Venerable Bede, and others.

[53] *Summa theol. III, Q. 76, Art. 3.*

[54] Augustine explains John 6:54: 'Eating that food and drinking that drink to remain in Christ and to have Him dwelling in us' (in John 26:18; MPL 35, 1614). The famous *Crede et manducasti* (in John 25:12; MPL 35, 1602) does not refer to the Lord's Supper at all, but to the spiritual eating of Christ as the bread of life, John 6:27 ff.

is what is really essential, and this *res* can be received without a bodily reception of the *signum*. From this it follows that there are two ways of receiving this Sacrament, a bodily one and a spiritual one. Augustine had to admit, even in his anti-Donatistic period, that even Baptism could be replaced at least by suffering 'for the name of Christ', or by firm belief, as the story of the thief on the cross suggested.[55] From this the Ancient Church had already drawn the conclusion that there is a *baptismus sanguinis* for those who shed their blood for Christ before they were able to receive Baptism. Later, the mere desire to receive Baptism was regarded as another substitute. Thus, we have with Thomas the three kinds of baptism: *baptismus fluminis, baptismus sanguinis, baptismus flaminis* (baptism of water, baptism of blood, and baptism of desire).[56] Although Thomas regards baptism with water as the only sacramental Baptism, he admits that the grace of Baptism can be received also by the other two. If, then, even the fundamental Sacrament of Baptism can be received spiritually, how much more the Sacrament of the Eucharist? Thus, since Thomas's Catholic theology, based on Augustine, distinguishes between the sacramental and the spiritual reception of the Sacrament, both belong together for a worthy reception. The body of Christ is received unworthily also when it is received merely bodily. The recipient does not get the *res sacramenti*, which in this case is the unity of the mystical body of Christ. This *res* is received by spiritual communion, even if the outward, sacramental communion is missing. Thus, the spiritual reception of the Sacrament only is necessary for salvation. This is the answer of Thomas which was accepted by the Council of Trent,[57] and which *mutatis mutandis* also became the doctrine of the Lutheran church.[58] The doctrine of spiritual communion as the most essential in Holy Communion, an Augustinian heritage, deeply influenced the Late Middle Ages and helped to develop that spiritual

---

[55] *De baptismo contra Donatistas, cap. 22* (MPL 43, 173).

[56] *Baptismus aquae, sanguinis, flaminis (Summa theol, III, Q. 66, Art. 11).* Another term is: *baptismus fluminis, flaminis, sanguinis.* The *baptismus flaminis* is what is usually called *baptismus in voto.* All sacraments necessary for salvation, including the sacrament of penance, can be received, according to the Roman church, *in voto.* Thus the sentence is valid: '*Deus non alligatur sacramentis suis*'. This broadmindedness has always been kept in mind when the Roman doctrine on the sacraments is discussed.

[57] *Sessio XIII, cap. 8* (Denz, 881) distinguishes between three modes of communion: sacramental, spiritual, and sacramental-and-spiritual.

[58] *Form. Conc., Sol. Decl. VII, 61-66* (Trigl. 992-96).

understanding of the Sacrament of the Altar which we find in the *devotio moderna*, the piety of the Brethren of the Common Life, and in the humanist movement. In this way, contrary to the intention of Thomas, it paved the way for the destruction of the Sacrament in the more radical movements of the 15th and 16th centuries.

5. Medieval Criticism of Transubstantiation

The introduction of the dogma on transubstantiation into the church is one of the greatest tragedies in the history of the Sacrament, comparable only to the rise of the idea of the sacrifice of the mass in the first centuries. As we have seen, it was originally another, more definite, form of the old word 'conversion', which in itself was a very questionable expression of the biblical truth that the bread is the body, for in the New Testament we do not find the slightest trace of such a conversion. Conversion is an attempt to explain the inexplicable miracle of the Real Presence.

With the introduction of the term 'transubstantiation', the religious miracle began to acquire a philosophical aspect, especially when Albertus Magnus and his great disciple Thomas Aquinas interpreted transubstantiation in the terms of Aristotelian philosophy. It is not within the purpose of this book to show how this philosophy was applied also to other aspects of the Sacrament — for example, the understanding of the Word and the element as *forma* and *materia*, or the *dispositio* (preparation) as a condition for the blessed reception of the Sacrament. The idea of transubstantiation is sufficient to show how closely the biblical ideas of the Real Presence in this doctrine are bound up with philosophical speculation, not only with respect to the distinction of substance and accidents, but also with the assumption that accidents can exist without their proper substance, and vice versa. Whatever modern Roman theologians may say to minimize the philosophical content of their doctrine on the Sacrament of the Altar, they simply cannot get rid of the philosophical miracle which has been devised to explain the biblical miracle of the New Testament. Thus, we shall not be surprised to observe that, soon after Thomas had given his interpretation of the dogma of the year 1215, serious doubts arose as to whether this understanding of the relationship between the species and the body and blood of Christ was correct.

Since the decision of the Ecumenical Council of 1215 was irrevocable, corrections or improvements could be made by way of an interpretation of the dogma only. Hence, we find the later schoolmen making desperate attempts to reintroduce, under various names, the substance of bread and wine into the Sacrament without violating the dogma. Duns Scotus (1270-1308), for instance, teaches what he calls *transubstantiatio adductiva,* instead of *transubstantia productiva* which he finds in Aquinas. In other words, Duns Scotus assumes that the substance of the body of Christ is added to the substance of the bread. He and his school try to reconcile this idea with the official doctrine by assuming that the substance of the bread is being annihilated. Other thinkers, however, hold that the substance of the bread is retained. Thus, they arrive at the doctrine of consubstantiation, which teaches that the substance of the bread and the substance of the body are coexisting in the consecrated host. This theory could be maintained only with restrictions and qualifications necessary to avoid conflicts with the teaching office of the church by many theologians of the school of Occam (died about 1350), the representatives of the *via moderna,* in contradistinction to the men of the *via antiqua* who followed their great master Thomas. Luther, as we shall see later, was deeply impressed when for the first time he read in Peter d'Ailly's *Quaestiones on Peter Lombard* that the doctrine on consubstantiation, as requiring fewer miracles, would have to be preferred, if transubstantiation had not been decreed by the church. In studying the later stages of scholasticism, one gains the impression that consubstantiation was favoured by so many theologians that it seems very doubtful whether the dogma on transubstantiation would ever have become the official doctrine of the Roman church, if the decision of 1215 could have been postponed, like the doctrine on concomitance, for another 200 years. Why that had not been possible we shall understand if we look into the practical and devotional side of the matter.

It would be neither possible nor helpful for our purpose to enter into a discussion of the manifold and complicated ideas of later Scholasticism about the eucharistic doctrine. Some remarks will be made when we speak of Luther. However, it is of great interest to discuss briefly the views of John Wyclif, whose criticism of the doctrine on transubstantiation played an important role in the 15th century, and who paved the way for Reformed Protestantism, though at the present stage of historical research we are not able to state exactly the direct or indirect influence which he exercised on Reformed theology. To speak of him is the more necessary because his works are being read very rarely today, and many untenable statements on his eucharistic doctrine have been more or less canonized in current textbooks.

One must remember that Wyclif was not a reformer, but a medieval thinker who had the misfortune of becoming, in public opinion, a dangerous heretic. His opposition to transubstantiation originally had purely philosophical reasons. As a realist he protested against the form of the doctrine which he found among the Scotists at Oxford. He did not like their theory of 'annihilation', and could not agree with their solution of the problem of accidents existing without substance. Yet, for many years, he did not doubt transubstantiation itself, and tried to reconcile it with the doctrines of the Ancient Fathers. It was only in the last years of his life — probably not before 1379 [59] — that he realized that transubstantiation in any form contradicts reason, the Fathers, and Scripture. This doctrine, which had been unknown during the first 1,000 years of the church when Satan was bound, was now regarded by him as an invention of Antichrist. The Words of Institution must be taken figuratively. They are not a *praedicatio identica*,[60] a way of speech which establishes an identity between two beings (as, for example, the sentence, Christ is man), but, rather, a *praedicatio tropica* which must be understood

---

[59] H.B. Workman, *John Wyclif, II* (1926), 30 and 408.

[60] This is the original meaning of the much-debated phrase which Luther, owing to his necessarily fragmentary knowledge of Wyclif's theology, regarded as the genuine doctrine of Wyclif. Compare Wyclif, *De Eucharistia Tractatus Major*, ed. J. Loserth (London, 1892), 2, 22;35, 17;200, 2 ff; 291 ff, with Luther, *Vom Abendmahl Christi. Bekenntnis*, WA 26, where Luther (437-445) deals with what he regards as Wyclif's doctrine under the title *De praedicatione identica.* Luther is right in criticizing Wyclif as denying that the bread is the body. He understands *praedicatio identica* as a sentence in which subject and predicate are identical. As for the 'sophists', the consecrated bread is no longer bread, but the body of Christ, so for Wyclif, Luther thinks quite correctly, the bread is bread and not body. Thus he can say of the *praedicatio identica: 'Es ist auch keine da, sondern es träumet dem Wiclif und den Sophisten also'* (WA 26, 445, 1). For Wyclif, however, *praedicatio identica* is the opposite to *praedicatio figurativa.* He rejects the former and accepts the latter. To give another example we quote *De eucharistia,* 35, 17 ff: *'Identica (sc. praedicatio) est, quando praedicatum identice asseritur de subjecto, ut Christus est homo. Sed praedicatio tropica vel figurativa est, quando unum extremum notatur figurari per reliquum, ut prius exposui: Petra autem erat Christus'* (1 Cor. 10:4). A closer study of Wyclif's doctrine shows that the footnote WA 26, 437 f has to be corrected insofar as the editors follow the Reformed interpreters of Wyclif like Buddensieg (*Prot. Real-Enzyklopädie,* 3rd ed., Vol. 21, 225 ff) who find in Wyclif a representative of what they understand by Real Presence. The same applies to the book by H.B. Workman, *John Wyclif, II,* 36 f, excellent in its way. See also Wyclif's *De apostasia* (London, 1889) with the illuminating introduction by the editor, M. H. Dziewicki.

figurative vel tropice or *parabolice,* like the word of Christ that John the Baptist is Elijah.[61] The consecrated bread remains bread. This is the doctrine of remanence (*remanentia*) which later became one of the most characteristic features of Wyclifism.

Thus, Wyclif rejects not only transubstantiation, but also what he calls 'identification' and 'impanation'.[62] 'Identification', which he finds in Peter Lombard, is every theory which identifies the elements with the body and blood of Christ by stating that the bread is the body, the wine is the blood.[63] 'Impanation' (and 'invination') is the theory that we have already mentioned in speaking of Guitmund of Aversa, whose book against Berengar was carefully studied by Wyclif: Just as the Son of God assumes flesh in the incarnation, so the body and blood of Christ assume the earthly elements in the Sacrament of the Altar.[64] If Wyclif accepts the figurative meaning of the sacramental words, he still does not want to give up the Real Presence. He emphasizes his disagreement with the older views of Berengar. He approves of the rejection of these views by the church, and accepts wholeheartedly the declaration *Ego Berengarius* of 1079. But he reads into this declaration his own theory, which actually is the very doctrine condemned by that document. The Real Presence, as he understands it, is not the presence of the true body and blood of Christ.

> The consecrated host is neither Christ, nor any part of him, but the effectual sign of him (*efficax eius signum*),

he says in the first of his theses of 1381.[65] This is exactly the view of Berengar condemned by the church. If the fourth thesis states that the Eucharist contains 'truly and really' body and blood of Christ, this 'Real Presence' must be understood as a 'sacramental' presence. Wyclif compares Christ's presence with the threefold presence of a king in his realm: the local, the potential, and the intentional presence. Locally, Christ is present in heaven; potentially, throughout the world; intentionally, in various ways and especially

---

[61] *De eucharistia,* 83, 18 with the quotation of Matthew 13:37-40.

[62] *op. cit.,* 190 f.

[63] *op. cit.,* 190 ff.

[64] Compare Guitmund (MPL 149, 1430 C): *'Alii . . . dicunt ibi corpus et sanguinem Domini re vera, sed latenter contineri et, ut sumi possint quodammodo, ut ita dixerim impanari'.* *Impanatio* and *invinatio* are mentioned in MPL 149, 1490. See also the passage on *impanatores,* quoted above, 27.

[65] *Fasciculi zizaniorum* [Bundles of Tares] *Mag. Joh. Wyclif,* ed. W. Shirley, *Roll's Series, V* (London, 1858), 105. The same expression is found in numerous places.

in the effectual sign of the host. Wyclif can also put it this way: Christ's body is virtually present in the host, or is present '*mystice*'. No unbeliever can receive it. This view he reads into all the Fathers, including John of Damascus.

We must be satisfied with this short presentation of Wyclif's doctrine on the Real Presence, for it cannot be our task to give a complete picture of his doctrine on the Lord's Supper. As for the two other doctrines concerning the Sacrament, the sacrifice and concomitance, it seems that Wyclif in the short period of his fight against transubstantiation did not deal with these problems. A criticism of the sacrifice was outside of his horizon. He speaks of the priest (*sacerdos*) who confects (*conficit*) the Sacrament. The concomitance would be meaningless without the Real Presence of the body and blood.

In order to understand Wyclif's place in the history of the Lord's Supper, one must always remember that he was a medieval theologian. It is impossible to understand him from the point of view of the churches of the Reformation. The questions he answers are questions of the Middle Ages, and his way of thinking makes him a neighbour of the schoolmen more than of the Reformers. The Reformers, Zwingli and Calvin, as well as Luther, did not know much of him. His writings were almost inaccessible to them. And yet he had a great influence on the doctrines of the 16th century, especially on those of Zwingli. It was an indirect influence. Wyclifism became a power in eastern Europe, in Bohemia, in the 15th century. But his ideas must have been known also in western Europe, especially in the Netherlands from where Zwingli received his tropical understanding of the Sacrament.

Thus, the close relationship between Zwingli and Wyclif must be explained. Both understand the Words of Institution figuratively. Both abhor the idea of a bodily eating and drinking and recognize a spiritual manducation of the Sacrament only. For both it is an especially-horrible idea that an unworthy priest could consecrate the bread.[66] Both refer to Scripture and reason. Zwingli uses almost the same proof-texts, such as John 6; 15:1; Matt. 11:14; 1 Cor. 10:4. Both refer to Augustine as the great patristic authority, especially with

[66]The value of a mass depends on the character of the priest. Thus, one mass may be damnable and hateful to God, another one acceptable: *De eucharistia,* 4, 112, 113. Notice here how the idea of an acceptable sacrifice is still upheld. The conclusion that Wyclif draws is that a pious layman can consecrate (*op. cit.,* 4, 15; 98, 28 ff).

respect to the idea that the body of Christ is in heaven and not on earth. To both, transubstantiation is the great corruption of the church because it leads to idolatry. In all these respects, Wyclif is like Berengar though he misunderstands him in many respects, a *Zwinglius ante Zwinglium.* These three men are for us the representatives of a theological tradition that runs through the centuries like a river which disappears for long stretches, only later to come to the surface again at some distant point.

6. Eucharistic Piety, Devotion, and Practice

The reader of the books written on the history of doctrine in the 19th century, and in the beginning of the 20th, easily gets the impression that during the Middle Ages the question of the Lord's Supper was merely or mainly a problem of theological thought and scholastic distinctions. Nothing could be more misleading than such an idea. It would be as incorrect as to understand medieval cathedrals primarily as a display of an amazing knowledge of mathematics and statics. As the medieval church was built for the celebration of the mass and the adoration of Christ as present in the Sacrament, so the eucharistic dogma of those centuries had a very practical side. This dogma cannot be understood without the liturgy of the Eucharist and the personal devotion connected with its doctrine.

This may be illustrated by an example. When Thomas Aquinas was taken ill in the year 1274 on his last journey from Naples to Lyons, where his presence at the Council was urgently needed for the union negotiations with the Greeks, he was brought to the Cistercian Abbey of Fossa Nuova — a man facing death at the age of not quite fifty. When his end approached, he received the Sacrament with the words:

> I receive Thee, the price of my soul's ransom. For love of Thee I have studied, passed watchful nights, and laboured. Thee I have preached and taught. Never have I said anything against Thee. If, however, I should have said something wrong on this or the other sacraments, I submit it for correction to the Holy Roman Church, in whose obedience I am about to depart this life.[67]

---

[67] *'Sumo te pretium redemptionis animae meae, pro cuius amore studui, vigilavi, et laboravi. Te praedicavi et docui, nihil contra te dixi umquam, sed quod male dixi de hoc sacramento et aliis, totum relinquo correctioni Sanctae Romanae Ecclesiae, in cuius obedientia nunc transeo ex hac vita'.* This is the text given by William of Tocco in his *Vita S. Thomae Aquinatis* (Paris, 1320), contained in *Acta Sanctorum,* for March, part I, and republished by Pruemmer, *Fontes Vitae S. Thomae Aq. Fasc. 1.* The report is confirmed by that contained originally in the Proceedings of the Inquisition of Naples concerning the canonization of Thomas.

According to another source (which, however, might not be free from legendary elements[68]), he prayed after having received the *viaticum* with the words of his great eucharistic hymn:

> *Adoro te devote / Latens Deitas / Quae sub his figuris / Vere latitas . . . ,*

a hymn that has always been regarded as one of the greatest confessions of the belief in the Real Presence, and which as such is still quoted, along with two communion prayers of Aquinas, by Johann Gerhard in the last chapter of his *locus, De coena Domini.*[69] It seems as if the greatest thinker of the Middle Ages in the hour of death forgot what the world regards as his real life-work, that mighty synthesis of Christian faith and Aristotelian philosophy in the greatest system of medieval thought, and nothing is left except the *unum necessarium,* faith in Christ as it is expressed in that hymn which adores the hidden Christ:

> *In cruce latebat / Sola Deitas / Sed hic latet simul / Et humanitas / Ambo tamen credens / atque confitens / Peto quod petivit / Latro penitens.* (God only on the cross lay hid from view / But here lies hid at once the manhood too / and I in both professing my belief / Make the same prayer as the repentant thief.)

That is the other side of medieval scholasticism as far as it is real theology. For theology in its deepest sense is not only thinking of God, but also thinking in the presence of God; not only speaking of Christ, but also speaking to him: 'Thee I have preached and taught'. No one can comprehend the endeavours of the Middle Ages to understand the mystery of the Real Presence unless he knows this secret background of scholastic theology.

The practical background, liturgical as well as devotional, of medieval eucharistic theology becomes evident if we observe the difference between the Eucharist of the Early Church and the medieval mass. They all, of course, have that in common which is really essential for the Sacrament of the Altar in the Catholic sense. One of the most convincing and impressive results of Dom Gregory Dix's *magnum opus* is the proof that what he calls 'the shape of the liturgy', including the most important formulas, is preserved throughout the centuries and makes the liturgy one, despite the fact that an amazing variety, not only of the many rites of the Eastern and

---

[68]Definitely legendary seem to be the story that upon entering the abbey he went straight to the church to adore the Blessed Sacrament, as well as some other traditions connected with his death.

[69]*Loci theologici, XXI* (ed. Preuss, V, 252).

Western churches, but also of the local traditions within these rites, lasted to a high degree even throughout the Middle Ages. However, a great change took place concerning the understanding and the performance of the liturgy during the centuries of the decay of the ancient, and the rise of the medieval, world. This change began when, after the time of Constantine, the Eucharist became a public instead of a private form of worship. It has sometimes been said that the difference between the Catholic and the Protestant churches of the 16th century was not so conspicuous as the difference between the pre-Nicene and the post-Nicene church. This applies especially to the history of liturgy. Certainly the fourth century, which brought the church into the centre of public life, made it possible to develop the old worship to that outward perfection which characterizes the Catholic liturgies. And yet there was a deep difference which has been observed not only by historians, but also by leaders of the modern Liturgical Movement within the Roman church.

The church of the first centuries, consisting of people who had entered the church out of deep convictions, assembled on Sunday as *ecclesia orans.* It was a body, and not an aggregation of individuals only, which prayed and celebrated the Sacrament as a 'corporate action'. It was the people of God, the Body of Christ at prayer. All Catholic liturgies have preserved this character as the people of God at prayer: '*nos, servi tui, sed et plebs tua sancta',* as the *Canon Missae* puts it. Theoretically, the mass has ever remained corporate worship. Practically, however, this consciousness of being one community began to dwindle when the masses of the Empire entered the church. The old corporate service went on, but it was a sort of *ecclesia representativa* (the members of a monastery, the clergy of larger churches like cathedrals) who performed the elaborate rites and held the prayer-services of the liturgical day. The laypeople became more or less spectators, or they were not present at all, as in the monasteries, being satisfied that the *ecclesia representativa* prayed and sacrificed for them. Their personal devotion became more and more independent of the corporate worship of the professional men of religion.

This development went on when the new pagan tribes and people which were conquering the western provinces of the Roman Empire were baptized. In contrast with the East, where the national language was used as liturgical language, the Western church imposed on the newly-converted a mass in a language unknown to the people. Thus, it was quite impossible for an *ecclesia orans* in the old sense to arise in

Western Christendom. One of the reasons why the Reformation (in some countries, within one generation) swept away the Roman church and its mass was the simple fact that now, for the first time, the people of western and northern Europe could have a real share in the liturgy, even if it was a poor liturgy in many cases. Never during the thousand years of the Middle Ages could the claim of the liturgy to be the worship of God's people, and the fact that the worshippers held their private devotion during mass, be brought into harmony. It is not the Reformation that made the 'congregation' an assembly of individuals only; this was a medieval heritage.

This development, and the impact it had on medieval Christendom, become evident if we ask what 'Holy Communion' meant in the Middle Ages. The Early Church could not think of a Eucharist in which not all present offered their gifts and received the body and blood of Christ. There was also private communion insofar as the members of the church took along some consecrated bread to eat at daybreak before they partook of any other food. Whatever has to be said from the point of view of the New Testament about this custom, it is a striking proof of the harmony which existed in the Early Church between 'corporate' and 'private' devotion. For centuries the idea prevailed that the whole congregation took part in the communion. If in Orthodox churches today the *eulogiai* (blessed, but unconsecrated, bread) are distributed after mass to all present, we still have a remnant of the old idea. The idea that the entire congregation could and should receive communion during mass was absolutely foreign to the medieval church (with the exception only of a special mass like that of Easter). It is a medieval heritage if, even today in Catholic churches, people receive communion before or after mass, while during mass the officiating clergy and perhaps some others receive the Sacrament. This is one of the points in which the Liturgical Movement seems to have been successful. Modern Catholics have a strong feeling that this should not be so because it destroys the real meaning of 'communion'. Thus, we shall not be surprised to learn that the Middle Ages was the time of infrequent communion.

It is not correct for Albert Hauck, the great historian of the German church in the Middle Ages, to assume that in the Frankish church in the sixth century the whole congregation that assembled for mass still received the Sacrament.[70] Only very pious people used

[70] *Kirchengeschichte Deutschlands, I* (1914), 187; see P. Browe, *Die häufige Kommunion im Mittelalter* (1938), 14.

to receive the Sacrament more than once a year. The decree of the Fourth Council of the Lateran in 1215, which made it compulsory for all Catholics to receive the sacraments of penance and of the Lord's Supper at least once a year, at the time of Easter, set a standard which so far had not been reached. One of our sources for the eucharistic practice at the time of Thomas Aquinas is Humbert of Rome, author of practical books for the parish priests, who died in 1277. According to him it was necessary for the layman to receive Holy Communion at Easter and at the hour of death, while pious people might receive the Sacrament a few times a year.

> The Middle Ages was the time when Christians went to Holy Communion from two to four times a year . . . This was called 'frequent' communion at that time,

writes one of the best-informed historians of medieval liturgy.[71] The great festivals of Easter, Pentecost, and Christmas, and sometimes a fourth festival like the Assumption of Mary, used to be occasions when Holy Communion was distributed to the people in a medieval parish church, but only a few people made use of all these opportunities. Although in the monasteries weekly communion was practised, even the old Cistercian rule limited the obligation of the monks to four communions (Christmas, Maundy Thursday, Easter, Pentecost). The four Communion Sundays which we find in many Protestant churches are a continuation of this medieval custom.

The question whether frequent or even daily communion was to be encouraged has played a great part in the pastoral theology and in the devotional literature from Caesarius of Arles in the fifth century up to books like the *Imitatio Christi* at the end of the Middle Ages.[72] Two ideas clashed with each other. On the one hand, there was the conviction that a Christian should receive Communion as often as possible since it was regarded as necessary for salvation, so that even the newly-baptized children were given at least some consecrated wine; on the other hand, a thorough preparation was demanded in order to prevent an unworthy reception of the Sacrament. This struggle between two principles was continued even after the

---

[71]P. Browe, *op. cit.*, 28, 29.

[72]St Francis never encouraged frequent communion, not even among his brethren. Aquinas gives a well-balanced decision in *Summa theol. III, Q. 80, Art. 10:* '. . .*si aliquis se quotidie ad hoc paratum inveniat, laudabile est quod quotidie sumat*'. For further deails, see the books by P. Browe, *Die häufige Kommunion im Mittelalter* (1938), and *Die Pflichtkommunion im Mittelalter* (1940).

Reformation: in the Roman church, for instance, in the controversies between Jesuits (who always favoured frequent communion as a means of fighting sin), and the Jansenists (who renewed the rigorism of the *devotio moderna* of the Late Middle Ages). It was not until the beginning of the 20th century that Pius X, the 'Pope of the Eucharist', gave a definite decision in favour of the frequent and even daily communion, and the communion of children. In England, the typically-Anglican divines and the Puritans had to fight the same struggle. The Reformed churches tended to keep their four Communion services, and were generally very broadminded concerning admission. The Lutheran church, which preserved the mass for nearly 200 years, was, as a rule, very strict in the demand that communion presupposed preparation and private confession. It is interesting to observe that the problem still exists in the Protestant churches of today. There is a general feeling that more frequent communion should be encouraged. This, however, led again to a discussion, especially in the Lutheran church, whether the custom of celebrating Holy Communion in connection with church meetings, where a thorough preparation is impossible, is really a restitution of a celebrating of the Sacrament of the Altar as it was understood by the Lutheran Reformation.

Despite this remarkable decline of Holy Communion during the Middle Ages, the Sacrament of the Altar did not cease to be the very centre of Christian worship. A new form of eucharistic service arose: the mass in which the priest only, or the priest together with his ministrants and, in some cases, a very few laymen, partook of the Sacrament. The rest, and that means practically the whole congregation, be it large or small, were satisfied with watching or knowing what happened at the altar. Actually, they could not follow the prayers and liturgical words of the priest, save for the Gospel (if it was read not only in Latin, but also in the mother tongue). Otherwise they observed the actions of the clergy. They could not answer the prayers with their Amen, or the *Dominus vobiscum* with the *Et cum spiritu tuo.* That was done by the ministrants or, in the case of very solemn masses, by the choir. Thus, the assembly ceased to be *ecclesia orans* and became a gathering of individuals, each of whom held his own private devotion.

There was one moment, indeed, when the thoughts of all were directed to the altar, namely, when during the *Canon Missae,* which was spoken with low voice, the transubstantiation took place. To indicate that moment, the blessed elements were shown to the people in the elevation for adoration. Not Holy Communion but elevation was now becoming the climax of the Catholic mass. It is obviously not accidental that the elevation was introduced into the church just at the time when the word and idea of transubstantiation arose in the late 12th century. The adoration of the consecrated host, or rather of the eucharistic Christ, the Christ present in the blessed host, more and more replaces Holy Communion. Catholic liturgists even speak of a communion with the eyes.[73] The host seems to be there to be seen and venerated, rather than to be partaken of. The Eucharist becomes, as in the Eastern church where a decline of communion also takes place,[74] a holy drama to be seen. In the West the elevation, the monstrance, the tabernacle in its various forms, the eucharistic procession during Holy Week and, later, at the Festival of Corpus Christi, are indicative of the deep change which Christian piety underwent from the end of the 12th to the end of the 13th century. This development has never taken place in the Eastern church. There the blessed Sacrament is also reserved for the purpose of giving communion to the sick. But a cult of the host never developed. In the West the veneration of the host is obviously closely connected with the simultaneously-arising idea of transubstantiation. For, if Christ, the God-man, remains present after the celebration, he has to be adored even outside the mass. When an Orthodox Christian enters his church, he kneels and prays before the icons, while a Roman Christian kneels before the tabernacle. According to the Early Church, the church-building is the house of God because the holy people of God assemble there to receive the body and blood of Christ, the Lord being in the midst of his people according to Matthew 18:20. In the Roman church since the year 1200, the church-building has been the house of God because Christ dwells in the tabernacle. Thus, quite a new form of eucharistic piety and devotion arose, the climax of which is the Feast of Corpus Christi, which after 1264 slowly spread over Western Christendom. It is significant that the beautiful liturgy of this festival, which served to bring the eucharistic Christ from the church to the public, was written at the request of the pope by Thomas Aquinas, including the great hymns, which are real treasures of medieval religious poetry.

---

[73] '*Augen-Kommunion*'.

[74] There have been movements at times in favour of frequent communion. Many Orthodox Christians are satisfied with receiving the Sacrament on Maundy Thursday or at Easter. See Fr. Heiler, *Urkirche und Ostkirche* (1937), 331.

The doctrine of concomitance, as it had been developed in connection with transubstantiation, justified a custom which is very old and which, originally against the will of the clergy, had spread more and more during the 12th century: the *communio sub una specie*. It was not, as the Reformers and later Protestants believed, a sort of arrogance on the part of the clergy that caused them to withhold the chalice from the laymen. There had been a *communio sub una* in the Ancient Church, at least in the custom of preserving the Eucharist (the consecrated bread) at home and eating from it in the early morning. Another form of the *communio sub una* occurred in the Middle Ages, up to about the year 1200, when newly-baptized children who were not yet able to swallow even a particle of the host were given a little consecrated wine.[75] In the Early Middle Ages we find some reluctance on the part of the laymen to take the blood of Christ for fear of spilling some of it. The church at that time did not approve of such incomplete communion, especially in the case of adults, as several synods of the Early Middle Ages show.[76]. In order to prevent spilling the holy blood, either intinction was introduced, or the custom which had developed in the East of giving bread and wine simultaneously on a spoon. Another device was a little pipe (*fistula*) with which a little wine from the cup was taken by the communicant.[77] It seems that practical reasons favoured the communion under one species only. The larger gatherings, especially at Easter, required not only much wine, but also large cups, sometimes with two handles. The priest consecrated the wine in a small cup on the altar. This consecrated wine was mixed with unconsecrated wine in the large cup, the consecration being thus performed 'by contact'. Thus, the *communio sub utraque* presented practical problems at that time, even as it does today. The doctrine of concomitance allowed a drastic solution of all these problems. Once again it has to be stated that the initiative was with the laity. The decree of 1415 sanctioned a custom which had been introduced by laymen, though at that time it was already understood by many as an interference on the part of the clergy with the genuine Sacrament.

---

[75]For details, see Peter Browe, *Die Pflichtkommunion im Mittelalter* (1940), 130 ff.

[76]Braga 675, Clermont 1095, and others. For details, see PRE 12, 722, 9 ff; Hefele, *Conciliengeschichte, V*, 224.

[77]As the pope still communes at solemn High Mass.

7. The Great Struggle of the Late Middle Ages

In the meantime a new movement had begun. If the church, as many pious Christians already believed in the 13th century, had to undergo a reformation, it could easily be foreseen that such a reformation would not leave the sacramental life of the church untouched. Every religious movement in the Middle Ages, as also later the Reformation itself, began with the quest for the Sacrament. The first indication of an approaching change became visible when, in the second half of the 14th century, a strong religious movement arose which again stressed Holy Communion instead of the adoration of the host by demanding frequent, if not daily, communion of the laity. The centre of this movement was in Bohemia, though it was not at all confined to that country.

The Hussite Movement, which started around the year 1400, was preceded by a religious revival stirred up by preachers of the surrounding countries. Outstanding among these men was John Milic of Kremsier, Moravia. He was for some time canon, then archdeacon, in Prague, and later became a powerful and popular preacher, very much given to apocalyptic ideas. After an adventurous life he died in 1374. More than anyone else this man became instrumental in propagating the idea of frequent and even daily communion, which was a topic widely discussed during his lifetime among clergy and laity in various countries. Matthias of Janov was one of his disciples. He had studied in Paris, and also became a powerful preacher of repentance. In 1394 he died as a canon in Prague. Like the Jesuits of later times and like modern Catholics, he regarded daily communion as the strongest means to prevent sin and to attain perfection. In his *Regulae,*[78] 'the only greater writing of the Middle Ages on frequent communion . . . written a few centuries too early', as a modern Catholic scholar remarks,[79] he seems to have anticipated certain ideas of the Liturgical Movement of our time. Referring to the custom of the Ancient Church, he wrote among other things:

> The eating and drinking of this our sweetest sacrifice which is full of the sweet Spirit of God must be done by all, consequently not only by priests, but also by the people.[80]

---

[78]*Regulae veteris et novi testamenti,* ed. by V. Kybal in the edition of the works of Janov, 1908-13: quoted by Peter Browe, *Die häufige Kommunion im Mittelalter* (1938), 33.

[79]Browe, *op. cit.,* 34.

[80]'*Manducatio et potacio nostri huius sacrificii dulcissimi et pleni Dei suave spiritu*

Matthias was, by the way, a man of blameless Catholic orthodoxy. He submitted readily to a synod which in 1389 rejected his ideas about frequent communion. Influences of Wyclif (whose writings became known in Prague during his last years) cannot be found in his writings on the Sacrament of the Altar. Nor are the views on this Sacrament which Wyclif held during the last few years of his life shared by Matthias and his contemporaries. The question of frequent communion, by the way, did not play any role with Wyclif. Thus, the interest in the Sacrament of the Altar, a real hunger and thirst for the Sacrament, was alive in Bohemia, as in other parts of Europe, before the Hussite Movement started, making the Sacrament the centre of its fight. It seems that this keen interest in the Sacrament is the spiritual contribution of the Bohemian people to the Hussite Movement.

In other respects (apart from its being a nationalistic movement of the Czech people) Hussitism, as it arose in Prague when John Hus made his appearance on the scene of church history at the turn of the century, was Wyclifism transplanted from England to Bohemia. Modern scholarship has discovered to what an astonishing degree Hus was dependent on Wyclif.[81] Entire writings of Hus were taken, sometimes literally, from the works of Wyclif. It is all the more interesting to observe that only in the doctrine on the Lord's Supper Hus did not follow his English master, although he knew, and at first seems to have been impressed by, what Wyclif had written toward the end of his life (after 1379) against the doctrine of transubstantiation as the worst invention of Antichrist. Hus, however, neither accepted this criticism nor Wyclif's theory on the remanence (*remanentia*) of the substance of bread and wine after consecration. Even if he might have been influenced in this respect by Wyclif for a very brief period, he could rightly say at his trial in Constance that he was unjustly accused of denying transubstantiation. There were, indeed, others who had accepted the theory of remanence, especially since this theory was in agreement with the doctrine of consubstantiation, which at that time had already become very popular with theologians. But it is very noteworthy that the Hussite Movement

---

debet esse communis et omnium, et per consequens plebeiorum et non tantum sacerdotum.' V. Kybal, quoted by Browe, *op. cit.*, 33.

[81]The standard work is *Huss und Wiclif. Zur Genesis der Hussitischen Lehre* (1925) by Johann Loserth, to whom research on Wyclif also owes so much.

from the very beginning was divided on the doctrine of the Sacrament of the Altar.

All shades of possible interpretations of the Lord's Supper are to be found in the rich literature that was produced in both the Latin and Czech languages in Bohemia during the 15th century.[82] They range from transubstantiation and consubstantiation to more spiritual ways of understanding the Sacrament, and even to the radical views of the Pickards who, like certain radical enthusiasts at the time of the Reformation, and like the Quakers, rejected all outward sacraments.[83] The variety of opinions that existed among the Hussites is a striking parallel to the variety of views on the Lord's Supper to be found later in the 16th century. Just as in the time of the Reformation the views on the sacraments constituted the main frontiers between the parties and denominations, so in the 15th century the Czech nation was divided on the question of the Sacrament. This small nation was the first to break away from the papal church, a hundred years before the Reformation. Its independence, however, resulted in a process of disintegration such as the whole of European Christendom had to experience in the 16th and 17th centuries when the medieval church broke down. The main parties in Bohemia were, apart from those who wanted to remain faithful to the papal church: the moderate Utraquists (or Calixtines) who also wanted to stay within the church provided the *communio sub utraque* (the chalice) was granted to them, and certain other demands of the Law of God were carried out; and the radical Taborites who as strict Wyclifites fought the church of the Antichrist, and demanded a new social order in accordance with what they regarded as the Law of God. While among the Utraquists there were found even representatives of the doctrine of

———

[82]Numerous authors and writings are quoted by Loserth, *op. cit.* A valuable supplement to the work by Loserth is given by Erhard Peschke, *Die Theologie der Böhmischen Brüder in ihrer Frühzeit, I. Das Abendmahl:* Part 1: *Untersuchungen* (1935), Part 2: *Texte aus alttschechischen Handschriften übersetzt* (1940). The texts which Peschke has translated into German are works by Peter of Chelcic (a layman, 1390-1460) and Luke of Prague (a bishop and leader of the *Unitas Fratrum,* 1460-1528). Peschke's work (unfortunately unfinished) discloses hitherto-unknown sources, and discusses the relationship of the early Brethren with Luther. Many valuable manuscripts on the problem of the Sacrament should still be in existence in Prague.

[83]'Pickards' is the name of heretics (Beghards?) who were persecuted in northern France after 1411. A number of them fled in 1418 from Lille and Tournay to Bohemia where even the Taborites rejected them.

transubstantiation, the Taborites attacked this doctrine with great vehemence, though they themselves were divided concerning the positive doctrine of the Sacrament, since they interpreted Wyclif's utterances differently. The Pickards, again, rejected all sacraments. After the final military defeat of the Taborites in the middle of the century, small groups of deeply religious Hussites founded the *Unitas Fratrum* in 1467. Under the leadership of men like Peter of Chelcic and Luke of Prague, this community grew into a church which at the time of the Reformation comprised about 400 congregations in Bohemia and Moravia.

But even within each of these parties and groups, various opinions on the Lord's Supper existed.

> Just as at one time the *homoousion* had separated the parties from one another, so in Bohemia the attitude toward the Lord's Supper was the foremost feature of all political and social programs of Utraquists, Taborites, and Pickards. The chronicler relates that no one family was unanimous in their views. The wife was opposed to her husband, the father to the son, the family to their guest. Everyone had a different view on the sacraments and the rites of the church. The question of the Lord's Supper was the foremost topic of synods and religious colloquies. The party of the Utraquists (or Calixtines) had its name from the main demand of its doctrine. The Pickards regarded the Sacrament as an object of contempt. Extreme Taborites who were close to the Pickards and harboured heretical thoughts concerning the Lord's Supper were exiled or even burned. In trials an attempt was made to find out what the heretics were thinking . . . Accustomed to the methods of the Inquisition, the defendants used to appeal to the teaching of Jesus and the apostles . . . The controversies about the Lord's Supper lasted up to the 16th century. The Bohemian Brethren were persecuted mainly on account of their views on the Lord's Supper, their main heresy.

Thus a well-informed scholar describes the situation in Bohemia in the second half of the 15th century.[84]

If the question is asked what the result of these endeavours and controversies was, the answer must be that it was surprisingly small as far as theology is concerned. We find among the Czech theologians representatives of all sacramental doctrines put forward by late medieval schoolmen, but they seem to have added no new theory. Like Hus they were not productive, but more or less reproductive, thinkers. This is true even of the writers of the *Unitas Fratrum* who, in contradistinction to many Utraquists, did not accept the scholastic theories, but rather followed Wyclif. From him they took over the strong criticism of transubstantiation, the

---

[84]Erhard Peschke, *op. cit.*, I, 1, 2.

figurative understanding of the sacramental words, the spiritual understanding of Christ's presence, the idea that a good priest only can effectively consecrate (and, in a case of emergency, a layman).

What touches the reader of the treatises by a man like Peter of Chelcic is the great piety and seriousness with which he wrestles with the problem of the Lord's Supper. The same is true of Luke of Prague. We understand why these laymen exercised such a great influence on the most serious Christians in Bohemia. If we consider the vast amount of literature on the Lord's Supper produced by that small country in about 150 years — most of it inaccessible to Western theology today — and if we ponder over the meaning of these endless controversies, we cannot but feel that the earnestness of this search for the real meaning of the Sacrament, this longing for the genuine Sacrament of the Altar, is what really matters.

The deeper reason for the lack of real results lies in the fact that all these Christian thinkers, theologians as well as laymen, were still medieval Catholics, or medieval 'heretics' revolting against the Roman church. All of them, even the most evangelical among the Brethren, represent a type of late-medieval piety which was not yet able to distinguish between Law and Gospel and to understand the Sacrament of the Altar as the heart of the Gospel. This is the reason why the Hussites of varying opinions could never get rid of Wyclif's legalism, moralism, and Donatism. Luther's understanding of the Lord's Supper, as we shall see, was determined by the discovery that this Sacrament is a form of the Gospel. How can one rightly expect such insight from Christians who lived before the Reformation?

This also explains the fact that the controversy in Bohemia centred around the question whether or not a certain law of the church, the decree of the Council of Constance of 1415, which established the communion under one species, was in accordance with the law which Christ had given concerning this Sacrament in the New Testament. Not a common understanding of the Lord's Supper, but the demand for the chalice, kept the various branches of Hussitism together (excepting, of course, the radical Pickards) and became the great symbol of the common fight against the papal church. This question became the issue of the Hussite controversies, and even wars; the flames at the stake at which John Hus died, as a martyr of his faith and of the Czech nation, set the Czech people afire and caused the religious movement to become a real revolution.

How just the question of the chalice became the crucial issue, no one knows. Shortly before he was imprisoned, Hus himself had defended the thesis that the *communio sub utraque* is the proper form of celebrating the Sacrament.[85] The emphasis, however, which was placed by the Hussites on this very point cannot be explained simply by reference to these statements of Hus. It has been suggested that the proximity of the Eastern Orthodox church played a part. But this is only a conjecture, especially since in that church the wine was no longer distributed from the cup. It may be that the coincidence of the condemnation of Hus by the Council on July 6 and of the decree on the *communio sub una* on June 15 is a sufficient explanation.

At any rate, the whole question of the chalice as it was presented by the Hussite Movement remained a medieval one. What an amazing example of medieval confusion of Law and Gospel, State and Church, things temporal and things spiritual, is presented by this movement! A whole European nation, though a small one, was fighting against its German rulers, and at the same time against the Roman hierarchy which supported them. It fought at the same time for political freedom and cultural independence, and against the Roman mutilation of the Sacrament of Christ. The *sub utraque* became an ecclesiastical and a political slogan. One must imagine these Czech armies invading the surrounding countries, hosts fixed to their lances, in order to understand this climax of the great synthesis of church and world, this confusion of Law and Gospel which characterizes the Middle Ages.

On the other hand, it is a manifestation of the longing for the pure Sacrament, so deeply rooted in the souls of Christian people on the eve of the Reformation. No one can understand the controversies of the Reformation on the Sacrament of the Altar unless he has understood that longing, so inconceivable to modern man. It happened in the 16th century that the strictly-Catholic dukes of Bavaria had to compel their bishops to allow communion under both species in order to prevent their subjects from becoming Lutherans.[86] Thus, it was not only the Czech nation that felt very strongly about the *sub utraque specie.* One must keep this in mind in order to understand that mighty hunger and thirst for the Sacrament which lies at the root of the controversies on the Lord's Supper at the time of the Reformation.

---

[85] J. Loserth, *Huss und Wiclif,* (2nd edition, 1925), 190.

[86] The history of this highly-important, though almost unknown, movement was written by A. Knoepfler, *Die Kelchbewegung in Bayern* (1891). The book contains very interesting documents which show that the desire for the cup was strong even among Catholics.

CHAPTER II

Luther in His Early Period

(1517-1524)

1. The Source of Luther's Doctrine on the Lord's Supper

At first sight it would seem that we have given comparatively too much space to the medieval background of the controversies of the Reformation on the Sacrament of the Altar. However, no one can study these controversies of the 16th century without realizing that to a large degree they are a continuation, if not the consummation, of medieval debates and strife. This appears not only from the Roman doctrine on the sacraments which was completed at the Council of Trent. It is surprisingly true also of Luther, Erasmus, Zwingli, Bucer, Calvin, Cranmer, and the leaders of the Anabaptist movements. Each of these men carries with him the heritage of the Middle Ages, which determines his thoughts more than he himself knows. Just as Ambrose and Augustine in their understanding of the Sacrament live on in the Middle Ages, so the various schools of thought that made their appearance in the medieval church (and sometimes in sects outside the church) are still living realities in the 16th century. Their arguments are repeated incessantly; the Bible passages and the quotations from the Church Fathers are the same down through the centuries. For that reason a superficial observer could come to the conclusion that, as far as the Sacrament of the Altar is concerned, the century of the Reformation still belongs to the Middle Ages, especially since very few modern Protestants understand the deep interest that 16th-century Christians of every persuasion had in the Sacrament. And yet such judgment would be quite incorrect. It would be based on a superficial perusal of the controversial literature of that time only, not on the theology of the Reformers or on the actual life of the church. This becomes evident if we try to understand the view on the Lord's Supper that Luther developed from the beginning of the Reformation up to the outbreak of his controversy with Zwingli.

What Thomas Aquinas in his doctrine on the Eucharist means to the medieval church and to the Roman church of all ages, Luther was and is to the church of the Reformation: the great theologian of the Sacrament of the Altar. Like Aquinas and like every great theologian, Luther was simultaneously a dogmatician and a liturgist. His dogmatical work concerning this Sacrament is inseparably connected with the old Lutheran mass that he created, the liturgy of Holy Communion, which he left to the Lutheran church as an invaluable heritage. It should never be forgotten what the evangelical mass in the mother tongue meant to Christian people who were accustomed to a celebration of the Sacrament in a foreign language, having not even a translation of the sacred text in their hands, as Roman Catholic Christians have today. It was a Catholic scholar that tried to explain the victory of the Reformation by pointing to its liturgical aspect. Although, of course, he strongly disapproves of Luther's criticism of the Roman mass, the Oratorian Father Felix Messerschmidt writes of the Reformation as a liturgical movement:

> It is necessary to get from the contemporary reports an impression of the unheard-of actuality of those services, of the religious power with which they were celebrated by the same congregations that thus far had been silent spectators and listeners in church, of the deep impression which these services made on the people . . . of the power with which the new hymns were sung by young and old in all walks of life . . . Jesuit witnesses have stated that these hymns have won more adherents to the new doctrine than all sermons and other means of propaganda.[1]

Anyone who wants to understand the lively discussions about the meaning of the Words of Institution must not forget that these words, the most sacred words of the Christian liturgy, were heard in church for the first time by people at the time of the Reformation. Previously they were spoken in a low voice by the Catholic priest, and were therefore inaudible to the people. Article 10 of the *Augsburg Confession* on the Lord's Supper cannot be understood without Article 24 on the Mass, where the old Lutheran church could declare what few Lutheran churches today could certainly say:

> It does not appear that the mass is more devoutly celebrated among our adversaries than among ourselves.[2]

---

[1]Felix Messerschmidt, *Liturgie und Gemeinde* (Wuerzburg, 1939), 49.

[2]AC Article 24, 2, Jacobs edition, following the German text: *'Denn das ist öffentlich, dass die Messe, ohn Ruhm zu reden, bei uns mit grösserer Andacht und Ernst gehalten wird denn bei den Widersachern'.*

Despite the rich Catholic heritage, doctrinal as well as liturgical, which Luther had received from the Middle Ages and which he preserved as far as possible, it would be quite wrong to regard this heritage as the source of his doctrine on the Sacrament of the Altar. Otherwise, he would not have gone through the depths of those inner struggles which he describes in 1533:

> Once when I woke at night the devil started a disputation with me in my heart . . saying: 'Listen, most learned Sir, do you know that for fifteen years you have committed sheer idolatry by adoring and showing for adoration to others, not the body and blood of Christ, but mere bread and wine?'[3]

This, of course, does not imply a denial of the Real Presence in the Lord's Supper. What Luther denies is rather that a private mass without communicants is the Sacrament of the Altar as instituted by Christ. The man who thus looks back to his own daily celebration of the mass was not bound by tradition, but solely by the Word of God, by which private mass could not be justified. That it was the Word of God and nothing else that made him a fervent believer in the Real Presence also becomes evident from the famous words which he wrote in 1524 at the beginning of the great controversy about the Lord's Supper, and which he addressed to the Christians of Strasburg in answer to the question the Strasburgers had put to him after Carlstadt had tried to win them for his own view on the Sacrament of the Altar:

> That I admit: if Dr Carlstadt or someone else had told me five years ago that in the Sacrament there is nothing but mere bread and wine, he would have rendered me a great service. I passed through great inner struggles in that respect, and had to fight hard to overcome that temptation. For I was well aware that by these means I could strike the hardest blow against the papacy. Besides, there were two men who wrote to me about this in a far more able way than Dr Carlstadt, without torturing the words according to their own ideas as he does. **But I am captured by the Word of God** and cannot find a way out. **The words are there, and they are too strong for me.** Human words cannot take them out of my soul. Yea, even if it should happen today that someone should prove with strong reasons that only bread and wine are there, it would not be necessary to attack me so furiously. For, according to my Old Adam, I am,

---

[3] *Von der Winkelmesse und Pfaffenweihe* (WA 38, 197, 18 ff). This passage shows, by the way, that in Luther's monastery daily celebration was customary for the ordained monks. This was not the case in all monastic orders of that time, let alone with the secular clergy. Even high ecclesiastics used to celebrate very rarely. According to 805 of the Canon Law, the minimum requirement for the priest is to celebrate on all Sundays and feasts of obligation. Practically daily celebration, if possible, is the rule today. It is interesting that Luther, in contradistinction to Thomas, used to celebrate daily (*'fast alle Tage'*).

> unfortunately, very much inclined to that view. However, the way Dr Carlstadt talks wantonly about it does not tempt me at all. On the contrary, it only confirms me in my opinion (*emphasis mine*).[4]

These were the words of the theologian for whom the only source of Christian doctrine was God's Word. He would have given up the Real Presence as easily as Zwingli, had it not been for the Word of God, which offered no other choice. The question arises whether he had ever been really tempted to accept a figurative understanding of the Words of Institution. He himself seems to admit that, for the phrase 'five years ago' would lead to 1519. We do not know who the two correspondents were that Luther mentions, or at what time they attempted to convince him that the sacramental words must not be understood literally. What we do know is that, after the Leipzig Colloquy of June and July, 1519 (when Luther had admitted that among the sentences of John Hus condemned at Constance there had been orthodox, Christian opinions), contacts were more and more established between Wittenberg and Bohemia. Among the various views on the Lord's Supper put before Luther by theologians from Bohemia, there were such as denied the Real Presence in the orthodox sense. It is very likely, then, that the correspondents mentioned by Luther in 1524 are to be sought there. But this correspondence could not have taken place before 1520, and we cannot state with certainty that it was the cause of the great temptation to give up the traditional doctrine of the Real Presence. If anywhere, one would expect traces of such an inner struggle to be found in Luther's writings of 1519-1520. But, if he ever had doubts about the literal meaning of the words of the Sacrament during those years, they found no expression either in his books or in his correspondence, and he must have already overcome them when he wrote his *Treatise on the Blessed Sacrament of the Holy and True Body of Christ and on Fraternities* which appeared in December 1519.

We have no utterance of Luther's in which he expresses any doubt concerning the belief that the body and blood of Christ are truly present in the Lord's Supper and distributed to the communicants.

2. Criticism of the Roman Mass: Opus Operatum and Sacrifice

That Holy Scripture, and not the Catholic tradition in which he had grown up, determined Luther's understanding of the Sacrament of the Altar is evident from the development of his doctrine. He was

---

[4]WA 15, 394, 12 ff.

the most conservative among the Reformers and preserved the Catholic heritage as far as possible. This conservatism, however, goes hand in hand with the most serious and unambiguous rejection of everything that contradicts Scripture and is based on tradition only — even the most ancient and venerable tradition. Consequently, we can understand that in some cases Luther's development was very slow. Piece by piece, he gives up such points of Catholic doctrine and practice as the *opus operatum,* the sacrifice of the mass, the use of a foreign language in the mass, the *communio sub una,* transubstantiation. In some of these matters, there is even a certain lack of resoluteness and consistency. Luther tried to keep what could be kept, until he was convinced that God's Word demanded a different course of action.

The first sign of a new understanding of the Sacrament appears in the controversy on indulgences. In the *Sermon on Penitence,*[5] in the *Resolutiones,*[6] and in the *Asterisci,*[7] — all written in 1518 — Luther rejects the doctrine that the sacrament is efficacious *ex opere operato*, that is, produces its effect unless the recipient obviates this effect by an actual sin or by the intention to commit a sin.[8] In the passages concerned, the Reformer refers to the old sentence: 'Not the sacrament, but the faith of the sacrament, justifies'. Faith must precede, not only accompany, the reception of the Sacrament. Divine grace, then, is active in us even before we receive the Sacrament, and this is true, according to Luther, even of Baptism.[9]

———

[5]*'Talis nullus est in mundo, qui non ponat obicem, nisi solus is, qui credit, cum sola fides iustificet, et accedentem ad Deum oporteat credere. Verissimum enim est enim doctum illud commune: Non sacramentum, sed fides sacramenti iustificat'* (WA 1, 324, 14 f).

[6]Luther declares in *Conclusio VII* that it is *'impossibile sacramentum conferri salubriter, nisi iam credentibus et iustis et dignis. Oportet enim* ***accedentem*** *credere, deinde non sacramentum, sed fides sacramenti iustificat'* (WA 1, 544, 39 ff).

[7]*'Dico . . . sacramenta novae legis non efficiunt gratiam, quam signant'* — as the schoolmen, especially Thomas, had taught — ***'sed requiritur fides ante omne sacramentum.*** *Fides autem est gratia. Ideo* ***gratia semper praecedit sacramentum'*** (WA 1, 286, 15 ff).

[8]*'Obicem ponere'.*

[9]*'Igitur remissio Dei gratiam operatur, sed remissio sacerdotis pacem, quae et ipsa est gratia et donum Dei, quia fides remissionis et gratiae praesentis.'* This, Luther continues, is true not only of absolution but also of Baptism: *'At baptisatum oportet etiam credere se recte credidisse et accessisse, aut pacem non habebit, quae non nisi ex fide habetur'* (*Resolutiones, Conclusio VII,* WA 1, 542,7 ff). The whole problem has been discussed by A.W. Dieckhoff, *Die evangelische Abendmahlslehre im Reformationszeitalter* (1854), 181 ff. If modern Catholics, Anglicans, and even some modern Lutherans, cannot see how the *sola fide* can be reconciled with a very serious

This understanding of the relationship between faith and sacrament means, indeed, the end of the *ex opere operato,* though by no means a rejection of the objective character of the Sacrament. It was modern Protestantism that read its negation of the objective means of grace into the words of the 'young Luther'. The Sacraments do not create faith; they are rather accepted by faith, and serve, as acts of God, to assure the faithful of God's grace. This is, of course, no exhaustive description of the meaning of the Sacrament, but it expresses something which for Luther always remained a most important aspect.

Closely connected with his rejection of the *ex opere operato* is Luther's objection to the idea of the mass as a sacrifice. Gradually he arrived at the conclusion that the mass as a sacrifice brought by the priests for the living and the dead has no foundation in the New Testament. He does not touch on the subject in his *Treatise on the Blessed Sacrament of the Holy and True Body of Christ and on Fraternities* of December 1519, nor in the *Explanation* of that treatise published a few weeks later in the beginning of 1520. This silence is all the more significant, since the main purpose of such 'fraternities' was to gain the fruits of masses said for their members. In his discussion of the mass in the *Treatise on Good Works* a few months later, his silence on that matter is still more surprising. He promised, however, to take up the problem when occasion arises.[10] He kept that promise when he wrote his *Treatise on the New Testament, that is, on the Holy Mass,* which appeared in August 1520. There Luther discusses the problem in what sense the mass can or cannot be called a sacrifice.

> We must let the mass be a sacrament and a testament, and this is not and cannot be a sacrifice . . . We should, therefore, give careful heed to this word 'sacrifice', that we do not presume to give God something in the sacrament when it is He who therein gives us all things. We should bring spiritual sacrifices . . . What sacrifices, then, are we to offer? Ourselves, and all that we have, with constant prayer, as we say, 'Thy will be done on earth as in heaven'. Hereby we are to yield ourselves to the will of God . . . in addition, we are to offer Him praise and thanksgiving with our whole heart . . .And although such a sacrifice occurs apart from the mass, and should so occur . . . yet it is more precious, more

---

appreciation of the objective side of the Sacraments, they should at least study Luther's *Catechism* before criticizing him. The *Large Catechism* puts it this way: 'Since these blessings are here presented and promised in the words in and with the water, they cannot be received in any other way than by believing them with the heart' (Trigl. 741). Even in the Roman rite of Baptism, the profession of faith precedes the baptism proper.

[10] WA 6, 231, 15; Philad. I, 224.

> seemly, more mighty, and also more acceptable when it takes place with the multitude and in the assembly... To be sure, this sacrifice of prayer, praise and thanksgiving, and of ourselves, we are not to present before God in our own person, but we are to lay it on Christ and let Him present it, as St Paul teaches in Hebrews 13: 'Let us offer the sacrifice of praise to God continually, that is, the fruit of the lips which confess Him and praise Him', and all this through Christ. For He is also a priest, as Psalm 110 says: 'Thou art a priest for ever after the order of Melchizedek', because He intercedes for us in heaven, receives our prayer and sacrifice, and through Himself, as a godly priest, makes them pleasing to God, as St Paul says again in Hebrews 9: 'He is ascended into heaven to be a mediator in the presence of God for us'... From these words we learn that we do not offer Christ as a sacrifice, but Christ offers us. And in this way it is permissible, yea, profitable, to call the mass a sacrifice, not on its own account, but because we offer ourselves as a sacrifice along with Christ; that is, we lay ourselves on Christ by firm faith in His testament, and appear before God with our prayer, praise, and sacrifice only through Him and through His mediation; and we do not doubt that He is our priest and minister in heaven before God. Such faith, forsooth, brings it to pass that Christ takes up our cause, presents us, our prayer and praise, and also offers Himself for us in heaven. If the mass were so understood and therefore called a sacrifice, it would be well.[11]

We have quoted this passage extensively in order to show that Luther's polemics against the Roman understanding of the sacrifice of the mass had a very positive side. And this was, by no means, the attitude of the Reformer only in the first years of his fight. We find the same ideas, for example, in his *Vermahnung zum Sakrament des Leibes und Blutes unseres Herrn* of 1530, where he distinguishes between the spiritual sacrifice of prayer, thanksgiving, and remembrance, and the meritorious sacrifice as the work of the priest.[12] It is the understanding of the sacrifice of the Christians found in the New Testament that compels Luther to attack the Roman conception of the mass in the great Reformation writings of 1520: *To the Christian Nobility,* and *De captivitate Babylonica.* While in the *Treatise on the New Testament, that is, on the Holy Mass* he avoids polemics (as befits a devotional writing), he must speak very frankly against the Roman idea of the sacrifice of the mass and the misuses which grew out of it. In the book addressed to the Nobility, he attacks the multitude of masses, and remarks parenthetically that masses are

> regarded only as sacrifices and good works though they are really sacraments, just like baptism and penance.[13]

---

[11] WA 6, 368, 1 to 369, 12; quoted from Philad. 1, 312 ff.

[12] WA 30, 2, 610 ff.

[13] WA 6, 451, 24 f; quoted from Philad. 2, 136. The parallel to the other sacraments is also found in WA 6, 367, 13 ff; Philad. 1, 312.

In his great book on the Babylonian captivity of the church, Luther sees the 'captivity' of the Sacrament of the Altar, first, in the withholding of the cup from the laity, then, in the doctrine of transubstantiation, and finally, in the understanding of the mass as a good work and a sacrifice. This is

> that most wicked abuse of all . . . And this abuse has brought an endless host of others in its train, so that the faith of this sacrament has become utterly extinct . . .[14]

Luther foresees that this question would lead to a severe struggle:

> I am attacking a difficult matter, and one perhaps impossible to abate, since it has become so firmly entrenched through century-long custom and the common consent of men that it would be necessary to abolish most of the books now in vogue, to alter well-nigh the whole external form of the churches, and to introduce, or rather reintroduce, a totally different kind of ceremonies. But my Christ lives; and we must be careful to give more heed to the Word of God than to all the thoughts of men and of angels . . . I will faithfully do my part that none may cast on me the blame for his lack of faith and knowledge of the truth, when we appear before the judgment-seat of Christ.[15]

Luther knows full well how bitter the struggle will be at this point between the oldest and most venerable tradition of the church and the *sola Scriptura*.

The attitude he adopts here has always been Luther's attitude toward the Eucharist as he found it in the Roman church. In contradistinction to the great critics of the Roman mass from Wyclif to Calvin, he did not see the great heresy in the doctrine of transubstantiation and concomitance, and in the mutilation of the Lord's Supper through the *communio sub una,* but rather in the sacrificial character of the mass.[16] This conviction grew out of his understanding of the Gospel. The idea that a priest could sacrifice the body and blood of Christ was for him the great blasphemy, a real manifestation of the Antichrist, who had taken his seat in the temple of God, the Church. The question arises whether in this view he was influenced from outside. For about 300 years the question had been discussed in Western Christendom whether the pope was the Antichrist. He was regarded as such by very pious Christians because

---

[14]WA 6, 512, 7 ff; Philad. 2, 194.

[15]WA 6, 512, 16 ff; Philad. 2, 194 f.

[16]Calvin, *Institutio IV,* where chapter 17 with its discussion of the Real Presence and transubstantiation precedes ch. 18 about the mass as sacrifice, thus suggesting that the wrong understanding of the Words of Institution is the root of the perversion of the mass into a sacrifice.

he did not obey the Law of God. For Wyclif and his adherents, one of the inventions of Antichrist was the doctrine of transubstantiation. But Wyclif never developed his criticism into a criticism of the sacrifice of the mass. In Bohemia all moderates, Utraquists as well as Brethren, seem not to have rejected the sacrifice as such, for they kept the offices of bishop and priest in the Catholic sense. Only the radical Pickards rejected also the eucharistic sacrifice along with all outward sacraments.

The first direct rejection of the sacrificial character of the mass among the more conservative Bohemians seems to be found in an answer that Luke of Prague wrote to the *Conclusiones Beghardorum*. These *Conclusions* called the celebration of the mass a 'doctrine of Antichrist', since it was not found in the Law of Christ and in the writings of the apostles. In his answer, Luke remarks that 'Christ did not intend to sacrifice the Eucharist and to institute it as sacrifice', but rather to establish it as a memorial feast.[17] Luke, however, when he wrote this, was already under the influence of Luther, and it is likely that Luther's criticism of the sacrifice of the mass in the great writings of 1520 had influenced him. At any rate, the sacrificial mass did not play any considerable role in Bohemian theology, at least, not before the Reformation. Not from the Law of the New Testament, which for the various branches of the Bohemians was the norm of teaching, but from the Gospel only, as the message of *sola gratia, sola fide,* could it be seen why the mass must not be understood as a sacrifice that man could bring. For, even if the priest theoretically is supposed to act only as a representative of Christ, even if the identity of the sacrifice of the mass with the sacrifice of Calvary is asserted, it remains a fact that not only Christ, but also man, offers the sacrifice of the mass. Or, what else can the prayer mean which the priest says at the end of each mass, asking the blessed Trinity:

> Grant that the sacrifice which I, though unworthy, have offered in the sight of Thy majesty may be acceptable to Thee and through Thy mercy be a propitiation for me and for all those for whom I have offered it up?

Luther, as a Catholic priest and monk, knew full well what could be said in favour of the Roman mass. As the discoverer of the Gospel of *sola gratia*, however, he also knew that this synergism was incompatible with the New Testament. The Council of Trent, in spite

[17]Erhard Peschke, *op. cit., I,* 2, 260.

of its careful formulas, and modern Catholicism, with its attempt to read *sola gratia* into the text of the mass, have not succeeded in altering the situation that Luther saw so clearly. Anyone who understands the Gospel will understand the words with which Luther in the *Smalcald Articles* expressed his verdict on the Roman mass as the worst violation of the *articulus stantis et cadentis ecclesiae:*

> The mass in the Papacy must be the greatest and most horrible abomination as it conflicts directly and powerfully with this chief article, and of all other popish idolatries it is the chief and most specious.[18]

3. Communio sub una and sub utraque

There is hardly anything more elucidating than the difference between the Bohemians and Luther in their attitude toward the question of the chalice for the laity. Although it had started as a renunciation of the cup on the part of the laity — which no one knew, especially since the decree of 1415 — the withholding of the cup had been the great corruption of the Sacrament, or at least the visible sign of this corruption, for Utraquists, Taborites, and Brethren alike. The restoration of the Sacrament according to the institution of Christ as divine law was the common demand that bound together those who otherwise were separated by insuperable differences concerning the eucharistic doctrine. In his *Treatise on the Blessed Sacrament,* Luther admits that the withholding of the cup is not right. However, he does not think that this invalidates the Sacrament.

> For this sacrament signifies the complete union and the undivided fellowship of the saints . . . and this is poorly and unfittingly indicated by only one part of the sacrament.[19]

But the Sacrament remains what it is, even if given to the laity under one species only:

> Although at present the two kinds are not given the people daily, as of old — nor is this necessary — yet the priesthood partakes of it daily in the sight of the people, and it is enough that the people desire it daily and receive one kind at the proper time, as the Christian Church ordains and offers.[20]

He wishes communion under both species to be restored. At that time, however, he can visualize no other way than

> that the Church in a general council should again decree that all persons, as well as the priests, be given both kinds. Not that one kind would be insufficient . . .[21]

---

[18]*Smalcald Articles, II, 2* (Trigl. 463).
[19]WA 2, 742, 33 ff; Philad. 2, 10.
[20]WA 2, 742, 20 ff; Philad. 2, 9.
[21]WA 2, 742, 26; Philad. 2, 9 f.

In other words: The decree of Constance in 1415 can and should be revoked by that authority which at one time established the law, viz., by an ecumenical council. This was still Luther's position in the *Explanation* of 1520, which had been necessitated by his being attacked as an adherent of the Bohemian heresy. Again he emphasizes that communion under both kinds is according to the institution of Christ and the usage of the church through many centuries. The Bohemians were right in demanding it, and could not be called heretics on account of their demand. However, they were schismatics because they did not leave the decision to a general council. Both have sinned, Luther states: the Roman church ('**we** Romans') in declaring the Bohemians to be heretics although the Council of Basle had already conceded them the cup; and the Bohemians ('**you** Bohemians') by insisting on the chalice.

> As Christ did not command everybody to take the Sacrament,[22] it might be allowable to receive one species only or even no species at all, as some old Fathers did in the desert.[23] Therefore I disapprove of the Bohemians for not having followed the major part of the church or obeyed authority by being content with one species. Whether the Roman church is right or wrong, such order of the Sacrament does not matter since no species was commanded by Christ.[24]

It is remarkable how slowly Luther moves forward from this position. In August 1520 his great appeal, *To the Christian Nobility,* made its appearance. This book had been written in those very days in June when Luther's trial in Rome came to an end and the Reformer was practically excommunicated by the bull *Exsurge Domine* (although, indeed, he did not know it until October). This book, which denies that there is a priestly order besides the universal priesthood of all believers, and which rejects the Roman claims that the pope alone can summon a universal council, signifies in many respects Luther's final breach, not only with the papacy, but also with what is commonly understood as Catholic Christianity. But how conservative is what it has to say about Hus and Bohemians! The way Luther enlarges on the Bohemian schism seems to indicate that the

---

[22]According to Luther, only spiritual communion is necessary for salvation. This is his understanding of John 6, 54 ff. Luther is here in agreement with Thomas (*Summa theol. III, Q. 73, 3; Q 79, 1*) and the Roman church.

[23]Basil the Great recommends daily communion by pointing out that the hermits in the desert used to have the Eucharist in their cells (*Ep.93*). The opinion of Luther, then, cannot be upheld generally.

[24]WA 6, 79, 32.

doctrines of the Bohemians and their relationship with the Roman church occupied his mind quite considerably during those very months when Rome was busy preparing for him the destiny of Hus. But he still feels himself a member of the Roman church as compared with the schismatics of Bohemia. Nor does he take sides with Hus and his followers.

> Although it is the impatience of the Bohemians that is at fault, yet the Pope and his followers are still more to blame for all the trouble, error, and loss of souls that have followed upon that Council [of Constance].[25]
>
> I do not wish . . . to make John Hus a saint or a martyr, as do some of the Bohemians, though I confess that injustice was done to him and that his books and doctrines were unjustly condemned.[26]

The only progress beyond the *Explanation* of 1520 lies in the fact that Luther no longer demands a new general council to revise the decree of Constance. Instead, he puts forward a well-considered, detailed suggestion as to how the schism in Bohemia could be overcome by mutual agreement.

> The Pope has no right to oppose such an agreement, and if he does oppose it, he becomes a wolf and a tyrant; no one could follow him, and his ban should be met with a counterban.[27]

It is most surprising that Luther with this attitude toward the pope still retains his old view concerning the chalice. The chalice remains an *adiaphoron.*

> I would also advise against compelling them to abolish both kinds in the sacrament, since that is neither unchristian nor heretical. They should be allowed to retain their own practice, **if they wish.** The new bishop should be tactful, so that no discord may arise because of such a practice, and should kindly instruct them that **neither practice is wrong**; just as it ought not to cause dissension that the clergy differ from the laity in manner of life and dress (*emphasis mine*).[28]

Precisely during the days in August 1520 when *To the Christian Nobility* was published, Luther was writing his next great book, *De captivitate Babylonica,* in which he attacked the Roman doctrine on the Sacraments. Here, if anywhere, the final answer to the question of the cup for the laity is to be expected. We do find, indeed, in Luther's discussion of the Sacrament of the Altar, a new defence of the Bohemians and of their demand for the chalice.

---

[25]WA 6, 454, 31 ff; Philad. 2, 141.
[26]WA 6, 455, 7 ff; Philad. 2, 141.
[27]WA 6, 455, 40 ff; Philad. 2, 143.
[28]WA 6, 456, 16 ff; Philad. 2, 143, 144.

> Matthew, Mark, and Luke agree that Christ gave the whole sacrament to all the disciples, and it is certain that Paul delivered both kinds . . . Both Matthew and Mark attach the note of universality to the cup, not to the bread — as though the Spirit saw this schism coming, by which some would be forbidden to partake of the cup, which Christ desired should be common to all.[29]

From this it follows:

> In the Lord's Supper . . . the whole sacrament, or communion in both kinds, is given only to the priests or else it is given also to the laity. If it is given only to the priests, as they would have it, then it is not right to give it to the laity in either kind; for it must not be rashly given to any to whom Christ did not give it when He instituted it. For if we permit one institution of Christ to be changed, we make all of His laws invalid . . . But if it is given also to the laity, then it inevitably follows that it ought not to be withheld from them in either form. And if any do withhold it from them **when they desire it**, they act impiously and contrary to the word, example, and institution of Christ (*emphasis mine*).[30]

Here again we find what at first seems to be an inconsistency. Luther's argument is: Since Christ instituted the Sacrament under both species, it is a violation of his institution to deny the cup to those desiring it. That is why the Roman church is wrong:

> If any are to be called heretics and schismatics, it is not the Bohemians or the Greeks, for they take their stand upon the Gospel, but you Romans [notice that Luther no longer says 'we Romans' as he did half a year earlier] are the heretics and the godless schismatics, for you presume upon your own fictions and fly in the face of the clear Scriptures of God.[31]

The advancement of *De captivitate* lies in the understanding that the Bohemians, who insist on the cup, are not heretics and schismatics, but the Roman church is guilty of schism and even of heresy if she withholds the chalice from those who desire it. What surprises most is that Luther, in spite of the fact that Jesus instituted both kinds, as he clearly points out, does not regard it as a violation of the Sacrament if a person takes one species only. Thus, this 'captivity' of the Sacrament is for him the most lenient one:

> The first captivity of this sacrament . . . concerns its substance or completeness, of which we have been deprived by the despotism of Rome. Not that they sin who use the one kind, for Christ did not command the use of either kind, but left it to everyone's free will when He said, 'As often as ye do this, do it in remembrance of me'.[32]

---

[29] WA 6, 502, 30 ff; Philad. 2, 179.
[30] WA 6, 503, 10 ff; Philad. 2, 180.
[31] WA 6, 505, 21 ff; Philad. 2, 184.
[32] WA 6, 507, 6 ff; Philad. 2, 186.

It is obvious that the man who did not cease to regard the taking of the cup on the part of the laity as an *adiaphoron* was not a follower of the Bohemians. They made a deep impression on him; they compelled him to rethink again and again the questions of the Lord's Supper in general, and the chalice in particular. But a world separated him from them: to them the Gospel was a new Law, and the Sacrament of the Altar was, consequently, an ordinance that had to be carried out to the letter. Modern Protestants, even Lutherans, who have learned to regard communion under both kinds as one of the great issues of the Reformation, and who do not know that in reality it had already been the issue between Rome and Catholic sects of the 15th century, are hardly able to understand the evangelical freedom with which Luther dealt with this problem during those early years of the Reformation.

It is interesting to observe how slowly Luther changed his mind in the course of his work as a reformer. When Carlstadt in 1522 declared it to be a sin to take Holy Communion without a cup, Luther stated that he, too, would like to introduce the *communio sub utraque;* if, however, pious Christians were refused the cup by tyrants, they should be satisfied with the bread.[33] In his writing about the communion under both species (which comprises what Luther had said about the Lord's Supper in his Invocavit sermons of 1522), he still puts the *communio sub utraque* on the same level as allowing the laity to touch the sacramental bread with their hands.[34] Though criticizing severely those who through human law take away the cup from the laity, he recognizes, on the other hand, the danger of making a law to the contrary:

> Thus I see how Satan intends to make both species a common rule, just as the Pope has made one species his rule, **before there are Christians who should do it.** He intends to make it worse on the right-hand side than it was on the left-hand side. We need, therefore, to remain in the middle of the road and to pray that God may help and keep us there. For Satan is seriously snaring us *(emphasis mine).*[35]

In order to understand this utterance we must remember that it was made at one of the most critical moments of the Reformation, when the revolutionary enthusiasts under the leadership of Carlstadt threatened the Gospel and the existence of the church of the Gospel.

---

[33]Enders 3, 207 (No. 449, 76 ff); see Köstlin, *Martin Luther, I,* 471.

[34]*Von beider Gestalt des Sakraments zu nehmen und anderer Neuerung.* WA 10, 2, 2, 11 ff.

[35]WA 10, 2, 24, 22 ff.

Carlstadt, indeed, did what Luther criticized in the words quoted: He replaced the law of the pope with another law, not taking into account that the Sacrament is primarily a gift of the Gospel, and not an ordinance of the Law. The Lord of the Sacrament is not a second Moses who watches over a ceremonial law, but the Saviour who wants to save sinners from eternal death through the grace which he freely offers through the Sacrament as a real means of grace. It was Luther's understanding of the Sacrament as a manifestation of the Gospel, and his tender pastoral care for the souls Christ wants to save, that caused him to believe that a certain amount of freedom with regard to the *communio sub una* or *sub utraque* is according to the mind of Christ. Luther never doubted that Christians, during the centuries when the cup was denied them, received the real Sacrament of the body and blood of Christ.[36] The same, he thinks, is true of those believing communicants from whom the cup was withheld by the pope and his bishops in his (Luther's) own day. He is prepared to admit *communio sub una* even in Lutheran Saxony for that time of transition in the 1520s. As late as 1528, the *Instruction for Visitors* provided that people who for conscience' sake did not want to receive the cup could take the bread only.[37] The rule that Luther followed here, as in his entire work as a practical reformer, was to take into account the weak brother's conscience. In this particular case, it was a great concession to those who had not yet heard the Gospel. To those who after careful indoctrination on the Sacrament still refused to take the Lord's Supper under both kinds, Luther recommended as early as 1523 to abstain from the Sacrament.[38] This later became the

---

[36]The problem is thoroughly discussed in *Von der Winkelmesse und Pfaffenweihe* (1532), WA 38, 171 ff, especially 245, 13 ff, 'The Church as well as common Christians who could not receive both kinds cannot be blamed because they were cheated and misled by Antichrist into receiving one species only. For the faith still remained firm and pure in the Church that Christ instituted and commanded all Christians to receive His body and blood as is indicated in many hymns, in particular the well-known "*Gott sei gelobet und gebenedeiet / Der uns selber hat gespeiset Mit seinem Fleisch und mit seinem Blute . . . Herr, durch deinen heiligen wahren Leichnam / Der von deiner Mutter Maria kam, / Und das heilige Blut / Hilf uns aus aller Not*", etc.' Still more positive are the affirmations as to the validity of the medieval sacrament in spite of the denial of the cup in the *Brief D. Martin Luthers, von seinem Buch der Winkelmessen* (1534), especially WA 38, 264, 26 ff.

[37]The *Unterricht der Visitatoren* was written by Melanchthon and prefaced by Luther. The passage mentioned was inserted by Luther; the Elector was very hesitant with respect to such a concession.

[38]*Formula Missae et Communionis,* WA 12, 217, 12 ff. Compare the letter written to Spalatin on April 4, 1524: If a person either for conscience' sake or for fear of men

rule of the Lutheran church also for those who for various reasons could not drink wine.[39]

The time of transition in this respect had definitely passed when the theologians discussed this problem at the Diet of Augsburg, and the *Augsburg Confession* in Article 22 declared the custom of the *communio sub una* to be

> not only contrary to Scripture, but also contrary to the old canons and the example of the Church.[40]

After that time Luther took a firm stand against the possibility of permitting the renunciation of the cup in certain cases, while Melanchthon in 1537 still would admit such possibility in special cases, in the sense of the *Instruction for Visitors.* Luther's first statement of his definite view seems to be a letter, written from Coburg on August 26, 1530, to Melanchthon at Augsburg. Here he approves of Melanchthon's rejection of the *communio sub una,* and points out that the Sacrament was instituted by Christ under both kinds, and that the church has no right to alter this institution. The chalice could not be regarded as an *adiaphoron* (*'indifferens'*), since it is a clear precept of Christ that we should take both kinds when receiving the Sacrament.[41] The classical expression of Luther's position is to be found in the words of the *Smalcald Articles:*

> And that not only one form is to be given. For we do not need that high art which teaches us that under the one form there is as much as under both, as the sophists and the Council of Constance teach. For although it may perhaps be true that there is as much under one as under both, yet the one form is not the entire ordinance and institution established and commanded by Christ. And we especially condemn and in God's name execrate those who do not only omit both forms, but also tyrannically prohibit, condemn and blaspheme them as heresy, and so exalt themselves against and above Christ, our Lord and God.[42]

---

cannot commune under both kinds, Luther's advice is to abstain from the Sacrament for the time being, because such abstention is not dangerous (Enders 4, 316; WA BR 3, No. 727).

[39]Johann Gerhard, *Loci XXI, cap 21 (De convivis . . .),* q. 2 (ed. Preuss V, 221 f) answers the question as to how to deal with the *abstemii,* who cannot drink wine because it does not agree with them, by stating that they should abstain from communion altogether. This question is not to be confused with the problem of those 'who regard wine as a creature of the devil', such as the Manicheans of old. Johann Gerhard deals with this question as a historical problem in a quotation from the Jesuit J. Hack, *Confessio Catholica, Liber II, Pars II, Art. XIV, cap. 7 'De communione sub utraque specie'* (ed. Preuss III, 1091).

[40]Trigl. 61.

[41]Enders 8, 219; WA BR 5, No. 1699. This letter was enlarged and published in German in the older editions of the works of Luther, e.g. EA 45, 46.

[42]*Smalcald Articles III, 6* (Trigl. 493).

It is quite obvious that a development had taken place in Luther's attitude toward the cup. It is impossible to explain this merely by referring to the practical problems of pastoral care that confronted the Reformer when people who had grown up in the papal church had to be led, step by step, to a new understanding of the Gospel and a corresponding ecclesiastical practice. No practical consideration could justify communion under one species if such communion was clearly against the Word of God. The only possible explanation is that Luther arrived only later at a clear understanding of the problem of *communio sub una* and *sub utraque*. If, in the passage quoted from the *Smalcald Articles*, Luther still thinks, as the normative German text suggests, of a remote possibility that the idea of concomitance might be correct, we shall not be surprised to find him to be a defender of that doctrine in the early years of the Reformation. When the Bishop of Meissen in 1520 rejected Luther's demand for communion under both kinds by appealing to the doctrine that the whole Christ is under either species, Luther confessed that this was his belief too:

> Who has ever doubted that the whole Christ is under either species?[43]

When Speratus in 1522 transmitted to him precise questions concerning concomitance which had been raised by a Bohemian theologian, his answer was that such questions should not be asked at all because the Sacrament should not be made an object of philosophical discussion.[44] Only later, in his fight against the denial of the Real Presence and in his protest against the Roman *communio sub una*, he rejects the doctrine of concomitance, but always as the source of the mutilation of the Sacrament.[45] What a Christian receives who in faith partakes of the bread only, as the people in the Late Middle Ages did, is a question that cannot be answered any more than we can answer the question whether or not the Real Presence of the body and blood of Christ can be separated from the presence of his soul and his divinity. Whatever the truth of the theological speculation on concomitance may be — it cannot be a doctrine of the church because it is not found in Scripture — for Luther the doctrine of the presence of Christ in the Lord's Supper, based solely on the Words of Institution, was always an article of Christology. Moreover, his firm conviction that God can give, and

[43] WA 6, 139, 25 f. Cf WA 6, 151, 29 ff; 152, 26.

[44] WA BR 2, No. 509, 41 ff.

[45] WA 26, 495 (*Vom Abendmahl Christi*); WA 39, 1, 27, 4 ff (*Against the Council of Constance*, 1535).

has in the past given, the full blessing of the Sacrament also to such believers as for outward reasons had to be satisfied with the bread, is not based on something like concomitance, but rather on the belief that in such a case a spiritual communion takes place, just as Christians who live in pagan surroundings without the possibility of receiving the outward Sacrament still receive the full blessing of the Sacrament by a mere spiritual communion. These ideas, which go back to Augustine and which were revived by Thomas, were shared by all Christendom in the Late Middle Ages. They play a great role in the theology of Luther in his first years as a reformer, until the fight against such 'sacramentarians' as Carlstadt and Zwingli helped him to realize the dangers of sacramental spiritualism, and compelled him to stress the institutional aspect of the Sacrament of the Altar, which included indispensable communion under both kinds.

4. The Real Presence

There was a development in Luther's attitude to several questions of the Sacrament of the Altar, as, for example, the questions of concomitance, and such practical problems as the retaining of the Latin language in the mass,[46] and elevation.[47] But there was never a time in Luther's life when he did not believe the Real Presence of the true body and blood of Christ in the Sacrament. He did, in fact, have to go through a short period of inner struggle, as we have learned from his own words. But the lack of any evidence of another understanding of the Sacrament proves that he must have overcome at once whatever doubts he had. As he repeatedly pointed out in later years, he also was prepared to accept the figurative meaning of the Words of Institution as by far the easier one, if only it could be proved that this could be, and was, the correct understanding of the Scripture. His belief in the Real Presence was never a blind belief in the sense that he did not realize the difficulties implied; it was no *credo quia absurdum*. But it was an unshakeable belief from the beginning to the end of his life as a theologian.

---

[46]In opposition to the revolutionary attempts of Carlstadt and Muenzer, who introduced masses in German, Luther returned in *Formula Missae et Communionis* to the Latin text, having regard for the weak. But he anticipated a time when the whole service would be in the vernacular. Latin parts (*Gloria, Agnus Dei*) were sung up to 1700 in Lutheran churches that had a choir of schoolboys at their disposal. The average service, however, was in the mother tongue.

[47]Elevation was abolished by Bugenhagen at Wittenberg in 1542.

Up to 1519 Luther understood the Real Presence in the sense of the official doctrine on transubstantiation. The first doubt, at least of the speculations connected with this theory, is to be found in the *Treatise on the Blessed Sacrament of the Holy and True Body of Christ* of 1519, where we read:

> There are those who practise their arts and subtleties to such an extent that they ask where the bread remains when it is changed into Christ's flesh, and the wine when it is changed into His blood; also in what manner the whole Christ, His flesh and His blood, can be comprehended in so small a portion of bread and wine. What does it matter? It is enough that it is a divine sign, in which Christ's flesh and blood are truly present — how and where, we leave to Him.[48]

This means that the Real Presence, in the form of a change of the elements into the body and blood, is preserved, while the question of the mode of this change, whether transubstantiation or otherwise, is left open, and all discussions of this mode are rejected.

The next step in Luther's discussion of the problem of transubstantiation is the famous passage in *De captivitate* which we have already mentioned. Looking back on his theological studies, he describes his surprise when he came across some comments on the doctrine of transubstantiation made by Peter d' Ailly, the famous theologian of Paris (and later Bishop of Cambrai and Cardinal) to the effect that it would be more probable and require fewer miracles (and superfluous ones at that) to assume that after consecration there are on the altar real bread and wine, and not accidents only, had not the church decreed otherwise.[49] Later, so Luther continues, he saw what church had defined the dogma on transubstantiation, namely, the Thomistic or Aristotelian church. He came to understand that such opinions of the Thomists, even if confirmed by the pope or a council, remained opinions, and could never become articles of faith, binding on conscience, even if an angel from heaven decreed otherwise:

[48] WA 2, 749, 36 ff; Philad. 2, 20.

[49] WA 6, 508, 7 ff; Philad. 2, 188 f. This passage has been dealt with not only by Roman critics of Luther, like H. Denifle (*Luther und Luthertum, I,* (1904), 239), who accuses Luther of 'crass ignorance' because he regarded transubstantiation as a Thomistic doctrine, but also by Reformed theologians who, like R. Hospinian, *Historia Sacramentaria*, (new edition Geneva, 1681) II, 6, understand Luther's words as meaning that he had his doctrine on the Real Presence not from the Bible, but from scholasticism. Compare the quotation given by W. Elert, *Morphologie des Luthertums, I* (1931), 264, note 1 (which, by the way, is not to be attributed to the people of Brandenburg, but to the Elector).

> For what is asserted without Scripture or an approved revelation, may be held as an opinion, but need not be believed.[50]

From this passage the conclusion has been drawn that Luther had accepted consubstantiation instead of transubstantiation, and even Lutheran theologians have regarded consubstantiation as a genuinely-Lutheran doctrine.[51] It should not be overlooked, however, that Luther neither here nor in any other passage uses the word 'consubstantiation', and that the Lutheran church has never accepted it. Luther quotes d'Ailly in order to show that even distinguished Roman theologians would have liked to give up transubstantiation in favour of a theory that did not deny the existence of the substance of bread after consecration. If Luther had had to choose among the various scholastic theories, he would perhaps have chosen the theory of consubstantiation; what he thought about the presence of the body of Christ and the presence of the bread came closer to that theory than to any other current opinion. But his doctrine was not a philosophical theory of two *substantiae* existing together. The same is true even of the only passage in the *Book of Concord* in which the doctrine on consubstantiation might be found. The English translation reads:

> Even as many eminent ancient teachers, Justin, Cyprian, Augustine, Leo, Gelasius, Chrysostom and others, use this **simile** concerning the words of the sacrament: 'This is my body', that just as in Christ two distinct, unchanged natures are inseparably united, so in the Holy Supper the **two substances,** the natural bread and the true natural body of Christ, are present together here upon earth in the appointed administration of the Sacrament (*emphasis mine*).[52]

The translator here has followed the Latin text, which speaks of *substantiae,* while the German text, the original text of the *Formula of Concord*, uses the expression *'zwei Wesen'*. This does not perhaps make a big difference, but taken together with the quotation from the Ancient Fathers who did not know of a theory of consubstantiation, it shows that the passage was originally not meant to express the doctrine of consubstantiation in its technical sense. This is borne out by the fact that even one of the authors of the *Formula of Concord,* N. Selneccer, belonged to the theologians of the 16th century who

---

[50] WA 6, 508, 19 f; Philad. 2, 188.

[51] For instance: R. Seeberg, *Lehrbuch der Dogmengeschichte,* IV, 1 (1933), 399; E. Peschke, *op. cit., I, 1,* 334.

[52] *Form. Conc., Sol. Decl. VII, 37* (Trigl. 985).

always strongly protested against the insinuation that the Lutherans taught consubstantiation.[53]

What, then, is the Lutheran understanding of the Real Presence, if it is not consubstantiation? What takes the place of the Roman doctrine on transubstantiation for Luther and the Lutheran church? The answer is clear if one looks at Luther's criticism of the medieval theories. We have seen in the *Smalcald Articles* how he deals very gently with the doctrine on concomitance, although he rejects it. Similarly cautious is his verdict on transubstantiation:

> We care nothing about the sophistical subtlety by which they teach that bread and wine leave or lose their own natural substance, and that there remain only the appearance and colour of bread, and not true bread. For it is in perfect agreement with Holy Scriptures that there is, and remains, bread, as Paul himself calls it, 1 Cor. 10:16: 'The bread which we break'. And 1 Cor. 11:28: 'Let him so eat of that bread'.[54]

Transubstantiation, according to Luther, is an unnecessary philosophical theory to explain the miracle of the Real Presence, which defies such explanation. It must be rejected because Paul speaks of the consecrated bread as being bread. But Luther never put this error on the same level as withholding the cup from the laity, or the sacrifice of the mass. While these latter errors destroy the Sacrament, transubstantiation is only a wrong attempt to explain the miracle of the Real Presence. This miracle can be stated only as an article of faith, as Luther does at the beginning of the Article quoted:

> Of the Sacrament of the Altar we hold that bread and wine in the Supper are the true body and blood of Christ, and are given and received not only by the godly, but also by wicked Christians.[55]

Nothing else is Lutheran doctrine: The consecrated bread **is** the body; the consecrated wine **is** the blood of Christ. How that is possible, no person on earth can say. What we know is that Christ himself gave this explanation by saying: 'This **is** my body . . . This **is** my blood of the new covenant'. On the basis of these words of Christ, Luther believes in the Real Presence without trying to build up a theory comparable to the theories of impanation, transubstant-

---

[53]As in N. Selneccer, *Vom hl. Abendmahl des Herrn etc.* (1591) Bl. E 2: 'Although our churches use the old expressions "in the bread", "with the bread", or "under the bread" . . . they do not teach an *inclusio*, *consubstantiatio*, or *delitescentia* [i.e. being locally hidden]. The meaning is rather that Christ, 'when giving the bread, gives us simultaneously His body to eat . . . '

[54]*Smalc. Art., III, 6* (Trigl. 493).

[55]Trigl. 493.

iation, consubstantiation, or whatever else the subtle minds of philosophers and theologians may have devised in order to answer the question: How could the Real Presence be possible?

It has rightly been observed that during 1523 the Real Presence began to step into the centre of Luther's theology. It is not true (as certain modern admirers of what they call the 'young Luther' have tried to make us believe) that the earlier writings, especially the treatises of 1519 and 1520 with their strong emphasis on the faith of the communicants, and with their impressive descriptions of the manifold blessings of the Sacrament, represent a stage in the theology of Luther in which the Real Presence was unimportant. From this point of view, the emphasis on the presence of the true body and blood, which we find some years later, seemed to be a sort of apostasy of the Reformer from his original doctrine. But this understanding of Luther's development cannot be maintained. Every single sentence of these early writings of Luther on the Lord's Supper presupposes the miracle of the Real Presence as an obvious truth that nobody dared to doubt and which, therefore, did not need to be stressed. It was only when he met with the denial of the Real Presence that Luther found himself compelled to speak clearly and emphatically of that which during his whole life had undoubtedly been fundamental in his view of this Sacrament. The occasion arose when he received from some Bohemian Brethren a pamphlet on the Lord's Supper in which the true and substantial presence of the body and blood of Christ was denied. This caused him to write his book *Of the Adoration of the Sacrament of the Blessed Body of Christ* (1523).[56]

Here he distinguishes four errors which must be rejected. The first is to assume that in the Sacrament there is nothing else than bread and wine, which signify the body and blood of Christ:

> Beware of this opinion. Let go reason, which asks in vain how flesh and blood may be there, and refuses to believe, since it cannot understand. Embrace the word spoken by Christ: This is my body, this is my blood. It is not permissible to deal so blasphemously with God's words.[57]

The second error is the attempt to give the Words of Institution a different meaning. Some people understand the words of Christ, 'This is my body' to mean: 'If you take the bread and wine, you will be incorporated into my spiritual body'. This, however, is to read a

[56] WA 11, 417 ff: *Vom Anbeten des Sakraments des heiligen Leichnams Christi.*
[57] WA 11, 434, 17 ff.

different meaning into the text, Luther retorts. For 'the body which is given for you' cannot be referred to the spiritual Body of Christ, which is the Church.

> The third error is that the bread does not remain in the Sacrament, but only the species of bread. This error, however, is not of very great importance, if only Christ's body and blood are left there, along with the word, though the papists have seriously fought about this new article of theirs, and are still fighting and calling everybody a heretic who does not regard as a necessary truth that monastic dream confirmed by Thomas Aquinas and approved by the popes, namely, that no bread remains in the Sacrament.[58]

It is noteworthy, also here, how lenient Luther's verdict on the doctrine of transubstantiation is. Quite different are his words on the sacrifice of the mass:

> The fourth error, which is the most injurious and the most heretical one, invented by the Antichrist, the pope and his adherents, is this: that they have made of the Sacrament a sacrifice and good work.[59]

How important the Real Presence as the very core of the Sacrament is for Luther becomes evident in the second part of the book where he speaks of the 'adoration (*Anbeten*)' of the Sacrament. He rejects, of course, the adoration of the consecrated host in the tabernacle or in the procession of the Feast of Corpus Christi. He also doubts whether the German word *Anbeten* is the correct translation of the Latin *adorare* in this case. He would prefer to speak of *Ehrerbietung* (reverence), that showing of reverence which in the Old Testament is called 'to bow', 'to prostrate'. It is a reverence born out of deep faith, a spiritual awe, which, however, finds its expression in bodily gestures, too. The object of this adoration is Jesus Christ, as he is present in the Sacrament — not the bread and wine. How the whole Christ, not only his body and blood, but also his human soul and his divine nature, are present, we should not ask, as did the theologians of concomitance. Such adoration is not divinely commanded; for example, the apostles did not adore Christ at the Last Supper. Neither those who practise it, nor those who do not practise it, should be regarded as heretics. What is necessary is

> that you in faith embrace the words: 'This is my body which is given for you'. Thus eat and drink (spiritually) and nourish your faith. Then take the body and blood as a confirmation of such words of God and say: I have not been ordered to search and to know how God the Father, Son, and Holy Ghost, or the soul of Christ is in the Sacrament. It is enough for me to know that the word which I hear and the body which I take are truly those of my Lord and God. Let the subtle and faithless sophists search for such inscrutable things and bring the

[58] WA 11, 441, 18.
[59] WA 11, 441, 32.

> deity into the Sacrament by magic. The body which you take and the word which you hear are his who holds in his hands the entire world and who is everywhere. Be satisfied with that.[60]

In these words, which were written before the great controversy on the Lord's Supper broke out which led to the Marburg Colloquy, we find the gist of Luther's doctrine on the Sacrament of the Altar. His belief in the Real Presence rests solely on the words of Christ. He was well acquainted with the scholastic theories on the Eucharist. He himself had to make use of them in subsequent years when he had to refute the objection of adversaries that the doctrine of the Real Presence was nonsense. But important as such ideas from medieval theology and philosophy might become for him as means of apologetics, they never became the basis of his convictions. Even if all theories of the Middle Ages concerning the possibility that a body can exist without space were wrong, his belief in the Real Presence would have been unshattered. It was not stubbornness that moved Luther to retain the words 'This is my body' in their literal sense; it was simply reverence for him who spoke these words and neither gave, nor commanded to give, another explanation. We must not forget that this reverence has always been the deepest motive for the realistic understanding of the sacramental words. Luther could have made his own the words of Thomas Aquinas which were later quoted by the Lutheran church:

> *Credo, quidquid dixit Dei Filius / Nil hoc verbo veritatis verius* (I believe whatever the Son of God has said; nothing is more true than the Word of truth).[61]

But where do we find the difference between Thomas and Luther, between the belief of the Middle Ages and the faith of the Lutheran Reformation in this respect? Both assert that these are the words of Christ, the God-Man, and his words must be accepted as absolute truth. They agree that he who spoke these words can do what he says; they are the words of almighty God who can do everything and is not bound by the limitations of our human power and reason. It is interesting, incidentally, that here, where Luther speaks of omnipotence of God or of the Lord of the universe, the idea that this Lord is everywhere is expressed for the first time. We shall come back to this idea later when we shall observe how the 'ubiquity' of Christ plays an important role in the controversy of the ensuing years. The difference between Thomas and Luther is to be sought at another

---

[60] WA 11, 450, 8.

[61] From *'Adoro te devote'*. See above, 37, footnote 39.

point. *Ad firmandum cor sincerum sola fides sufficit* was the answer of Thomas in view of the fact that our human senses can never find Christ's body and blood in the Sacrament.[62] But, according to Thomas, the 'faith' which supplements the failure of our senses to realize Christ's presence is that divine virtue of 'assent' which takes as true that which our reason never can comprehend. How different is the faith of Luther in the words of the Sacrament! His is a faith in the Gospel, a faith that is not only the acceptance of a dogma, but the acceptance of Christ. For the sacramental words are not only the expression of a doctrine, a dogmatical statement that has to be accepted; they are the Gospel itself. You cannot accept the words, 'This is my body', without believing also 'which is given for you'.

This is the great return of Luther to the New Testament, the return from the medieval mass to the Holy Communion of Jesus and the Early Church; the Lord's Supper is again understood as the Gospel itself, the Gospel in action. The entire content of the Gospel is the content of this Sacrament. Christ, the eternal Son of God; Christ who became man for us and for our salvation; Christ who was made really flesh; Christ who was born of the Virgin Mary; Christ who suffered under Pontius Pilate and died on Calvary as the one and final sacrifice for the sins of the world; Christ who shed his blood for us; Christ who is the Saviour and Lord of his Body, the Church; Christ who is not separated from us by space and time; Christ who gives us forgiveness of sins and, with that forgiveness, eternal life and eternal salvation; Christ who enters our whole life, spiritually as well as bodily in order that we may belong to him for ever, body and soul, as his members: all this is contained in the Words of Institution. They are the Gospel itself, and to believe in them is to believe in the Gospel. To destroy or to extenuate these words was for Luther a violation of the Gospel itself.

> These are the words on which everything depends, and every Christian should know and retain them well, not allowing them to be taken away by any other doctrine, even if an angel from heaven should try to do it. These are the words of life and blessedness. He who believes them has by his faith the forgiveness of all his sins and is a child of life, having overcome hell and death. It is unspeakable how great and powerful these words are; for they are the sum total of the whole Gospel.[63]

---

[62]From *'Pange lingua, gloriosi corporis mysterium'*, one of the hymns of Corpus Christi.

[63]*Denn sie die Summa sind des ganzen Evangelii,* WA 11, 432, 19 ff. Compare *Denn dies Sakrament ist das Evangelium,* WA 11, 442, 22 f.

What faith in these words as faith in the Gospel means has never been stated in a more childlike and more impressive way than in his *Large Confession* of 1528 after the great literary controversy with Zwingli:

> Therefore you can joyfully say to Christ, both at your death and in the Last Judgment: My dear Lord Jesus, there has arisen a strife about Thy words at the Last Supper. Some want them to be understood differently from what they say. However, since they cannot teach me anything certain, but only lead me into confusion and uncertainty . . . I have remained with Thy text as the words stand. If there should be an obscurity in them, Thou wilt bear with me if I do not completely understand them, just as Thou didst forbear with Thine apostles when they did not understand Thee in many things — for instance, when Thou didst speak to them about Thy suffering and resurrection, and yet they retained Thy words and did not alter them. As also Thy dear mother did not understand when Thou didst tell her, Luke 2, 'I must be about my Father's business', and yet she kept these words in her heart and did not alter them. Thus, I also have remained with these Thy words: This is my body, etc. Lo, no enthusiast will dare to speak thus with Christ.[64]

We must understand this deep reverence for the Words of Institution as the words of Christ and the sum total of his Gospel if we want to understand the doctrine on the Sacrament of the Altar which Luther held when the Great Controversy with Zwingli began.

5. The Fruits of the Sacrament

A few words should be said on the effects, or the fruits, of the Sacrament of the Altar according to Luther in his early period before we try to understand the Great Controversy. It is a remarkable fact that the church has always felt at a loss in defining the effects of the Sacrament.[65] While it is very easy to define the gift imparted by Baptism, the fruit or fruits of the *sacramentum sacramentorum* have always been the object of discussions among the theologians even of one and the same church. Luther's first utterances are to be found in his *Treatise on the Blessed Sacrament of the Holy and True Body of Christ and on Fraternities* of 1519. Here we find all emphasis being laid on the idea of the Lord's Supper as Holy Communion.

> The significance or purpose of this sacrament is the fellowship of all saints, whence it derives its common name *synaxis* or *communio,* that is, fellowship; and *communicare* means to take part in this fellowship or, as we say, to go to the sacrament, because Christ and all saints are one spiritual body . . . On the other hand, *excommunicare* means to put out of the community and to sever a member from this body . . .[66]

---

[64] *Vom Abendmahl Christi. Bekenntnis* (1528), WA 26, 446, 32 ff.

[65] This may be one of the reasons why the idea of the eucharistic sacrifice spread so rapidly throughout the Ancient Church. For the purpose of a sacrifice presents no problem whatever.

[66] WA 2, 743, 7 ff; Philad. 2, 10.

This idea, deeply rooted in the passage 1 Cor. 10:17, which Luther quotes as scriptural proof, had determined Augustine's doctrine on the unity of the Body of Christ as the *res sacramenti*, which had become the doctrine of the medieval church.[67] It is not by accident that the young Luther takes this very idea as the starting-point for his thinking about the effects of the Sacrament. Not only in this and subsequent writings, but especially in his sermons on the Lord's Supper, he makes use of the imagery of the Ancient Church in a remarkable way as he compares the unity and communion of the church with the one bread, which has been made from many grains, and the wine, which has been produced from many grapes.[68] It is significant for Luther and his *theologia crucis* that he stresses the fact that the individual grain of wheat or the individual grape has to give up its own separate existence in order to become a part of the whole:

> Just as the bread is made from many grains that have been ground and mixed together, and out of the many bodies of grain there comes the one body of the bread, in which each grain loses its form and body and acquires the common body of the bread, and as the drops of the wine,[69] losing their own form, become the body of one wine: so it should be for you, and indeed so it is, if this sacrament is used aright. Christ, with all saints, by His love, takes upon Himself our form, fights with us against sin, death, and all evil; this enkindles in us such love that we take His form, rely upon His righteousness, life and blessedness, and through the interchange of His blessings and our misfortunes become one loaf, one bread, one body, one drink, and have all things in common. This is a great sacrament, says Paul,[70] that Christ and the Church are one flesh and bone.[71]

Luther then goes on to admonish the Christians to practise such fellowship.[72]

Two questions arise here: first, what the **Real Presence** means in this understanding of the Sacrament, and secondly, in how far the

---

[67]It is interesting to observe how Luther interprets this medieval doctrine in terms of the Reformation.

[68]The oldest example, unknown until 1887, but probably the source of the later liturgies and Fathers is *Didachē 9,* 4, Serapion, *Euchologion 3,* 7; Cyprian, *Ep. 63,* 7 (CSEL III, 2, 705 f); *Ep. 69,* 5, (CSEL *loc. cit.,* 754); Augustine in *Joh. 26,* 17 (MPL 35, 1614, quoted by Thomas, *Summa theol. III, Q. 79, Art. 1*).

[69]In other places Luther, following the example of the Fathers, speaks of 'grapes' (*Beeren*).

[70]Here Luther still accepts the word *sacramentum* used by the Vulgate in Eph. 5:32.

[71]WA 2, 748, 7 ff; Philad. 2, 17,18.

[72]For the practical application which Luther made in his sermons, see the Sermons for Maundy Thursday 1523 (WA 12, 472 ff; EA 17, second edition 39 ff) and 1524 (WA 15, 497 ff; EA 11, second ed. 164 ff).

remission of sins belongs to the fruits of the Lord's Supper. Luther gives the answer:

> This holy sacrament is naught else than a divine sign, in which Christ and all saints are pledged, granted, and imparted, with all their works, sufferings, merits, mercies, and possessions, for the comfort and strengthening of all who are in anxiety and sorrow, and are persecuted by the devil, sin, the world, the flesh, and every evil; and that to receive the sacrament is nothing else than to desire all this and firmly to believe that it shall be done.[73]

It is not permissible to understand this and similar sayings, as sometimes has been done, as a denial of the Real Presence or of the necessity to receive the true body and blood of the Lord. The 'sign' is by no means the mere sacramental action, or the element, but rather the true body and blood which cannot be separated from the elements:

> For just as the bread is changed into His true natural body and the wine into His true natural blood, so truly are we also drawn and changed into the spiritual body. . . [74]

Thus, Luther's idea of the reality of the *corpus Christi mysticum* is inseparably connected with his understanding of the reality of the *corpus Christi sacramentale.* However, he is not quite able to show why the *corpus mysticum* depends on the *corpus sacramentale.* If the body and blood of Christ are a sign to us, could we not do without this sign? If Luther here, as in subsequent writings, and in all his writings for that matter, emphasized faith in the words of Christ as that which is really essential for the blessed reception of the Sacrament, must this faith necessarily include belief in the Real Presence? This is, indeed, Luther's opinion. How can, and will, he who does not believe the words, 'This is my body', believe the words 'which is given for you'? But it cannot be denied that in these early writings, where Luther had to fight the Roman doctrine, the main emphasis is on the *corpus mysticum* and on faith. In that situation, which was not yet determined by the fight against the enthusiasts, Luther could say:

> It is more needful that you discern the spiritual than that you discern the natural body of Christ, and faith in the spiritual is more needful than faith in the natural. For the natural without the spiritual profiteth us nothing in the sacrament. . . [75]

---

[73]WA 2, 749, 23 ff; Philad. 2, 19.
[74]WA 2, 749, 10 ff; Philad. 2, 19.
[75]WA 2, 751, 13 ff; Philad. 2, 22.

In order to understand such sentences, one must always remember that for Luther even in his early years the 'natural' and the 'spiritual' belong together, and that 'sign *(signum)*' to him was not the same as what Honius (Cornelius Hoen) and Zwingli later understood by 'sign'. The word *signum* as a definition of the Sacrament was given to him by the tradition which goes back to Augustine. How Luther understood it in the case of the Lord's Supper is shown in the answer which on a later occasion he gave to the question whether the Supper could be called a sign. He distinguished between a philosophical sign, which denotes something that is absent, and a theological sign, which denotes something present.[76]

After 1520 it becomes evident that for Luther **the real gift** and fruit of the Lord's Supper **is the forgiveness of sins**. His *Treatise on the New Testament, that is, on the Holy Mass* of 1520 and *De captivitate* proves that. The effects of the Eucharist, which Thomas enumerates and discusses (*Summa theol., Pars III, Q. 79*), are the reception of grace, the preparation for future glory, the preservation from future sins, the forgiveness of venial sins, but by no means forgiveness of mortal sins. On the contrary, Thomas emphasizes the necessity of being free from mortal sin for a worthy communion. A sinner, a person who is not in the state of grace, cannot enter into the union with Christ in the Eucharist.[77] According to Roman doctrine Holy Communion is for the righteous only, for those who through the sacrament of penance have been made righteous. According to Luther, Holy Communion is for sinners only, for people who remain sinners even after they have received absolution. For Christ came from heaven, where he dwelt among sinless saints, in order that he might dwell on earth among sinners. If this is the meaning of his incarnation, it is also the meaning of the Real Presence of his body and blood in the Sacrament.

Thus, the discovery of the Gospel led to the rediscovery of the meaning of the Lord's Supper. The 'new testament' is the Sacrament of the Altar; the Words of Institution are the Gospel. To believe the Gospel means to believe all the words with which Christ instituted the Sacrament, and especially the promise: 'Given and shed for you, for the remission of sins'. This is the 'testament' of Christ.

---

[76] '*Duplicia sunt signa: philosophica et theologia. Signum philosophicum est nota absentis rei, signum theologicum est nota praesentis rei*' (*Table Talk of 1540*, WA TR 4, 5106).

[77] '*Non potest uniri Christo . . . dum est in affectu peccandi mortaliter*' (*op. cit.* Q. 79, 3).

> He has attached a most powerful and noble seal and sign to the words of His testament. This seal and sign is His own true flesh and blood under the bread and wine. For while we poor men live in our five senses, we need . . . an outward sign besides the words to keep to it and to gather around it.

Such sign, however, must be something

> external, and still contain and signify something spiritual, in order that we may be drawn by that which is external into that which is spiritual, perceiving the external thing with our bodily eyes and the spiritual and internal thing with the eyes of the heart.[78]

From this passage it becomes quite clear that Luther, when speaking of the Sacrament as a seal, sign, or pledge, attached to the word of the evangelical promise, never thinks of the external bread or of the external action only. This external element is, rather, inseparably bound up with what the Catholic doctrine would call *sacramentum et res,* the true body and blood of Christ. The question then arises: Would not the visible, external element suffice as pledge, seal, and sign, since the invisible, internal body and blood are in themselves objects of faith, to be perceived with the eyes of the heart? Is it not enough to believe in the words of Christ and regard the external element as the sufficient seal? It was to be expected that this question would be put to Luther during the Great Controversy with Zwingli. But the writings of his early period already indicate what his answer would be: You cannot believe the second part of the Words of Institution: 'given and shed for you, for the remission of sins', without believing the first part: 'This is my body', 'This is my blood'. And if the question were asked: Why not?, his answer would be: I do not know; Christ said so; that must be sufficient.

[78] WA 6, 359, 4 ff; Philad. 1, 301.

CHAPTER III

Zwingli

1. The Background of Zwingli's Theology

The difference between Luther and Zwingli that proved to be so fateful for the Reformation cannot be explained by the difference in their characters or by the contrast between their cultural and political backgrounds in Saxony and Switzerland. This does not mean, of course, that these non-theological factors in the development of the German and the Swiss Reformers are insignificant. On the contrary, the fact that Zwingli, the son of democratic Switzerland, was by nature a politician who, as a citizen of the Republic of Zurich, had to act as a politician in order to gain a majority for his ecclesiastical plans, is of importance even for the understanding of some of his decisions on the question of the Sacraments.[1] More illuminating, however, is the dissimilarity between Luther's and Zwingli's education and religious background.

Luther was a priest of a monastic order, a theological scholar, well trained in the philosophy and theology of the *via moderna,* the school of Occam and his disciples. Though in many respects deviating from this school of thought, especially from Occam's belief in the free will of man, he learned much from his 'dear master', such as the antithesis of reason and revelation. A great Christian character, matured by profound inner struggles, he was imbued at the beginning of the Reformation with the other-worldliness of a strict monastic life and with a living experience of Augustine's *sola gratia.* He had learned to despair of man and to believe in God, not

[1]It should never be overlooked that the majority of the independent territories of Germany which in the earlier period accepted the Lutheran Reformation were Free Cities, i.e. republics. Even the *Formula of Concord* was signed by 35 republics. This fact should suffice to refute the popular prejudice that the Lutheran Reformation was mainly the work of the princes, and that Lutheranism is essentially related to a form of government that relieves citizens of their responsibilities for the management of public affairs.

the God of the philosophers, but the God of the Bible. Preaching and teaching him, he had become, as a doctor of divinity and a professor of exegesis, the beginner of a new theological school that was characterized by anti-Aristotelian biblicism. The God he found in the Bible is God who is hidden (*Deus absconditus*) outside Christ, and revealed (*Deus revelatus*) in Christ only, but revealed in such a way that even Christ's divinity is hidden behind his humanity. Thus, Luther, as he had become the theologian of *sola gratia* and *sola fide,* was at the same time the great theologian of the cross, and, along with Irenaeus, Athanasius, and Anselm, one of the greatest theologians of the Incarnation. In a wonderful explanation of 'He made darkness his secret place' (Psalm 18:11; 17:12 Vulgate), Luther had spoken in 1513 about God who hides himself in the enigma and riddle of faith. Hidden and incomprehensible, God is in an inaccessible light. Even in the mystery of Incarnation, where we can know him, he remains hidden in his humanity. He is hidden in the Church, as he is in the Sacrament of the Eucharist, where he is 'most hidden'.[2]

One must keep in mind this character of Luther's theology in order to understand Zwingli. This Reformer of German-speaking Switzerland was a secular priest. He had never studied in a theological faculty, but had taken holy orders (as was not uncommon at that time) after he had attained the degree of Master of Arts. The Faculty of Arts, especially that of Basle, had given him a considerable knowledge of the *via antiqua*, the philosophical and theological system of Thomas. Although he had also carefully read Duns Scotus, he was at heart a Thomist, which he remained even as a reformer — a Thomist for whom revelation can never contradict reason. For him, as for Thomas, God was *primum movens* and *prima causa,* the first cause of, and the deepest reason underlying, all things.

> What reason is in man, that God is in the world (*Hoc est Deus in mundo, quod ratio in homine*).
>
> God is truth and he is light. He gives light and does not lead us into darkness,

as Zwingli said at Marburg.[3] Here is, perhaps, the deepest contrast between him and Luther (who in the Word of God always found that which contradicts human reason). That the wisdom of God is hidden

---

[2]'*Sacramentum Eucharistiae, ubi est occultissimus*', in *Scholia ad Ps. 17:12;* WA 3 124, 37 f.

[3]See below, 191-193.

under the appearance of foolishness, the truth of God under what seems to human reason to be a lie, and that the Word of God always comes to us as something that contradicts our mind,[4] Zwingli would never have been able to say.

The Thomistic heritage was strengthened by the second school of thought that shaped Zwingli's thinking: Erasmian humanism. From Erasmus, Zwingli learned the idealistic separation of matter and mind, body and soul, the spiritual understanding of Christianity and Christian salvation, as it had been cultivated by the *devotio moderna* of the Late Middle Ages, the moralistic understanding of the Gospel and a high respect for the high ethics of ancient paganism. He kept this heritage even after the breach with Erasmus. At Marburg, before the arrival of Luther, he preached a sermon on Divine Providence, one of the favourite topics of his theology.[5] In this sermon it became obvious that, whatever he had learned from the New Testament in the meantime, at the bottom of his heart he was still a Thomist who believed in the harmony of reason and revelation, as well as a humanist who never could imagine heaven without the great ethical heroes of pagan antiquity. Though he never doubted the miracles of the Bible, or the great doctrines of the Creed, there is in his theology a rationalistic element, side by side with traditional Christian dogmatics, as we find in many humanists. As a friend of Erasmus, in the early years of his ministry he was a shining light among the men of letters in his country, a hope of what the humanists called *Christianismus renascens.* For one must never forget that the Humanistic Movement, as it was represented by Erasmus and his friends in England, Germany, and the Netherlands, had as its most important aim a reformation of the church. Zwingli, who later used to emphasize his independence from Luther, began his activity as a reformer of the Erasmian type. Following the humanist slogan, *ad fontes*, he studied the Bible (especially the Greek New Testament that Erasmus had edited), and the early Church Fathers, as the 'sources'

---

[4] '*Sicut . . . Dei sapientia abscondita est sub specie stultitiae et veritas sub forma mendacii — ita enim verbum Dei, quoties venit, venit in specie contraria menti nostrae . . .*' Luther, *ad Rom. 12,* 1 ff; WA 56, 446, 31 ff.

[5] Walther Koehler, *Huldrych Zwingli* (1943), 202 f; *Zwingli und Luther, II* (1953), 75. O. Farner, *Zwingli the Reformer, His Life and Work,* English translation by D.G. Sear (London, 1952), 120, assumes that the sermon was preached during the colloquy, on Sunday Oct. 3. In that case Luther's criticism of Zwingli's rhetorical way of preaching at Marburg (*Table Talk of 1539,* WA TR 4, 4719, 16 ff) would refer to that sermon.

of pure, original Christianity — as his great master and friend had understood it. Although he later gained a deeper understanding of the Christian faith, especially after Luther had begun to influence him (for the courageous German Reformer overshadowed Erasmus, the man of theory and compromise), he was never able to relinquish the legalistic understanding of Christ and the Gospel. Thus, the Swiss Reformer remained a man of affairs, an ever-active politician, who never could understand Luther's idea that the minister of the Gospel should not meddle in politics.

> One must help the Lord Jesus to become the ruler of the country.

With such words he justified the attempt by political means to force the Catholic cantons of Switzerland to accept the Reformation. The sword with which he appeared at Marburg (to the amazement of the Lutherans) was a symbol of the way things ecclesiastical and things secular belonged together, as far as he was concerned. It symbolized at the same time the tragedy of his life as a minister of the Gospel, which led him from the battlefields of Pavia and Marignano, where he served as a chaplain, to the battlefield of Kappel, where he was killed in 1531 in a bloody massacre as a brave soldier who gave his life for the ideals, ecclesiastical and political, for which he had fought for so many years as a Christian politician and a Christian soldier.

When these two contemporaries, Luther and Zwingli, searched the Scriptures to find the real meaning of the words of Christ in contradistinction to the errors of the papal church, the results were bound to be very different. If anywhere, the difference was to become quite clear in their understanding of the Sacrament of the Altar.

2. Zwingli's Understanding of the Sacraments

The older Reformed theologians tried to show that Zwingli from the very beginning of his activity as reformer held the doctrine which he later defended so forcefully against Luther and the Lutherans. This legend was definitely overthrown by Walther Koehler in his *magnum opus, Zwingli und Luther.*[6] Actually, Zwingli confessed the Roman doctrine on transubstantiation up to the year 1523, although it seems that he, like many priests at that time, did not take it very

———

[6] *Zwingli und Luther. Ihr Streit über das Abendmahl nach seinen politischen und religiösen Beziehungen.* Vol. I: *Die religiöse und politische Entwicklung bis zum Marburger Religionsgespräch* (1934). Vol. II: *Vom Beginn der Marburger Verhandlungen 1529 bis zum Abschluss der Wittenberger Konkordie von 1536* (1953), edited after Koehler's death by Kohlmeyer and Bornkamm.

seriously. This is indicated by a word spoken not only against Lutherans, but also against Catholics:

> In my opinion no one has ever believed that he eats Christ bodily and essentially, though almost all have taught this or at least pretended to believe it.[7]

From these words the conclusion must be drawn that Zwingli in his earlier years, like many theologians especially of humanist persuasion, accepted this dogma as he did all doctrines of the church, but attempted to interpret it in a more spiritual way. As to the Real Presence itself, however, he had no desire to give it up. Still, in his treatise on fasting, one of the great documents of the Reformation at Zurich, he uses terms for eating and drinking the Eucharist that exclude a figurative understanding.[8] His first criticism of the Roman mass is directed against the *communio sub una* and against the sacrifice of the mass, but by no means against the Real Presence. For him, according to the 18th of his *Theses* (*Schlussreden*) of January 1523, the mass is

> not a sacrifice, but a remembrance of the sacrifice and an assurance of the redemption that Christ has gained for us.[9]

In his letter to Th. Wyttenbach in June of 1523, where he attacks transubstantiation for the first time, he still maintains the Real Presence in a certain way. All the same, it is not that Presence which Luther taught. Zwingli's view at that time was: The believer eats Christ, who otherwise is in heaven, seated at the right hand of the Father, but who miraculously descends in this Sacrament. How this is possible, no one knows. By an inscrutable miracle Christ enters the soul of the believer. What the actual relationship between the elements and the body and blood of Christ is, Zwingli is unable to say. Nor is he able to answer the question: What do the unbelievers receive? Although he uses the old terminology in speaking of 'eating the body', 'drinking the blood', the meaning of these expressions remains ambiguous and obscure. In fact, the believer receives Christ in the Sacrament by faith only. Here the question necessarily arises whether the Sacrament gives anything that we do not receive outside the Sacrament by faith, especially since Zwingli already refers to

---

[7]Quoted by W. Koehler, *Zwingli und Luther*, 74, from *Zwingli's Works,* Critical Edition in *Corpus Reformatorum,* III, 350, 6 ff.

[8]*Vom Erkiesen und Freiheit der Speisen, Zwingli's Works,* I.

[9]E. F. K. Mueller, *Die Bekenntnisschriften der Reformierten Kirche* (1903), 18. See also W. Koehler, *op. cit.,* 19 f with the explanation of *'des Opfers ein Wiedergedächtnis'* (*anamnēsis*).

John 6 in his writings of 1523, and concludes from that chapter that when we firmly believe in Christ's redeeming death, our soul eats the body and drinks the blood of our Lord.[10]

The characteristic feature of this early stage of Zwingli's doctrine on the Lord's Supper is an attempt to spiritualize the Catholic doctrine. In this respect Zwingli followed his master Erasmus, who, while rejecting the theory of transubstantiation, believed in a miraculous, inexplicable presence of Christ in the Sacrament. This seems to have been a widespread view among the clergy of humanistic leanings. The difference, as compared with the views of Erasmus, lies in the strong emphasis on the faith of the recipient. In this respect Zwingli seems to have been influenced by Luther's early writings on the Sacrament. It is noteworthy that in this early stage of Zwingli's development there are not the slightest traces of a figurative understanding of the Words of Institution. For a spiritual understanding of the Lord's Supper does not necessarily include a figurative interpretation of the sacramental words.

The second and final stage in Zwingli's doctrine was reached in 1524, under the influence of the famous letter, or, rather, treatise, in which the Dutch humanist Honius (Cornelius Hoen) placed a new view of the Lord's Supper before the theologians of his time. This letter, the origin of which is somewhat shrouded,[11] belongs to the great events in the history of the Sacrament insofar as it introduced into the discussion of the 16th century the figurative understanding of the Words of Institution. Honius takes up an older tradition which we have already encountered in Berengar and Wyclif, and which he seems to have borrowed from Wessel Gansfort (1420-89). This disciple of Thomas à Kempis and of the *devotio moderna* of the Low Countries had developed a purely spiritual doctrine on the Sacraments, and had written a book on the Eucharist, which, while not denying the bodily presence of Christ or even the doctrine of the church on transubstantiation, laid all emphasis on the faithful commemoration as the real communion. For Gansfort the real eating and drinking were the spiritual eating and drinking in the

---

[10]Koehler, *op. cit.,* 35.

[11]The letter was formerly regarded as addressed to Luther, and consequently included in *Luthers Briefwechsel* by Enders, Vol. 3, 412-23 (No. 552). The real addressee, however, is unknown. W. Koehler, *Huldrych Zwingli*, 175, thinks of Erasmus. Messengers brought the document to various persons, first of all to Luther in 1521, and then to Zwingli in 1524. The letter was published by Zwingli in 1525.

sense of John 6, which could take place, with the same blessing, also outside the Lord's Supper. This is the reason why Gansfort was not interested in the fight for the cup for the laity. The logical consequence of this spiritual view of the Sacrament (traces of which we found as an Augustinian heritage even in Thomas and Luther) is the fact that the outward Sacrament becomes more or less superfluous. What does it actually mean? This question was answered by Honius. We must sketch his theory briefly because it definitely shaped the doctrine of Zwingli.

Honius understands the Sacrament of the Altar as a visible pledge that Christ added to the promise of the Gospel, just as a bridegroom as a token of his love gives his bride a ring which will always remind her of his promise. Likewise, through the Lord's Supper we are reminded to trust Christ's promise. To have such confidence in him means, according to John 6, to eat his body and to drink his blood. Roman scholasticism replaced this justifying faith by the belief that bread and wine after consecration are no longer bread and wine, but the true body and blood of Christ. This belief led to the adoration of the host, and, in turn, to idolatry that puts Christians on the same level with pagans adoring objects of wood and stone. If the objection is raised that we need simply to believe Christ's Words of Institution, the answer is that Christ himself said: 'If any man shall say unto you: Lo, here is Christ, or there; believe it not' (Matthew 24:23). Nor did the apostles speak of this Sacrament in that way. They always speak of the bread as bread, and even Paul (in 1 Cor. 10:16) calls the bread not the body, but the communion of the body, even as he asserts in the same chapter that the Fathers in the desert did eat the same spiritual food as we receive. Hence, the bread signifies the body; *est* is to be understood as meaning *significat*. The Incarnation was predicted by the prophets, shown by Christ's life and death, and proclaimed by the apostles. Nothing of that kind may be said of the daily 'impanation' of Christ which is taught solely on the basis of the words: 'This is my body . . . this do in remembrance of me'.[12] These words must be understood figuratively, like Matthew 11:14 (John is Elijah), John 19:26 ('Behold thy son'), Matthew 16:18 (Peter the rock), 1 Cor. 10.4 ('The rock was Christ', that is, it represented Christ), and like the words in which Christ calls himself the door, the way, the true vine. Honius finds a threefold spiritual bread in the

[12]'*Christus quotidie impanatur (ut ita loquar)*'. Enders 3, No. 552, lines 83, 84.

Bible: Christ eaten by faith according to John 6:48-50; the manna given to the Fathers; the eucharistic bread of the Christians. The manna points forward to, while the eucharistic bread reminds us of, Christ crucified, who is our true bread of life. As the passing through the sea signified to the believing Fathers the passing from death to eternal life, so Baptism signifies for the believer the resurrection to a new life. In a similar way, the eating of the Eucharist signifies for the true believer the eating of the true and living bread of life by faith. Refuting the Roman doctrine, Honius shows that no article on the eucharistic transformation is to be found in the Creed. This doctrine is rather a papistic or even a satanic invention. For Christ can be seen only by faith and not, like the host, by human eyes. Thus, '*Hoc est corpus meum*' can be understood only as meaning: 'This signifies my body', for the word *est* is used often in that sense in Scripture, like Gen. 40:12: 'The three branches **are** three days'; v 18: 'The three baskets **are** three days'; Gen. 41:26: 'The seven good kine **are** seven years, and the seven good ears **are** seven years'.[13] Nor is it possible to understand the Lord's Supper as a miracle, for all miracles performed by Jesus were not contrary to experience.[14]

When Luther learned about this document, he at once rejected it. It was different with Zwingli when it was brought to him in 1524. He wholeheartedly accepted the theory of Honius. Henceforth, the spiritual understanding of the Real Presence that he had shared with Erasmus was replaced by the figurative understanding of the sacramental words, and the idea of a miraculous presence was given up. This change of mind took place just at the time when he was compelled to break with his former master on account of the attitude that Erasmus took toward the Reformation. In the same year that Zwingli made the doctrine of Honius his own, Carlstadt, who had found a refuge at Strasburg, published his anti-Lutheran treatises on the Lord's Supper. Carlstadt's criticism of Luther (who the previous

---

[13]Honius follows the text of the Vulgate where the copula is used: *'sunt'*. The Hebrew text, of course, has no copula, as in the original Aramaic text of the Words of Institution the copula *est* could not be expressed. The words as Jesus spoke them were probably *'den bisri'*, *'den idhmi'*. Our normative Greek text is a correct translation, for the copula is contained in the Aramaic words.

[14]This argument is repeated by Zwingli and also by Bucer. Zwingli never doubted the biblical miracles. A miracle like the virgin birth, however, was apparent to those concerned. What Zwingli fails to recognize is the fact that there are miracles that are beyond human experience, such as the Incarnation, the presence of Christ according to his divine nature (as Zwingli confesses), baptismal regeneration, and many works of the Holy Spirit.

year had defended the Real Presence against the Bohemians in the book we discussed in the previous chapter) made a deep impression on Zwingli, as well as on the radical group that was just inaugurating the Anabaptist movement at Zurich, partially under the influence of the enthusiasts in Saxony. To be sure, Zwingli did not accept Carlstadt's doctrine (namely, his interpretation of the Words of Institution, that Christ pointed to himself when he said, 'This is my body') or Carlstadt's denial that the Lord's Supper is a pledge (*pignus*) that assures the believer of the forgiveness of sins. His criticism of Carlstadt, however, was very lenient. Despite the differences existing between them, they regarded each other as allies, and were rightly considered as such in Wittenberg as soon as Zwingli declared war on Luther's doctrine on the Sacrament.

What Zwingli seems to have learned from Carlstadt is the Augustinian argument that Christ's body is in heaven and cannot, therefore, at the same time be in the bread. Thus, Zwingli's doctrine on the Lord's Supper was completed in the same year in which the Great Controversy on the Sacrament of the Altar was inaugurated by Carlstadt's attack on the doctrine of Luther. What Zwingli learned during the next years was to make more use of Scripture passages that he regarded as favourable to his view. These were especially: his 'diamond', John 6:63 ('The flesh profiteth nothing'); Exodus 12:11 ('This is the Lord's passover'), the passage that occurred to him in a dream as a sort of revelation; and Matthew 26:11 ('Me ye have not always'). As regards John 6, which was always Zwingli's starting-point for the understanding of the Lord's Supper, it is to be noted that in this period of his theology (for him, as for Luther) this chapter did not deal with the Lord's Supper. They were agreed that John 6 spoke of that spiritual eating and drinking which is faith. As Zwingli understood this chapter, it was of utmost importance insofar as it clearly taught that Christ recognized only a spiritual eating, and expressly rejected (in v 63) all bodily eating as was taught by the Roman church and by Luther. Thus, when he entered the Great Controversy with Luther, two convictions clashed which were fully developed, and between which a compromise was not possible.

If, at this juncture, we try to understand the contrast between Luther and Zwingli as it existed at the beginning of the Great Controversy, it may be described in this way. Luther retained the Real Presence, not because he could not get rid of the orthodox Catholic tradition, but because he was convinced that the Real Presence was deeply rooted in Holy Scripture. Repeatedly — not only in his letter to the Christians of Strasburg in 1524, which we have mentioned — he expressed the opinion that it would have been far easier for him to accept the figurative understanding than what to human reason must seem to be an absurdity.[15] But when the letter of Honius was presented to him, he saw at once that the words '*Hoc est corpus meum*' defied a figurative interpretation.[16] This letter was no temptation for him. Zwingli, on the other hand, abandoned without scruples the Catholic tradition, which he as a disciple of Erasmus for many years already had understood spiritually, on reading Honius's interpretation that recommended itself through its simplicity and seeming clarity. For Zwingli, clarity was always a mark of the Word of God, even if such clarity was reached at the expense of the inexhaustible depth of the divine Word. He was not able to realize, for instance, that 'I am the true vine' cannot be put on the same level with 'the three branches are three years'. In the former case, we have an assertion of the inscrutable mystery of the eternal Son of God; in the second case, an interpretation of a dream.

The difference between Luther and Zwingli at this point is closely connected with the fact that the Reformation in northern and southern Germany as well as in Switzerland in those years had to fight its way in a two-front war against Romanism and Enthusiasm. It is illuminating to see how this situation influenced Luther's and Zwingli's doctrines on the Sacrament. While Luther, despite his strong opposition to the Roman errors concerning the *opus operatum,* the sacrifice of the mass, the withholding of the cup from the laity, and the scholastic doctrine of transubstantiation, retained the Real Presence and the character of the Sacraments as real means of grace, Zwingli regarded this conservatism as an impermissible concession to the papal church. In Zurich, where Zwingli met with the strong resistance of some serious adherents of the old church, who were backed by the interest of the Catholic cantons and by the concern for the religious unity of Switzerland, belief in the Real

———

[15]'No reason is too simple to prefer the belief that mere bread and wine are there and not Christ's flesh and blood. . . It would have been much easier for me to believe and to preach that' (*Wider die himmlischen Propheten,* WA 18, 143, 8 ff). 'If they could give me assurance that the word *est* in this passage means the same as *significat,* I should believe them. They have not the temptations that I had. . . I do not know of any temptation in matters of faith except about anabaptism and the sacrament' (*Table Talk of 1533,* WA TR I, 515). More passages are quoted by H. Grass, *Die Abendmahlslehre bei Luther und Calvin* (1940), 8.

[16]We do not know the exact date. It may be as early as 1521.

Presence soon became a mark of Romanism. Since the Swiss Romanists did not fail to appeal to the fact that even Luther maintained the Real Presence, the Wittenberg Reformation soon came to be regarded by Zwingli and his adherents as a half-way Reformation, notwithstanding Luther's powerful fight against Rome. It belongs to the tragedies of the history of the Reformation that in Zurich the Real Presence, based on the literal understanding of the Words of Institution, was looked upon as an inexplicable relapse by Luther into Romanism. It was impossible, therefore, that Zwingli in the ensuing controversies, and even at Marburg, could go back to a mild formulation of the Presence as he had held it before 1524.

For Luther, on the other hand, Zwingli belonged to the enthusiasts, despite his fight against the Anabaptists at Zurich. And was he not an enthusiast in Luther's sense? Was not the fight against the Anabaptist movement, theologically speaking, an inconsistency? Seen from Wittenberg, the difference between Zwingli and the radical reformers was almost non-existent. For both Zwingli and the Anabaptists the Sacraments ceased to be means of grace, and became mere signs of that divine grace which may be, and is being, received even without them. How close Zwingli (without knowing it) was to his radical adversaries theologically, becomes evident from the fact that he was never able to justify infant baptism except by referring to Old Testament circumcision. As he himself, before the rise of the Anabaptist movement, had been inclined to postpone baptism to a later age, likewise, after he had become a defender of infant baptism against the radicals, he could never realize the necessity for emergency baptism. Why must a person in danger of death receive the Sacrament if the Sacrament is not a means of grace? The Reformed church never, not even at the time of Calvin and later, recognized emergency baptism. It seems that Karl Barth, in his fight against the practice of infant baptism, represents the genuine understanding of Baptism in the Reformed church, although he, of course, is not a Baptist since he recognizes the validity of Baptism received in infancy.

The Anabaptists at the time of Zwingli were not all wrong when they appealed to what they had learned from the Reformer of Zurich about the Sacrament as a mere sign of grace. They applied this to the Lord's Supper, too. Their understanding of the Sacrament as a sign of what takes place in the soul of the believer — self-surrender to Christ, personal assuredness of one's salvation — made it necessary for Zwingli to rethink his concept of the Sacrament. He now liked to stress the old meaning of the Latin *sacramentum* as the soldier's oath of allegiance. Thus, he arrived at an understanding of the Sacrament in which the last remnants of a divine activity had disappeared.

The Sacrament, curiously enough, again became what it had become when the idea of the sacrifice of the mass had made it something that man performs. The Sacrament represented, not what God's grace does in the soul, but rather what man does as a *miles Christi,* as a member of the church. Baptism is a sign indicating man's belonging to the church, just as the white cross that a Swiss soldier puts on his arm shows his nationality — a very inadequate simile, for infants are not soldiers, and baptism that has once been performed in the past is no longer visible to the world. The whole idea can be explained only by Zwingli's identification of nation and church. The Lord's Supper, then, becomes a feast of remembrance, an assembly (*synaxis*), a joyful act of thanksgiving. Seen from the Lutheran point of view, the difference concerning the Sacrament of the Altar becomes insignificant. As both deny the Real Presence, so both deny the idea that grace is given through the Sacrament. The Sacraments give nothing that the Christian cannot and does not receive outside and before Baptism, outside and before the Lord's Supper. This is, indeed, the end of the Sacrament. For a sacrament that is a sign only (*signum*), and not an effective sign (*signum efficax*), ceases to be a sacrament, which always is a means of grace.

Thus, Zwingli, certainly against his own will, through his spiritual understanding of the Gospel, assisted more than anyone in the destruction of the Sacrament in the Protestant world. For there can be no doubt that the majority of modern Protestants, even in nominally-Lutheran churches, as children of the Renaissance and of modern Enlightenment, would take sides with Zwingli against Luther on the question of the Sacrament. This is true even of people who, like Zwingli, want to take Scripture seriously. The least they would say is that Honius's and Zwingli's interpretation of Scripture appeals to them more than that of Luther. It seems that Luther foresaw this, perhaps on the basis of his own experience, when he came to regard Zwingli as one of the worst enemies of the Church of Christ.

3. The New Liturgy

Like the Catholic and the Lutheran doctrines on the Lord's Supper, Zwingli's doctrine, too, was accompanied by a corresponding liturgy. Before we say a word about it, it may be pointed out that even the Reformed liturgies, which at first may seem to represent the most revolutionary destruction of the medieval mass, have their devotional and liturgical background in the Middle Ages. They have not only kept several parts of the old liturgy, like the Gloria, the Salutation, and the Words of Institution, but they have their origin, at least partly, in devotional books written at the end of the Middle Ages for the use of pious laymen to help them to receive the Sacrament spiritually while attending mass. Dom Gregory Dix gives a very illuminating example of such 'Meditations in the Time of Mass' from an English source.[17] The private prayers that Christian laypeople were taught to say during mass are, in a certain way, prototypes of the prayers used in those liturgies that recognized no other kind of communion than a spiritual one — and for Zwingli and his adherents, this was the only communion which they acknowledged. An example of this connection between the reformed liturgies and medieval devotional literature is the liturgy introduced by Oecolampadius in Basle in 1525. The same Oecolampadius, who two years before had written such a devotional explanation of the mass,[18] now gave to his church a liturgy which in all its simplicity and beauty was nothing but a celebration of the remembrance of Christ's atoning death.[19] The liturgical reform in Zurich was carried out the same year.

It is remarkable how slowly changes in liturgy followed doctrinal development in Switzerland as well as in Wittenberg. The liturgy is as a rule the most conservative element in the church. The mass was not definitely abolished in Zurich until Easter 1525, when the Lord's Supper was celebrated with a new liturgy. The altar was replaced by a movable table covered with a white tablecloth. Cans, wooden cups, and wooden plates with unleavened bread were placed on the table. Deacons carried the gifts to the assembled congregation, and everyone broke for himself a small piece from the bread and drank from the cup. Zwingli had written an impressive liturgy for that occasion. Parts of the old mass had been preserved, like the Gloria, the Salutation, the Lessons (including the kissing of the holy book), the Creed, the Lord's Prayer, and the narrative of the Institution. The

[17]Gregory Dix, *op. cit.*, 605 ff.

[18]*Das Testament Jesu Christi, das man bisher genannt hat die Messe* . . . (1523).

[19]*Form und Gestalt wie des Herren Nachtmahl . . . zu Basel gebraucht und gehalten* . . . (1525-26).

first celebration was held on Maundy Thursday for the young people, then on Good Friday and Easter for the rest of the congregation. It was henceforth to be repeated four times a year: at Easter, Pentecost, September 11 (as church dedication day), and at Christmas — the four communion days of the Middle Ages thus being revived. Impressive as the liturgy of Zurich may have been, it was no longer the old Sacrament of the Altar, but a new rite, 'a memorial of thanksgiving and joy, not the *mysterium tremendum* of the Lutherans', as W. Koehler puts it.[20] Nothing is more significant for the new understanding than the fact that in the admonition that preceded communion the words 'guilty of the body of the Lord' were referred to his spiritual body, the assembled congregation, as though Paul did not speak of 'the body and blood of the Lord' (1 Cor. 11:27). It was a beautiful rite in which man remembers Christ, but no longer a sacrament in which Christ comes to man. An unconscious feeling of this profound change must have been in the souls of the people of Zurich, for, before they took part in the new celebration, they crowded the Great Minster on Wednesday of that memorable Holy Week, April 12, 1525, when mass was said for the last time — as if they wanted to take leave of him whose blessed presence in the Sacrament of the Altar had accompanied their lives and those of their fathers throughout the centuries. Henceforth they would never again receive the true body and blood of their Saviour.[21] This great

---

[20] W. Koehler, *Huldrych Zwingli,* 123; cf Koehler, *Zwingli und Luther,* I, 193 f: 'The new liturgy has no catholicizing or even sacramental character'. The expression '*mysterium tremendum*' goes back to the early Fathers.

[21] How deeply Zwingli himself must have been moved by this irrevocable step seems to be indicated by the fact that the dream mentioned earlier occurred in the very night after the last mass, and before the first new celebration on Maundy Thursday. While continuing in a dream the discussion which had been held in the Council before the great change was sanctioned, a messenger (*monitor*) appeared and called his attention to Exodus 12:11 ('it is the Lord's passover') as a decisive argument for 'is' in the sense of *significat*. 'Whether he was "black" (*ater*) or "white" (*albus*), I do not remember', he writes in his *Subsidium* (V. E. Loescher, *Historia Motuum, I,* 63). This led to a discussion between Lutheran and Reformed theologians about the true colour of that mysterious *monitor.* It is interesting to observe that in his monastic days Luther also had experiences that made him sure of his understanding of the Sacrament. When Gr. Casel in 1525 had gone from Strasburg to Wittenberg for negotiations on the question about the Eucharist, Luther told him of such experiences, which had convinced him of the Real Presence. He had seen horrible visions ('*visiones horribiles*'), often even angels, so that he had been forced to leave the altar (quoted by Koehler in *Zwingli und Luther,* I, 813 from Theo. Kolde, *Analecta Lutherana,* 72). This would be in agreement with the well-known scene at his first mass in 1507, when he was so overwhelmed by the *mysterium tremendum* that he was almost unable to

loss was not their fault, but the fault of those who, by making the Sacrament of the body and blood of Christ a human sacrifice and a beautiful spectacle, had already destroyed the Sacrament as the gift of God's *sola gratia*.

---

continue with the *Te igitur,* the first prayer of the *Canon Missae*. Such experiences may have occurred often ('*saepe*' in Casel's report). It is not necessary to prove that the Word of God, and not such visions, determined his doctrine on the Lord's Supper. They show, however, how at all times in his life, up to the last celebration of the Sacrament at Halle on his journey to Eisleben, the Sacrament of the Altar stood in the very centre of his spiritual life. This could not be said of Zwingli. See also the paragraph on consecration in the following chapter.

CHAPTER IV

The Great Controversy

1. Doctrinal Controversies in the Church.

There is nothing more depressing for the student of church history or for the Christian layman than to read about the great controversies on doctrinal matters that time and again have divided Christendom. At the same time, nothing has provoked more mockery from the world than those occasions when the old saying about the Early Church, 'Behold how they love one another', could be changed into an ironical 'Behold how Christians bite and devour one another' (see Gal. 5:15). How often such controversy has destroyed the missionary opportunities of the church! Was there a greater missionary possibility than at the moment when Constantine recognized Christianity as the religion of the Roman Empire? But, to his amazement, the Donatist controversy in Africa, and the Arian controversy in the East (which was soon to spread throughout Christendom), absorbed the strength of the church for generations to such a degree that it could not live up to the task of preaching the Gospel to the millions of Roman citizens as it should have done. Is not the same true of our centuries, and even of our own age, when Christianity, in a state of obviously-incurable divisions, meets the great world-religions on the mission fields? Politicians inside and outside the church have always regarded these divisions as incomprehensible foolishness and a lack of Christian charity on the part of theologians. Just as Constantine wrote to Athanasius and Arius, expressing his astonishment that they regarded their disagreement on the meaning of a certain Bible passage (Prov. 8:22-31) as church-divisive, and admonishing them to follow the example of the philosophers, who in similar cases always found it possible to agree on a compromise, so Philip of Hesse, the far-sighted politician of the Reformation, did his utmost, in the interest of the common Protestant cause in those fateful years of the Reformation, to bring about an agreement between Luther and Zwingli on the basis of a formula acceptable to both parties. In both cases the well-meant attempt of the secular ruler to restore the unity of the church was unsuccessful.

As Christians we are not allowed to excuse even the slightest of the many sins that have been committed time and again in connection with such controversies. Pride and self-glorification, lack of love and humility, failure to understand the other side's point of view,[1] and acrimonious speech are some of the sins that threaten the souls of those who have to fight doctrinal controversies. There are sins and dangers in orthodoxy that the world sees with greater clarity than we theologians do, and in many cases the judgment of God on the orthodox defender of the faith may be far more severe than his verdict on the erring soul of a heretic. In saying this, we do not want to exonerate Luther and Zwingli from the harsh words they spoke against each other. Although the 16th century was used to very rough language, this language is nothing if compared with the cruelty with which other churches and even some non-Roman nations tried to suppress what they regarded as heresy. Neither the night of St Bartholomew nor the bloody persecution of Catholics in England can justify the way in which Lutherans and Reformed wrote and spoke against each other.

In order to understand the doctrinal controversies that accompany the history of the Reformation, we must keep in mind that according to the New Testament such controversies belong to the history of the church from the days of the apostles to the end of the world: 'There must be also heresies among you, that they which are approved may be made manifest among you' (1 Cor. 11:19). The heretics that Paul wanted rejected after the first and second admonition probably felt themselves to be genuine followers of Christ. The Christian gnostics that John, the apostle of love, criticized so harshly as antichrists, and to whom he refused the courtesy of a greeting, may have been, in their way, lovers of Christ who complained bitterly of narrow-minded dogmaticians that made the doctrine of the Incarnation a church-divisive dogma. Much of the criticism that has been launched against the church of all ages on account of controversies that have divided Christendom could be, and has been, directed against the church of the New Testament.

---

[1]In defending Luther against Koehler's criticism in this respect, Karl Barth, *Ansatz und Absicht in Luthers Abendmahlslehre, Ges. Vorträge, II,* (1928), 71, remarks that this failure would not necessarily be a sin: *'Es waren zu allen Zeiten nicht die schlechtesten Theologen, die zum wirklichen Nachdenken der Gedanken anderer einfach kein Organ hatten'.*

However, in order to understand that the condemnation of soul-destroying error is more than the rejection of opinions that we do not like, we need only ask what would have become of the Gospel in the world if the apostles and the church after them had been less orthodox and more tolerant, if they had shown more of what the world calls 'love' and 'toleration'. Just as the distinction between true and false prophets or true and false apostles belongs of necessity to the history of God's revelation, so the fight against heresy and serious doctrinal controversy belongs to the very nature of the Church of him who called himself the truth. If this is true of the entire history of the church, how could one expect the church of the Reformation to be an exception to this rule? On the contrary, if in an age of religious decay in the Christian world the question should be raised again as to what the Gospel really is, how could this question find an answer without incurring the most earnest controversies? And how could it be avoided that these controversies centred in the Lord's Supper, which always has been a centre of discussion, because doctrine and liturgy, as well as the life and faith of the church, meet in this Sacrament as nowhere else?

2. The First Years (1524-1526)

The year 1524 marks an epoch in the history of the Sacraments in Western Christendom, for in that year the controversies on Baptism and the Lord's Supper began simultaneously. It was the year when Zwingli completed his doctrine by accepting Honius's understanding of the Sacrament of the Altar, and Carlstadt in Strasburg wrote not less than five treatises on the same subject which soon became widely known in southern Germany and Switzerland. At the request of the city council of Strasburg, Luther and Zwingli gave their opinions on Carlstadt's doctrine almost simultaneously, thus inaugurating the great discussion. It is noteworthy that Carlstadt's doubts concerning the Real Presence were closely related to doubts as to the correctness of infant baptism, doubts he shared with other enthusiasts in Saxony, such as Thomas Muenzer. Personal relationships between the adherents of a radical Reformation in Saxony and Zurich had been established when Carlstadt visited Zurich, in the autumn of 1524; at the same time, Muenzer, who was staying at Schaffhausen, was met by Grebel and Manz, who at that time became the leaders of the Anabaptist movement at Zurich. The fact that the denial of the Real Presence and the rejection of infant baptism originated in the same circles, and at the same time, shows more than anything else that there must be a close connection between the two Sacraments. Historically speaking, a movement was in progress, the origins of which we have already observed in the Late Middle Ages. The disintegration of the sacramental system of the medieval church was accompanied, or rather indicated, in considerable parts of Christendom by a profound change in the understanding of the Sacrament. This change found its expression in a great variety of opinions on Baptism as well as on the Sacrament of the Altar. There were people who, like Erasmus, remained faithful members of the papal church though they no longer believed in transubstantiation. Others, like Zwingli, accepted the figurative understanding of the sacramental words which was widely disseminated through Honius's letter, while they (inconsistently, so the radicals thought) rejected the Anabaptist idea. The Anabaptists, in turn, were convinced that the denial of the Real Presence must necessarily also mean the denial of a baptismal grace. Luther and his adherents, on the other hand, unshakeably maintained the Real Presence and baptismal regeneration. In their understanding of the Sacraments as objective means of grace, they went even beyond the Roman doctrine in some respects by rejecting, for example, the necessity of 'intention' for the validity of the Sacrament, or the possibility of receiving certain sacraments *in voto*.[2] The variety of opinions that were to clash during subsequent years was not less colourful than that which we found in Bohemia during the 15th century.

It cannot be our task to tell the whole story of the controversies that preceded the Marburg Colloquy,[3] for, in almost every country and every city where the Reformation took root, the great discussion on the Sacrament began, especially since the entire life of the church (also its economic and financial side) was bound up with the mass. Innumerable sermons were preached on the Lord's Supper, and an immense number of writings was published, especially in the cities of south-western Germany, where influences from Wittenberg (Brenz

---

[2]See above, 42f. Luther, *Large Catechism, IV, 54* (Trigl. 744), declares the baptism of a Jew whom we baptize in good faith, though he comes 'dishonestly and with evil purpose', to be genuine, while Thomas, *Summa theol., III, Q. 68, Art. 7,* holds that in the case of an adult the intention to receive the true baptism would be indispensable for the validity of the sacrament.

[3]For the details of the complicated history, see Walther Koehler, *Zwingli und Luther. Ihr Streit über das Abendmahl nach seinen politischen und religiösen Beziehungen.*

in Schwäbisch-Hall), Strasburg (Carlstadt, Bucer), Zurich, and Basle (Oecolampadius) met. For an outsider it was a sort of *bellum omnium contra omnes,* like the fight in Bohemia some decades earlier. In contrast to the Hussite struggles, the number of the fighting parties decreased with the defeat of the enthusiasts after the Peasant's War of 1525. Eventually two great fighters and their parties remained on the battlefield: Luther and Zwingli — and between them the man of negotiation and compromise, Martin Bucer, together with his political followers. But even the Great Controversy between these leading men cannot be given here in detail.

What is most surprising to anyone who has been imbued with the popular legend that Luther was unable to keep peace, and is responsible, through his stubbornness, for the split between the churches of the Reformation, is the simple fact that for years Luther neither attacked Zwingli nor answered directly the attacks launched against him from Zurich and Strasburg. We have the strong impression that he tried to avoid a controversy with Zwingli. Of course, he had to refute Carlstadt's treatises of 1524, and he did so in his writing, *Wider den himmlischen Propheten. Von den Bildern und Sacrament,* which was published in January 1525.[4] But he refrained from mentioning the name of Zwingli in the second part of that book, when he dealt with the denial of the Real Presence, although he had been informed about Zwingli's doctrine since August 1524.[5] Luther, as all modern scholars are agreed, was not the aggressor.[6] On the other hand, Zwingli was so strongly convinced that his new understanding of the Lord's Supper was the only possible one, being in agreement with the New Testament and, therefore, necessary for the fight against papal superstition and idolatry, that he could not avoid attacking what he believed to be a remnant of medieval superstition. Shortly after he had accepted the view of Honius in 1524, he attacked the Lutheran doctrine on the Sacrament in a letter addressed to M. Alber, a Lutheran pastor in the city of Reutlingen. The following year, Zwingli published this letter,[7] together with his answer to the

---

[4]WA 18, 62 ff.

[5]In a private letter from F. Kolb in Wertheim who asked Luther for his opinion, WA BR 3 No. 709, 78 ff.

[6]'*Stehen die Dinge aber so, dann ist die bisherige . . . Ansicht, dass Luther der Angreifer im Streite der Reformatoren gewesen sei, nicht zu halten. . . Zwingli vielmehr hat die Trennung in der Abendmahlsfrage zuerst vollzogen*' (W. Koehler, *Zwingli und Luther, I,* 73).

[7]*Zwingli's Works* (CR), III; St Louis, XVII, col. 1512 (reprinted from Walch). In Reutlingen the Latin mass had been abolished in 1524.

city council of Strasburg and the letter of Honius. A few months later, Zwingli's important writings, *Commentarius de vera et falsa religione* and *Subsidium sive coronis,* made their appearance.[8] In both books he defended the figurative understanding of 'This is my body', and accepted the argument of Carlstadt that the body of Christ would remain in heaven until the Second Advent.

Meanwhile, the Lutheran cities of south-western Germany (suzerain states within the Empire and therefore practically free to introduce the Reformation) under the spiritual leadership of Brenz, a faithful disciple of Luther, strongly resisted efforts by Oecolampadius (himself a man from Swabia) to win over south-western Germany to a symbolical understanding of the Sacrament. In August 1525, the Reformer of Basle, whose personal piety and theological learning Luther always acknowledged, published and dedicated to his Swabian countrymen a learned book in which he tried to enlist the Church Fathers as allies in his fight for his symbolical doctrine on the Lord's Supper. His own interpretation of the Words of Institution differed from that of Zwingli. Since Jesus spoke Aramaic, which does not have the copula *est*, the trope is not to be found in the *est*, but rather in *corpus*. The meaning originally was not: 'This signifies my body', but: 'This is the figure of my body'. He took this from Tertullian — without asking (for no one at that time asked in such cases) whether Tertullian's '*figura corporis mei*'[9] really corresponded to what the humanists of the 16th century understood by *figura,* namely, a mere figure or symbol of something that is absent, as a crucifix shows or symbolizes the absent body of Christ. The Lutheran movement in this part of Germany found its expression in the *Syngramma Suevicum,* written by Brenz and signed by fourteen Lutheran pastors of Swabia who met for that purpose in October 1525. The *Syngramma* was published the following year in Latin and German, the German editions being prefaced by Luther himself (although the *Syngramma* is not simply a repetition of Luther's thoughts but an independent work written by a man who was a theologian in his own right, but who agreed, with his colleagues, with Luther's belief in the Real Presence).[10] In his preface of 1526, Luther

[8]Both writings in *Zwingli's Works* (CR), III.

[9]See above, 23.

[10]The German text is to be found in St Louis XX, col. 520 ff. It has been suggested that the *Syngramma* does not contain the entire doctrine of Luther. However, it teaches clearly not only the Real Presence ('the bread is the body'), but also the

for the first time mentions Zwingli and Oecolampadius, together with Carlstadt, as the heads of the 'new pernicious sect'.[11]

Independently of this discussion in southern Germany, a controversy was in progress at the same time between Bugenhagen in Wittenberg and Zwingli, inaugurated by a letter from Bugenhagen to Hess in Breslau, and continued by Zwingli's *Responsio* in October 1525.

The scene was now set for the final struggle between Zwingli and Luther, which had become inevitable, especially since the literary discussion went on unabatedly. Everyone wondered why Luther refrained from writing directly against Zwingli. On the other hand, there seemed to be hesitation on the part of Zwingli to write against Luther. Luther did not even mention Zwingli's name in his next book on the Sacrament, *Sermon* [treatise] *on the Sacrament of the Body and Blood of Christ against the Enthusiasts,*[12] a book consisting of three of his Easter sermons (compiled by some friends, but, of course, with his consent). In Zurich and Strasburg his silence was interpreted as weakness. It can be explained only as a strong desire to avoid, if possible, an open clash with Zwingli, though he had compelling reasons to refute the church politics of his adversaries.

In September 1526 Luther wrote to J. Herwagen, a publisher at Strasburg, complaining about forgeries that Bucer had made in his edition of Bugenhagen's *Commentary on the Psalms,* and about explanatory notes made by Bucer in the Latin translation of Luther's *Church Postil.*[13] Very questionable means, indeed, had been employed by the church politicians of Zurich and Strasburg in order to alienate the Lutherans in southern Germany from Luther. The whole atmosphere seemed to be poisoned. It was especially Bucer (who had become an adherent of Luther at the Heidelberg Disputation of 1518, but who after 1524 had been a convinced believer in the symbolical understanding of the Words of Institution) who kindled the fire and demanded from Zwingli that for the glory of God he should challenge Luther's 'arrogance'.[14] Is it not comprehens-

---

manducatio oralis ('We assert that we eat the body of Christ bodily — *carne',* St Louis, XX, col. 564, par. 54) and the *manducatio impiorum* ('Just as the believer is sanctified by the Word, so also the body; and just as the impious is polluted by the Word, so also is he who eats impiously polluted by the body', *op. cit.*, col. 570, par. 61).

[11]WA 19, 457 ff.

[12]WA 19, 474 ff.

[13]WA 19, 462 ff.

[14]Quoted by Koehler, *Zwingli und Luther, I,* 462.

ible that Luther, when he was forced to speak, spoke very acrimoniously?

> I like my frank, public, unsophisticated biting against the devil much more than their poisonous assassination,

he wrote in his *Large Confession* of 1528.[15]

3. The Controversy Between Zwingli and Luther (1527-1528)

At last, the long-delayed open war between Zwingli and Luther broke out. At the urgent request of Oecolampadius in Basle, and Capito and Bucer in Strasburg, Zwingli opened the fight with his *Amica exegesis, id est expositio eucharistiae negotii ad Martinum Lutherum* of February 1527, and a German article against Luther's *Sermon on the Sacrament* of the previous year.[16]

The *Amica exegesis* is an attempt to be as friendly as possible, but the author does not quite succeed. He criticizes very harshly the *Syngramma Suevicum* and almost all the writings of Luther on the subject. He cannot but see the Antichrist as the real author of Luther's understanding of the Words of Institution. Deeply convinced that his own understanding of the Lord's Supper is the only correct one, he expresses the hope that Luther will accept it. One notices how deeply Zwingli is shocked by what he thinks to be a relapse of the great Reformer into papalism. He expresses his wish to come to an agreement with Luther, but, of course, only on the basis of that understanding of the Sacrament which he with his humanist feeling of superiority thinks to be the only correct one. He addresses his readers:

> If Luther continues to offer stubborn resistance, we shall doubtless prevail,[17]

but he does want a victory that consists in a real change of Luther's opinion.

Luther's reply was *That These Words: 'This is My Body', Still Stand against the Enthusiasts,*[18] whereupon Zwingli replied with *That These Words: 'This is My Body', Shall For Ever Retain Their Old Meaning.*[19] Luther's final word was his great book, *Vom Abendmahl*

---

[15]WA 26, 402, 31 ff.

[16]*Zwingli's Works,* ed. Schuler and Schulthess, III.

[17]Koehler, *Zwingli und Luther, I,* 486.

[18]WA 23, 38 ff : *Dass diese Worte Christi: Das ist mein Leib, noch feststehen wider die Schwarmgeister.*

[19]*Zwingli's Works* 2 b, 16 ff: *Dass diese Worte . . . ewiglich den alten Sinn haben werden.* St Louis XX, col. 1122.

Christi. Bekenntnis of 1528.[20] This was answered by Zwingli and Oecolampadius in their *Answers to Dr Martin Luther's Book called Confession.*[21]

THE EXEGETICAL PROBLEM

Instead of relating the contents of these single writings with their unavoidable repetitions and digressions, we shall make an attempt to understand the arguments put forward by either side.

> *De intellectu Verborum est contentia* (The understanding of the Words of Institution is the problem at stake).

Thus Zwingli formulates the issue. Are these words, spoken by the Son of God at the most solemn occasion, to be understood literally or figuratively? This old question is the real problem; all further questions are contained in this fundamental exegetical problem. That was the conviction of either side. The fact that the discussion of that problem did not lead to an agreement seems to indicate, first, that there is no middle road between Zwingli and Luther, as both realized, and secondly, that the exegetical problem is closely connected with a fundamental doctrine on the Word of God and the Person of Jesus Christ.

In order to understand Zwingli's arguments, we must remember that the Swiss Reformer, despite some rationalistic elements in his theology which he shares with all humanists, wanted to be, and was, a Bible theologian. The Reformation in Switzerland was a Bible movement. Not only were the discussions between the Zwinglians and the adherents of the papal church settled on the basis of what each side understood to be the teaching of the Bible, but also the Anabaptist movement claimed to follow the Scriptures alone. Just as people in Catholic countries were burned because they did not accept the Roman understanding of the Bible, so men in Zurich were drowned because they could not find in the Bible the official doctrine on infant baptism, and acted accordingly. Consequently, Zwingli was soon confronted with the problem of the correct interpretation of Scripture.

To him Holy Scripture, as given by inspiration of God, is absolutely clear, even if it requires careful study to find its real

---

[20] WA 26, 241 ff; quoted under the title: *Grosses Bekenntnis vom Abendmahl.*

[21] *Zwingli's Works*, ed. Schuler and Schulthess, II, part 2, 94 ff ; St Louis, XX, col. 1228.

meaning in certain cases.[22] Passage must be compared with passage, and dark passages are to be explained according to those that are clear from the outset. In certain cases the Bible makes use of figurative speech, of tropes and *alloiōsis*. While Zwingli's view of the Scriptures rests mainly on the doctrine of Augustine, a certain influence of Origen and his allegoric interpretation of the Bible is noticeable. The clarity of the Bible, however, does not mean that everyone can understand it; the Scriptures are clear and intelligible to the faithful only.[23] Now, faith comes from the Word of God, but only if and when the Holy Spirit moves the human soul. Such faith is the true master of a correct understanding of the Divine Word. Thus, Zwingli, in spite of his Augustinian biblicism, recognizes something as higher than the letter of the Bible.

Here a strong contrast between Luther's and Zwingli's understanding of the Word becomes evident. For Luther the content of the Word is bound up with the letter. The Holy Spirit comes to us in the external word. In Zwingli's opinion, the external word (the letter) in itself has no power over the human soul.

> Not the content of the Word as such overpowers the soul by virtue of the Spirit that dwells in the Word, but the Spirit contacts the soul directly and thus enables the soul to understand the real meaning of the Word —

so Reinhold Seeberg puts it, and underlines the parallel existing between the understanding of the Word and the Sacrament.[24] According to Luther, the meaning of the sacramental words can be found in those words only, since they are words of Christ and, therefore, words in which the Holy Spirit dwells. For Zwingli they cannot be understood from the letter, but by the Spirit, who makes the believer understand the words when he compares Scripture with Scripture and asks for the analogy of faith. Starting from this understanding of the Word, Zwingli arrives at the conclusion that *est* in the Words of Institution must be understood, as in other passages of the Bible, as *significat*. Tirelessly he adduces all the Scripture passages that had been used by Honius and his medieval predecessors, adding those that he found for himself which we have mentioned earlier.

---

[22]See *On the Clarity and Certainty of the Word of God* (1523).

[23]Koehler, *Zwingli und Luther, I,* 474; see also O. Ritschl, *Dogmengeschichte des Protestantismus, III* (1926), 34 ff, and below, 182.

[24]*Lehrbuch der Dogmengeschichte IV,* 1 (1933), 437.

But why must *est* be taken as *significat*? There are many passages where Zwingli himself would retain the literal meaning. The reason why a figurative understanding is necessary in this case, Zwingli contends, is that otherwise an absurdity would arise, or even several absurdities. The greatest of these for Zwingli is the idea that bodily eating could have a spiritual effect. Spirit can be influenced only by spirit. It is the idealistic thinker, the humanist Zwingli, who simply cannot bear the idea of a bodily eating of the flesh of Christ in the Lord's Supper. He calls this idea 'a real pestilence'.[25] But even if there were such bodily eating, it would, according to John 6:63, profit nothing, let alone give such spiritual blessings as the forgiveness of sins. This passage excludes any other eating and drinking except that of which the whole chapter speaks and which Zwingli describes with the words:

> *Tunc corpus Christi editur, cum pro nobis caesum esse creditur* (We eat the body of Christ when we believe that it has been killed for us).[26]

In other words, eating and drinking here means nothing else than believing. Thus, Zwingli does not (as did Luther) explain the Words of Institution by themselves, but rather from other passages, and especially, of course, from John 6. The meaning he found there he applies not only to the sacramental words, but also to the eucharistic passage in 1 Cor. 10:16, 17. The communion of the body and blood of Christ, which, according to Paul, is established by participation in the consecrated bread and wine, is understood as the communion of the Church; 'body of Christ' means here, according to Zwingli, the Church; and 'the blood' refers to the blood shed at Calvary for us, for we Christians are, as Zwingli puts it, 'the people of the blood of Christ'.[27] This artificial exegesis of a passage of St Paul, which undoubtedly refers to the real body and blood of Christ (otherwise, the parallel between 'body' and 'blood' would be lost) shows the inadequacy of Zwingli's hermeneutical principles. His exegesis leads, against his will, to a violation of the sacramental texts of the New Testament, of the words of Jesus as well as of those in which Paul gives his authentic, apostolic commentary.

---

[25] *Zwingli's Works*, ed. Schuler and Schulthess, III, 365, quoted by Koehler, *op. cit.*, 473; cf *Fidei Ratio, Art. 8,* English translation: S. M. Jackson, *Huldreich Zwingli,* (1903), 470 ff.

[26] *Zwingli's Works,* III, 243 f, and other passages quoted by R. Seeberg, *op. cit.*, 460.

[27] Koehler, *op. cit.,* 475.

Luther, on the other hand, starts with the Words of Institution as they stand. His hermeneutical rule is that the literal meaning of a passage must be maintained either as long as there is no clear indication that the words are meant figuratively (as in the parables of Jesus) or unless literal sense would contradict an article of faith. In the passages put forward by Zwingli the figurative meaning for Luther is impossible, because the figure can never be in the *est*, but only in the predicate. Christ **is**, not **signifies**, the true vine, the rock, the way, etc. While generally denying that *est* can mean *significat,*[28] Luther admits the possibility of metaphors, but demands proof that in such cases figurative speech is used.[29]

> Where Holy Scripture establishes something which is to be believed, it is not permissible to abandon the words as they are, unless a clear article of faith would necessitate a different interpretation or arrangement of the words. What would otherwise become of the Bible? If, for example, we read in Psalm 18:3: 'God is my rock', we find the word 'rock', which otherwise means a natural stone. Since, however, **faith** teaches that God is no natural stone, I am compelled to understand 'rock' in that passage in a way different from the natural understanding. The same is true of Matthew 16:18: 'Upon this rock I will build my church' (*emphasis mine*).[30]

As for the sacramental words, *est* cannot be understood as *significat*, because the words are plain, and no explanation is attached to them, as would be the case if they were to be understood figuratively.

THE CHRISTOLOGICAL DIFFERENCE

There can hardly be any doubt that the deeper reasons for Zwingli's attitude toward the words of the Sacrament were not exegetical ones. No one — not even Zwingli — has ever doubted that grammatically the words can be understood as Luther understood them. He rejected this understanding only because he feared the 'absurdities' of a literal interpretation. One of these 'absurdities' we have mentioned already: the idea that a bodily eating can help the soul. Another 'absurdity' would be to assume that the body of Christ could be here on earth, while actually it is in heaven until the Second Advent. We remember that the deniers of the Real Presence have taken this argument from Augustine. Zwingli, by the way, never denied that the right hand of God is

---

[28] *Vom Abendmahl Christi,* WA 26, 271, 3 ff.

[29] See below, 187. The seeming contradiction is solved by the fact that, in a figurative use of *est*, not the copula *est* but the predicate changes its meaning.

[30] *Wider die himmlischen Propheten, Part 2,* WA 18, 147, 23 ff.

everywhere and that, consequently, Christ shares the omnipresence of God. This, however, is true of his divine nature only. His humanity is not in the same way on the right hand of God.

According to the divine nature He is present as God of equal power and eternity, without beginning, omnipresent, preserving all things and giving life to all things . . . according to His humanity He is present only with the nature which He later assumed and which cannot be from eternity; otherwise there would be two *infinita*.[31]

Thus, the humanity, the body of Christ, is in a certain place in heaven until the end of the world, otherwise it would not be a real human body. It is Zwingli's conviction that Luther's idea of a body that can be in heaven and on earth at the same time must lead to Marcionism, that is, docetism.[32]

This argument reveals the profound christological difference between the two Reformers, which soon became an important difference between the churches they represented. We cannot discuss here the entire problem of these various types of Christology. Both Luther and Zwingli wanted to maintain the orthodox doctrine as contained in the Ancient Creeds and maintained by the medieval church. Actually, however, there was a great difference between them which cannot be explained by their various views on the Sacrament only. Luther's Christology goes back to the very beginnings of his theology. In Christ crucified there is true theology and knowledge of God — nowhere else.[33] In the humanity of Christ we have God, the true God, hidden in the suffering and cross of him who cries: 'My god, my God, why hast Thou forsaken me?' That is Luther's understanding of God from the beginning to the end of his life.

Den aller Weltkreis nie beschloss / Der liegt in Marien Schoss Er ist ein Kindlein worden klein / ***Der alle Ding'*** *erhält* allein.

Es streit' für uns der rechte Mann . . . Fragst du, wer der ist / Er heisst Jesus Christ / ***Der Herr Zebaoth*** */ Und ist kein andrer* ***Gott*** *(emphasis mine).*[33A]

This understanding of the person of Jesus Christ belongs to the new discoveries of the Reformation.

---

[31] *Zwingli's Works,* ed. Schuler and Schulthess, II, part 2, 71. The Bible passages quoted by Zwingli for this view are: Mark 16:6; Matt. 26:11, 64; John 16:28; 17:11, cf. O. Ritschl, *op. cit.,* III, 101, and Hans Grass, *Die Abendmahlslehre bei Luther und Calvin* (1940), 54, where the quotation from Zwingli is given *in extenso.*

[32] *Zwingli's Works,* ed. Schuler and Schulthess, II, Part 1, 253; II, Part 2, 487.

[33] *'Ergo in Christo crucifixo est vera theologia et cognitio Dei.'* Heidelberg Disputation (1518), *Probationes Conclusionum 20,* WA 1, 362.

[33A] Excerpts from his hymns, *'Gelobet seist du, Jesu Christ'* and *'Ein feste Burg'.*

Contrariwise, Zwingli remained with the strict distinction between the natures of Christ which is characteristic of medieval scholasticism. It is noteworthy that all schoolmen (at least of the later Middle Ages) share the opinion of Zwingli that the body of Christ must be in a certain place in heaven — which is, by the way, one of the arguments for transubstantiation advanced by Thomas: since the body of Christ is in that heavenly place, it can be present on the altar only through a conversion of the substance of bread into the substance of the body. This medieval heritage made it impossible for Zwingli to accept Luther's view that God is revealed only in the humanity of Jesus Christ. The obvious weakness of his Christology is the inability to see the real unity of the God-man. Zwingli was not a Nestorian (just as Luther was not a Monophysite), but within the framework of the Chalcedonian Creed he came close to the Nestorian doctrine, which, while emphasizing the two natures, was unable to say how these two natures could be in one person. Zwingli did not recognize what the Lutherans call the *communicatio idiomatum,* a doctrine of the ancient Greek church that even medieval scholasticism did not understand.[35] He used the term, but actually

---

[34]The problem was discussed by the Greek Fathers of the 4th century. Gregory of Nazianzus was the first to use the simile of iron and fire to illustrate the relationship of the two natures (which later was used to explain the relationship between the bread and the body in the Sacrament). Gregory of Nyssa and later Leontius of Byzantium developed the doctrine of the *communicatio idiomatum,* which is to be found in the teachings of John of Damascus, *De fide orthodoxa, III, cap. 3 and 4* (MPG 94, 987 and 997).

[35]The question as to how far the glory of Christ was equal to the glory of the Father was discussed by the schoolmen of the 12th century (e.g. Gerhoch and Arno of Reichensperg) as a very important topic of theology. The representatives of High Scholasticism, however, do not deal with that problem. Even the expression *communicatio idiomatum* is not used by them. The passage that comes nearest to a discussion of the problem is Thomas, *Summa theol. III, Q. 3, Art. 6,* answer to obj. 3. Here Aquinas speaks of a *'communicatio proprietatum pertinentium ad naturam'* as a rule applying to the persons of the Trinity, but especially to the person of Christ since the Incarnation: That which belongs to one nature can be said of the person. The problem of Luther, whether and how the human nature can really share the properties of the divine nature, was really never discussed in the Roman church, except in polemics against Luther. There are Roman theologians who regret this (e.g. Scheeben, *Handbuch der kath. Dogmatik, III,* 39). *Zwingli's Works,* III, 525, gives the following definition: *'Est ergo alloiōsis . . . permutatio, qua de altera in eo natura loquentes alterius vocibus utimur'* (*Alloiōsis* is a way of speech in which we, speaking of one nature of Christ, use the expressions that belong to the other). When *'de altera natura praedicatur quod alterius, id tandem est alloiōsis aut idiomatum communicatio aut communio' (ibidem).* The expression *alloiōsis* goes back to Plutarch.

the *communicatio idiomatum* was for him only an *alloiōsis*, a figure of speech in which we attribute to one nature the qualities of the other. To take the famous example of the Nestorian controversy: Zwingli had no objection to calling Mary the 'Mother of God', but this was only a mode of speech; actually she is only the mother of his human nature. In the same way, when we speak of his suffering and death, according to Zwingli and the medieval scholastics, only the 'Son of Man' (which was understood as meaning the human nature) could suffer and die.

For Luther the idea was quite unbearable that only one nature of Christ should have done this for us and thus be our Saviour, and not the whole Christ. Luther saw clearly that this would mean the destruction of the one person of Jesus Christ, and, consequently, the full reality of the inscrutable mystery of the Incarnation. He discovered behind this theory the attempt of human reason to understand the person and work of Christ.

> Now if the old witch, Lady Reason, the grandmother of *Alloeōsis*, should say, The divinity cannot suffer or die, you should answer, That is true. Yet because divinity and humanity are one person in Christ, Scripture also, on account of such personal unity, attributes to the Godhead everything that belongs to the humanity, and in turn . . . the person who is God suffers in the humanity.[36]
>
> In truth, the Son of God has been crucified for us; that means the person who is God.[37]

The most characteristic feature of Luther's Christology, however, is what the theologians later called the *genus auchēmaticum* or *majestaticum,* that group of assertions in which it is stated that the human nature of Christ shares the properties of the divine nature, such as omnipotence, omnipresence, etc.

> Here you must take your stand and say, Where Christ is according to his divinity, there he is a natural divine person and is present in a natural and personal way, as his conception in his mother's womb shows. For if he was to be the Son of God, he had to be naturally and personally in the womb of his mother and had to become man. If he is present naturally and personally where he is now, he must be there also as man. For there are not two separate persons, but one single person. Where this person is, there he is as one undivided person. And when you can say, Here is God, then you must also say, Christ, the man, is also here. If, however, you were to show me a place where the divine nature is, and the human nature is not, the person would be divided, because then I could say in truth, Here is God who is not man and never has become man. That is not

———

[36] *Vom Abendmahl Christi* (1528), WA 26, 321, 19 ff.

[37] ibid, WA 26, 322, 20 f. These quotations are found in the *Form. Conc., Sol. Decl. VIII,* 41, 42 (Trigl. 1029).

> my God. For it would follow from this that space and place would separate the two natures and divide the person, though neither death nor all devils could ever separate and divide them.[38]

Here the profoundest difference between the two Reformers becomes apparent. For Luther, God is revealed (*Deus revelatus*) in Christ only. Zwingli could never understand that, closely associated with this difference in the understanding of God's revelation in Christ, there was a problem that had already been discussed by the theologians of the ancient school of Antioch. It was renewed in the controversies between the Lutheran and the Reformed churches of the 16th century under the name *Extra Calvinisticum.* On the basis of Colossians 1:19 ('that in him should all fullness dwell'), and John 14:9 ('he that hath seen me hath seen the Father'), Luther believes and teaches the biblical paradox that the fullness of the Godhead dwells in Jesus, not only after his resurrection and exaltation, but also since his incarnation. This is Luther's Christology.

If the old question is asked how the finite human nature can comprise the infinite divine nature, the answer can only be that, according to John 1:14, the Word became flesh, which cannot mean that part of the Word did not become flesh. The use of the terms 'finite' and 'infinite' shows that the Incarnation is being understood in terms of quantity. This must not be done; the miracle of the Incarnation is beyond all mathematics and beyond all philosophy. It is an attempt to rationalize the inexplicable miracle of the fullness of the Godhead dwelling in the man Jesus to believe with Zwingli and Calvin what the Reformed church later expressed in the *Heidelberg Catechism:*

> Because the Godhead is inconceivable and everywhere, it must follow that it is **outside** (*extra*) and nevertheless also **in** the humanity personally united with it (*emphasis mine*).[39]

For Zwingli this *extra* meant even more than for the later Reformed church. It meant for him that there is divine revelation even outside Christ. In the sermon on Divine Providence that he preached at Marburg before Luther arrived, and which in the following year was published in Latin, when he quotes ancient philosophers, he explains that by saying:

---

[38] WA 26, 332, 24 ff (cf Trigl. 1045).
[39] Question 48.

> I venture to call divine also such thoughts as are borrowed from pagans. Truth is always from the Holy Spirit, wherever and by whomsoever it has been brought forward.[40]

This would have been regarded by Luther as a blasphemy, just as he regarded as blasphemy Zwingli's claim that also great pagans like Aristides and Scipio are in heaven. If Luther and Zwingli disagreed to such a degree in their understanding of the Incarnation, how could they ever reach an understanding on the Sacrament of the Altar, which for Luther rested completely on the Incarnation, being, as it were, an extension of the Incarnation into our time and into our lives?

However, the insurmountable obstacle to an understanding between Luther and Zwingli was not only Christology in itself, but also the practical conclusions that were to be drawn from Luther's understanding of the Incarnation. Luther's understanding of Christ makes the Lord's Supper a miracle. For it is an unspeakable miracle that the inseparable union of the two natures causes the body of Christ, which is in heaven, to be present on the altar. Like Honius, Zwingli rejected the idea of such a miracle. He did not deny any miracle of the Bible, least of all the miracles connected with the Person of Christ. Thus, he even believed the miracle of Mary's perpetual virginity, which is a doctrine of the Catholic church, not the Bible. Hence, in Marburg he still rejected the doctrine of Helvidius, that Mary had become the mother of more children.[41] In this respect Zwingli was not a rationalist. But the miracles of the Bible (the healing of the sick, the resurrection, and so on) could be seen by those concerned; the Real Presence at the Last Supper would be a miracle that had not been seen by anyone.[42] Furthermore, God

---

[40]Quoted by W. Koehler, *Huldrych Zwingli,* 203; cf *Zwingli's Works,* ed. Schuler and Schulthess, IV, 89: *'attendentes veritatem, ubicunque et per quemcunque adferatur, a Spiritu Sancto esse'.* The same idea has been expressed repeatedly by Zwingli. For Luther's criticism of this view as it is found in Zwingli's *Expositio Fidei ad Franciscum Regem* (written shortly before his death in 1531, and published in 1536), see below, 223 ff (WA 54, 143, 15 ff).

[41]See below, 191, 192.

[42]One of the arguments is: How could Thomas refuse to believe in the resurrection if he had experienced the great miracle of the Lord's Supper? This question can easily be answered by the fact that other apostles, too, lost their faith temporarily, and one of them even betrayed Jesus right after he had received the blessed bread and wine, although he had seen all the visible miracles that Jesus had done. For a statement of the whole problem see above, 99, 100.

can, indeed, do any miracle, but he cannot cause black to be white. He has bound himself to logic, which requires that a body cannot be in more than one place at the same time. As to the visibility or invisibility of miracles, Luther could point out that many of God's miracles, especially the greatest ones, like the Incarnation, remain in the sphere of the invisible. It is enough to hear of them from the Word of God. In the case of the Last Supper, the apostles heard from their Lord what they were receiving, and, consequently, of the miracle of the Real Presence. This question had been answered already in a very evangelical way by Albert the Great and Thomas Aquinas when they pointed out that the senses were deceived, '*sed auditu solo tuto creditur* (but we can believe it on the basis of the word only)'. As to whether it is against the order of things to which God has bound himself if a body is present in more than one place at the same time, Luther could answer this philosophical argument only by employing a philosophical argument himself. If he was told: 'What you teach is impossible because it is against the rules of philosophy', he would, for apologetical reasons, be compelled to speak as a philosopher himself, not in order to prove the divine miracle, but simply to show that from a philosophical point of view the doctrine of the Real Presence could not be called impossible or nonsensical. He was not interested in mere philosophical arguments, only in those brought forward by theologians in the interest of theology.

THE POSSIBILITY OF THE REAL PRESENCE

The first answer that Luther gives to the question as to how the body of Christ, which is in heaven, can at the same time be in the Sacrament is merely a theological one. It is the doctrine that the Reformed later called 'ubiquity'. If Christ's human nature participates in his divine nature, it would follow that his body must share the omnipresence of his divinity. We have already mentioned this doctrine in quoting the following words from his book *Of The Adoration of the Sacrament* of 1523:

> The body which you take and the word which you hear are his who holds in his hand the entire world and who is everywhere.[43]

This seems to be the beginning of a development that takes form in the major writings of 1526, 1527, and 1528. Here in refutation of the denial of the presence of the body, the *ubique* (the 'everywhere') is

[43] WA 11, 450, 15 f.

expressly attributed to the body of Christ, which, though seated at the right hand of the Father, must still be everywhere, for

> the right hand of God is everywhere.[44]

Zwingli's objection was that then Christ's body would be in every piece of bread, and even in every part of nature; we could have it there without the Sacrament. Luther answers that there is a difference whether Christ's body is there or whether it is there **for you**; whether it is there or whether you can find it.[45] You can find it where Christ himself has promised that he would be found, and that is in the Sacrament. In order to understand this idea, one must realize that the presence here attributed to Christ's body is the presence of God. Luther speaks of God not only as being everywhere, but also as being nowhere:

> The right hand of God is the almighty power of God which at the same time can be **nowhere** and yet must be **everywhere** (*emphasis mine*).[46]

God is everywhere in the world, and yet he is also beyond the world. It is therefore a grave misunderstanding if the 'ubiquity' sometimes has been interpreted as a sort of pantheism. It is the mysterious way of God's presence, which Christ, even according to his human nature, shares — a mystery which necessarily is inaccessible to human reason.

If, however, philosophy asserts that such existence is impossible, Luther calls the attention of his opponents to the fact that even philosophers recognize more modes of presence than that which is called the local (*circumscriptive*) one. We have seen that even Thomas distinguished between a *praesentia localis sive circumscriptiva* and a *praesentia definitiva.*[47] The later schoolmen developed this theory until it reached its final form in the philosophy of Occam. From this school Luther adopted this distinction even while he was a student at Erfurt. In his *Large Confession* he accepts it as a correct philosophical theory and explains it to his readers.[48] A thing can be in a certain place *localiter* or *circumscriptive,* that is, in such a way that it fills the space, as wheat fills a bag or a human body fills a certain space. In this way Christ's body was present in his

---

[44]WA 26, 326, 32; see *Form. Conc., Sol. Decl. VII, 95* (Trigl. 1004, 6).
[45]WA 23, 151, 13 f.
[46]WA 23, 133, 19 ff; Compare 151, 1 ff.
[47]See above, 39.
[48]WA 26, 326, 12 ff.

earthly days when, for example, he was in his mother's womb, in the temple, on the cross.

> This mode He can still use whenever He will, as He did after the resurrection, and will use at the last day.[49]

This is the only way which Zwingli will admit. In this sense he understands passages like those in which the New Testament speaks of Christ as leaving the world and going to the Father. According to Zwingli and all other adversaries of the Real Presence, there cannot be an illocal presence of the body of Christ.

The second mode of presence is called by Occam and his school the *esse diffinitive.* The word *diffinitive* is a late form of what Thomas still calls *definitive;* these words are interchangeable in medieval Latin. There is, however, a difference of understanding between Thomas and Occam. Thomas and his contemporaries understood by *definitive* a mode of presence in which the thing present in a certain place does not fill the place. Thomas used this idea to show how the body of Christ could be in the host, but in an illocal way be present in each part of the host. For Occam *diffinitive* means a presence which is no longer bound to a certain space. Luther defines it in this way:

> Secondly, the incomprehensible, spiritual mode, according to which He neither occupies nor vacates space, but penetrates all creatures wherever He pleases; as, to make an imperfect comparison, my sight penetrates and is in air, light, or water, but does not occupy or vacate space; as a sound or tone penetrates and is in air or water or board and wall. . . This mode He used when He rose from the closed sepulchre, and passed through the closed door, and in the bread and wine in the Holy Supper, and, as it is believed, when He was born of His mother.[50]

This illocal, incomprehensible, spiritual presence, therefore, is the presence of Christ's glorified body. This was the presence of his body when at the Last Supper, standing before his disciples, he gave them with bread and wine his true body and blood. This miracle, like all miracles of Jesus, must be understood as a manifestation of his hidden glory. The glorification of Jesus Christ began, according to Lutheran doctrine, not with his resurrection and exaltation, but already with his incarnation.

The third mode of presence that Occam taught is what he calls the *esse repletive,* the presence of God who is present in all places, and yet is not contained in any space. It is the divine omnipresence, which Occam ascribes only to God. There are some passages in which Occam tentatively suggests that the presence of the body of Christ

---

[49]WA 26, 335, 31 ff, quoted in *Form. Conc., Sol. Decl. VII, 99* (Trigl. 1005).

[50]WA 26, 335, 38 ff (Trigl. 1005, 7).

may come under this category.[51] But as a rule he is satisfied with the *esse diffinitive* for the body of Christ. It was Luther who, on the basis of his Christology, understood the Real Presence in this way:

> Thirdly, the divine, heavenly mode, since He is one person with God, according to which . . . all creatures must be far more penetrable and present to Him than they are according to the second mode. . . For you must place this being of Christ, who is one person with God, very far, far outside of the creatures, as far as God is outside of them; and again as deep and near within all creatures as God is within them . . . Where God is, there must He also be . . . But how it occurs we do not know; it [this mystery] is above nature and reason, even above the reason of all the angels in heaven; it is understood and known only by God. Now, since it is unknown to us, and yet true, we should not deny His words before we know how to prove to a certainty that the body of Christ can by no means be where God is, and that this mode of being [presence] is false. This the fanatics must prove; but they will forgo it.[52]

The last words show clearly in what sense Luther makes use of these philosophical distinctions. It is not his intention to explain what even the angels in heaven cannot explain. He only wants to reply to those critics who, like Zwingli, declared the Real Presence to be quite impossible for philosophical reasons. How independent Luther was from medieval philosophy is indicated, among other things, by the fact that he dared to coin the famous sentence: '*Dextera Dei est ubique* (The right hand of God is everywhere)', which overthrows the entire view of the world of medieval science and theology.[53] For to all medieval men, heaven was a space within the

---

[51]Such as *Centilog. 25: 'Corpus Christi potest esse ubique, sicut Deus est ubique'.* Quoted by Fr. Loofs, *Dogmengeschichte,* 619, note 5; see the whole context, 618-20.

[52]WA 26, 336, 8 ff (Trigl. 1007).

[53]This has been rightly emphasized by W. Elert, *Morphologie des Luthertums, I* (1931), 363 ff. If modern Reformed theologians try to read back into Calvin the illocal understanding of the right hand of God, they fail to realize what the whole Reformed church of the 16th century actually taught (see below, 262). Zwingli as well as Calvin followed the Western medieval doctrine on heaven which had already been superseded by the Greek Fathers, who taught that the right hand of the Father is the glory of God, as John of Damascus puts it: 'If we say that Christ sitteth bodily at the right hand of God the Father, we do not teach a local right hand of God. For how could He who is not circumscribed have a local right hand? Only circumscribed beings have a right and a left hand. By the right hand of God we understand the glory and honour of the Godhead in which the Son of God exists as God and *homoousios* with the Father from eternity, and in which He now, after He has become incarnate in the last times, sitteth also bodily, His flesh being conglorified. For in one adoration He is adored with His flesh by the entire creation' (*De fide orthodoxa IV,* ch. 2). This is not a philosophical, but a theological argument. It is interesting to observe that Luther here, as in other points of the eucharistic doctrine (e.g. about the fruit of the sacrament, 177 ff), comes nearer to the Eastern Fathers, while Zwingli and Calvin remain dependent on the early Augustine. This is true also of the Lutheran Confessions, as the *Catalogus Testimoniorum,* the appendix to the *Formula of Concord,* shows.

universe. Thus, Luther's answers to the philosophers of his time do not claim to be of a theological, dogmatical nature. He himself suggests that what he says is by no means exhaustive. What he regards as binding truth is not expressed in the details of his philosophical argumentation, but in the four sentences that he calls his main reasons, and which have been adopted by the *Formula of Concord:*

> (1). . . Jesus Christ is essential, natural, true, perfect God and man in one person, inseparable and undivided. (2). . . God's right hand is everywhere (*Dextera Dei est ubique*). (3). . . God's Word is not false, nor does it lie. (4). . . God has and knows of many modes of being in any place, and not only the single one concerning which the fanatics talk flippantly, and which philosophers call *localem* or local.[54]

The very centre of these sentences is the first one, which contains Luther's doctrine of the Incarnation as we have discussed it. If Luther's Christology is right, according to which Christ's divine and human nature are inseparably connected since the Incarnation, as shown in John 1:14; 14:9; Colossians 1:19, then these four sentences must stand. Not the **way** in which the Real Presence may be understood is decisive, but the **fact** that it is acknowledged. As to the *how* of the Presence of the whole Christ, of his body and blood, of his human and divine nature, there is no dogma in the Lutheran church because Holy Scripture does not answer this question. Thus, Luther himself did not repeat in later years all that he had said about the 'ubiquity' in his controversies in the years before Marburg. Even at that time he emphasized that he

> left it to the wisdom and power of God as to the number of ways in which He might have the same effect, because we do not know either the measure or the end of His power.

Thus, in the *Formula of Concord*, the Lutheran church later recognized, side by side, Luther's understanding of the omnipresence of the body of Christ as he had developed it in the controversies with Zwingli,[55] and the doctrine held by Martin Chemnitz:

> That also according to that nature according to which He has flesh and blood He will [*velle*] be with us, and dwell, work, and be efficacious in us.[56]

This *velle* was later formulated as *multivolopraesentia,* the ability of Christ to be present with his body wherever he wishes.

---

[54]WA 26, 326, 29 ff, quoted in *Form. Conc., Sol. Decl. VII, 93 ff* (Trigl. 1005).

[55]This was done by including the quotations from WA 26, 335, 29 ff, especially 336, 8 ff, in the *Sol. Decl.* (Trigl. 1004-07).

[56]*Sol. Decl. VIII, 79* (Trigl. 1045).

Unio Sacramentalis

With all these arguments, Luther tries to answer the objection by Zwingli and Oecolampadius that the Real Presence of the body and blood in the Sacrament is impossible. The question which then arises (and which he certainly had to answer very early) is what the difference is between the Roman understanding of the Real Presence as transubstantiation and his doctrine. This implies the question of the relation between the body and the bread.[57]

Our review of the development of Luther up to the beginning of the Great Controversy on the Sacrament has shown how the Reformer early came to the conviction that the doctrine of transubstantiation was an insufficient and incorrect theory to explain the truth of the Real Presence. We have also stated that it is impossible to define his doctrine as consubstantiation.[58] Even the words 'in the bread', 'with the bread', 'under the bread', or 'in, with, and under the bread', were never regarded by Luther as more than attempts to express in these old, popular terms inherited from the Middle Ages the great mystery that the bread **is** the body, the wine **is** the blood, as the Words of Institution say.[59] In his *Large Confession* of 1528, he declares himself prepared to abandon them

> if it could be proved that it is not in conformity with the text 'This is my body' to say, 'In the Lord's Supper there is Christ's body'. In that case we would revoke this way of speech and simply say with the biblical text: 'This is my body'.[60]

In the same way he speaks of the expression 'under the bread'. However, Luther will under no circumstances give up the *unio sacramentalis,* the sacramental union between the elements and the body and blood of Christ. He maintains that what happens to the consecrated elements happens also to the body and blood. When the bread is eaten, Christ's body is eaten. In this respect he even goes farther than Thomas and the Roman church, assuming that if the

---

[57]This had also been the great question of Wyclif, as we have shown above, 45 f.

[58]See above, 81, 82.

[59]*In, cum, sub* were used during the Middle Ages almost synonymously. The same is true of the writings of Luther and the early Lutheran church. The *Small Catechism* says: 'Under the bread and wine'; *AC*, Article 10: *'Unter der Gestalt des Brots und Weins'*; *Apology*, Article 10: *'corpus et sanguis Christi exhibeantur cum illis rebus, quae videntur, pane et vino'* (Trigl. 246); *'Im Brot und Wein',* WA 26, 506, 22, quoted in *Form. Conc., Sol. Decl. VII, 32* (Trigl. 982); *'unter dem Brot, mit dem Brot, im Brot', Form. Conc., Sol. Decl. VII, 35* (Trigl. 982).

[60]WA 26, 265, 12 ff. See the entire context.

bread is crushed with the teeth the same happens also to the body of Christ.

> Therefore the enthusiasts as well as the *Glossa* of the Canonical Law are wrong if they criticize Pope Nicholas for having forced Berengar to confess that the true body of Christ is crushed with the teeth. Would to God that all popes had acted in such a Christian way in all things . . .[61]

Luther held this position for some years simply to emphasize the reality of the sacramental union. The Lutheran church later, in the *Formula of Concord*, rejected the idea 'as though His flesh was rent with the teeth', in connection with certain misunderstandings of the Lutheran doctrine by the 'Capernaites' of that time.[62]

But the sacramental union has remained a characteristic feature of Lutheran doctrine on the Lord's Supper, in contradistinction to Melanchthon and the Calvinists who denied this union, and found Christ's presence not in the elements but in the sacred action in the celebration of the Supper. The *unio sacramentalis* is the Lutheran counterpart to Roman transubstantiation, and Late Medieval consubstantiation, with which it is often confounded. Like consubstantiation, sacramental union presupposes that bread and body, wine and blood, exist together. Bread and wine are not destroyed or 'transubstantiated'. The difference, however, is that no theory is built up about the coexistence of two 'substances'. The difference over against Wyclif and his theory on remanence is this: For Wyclif, bread and wine remained what they were before; only sacramentally, that is, figuratively, they became the body and blood of Christ. For Luther, the bread is the body in an incomprehensible way; the union between the bread and the body cannot be expressed in terms of any philosophical theory or rational explanation; it is an object of faith, based solely on the words of Christ. The question which was put to him, not only by Zwingli, but also by his older adversaries, as to how the bread could be called the body of Christ if it still remained bread, was answered by Luther in pointing out the mode of speech called synecdoche. In his great controversy with Carlstadt he had already explained the words 'This is my body' as synecdoche.[63] 'This' referred to what Jesus held in his hands, the

---

[61] WA 26, 442, 39 ff.

[62] *Epitome VII, 42* (Trigl. 816).

[63] *Wider die himml. Propheten,* WA 18, 187, 14 ff ; *Large Confession,* WA 26, 444, 1 ff.

bread, not (as Carlstadt's impossible exegesis would suggest) to the body to which Jesus pointed. As a mother, pointing to the cradle in which her baby lies, says, 'This is my child', or as a man, pointing to a purse, may say, 'Here is a hundred dollars', so we say of the bread in a similar way, 'This is the body of Christ'. This is a common mode of speech called synecdoche, an abbreviated speech in which the containing vessel is mentioned instead of its content. The objection, especially by Zwingli, that thus Luther himself did not understand the sacramental words literally, but figuratively, was refuted by Luther as not being to the point, because the reality of the body was not denied. In all other figures of speech, the words 'body' and 'blood' are understood figuratively; the synecdoche takes the reality of the elements as well as the reality of body and blood seriously.

The Lutheran view, therefore, cannot be put on the same level with the figurative understanding on the one hand, or with transubstantiation on the other hand, as was done by its critics on both sides. Luther was quite clear about the fact that the synecdoche is, also, only an attempt to describe a fact that defies human explanation. The Real Presence remained for him an inexplicable mystery. All his answers are nothing more than attempts to refute the denial of this miracle as something impossible. No human reason can explore how this miracle can take place.

> We have not been commanded to inquire as to how it may come about that the bread becomes and is Christ's body. But God's Word is there to tell us so. With that we remain, and that we believe.[64]

CONSECRATION

Perhaps nothing reveals the profound difference between Luther's and Zwingli's understanding of the sacramental words more than the fact that for Luther and the Lutheran church the Words of Institution have always been also the words of consecration, while Zwingli and all Reformed churches reject the idea that the elements are consecrated by reciting the words of Christ. In fact, for Zwingli as for Carlstadt, the Lutheran idea of a consecration of bread and wine was a sure proof that Luther's understanding of the Sacrament was

---

[64] '*Uns ist nicht befohlen zu forschen, wie es zugehe, dass unser Brot Christi Leib wird und sei. Gottes Wort ist da, das sagts: da bleiben wir bei und glaubens*' (*Wider die himml. Propheten*, WA 18, 206, 20).

still papistic,[65] and the Reformed churches have followed Zwingli in this verdict, whatever their opinion on Zwingli's theology otherwise may be. This is borne out by the fact that none of the classical liturgies of the Reformed churches contains a consecration in the proper sense.[66] The Words of Institution are rather understood as a historical narrative addressed to the people.

Now, Luther never denied that the Words of Institution are the most important proclamation of the Gospel. He always blamed the Roman church for making these words a mere formula spoken by the priest in a low voice so that the congregation could not understand them. But, at the same time, they always were to him the words of consecration, even during his early years when he had to fight the Roman corruption of the mass, before Carlstadt began to deny the Real Presence, and with it the consecration.[67] Zwingli distinguished between the words 'Take, eat', as words containing a commandment, and the words 'This is my body . . .' as being a narrative only, a

---

[65]Compare the title of Zwingli's book: *Dass diese Worte Jesu Christi: Das ist mein Leichnam, der für euch gegeben wird, ewiglich den alten einigen Sinn haben werden und M. Luther mit seinem letzten Buch seinen und des Papstes Sinn gar nicht gelehrt noch bewahrt hat, Huldrychs Zwinglis christliche Antwort* (1527). Works, ed. Schuler and Schulthess, II, Part 2, 16; St Louis, XX, 1122 ff. The book by Luther referred to is, of course, *Dass diese Worte . . . noch feststehen wider die Schwarmgeister* (WA 23, 38 ff).

[66]In Zwingli's liturgy the Words of Institution were recited by a deacon, not by one of the officiating ministers. The later Reformed liturgies included these words either in an admonition or in a sort of eucharistic prayer, as is still done by Reformed congregations in the Prussian Union. This leads to an outward similarity with the Catholic liturgies, which also include the Words of Institution in the eucharistic prayer. The Reformed liturgies and confessions make it clear that the words are not consecratory. In the German Reformed churches the principle was always expressed '*dass die Erzählung der Einsetzung des Abendmahls nicht um des Brotes und Weines, sondern um des Volkes willen geschehe*', as the *Consensus Bremensis* of 1595 (E. F. K. Mueller, 787, 15) puts it. The *Confessio Helvetica Posterior* of 1562 in Art.19 defines consecration in the sacraments as putting aside the elements for the service of God. Reformed dogmaticians of the 17th century, like Heidegger, regard the blessing of bread and wine to be as necessary as the breaking of the bread. They deny, however, that the words 'This is my body . . .' have ever been or are today the blessing (*eucharistia, eulogia*) in the celebration of the Sacrament. This blessing is performed either by prayer or by the whole action. Compare Heidegger, *Corpus Theologiae* (Zurich, 1700) XXV, 79. This passage and many others from orthodox Reformed theologians are quoted by H. Heppe, *Die Dogmatik der evang. reform. Kirche*, ed. by E. Bizer (1935), 504 ff. For Calvin and the liturgy of Geneva see below, 264.

[67]In *De captivitate Babylonica* (WA 6, 516, 19; Philad. 2, 200) Luther complains: 'So mad are we priests that we arrogantly claim that the so-called words of consecration (*verba consecrationis, ut vocant*) may be said for us alone secretly, yet so that they do not profit even us, for we too fail to regard them as promises or as a

historical statement, namely, that Christ's body has been given, his blood has been shed for us, on Calvary.[68] These words, therefore, cannot 'make' the body of Christ. There is no such thing as a consecration that causes the body of Christ to be present.[69] Luther, on the other hand, rejects this distinction as artificial, and as not doing justice to the text. Jesus not only wanted his Church to eat the bread and drink the wine, but he also wanted it to repeat the whole action, which includes the blessing of the elements by speaking over them the same words as Jesus spoke.[70] Zwingli finds the 'blessing' in the prayer of thanksgiving which Jesus spoke before he broke the bread, the wording of which is not mentioned in the New Testament.[71] Just as all Reformed liturgies are based on the understanding of Zwingli and his followers regarding the Words of Institution, so all Lutheran liturgies presuppose that these words are really words of consecration. This is true even of Luther's *German Mass* of 1526,[72] where we find the suggestion that the bread should be

———

testament, for the strengthening of faith'. The same writing shows clearly, as we have seen, that Luther firmly believes in the Real Presence, although he rejects the philosophical theory of transubstantiation (above, 80 ff). In discussing the offertory and *Canon Missae* Luther states that in the offertory bread and wine are offered to be consecrated ('*panem et vinum consecrandum*'). The consecrated bread is not offered, but is received as a gift of God: '*Panis et vinum antea offeruntur ad benedicendum, ut per verbum et orationem sanctificentur. Postquam autem benedictus et consecratus est, iam non offertur, sed accipitur dono a Deo*' (WA 6, 524, 39; 525, 1 ff; Philad. 2, 215). The word *consecrare* is also used (WA 6, 525, 11) for the private mass: '*sibi ipsi consecrat*'.

68 *Dass diese Worte . . . ewiglich den alten Sinn haben werden* (*Zwingli's Works,* ed. Schuler and Schulthess II, Part 2, 54 f; cf W. Koehler, *Zwingli und Luther I,* 557). It is not easy to render the expressions *Heisselwort* and *Thetelwort,* which Zwingli uses to distinguish between the two kinds of works, a command and a narrative. Luther's answer is to be found in his *Large Confession* (WA 26, 282 ff).

69 Zwingli, *loc. cit.,* cf Koehler, 557.

70 WA 26, 282, 26 ff. Luther points out that the question is not whether the words are words of command or words of a historical statement, but whether or not they were true when Jesus spoke them. If they were powerful ('*Machtwort*') at the first celebration, then they remain powerful. 'I know that all Christians are bound by the institution and command of Christ to speak these words ("This is my body") in the Lord's Supper. I think even the enthusiasts would not dare to omit them with good conscience. If, then, they must be spoken, then they are words of command, and it is impossible to separate them from the [preceding] words of command.' WA 26, 283, 35 ff.

71 Even medieval interpreters of the *Canon Missae* understood the '*benedixit*' (He gave thanks) as consecration (from the time of Odo of Cambrai who died 1130. MPL 160, 1061 f). The doctrine is mentioned also by Erasmus and Honius (Enders 3, No. 552, lines 190 ff).

72 WA 19, 99, 5 ff.

distributed right after its consecration, and accordingly the wine right after the consecration of the cup. That the Words of Institution are really meant as consecration appears from the fact that they are clearly distinguished as '*Amt und Dermung*' from the preceding admonition.[73] The suggestion of the *German Mass* (which, by the way, has never been followed in the Lutheran church) stems from a misunderstanding of the words '*meta to deipnēsai*' (1 Cor. 11:25 and Luke 22:20), as though Paul and Luke had meant to say, 'after they had eaten the bread', instead of, as was the real meaning, 'after the [Passover] meal'.[74] Luther wanted to follow the principle, which he had repeatedly emphasized, that in celebrating the Sacrament we should follow the first celebration as closely as possible.

What, then, is consecration, according to Luther? Zwingli was not entirely mistaken when he saw a certain relationship between the Lutheran and the Roman doctrine on consecration. The question is only whether the Roman church, whatever her errors concerning this Sacrament may be, specifically in this case retained a truth without which there would be no sacrament at all. It is noteworthy, and should be kept in mind by every critic of the Roman understanding of the Sacrament that this church also regards the words of Christ as the *forma*, which makes the *materia* (the outward element) a sacrament. The Western church has never forgotten what Augustine taught about the Word as causing the element to become a sacrament. The Roman church has never been guilty of the heresy of modern Protestants who want to rediscover the sacrament by finding a mysterious quality in the natural things, water, bread, and wine. No Catholic theologian would disagree with Luther's words:

> The words are the first thing; for without the Word the cup and the bread would be nothing.[75]

---

[73]WA 19, 97, 12; *Amt* means '*mass*'; *Dermung* is a medieval German word for 'consecration', derived from the Latin *terminare*.

[74]According to Paul, whom Luke follows, the distribution of the bread took place during the meal, the distribution of the cup after the meal. In other words, the first celebration of the Sacrament was inserted into the Passover meal. This fact is still retained in Paul's narrative, which was written before the Gospels and goes back to the first tradition (this is the meaning of *parelabōn apo tou kyriou,* 1 Cor. 15:3; Paul does not refer, as our Fathers thought, to a special revelation, but to a tradition that goes back to what the Lord did and said). Later the Sacrament was, of course, celebrated without the framework of the Last Supper. Thus Mark, who was followed by Matthew, was no longer interested in that detail. Compare Joach. Jeremias, *The Eucharistic Words of Jesus* (1955), 133.

[75]*Large Confession,* WA 26, 478, 38 f.

The words, however, are effective only because Christ commanded us to say them in the celebration of the Sacrament.

> Even though I should pronounce over all bread the words: 'This is Christ's body', nothing, of course, would result therefrom; but when in the Supper we say, according to His institution and command: 'This is my body', it is His body, not on account of our speaking or word uttered, but because of His command... He has commanded us thus to speak and to do, and has united His command and act with our speaking.[76]

This is the explanation Luther gives in answer to Zwingli. The *Formula of Concord,* which quotes this passage from Luther's *Large Confession,* adds another quotation from the year 1533:

> This His command and institution have this power and effect that we administer and receive not mere bread and wine, but His body and blood, as His words declare . . . so that it is not our work or speaking, but the command and ordination of Christ that makes the bread the body, and the wine the blood, from the beginning of the first Supper even to the end of the world, and that through our service and office they are daily distributed.[77]

Could not the Roman church accept this statement? Indeed, it could; as a matter of fact, it does speak in a very similar way. The similarity is underlined by the fact that the theologians on both sides make use of the same patristic passages, for example, the words of Chrysostom which were quoted throughout the entire Middle Ages and which the *Formula of Concord* still repeats:

> Christ Himself prepares this table and blesses it; for no man makes the bread and wine set before us the body and blood of Christ — Christ Himself, who was crucified for us, does that. The words are spoken by the mouth of the priest, but by God's power and grace, by the word where He says: 'This is my body', the elements presented are consecrated in the Supper.[78] And just as the declaration in Genesis 1:28: 'Be fruitful, and multiply, and replenish the earth', was spoken only once, but is ever efficacious in nature, so that it is fruitful and multiplies, so also this declaration ['This is my body'; 'This is my blood'] was spoken once, but even to this day and to His advent, it is efficacious and works so that in the Supper of the Church His true body and blood are present.[79]

This apparent similarity, however, which led Zwingli and the later Reformed theologians to the assumption that Luther's doctrine on

---

[76]WA 26, 285, 13 ff; *Sol. Decl. VII, 78* (Trigl. 1001).

[77]*Von der Winkelmesse und Pfaffenweihe,* WA 38, 240, 8 ff; *Sol. Decl. VII, 77* (Trigl. 999).

[78]Thus the Greek *metarythmizein* has been translated. In the *Apology*, Article 10, Melanchthon still uses the word *mutare* ('change') in the quotations from the Greek mass and the Greek Fathers. The German translation by Justus Jonas leaves out these words in order to avoid a misunderstanding. The translation of the *Form. Conc.* here is not correct, but the 16th century was very broadminded with regard to such quotations. See above, 29,30.

[79]*De prod. Judae 1, 6* (MPG 49, 380), quoted *Sol. Decl. VII, 76* (Trigl. 999).

consecration was essentially identical with that of the Roman church, and therefore contradictory to the principles of the Reformation, cannot conceal the profound difference that becomes obvious as soon as an inquiry is made as to how a passage like that from Chrysostom is understood by either side.[80] Johann Gerhard made this difference quite clear in his great chapter on consecration.[81] He points out that, while the Reformed understand the recitation of the Words of Institution as a historical report, the Romans attribute the effect of the Words of Institution not to Christ only, but also to the spiritual power of the priest given him as a *character indelebilis* in ordination,

> so that the power of consecration is partly in the priest and partly in the consecratory words proffered.[82]

Although Roman theology has always emphasized that the priest in consecrating the Sacrament acts only 'in the person of Christ',[83] it cannot be denied that Gerhard was right in stating that actually a cooperation between Christ and the human priest takes place. This is already indicated by the fact that according to Roman doctrine the consecration is at the same time the immolation of Christ. In speaking the consecratory words, the priest offers the sacrifice of the mass.[84] In other words, the cooperation between God and man that we find in the sacrifice of the mass belongs essentially to the consecration according to Roman understanding. Thomas Aquinas says:

---

[80]Similar passages are quoted especially from Ambrose, *De mysteriis, c.9,* and *De sacramentis, c. 4,* by the Lutheran Fathers, e.g., Johann Gerhard, *Loci Theol. XXI* (ed. Preuss, V, 152 b).

[81]*Loci, XXI, cap. 13* (ed. Preuss, V, 148-156).

[82]*Ibidem,* 151 b.

[83]Thomas, *Summa theol. III, Q. 82, Art. 1: 'hoc sacramentum . . . non conficitur nisi in persona Christi'.*

[84]The question as to what actually constitutes the sacrificial act (*actus sacrificialis*) in the Eucharist has been extensively discussed in Roman theology. There is no dogmatic definition concerning this question except the negative decision of Trent (Sessio XXII, canon 1; Denz, 948) that the sacrifice is not the communion. Various theories have been put forward (e.g., the destruction of bread and wine or the breaking of the host being the sacrificial act; see the works on Catholic dogmatics), but today there seems to be an almost general agreement, based on the doctrine of Thomas (*Summa theol. III, Q. 78, Art. 3*) that neither the offertory, nor the prayers, nor the communion, nor what happens to the unconsecrated or consecrated host, constitutes the immolation, but solely the consecration: *'Die Konsekration ist wesentlich ein Opferakt', Deutsche Thomas-Ausgabe,* XXX (1938), 518 (Commentary in Q. 78). This view seems to be held by all modern dogmaticians.

> The consecratory power is not derived only from the words themselves, but also from the power given to the priest in his consecration and ordination when the bishop says to him, Receive the power to offer in the Church the sacrifice for the living as well as for the dead.[85]

Here lies the fundamental difference between the Lutheran and the Roman understanding of the consecration, which Zwingli and his followers failed to understand: For Luther it is the word of Christ, and nothing but this word, which is the cause of the Real Presence of the body and blood in the Lord's Supper; there is no secondary cause. The minister to whom the consecration is reserved is the minister of the Word and the Sacraments, the appointed administrator of the means of grace; he is not, however, a priest in any other sense than that which regards all believers as priests because they are members of the priestly people of God.[86]

Luther's understanding of the consecration raises a question which had already appeared on the horizon during the Great Controversy with Zwingli, though it did not become an issue of controversy among the Lutherans themselves until later. We have seen that Luther can express the fact that the Words of Institution effect the Real Presence by stating that the bread **becomes** Christ's body,[87] or that the words **cause** the bread **to become** the body.[88] Luther here follows the view held by the Catholic church of the West that the Words of Institution are the words of consecration and nothing else, not an *epiclēsis* after the Greek manner, nor another prayer. Does this imply the acceptance of the theory of the duration of the Real Presence which we found in earlier theology, Eastern and Western? When does the Real Presence begin? When does it end?

It seems that Luther would share the Roman view about the 'moment of consecration' if he regards the Words of Institution as effecting the Real Presence.[89] Actually, however, he never

---

[85]*Loc. cit. ad 1: 'Virtus consecrativa non solum consistit in ipsis verbis, sed etiam in potestate sacerdoti tradita in sua consecratione et ordinatione, cum ei dicitur ab episcopo: "Accipe potestatem offerendi in Ecclesia tam pro vivis quam pro mortuis".'*

[86]See chapter 1, 16 and 36.

[87]See the quotation from WA 18, 206, 20 on page 131, footnote 64.

[88]*'Ibi verba faciunt panem zum Leib Christi traditum pro nobis. Ergo non est amplius panis, sed corpus Christi hat das Brot an'* (*Sermons on the Catechism,* WA 30, I, 53, 23). See the entire *Sermon on the Lord's Supper,* WA 30, I, 52-57.

[89]Occasionally he seems to define the moment, as in his *Sermon on the Sacrament of the Body and Blood of Christ against the Enthusiasts* of 1526, WA 19, 491, 13: 'As soon as Christ says, "This is my body", his body is there by the Word and by the power of the Holy Spirit, Psalm 33:9.' The reference to this passage shows that Luther's emphasis was not on the time as such, but rather on the efficacy of the Word.

established a theory about this. The same is true of the question as to the precise moment when the body and blood of Christ cease to be present. It is not lack of clarity that causes him to refrain from answering such questions, but rather the fact that they cannot be answered from the Word of God. If Luther repeatedly confessed his ignorance as to the *how* of the Real Presence and its beginnings,[90] he could have used the words of Innocent III: 'He knows who knows all things'.[91] Still, *Ego Berengarius* of 1079 represents the older view that the sacred prayer and the words of Christ bring about the conversion.[92] When Eastern theologians tried to define the 'moment of consecration', they did not think of the Words of Institution, but of the *epiclesis,* the invocation of the Holy Spirit, which in the Eastern liturgy follows the words of Christ.[93] This is the official doctrine of the Eastern church,[94] which is in remarkable agreement with that of the Reformed churches which understand the Words of Institution as a historical report.[95] Modern Eastern theology, however, returns more and more to an earlier stage of the church when either the whole eucharistic prayer, including the Words of Institution, or even the whole celebration, was regarded as consecratory.

> The Christians of the first centuries certainly did not ask very closely at what exact instant the grace of any sacrament was given,

says the Roman Catholic scholar A. Fortescue;[96] he continues:

> They obeyed Christ's commands, said the prayers, and did the actions He had appointed, and they believed that God in answer would most certainly do His part. But they did not discuss the exact instant at which all conditions were fulfilled.[97]

---

[90]See the quotation from WA 18, 206, 20 on page 131; also WA 18, 166, 10 f; 23, 87, 32; 6, 510, 32 ff.

[91]'*Ego nescio, quomodo Christus accedit; sed et quomodo recedit, ignoro. Novit ille, qui nihil ignorat*' (MPL 217, 868). See above, 40.

[92]See above, 28.

[93]Thus the 'moment of consecration' is defined by Cyril of Jerusalem, *Cat. mystag. I, 7* and *V, 7* (MPG 33, 1072 and 1115) in contradistinction to Chrysostom, who regards the Words of Institution as consecratory. This difference between these two Greek Fathers shows that there was no definite doctrine in the Ancient Church.

[94]This doctrine is, of course, not binding, because it has not been sanctioned by an Ecumenical Council. But it has been stressed by modern Eastern churches in opposition to Rome, as in the answer of the Ecumenical Patriarch to Leo XIII. See this whole problem discussed by Fr. Heiler, *Urkirche und Ostkirche* (1937) 250 ff, where the sources are given in detail. See also Gr. Dix, *op. cit.,* 240 ff and 293 ff.

[95]A. Fortescue, *The Eastern Orthodox Church* (1929), 386.

[96]*Loc. cit.,* 387.

[97]*Loc. cit.,* 387.

In a similar way, Luther and the early Lutheran church avoided forming any theory about the 'moment' when the Real Presence begins, and the 'moment' when it ceases. Some later orthodox theologians advanced the theory that Christ's body and blood are present only at the 'moment' when they are being received.[98] This is frequently regarded as the genuinely-Lutheran doctrine both within,[99] and without,[100] the Lutheran church. Actually, this view is only another attempt to determine a time that only 'he knows who knows all things'. As far as Luther himself is concerned, there cannot be the slightest doubt that he ever limited the Real Presence to the instant of distribution and reception. He never abandoned the view that by the words of consecration bread and wine 'become' the body and blood of Christ. Otherwise, neither the elevation, which was in use at Wittenberg up to 1542, nor the adoration of Christ, who is present in the elements, could have been justified.[101] He always regarded it as Zwinglianism to neglect the difference between a consecrated and an unconsecrated host,[102] and it has always been the

---

[98]Egidius and Nicholas Hunnius and others.

[99]F. Pieper, *Christl. Dogmatik III,* 434, referring to F. Walther, *Pastorale,* 175, who gives a quotation from Egidius Hunnius.

[100]Fr. Heiler, *Urkirche und Ostkirche* (1937), 253, speaks of 'the Lutheran doctrine which recognizes the presence of Christ *in usu* only, i.e., at the moment of the reception'. As to the real meaning of *usus* in contradistinction to *sumptio*, see the following pages.

[101]The elevation had been explained in *De captivitate* (WA 6, 524, 21 ff) as a rite that should incite faith. In his *Short Confession* of 1544 (WA 54, 163) he repeats this interpretation, which would make it possible to retain the rite. It had been abolished, because it could be misunderstood as an admonition to adore the host. The adoration, in the sense in which we found it in his book *Of the Adoration of the Sacrament of the Blessed Body of Christ* of 1523 (WA 11, see above, 83, 84), was always upheld by Luther. Both elevation and adoration presuppose the presence of the body and blood, not only in the *sumptio*. Compare the *Table Talk of 1544* (WA TR 5, No. 5665, line 8). See also the *Table Talk of 1543* (WA TR 5, No. 5589): '*Praeterea cum Christus vere adest in pane, cur non ibi summa reverentia tractaretur et adoraretur etiam?*'

[102]Luther demanded the dismissal of a pastor who had given to a communicant an unconsecrated host instead of a consecrated one, which had been dropped. This unfortunate man was imprisoned. Luther does not approve of such punishment, but he thinks him to be unfit for the Lutheran ministry: 'He should go to his Zwinglians' (Letter of Jan. 11, 1546; WA BR 11, No. 4186). In 1543 Luther and Bugenhagen (WA BR 10, No. 3888) gave their opinion in a controversy about the question whether consecrated hosts could be preserved together with unconsecrated ones for another consecration. Luther criticizes this. Nothing of the consecrated elements should be saved, but must be consumed. In this connection he gives a clear definition of the sacramental 'time' or 'action': *'sic ergo definiemus tempus vel actionem sacramentalem, ut incipiat ab initio orationis dominicae et duret, donec omnes communicaverint, calicem ebiberint, particulas comederint, populus dismissus et ab*

custom of the Lutheran church to consecrate the new supply of bread or wine (or both) if more is needed than originally was provided for.[103] The rule that Luther followed, like Melanchthon and the Lutheran Confessions, was that there is no sacrament, and, consequently, no presence of the body and blood of Christ, 'apart from the use instituted by Christ' or 'apart from the action divinely instituted'.[104] Since the word *usus* is explained by *actio*, it cannot mean the same as *sumptio*. If it has sometimes been understood in this way, it must be said that neither Luther nor the *Formula of Concord* (which definitely stated what the Lutheran church teaches concerning this problem) identified the *sumptio* (eating and drinking) with the use or action of the Sacrament.

The controversies that arose in the Lutheran church, partly in Luther's lifetime,[105] partly after his death,[106] were finally settled by

---

altari discessum sit.' (WA BR 10, No. 3894, lines 27 ff). In the *Table Talk of 1540* Luther goes so far as to allow the blessed Sacrament to be carried to another altar (in the same church) or even, as was still customary in some churches, to be brought to the sick in their home (WA TR 5, No. 5314), provided this could be regarded as a part of the 'action'. This was tolerated as an exception. However, a reservation of the Sacrament was not allowed. The remnants of the elements should be either consumed or burned.

[103]Luther, June 26, 1542, Enders 14, No. 3155; WA BR 10, No. 3762. For present usage, see G.H. Gerberding, *The Lutheran Pastor*, 342: 'Should the supply of either or both run short, it will be necessary to consecrate the new supply, using the Lord's Prayer and the Words of Institution as found in the service. In fact, the latter alone would suffice.'

[104]'*Nihil habet rationem sacramenti extra usum a Christo institutum*' or '*extra actionem divinitus institutam*', quoted from *Sol. Decl. VII, 85* (Trigl. 1001; Bek. Schr. 1001 with literature). In the following words the *Sol. Decl.* gives the explanation: 'The use or action here does not mean chiefly faith, neither the oral participation only, but the entire external, visible action . . . the consecration . . . the distribution and reception . . .' (Trigl. 1003).

[105]See the above-mentioned cases of pastors Besserer (Enders 17, No. 3599; WA BR 11, Nos. 4186 and 3888) and Wolfrum or Wolferinus (Enders 15, No. 3291; WA BR 10, No. 3894).

[106]Joh. Saliger, first in Lübeck, later in Rostock, was accused of having taught that the Real Presence begins with the consecration (*ante asum* here to be understood as meaning *ante sumptionem*) and lasts even if no distribution takes place, or if the distribution should follow some days or weeks later. The rejection of this error is not to be understood as if the Real Presence takes place only at the moment of the *sumptio*, when the blessed bread and wine are touched by the mouth of the communicant, as the decision of the controversy expressly states. Chytraeus, the author of the decision (which later was partly incorporated in the *Formula of Concord, Sol. Decl. VII, 83-85*), refers expressly to the saying of Luther that 'We do not prescribe to God any time or moment', see J. Wiggers, *Zeitschrift fuer historische Theologie* (1848), 639 ff; H. Grass, *Die Abendmahlslehre bei Luther und Calvin* (1940), 111 f. The error of Saliger

the *Formula of Concord* in a statement that would have found the full consent of Luther:

> This blessing, or the recitation of the Words of Institution of Christ alone does not make a sacrament if the entire action of the Supper, as it was instituted by Christ, is not observed (as when the consecrated bread is not distributed, received, and partaken of, but is enclosed, sacrificed, or carried about), but the command of Christ, 'This do' (which embraces the entire action or administration in this Sacrament; that in an assembly of Christians bread and wine are taken, consecrated, distributed, received, eaten, drunk, and the Lord's death is shown forth at the same time), must be observed unseparated and inviolate, as also St Paul places before our eyes the entire action of the breaking of bread or of distribution and reception, 1 Cor. 10:16.[107]

The question as to what happens if the *actio* (celebration) is interrupted by an accident, so that no communion can follow the consecration, no one can answer.[108] Luther was right in leaving such questions to God, and the *Formula of Concord* confirmed his attitude when it says in the last of the condemnations that follow the article on the Lord's Supper:

> We reject and condemn also all presumptuous, frivolous, blasphemous questions and expressions which are presented in a gross, carnal, Capernaitic way regarding the supernatural, heavenly mysteries of this Supper.[109]

According to the *Short Confession* of 1571, one of the documents that preceded the *Formula of Concord*, such questions include: When and how does the body come into the bread? How long does the sacramental union last? When does the body cease to be in the bread?[110] In rejecting such questions, Luther not only followed his principle of avoiding theological statements that could not be based on Holy Scripture, but he was also in agreement with the church of the first 1,200 years. Besides, is not that which our human reason regards as a sequence of several actions in the celebration of the Sacrament one event in the sight of God? Much of the criticism on the part of Zwingli and the Zwinglians to which Luther's doctrine on

---

was not the view that the Real Presence cannot be limited to the moment of the eating and drinking — in this respect he had Luther on his side — but the 'papistic' way in which he expressed himself and his belief that the presence could last beyond the time of the celebration.

[107] *Sol. Decl. VII, 83f* (Trigl. 1001).

[108] The Roman church gave detailed advice as to such cases during World War II when masses were celebrated during air-raids. A mass may be interrupted before consecration, but it must be finished, even if privately, when the consecration has taken place.

[109] Trigl. 1015.

[110] These and other questions are quoted in Bek. Schr., 1016.

consecration was exposed had its origin in the rationalistic theories of Roman theology, which Luther never shared. Perhaps no Catholic ever had such reverence for the miracle of the Real Presence as Luther did. No one could think more highly of the consecration, no one could treat the consecrated elements more reverently,[111] and no one could receive the true body and blood of Christ with deeper piety.[112] However, as far as the theological theories are concerned, which tried to rationalize the unspeakable miracle, he could say only what he said about transubstantiation: '*Subtilitatem sophisticam nihil curamus*'.[113]

THE FRUITS OF THE SACRAMENT

On preceding pages we have had to go beyond the years of the Great Controversy in order to make clear the doctrine on consecration which Luther defended against Zwingli. We now return to the debate of the years 1527-28. Among the various points at issue between Luther and Zwingli, the most important one seems to be the problem of the sacramental eating of the body of Christ as Luther understood it. We have stated that of all 'absurdities' which Zwingli found in Luther's doctrine on the Sacrament, there was none greater or more dangerous than the idea that a bodily eating can help the soul.[114] All other objections which Zwingli raised were more or less determined (though Zwingli did not realize it) by logical — or, as Luther put it, 'mathematical' — considerations. Such 'absurdities' were the assertions that Jesus, standing with his earthly body before his disciples at the Last Supper, had given them his true body and blood to eat and to drink, or that at each celebration of the sacrament his body, which was sitting at the right hand of the Father in heaven, was also present here on earth, in many places at the same time. The protest against the eating of the body, however, came out of the depth of the religious convictions of Zwingli and his followers. Such an idea seemed to be a violation of the spiritual character of Christianity, and a relapse into pagan materialism, a sort of

———

[111]Some very significant traditions are extant about the great care with which Luther handled the consecrated elements. Compare also WA TR 3, No. 3824, and 5, No. 5984.

[112]Hans Preuss, *Martin Luther, der Christenmensch* (1942), 133 ff, especially 141, 2; *Luther als Kommunikant, Luth. Kirche in Bewegung. Festschrift für Fr. Ulmer* (1937), 205-14.

[113]*Smalcald Articles III, 6* (Trigl. 492).

[114]See above, 117.

anthropophagy or theophagy.[115] In his book of 1527, *That These Words 'This is my body' Shall For Ever Retain Their Old Meaning'*, Zwingli makes the statement:

> To eat the body of Christ contradicts [the Christian] faith,[116]

and he adds the argument:

> As man shall not live by bread alone, but by every word that proceedeth out of the mouth of God, so nothing can feed or save the soul except the Word of God, and even this does not save anyone but him whom God has drawn by His Spirit.

If Luther himself teaches that only the believer receives the benefits of the Sacrament, or if he admits that the believer receives them even outside the Sacrament, by trusting in the promise of the Gospel, what, then, is the peculiar gift of the Sacrament? What does it give which is not given through the Word? Furthermore, do not Luther and Zwingli agree, as was also later stated in the *Marburg Articles*, that the spiritual reception of the Sacrament is what really matters, that this spiritual communion alone is necessary for salvation? Finally, did not Jesus himself reject the idea of a bodily eating when he said in John 6:63: 'It is the spirit that quickeneth; the flesh profiteth nothing'?

Since this passage from John 6 was for Zwingli the most important argument against Luther, we may begin by discussing it briefly. We have already stated the noteworthy fact that neither Zwingli nor Luther regarded John 6 as dealing with the Sacrament of the Altar; they were agreed that in this chapter Jesus spoke of that spiritual eating and drinking which is nothing else than believing in Christ.[117]

---

[115]See Luther's complaint in the *Short Confession* of 1544 (WA 54, 146, 4 ff): *'Darum wussten sie wohl, dass wir keine Fleischfresser, Blutsäufer, Thyeste, Caperniten noch Localisten wären und unser Gott kein gebacken Gott, weinerner Gott, etc., sein konnte; noch mussten wir solche ihre mutwillige, erkannte Lästerung hören, und wer es nicht lassen will bei ihnen, noch lästert; denn sie lesen es in ihren Büchern.'* Such harsh words are to be found in Reformed literature from Zwingli to Beza. We are reminded of the old reproach of Jews and Gentiles that in the Christian Eucharist cannibalism was practised (*Thyesteia deipna,* cf the misunderstanding of the people of Capernaum, John 6).

[116]Translated from the German text of the book found in St Louis, XX, col. 1171 (par. 65).

[117]The *Formula of Concord*, following Luther and the exegetical tradition of the early Lutheran church, does not quote John 6 as a proof-text for the Sacrament, but for the spiritual eating ('of which Christ treats especially John 6:54', *Sol. Decl. VII, 61;* Trigl. 995) that occurs inside and outside the Sacrament. It is not, however, a dogma of the Lutheran church that no other connection between John 6 and the Lord's Supper may be assumed. The Reformers follow an exegetical tradition established in the

Zwingli was convinced that in verse 63 Jesus wanted to give a rule according to which the Words of Institution would later have to be interpreted, while Luther believed that a sound exegesis demanded that the words of Jesus in the narrative be understood by themselves first, and then in light of the commentary that Paul gives in connection with his narrative; John 6 must be understood from the Words of Institution, not vice versa. Thus, it is impossible to assume that the flesh of Jesus 'profiteth nothing'.

> Where spirit and flesh are opposed to each other in Holy Scripture, flesh does not mean the flesh of Christ, but the Old Adam.[118]

Western church by Augustine in his *Tractatus in Johannis evang*. 26, 11-20 (MPL 35, 1611 ff). Augustine has it from Eusebius, *Hist. Eccl. III, 12,* whose source is his great teacher Origen. In contradistinction to the neo-Platonic spiritualism of Origen and Augustine, the Eastern church has retained the realism of Ignatius and the Orthodox Fathers. The influence of Augustine on Luther, Zwingli, and Calvin in this regard is equally strong. Later Lutherans have admitted that there is a connection between John 6 and the Sacrament of the Altar (such as J. G. Scheibel, *Das Abendmahl des Herrn* (1823); Theodor Zahn). Our understanding of St John would take into account the specific character of this Gospel. All of chapter 6, from the feeding of the five thousand and the discourse on the new manna, the new 'bread from heaven', to the words on the eating of the flesh and the drinking of the blood, and to the rejection of this idea by the Capernaites and the apostasy of many disciples, was understood by the Ancient Church as a unit. Compare the first representation of the *fractio panis* in the Capella Graeca of the Catacomb of St Priscilla with the loaves, fishes, and baskets; J. Wilpert, *Fractio Panis* (1895). Even the walking on the sea has been understood as pointing to the divine-human mystery of the body of Jesus. If in the first part of the discourse Jesus calls himself the bread of life, while in verse 51b he speaks of his flesh and blood, it is neither necessary nor possible to harmonize this, as the exegetes of the 16th and 17th centuries did. The discourses of Jesus, as John has transmitted them to us, are not logically-constructed speeches, like those of Cicero. In some respects the present discourse reminds us of the discussion between Jesus and Nicodemus, in which Baptism is not directly mentioned, though it is the secret topic, as the Christian reader could not fail to notice. John deliberately left out the institution of the sacrament in his narrative of the Last Supper, not because he wanted to supplement the Synoptic Gospels — in fact he often relates a story already contained in the older Gospels — but because at his time, when the persecutions had begun, he did not want the pagan readers to know everything. This is the reason why the Sacraments are not directly mentioned. Chapter 6 shows that Jesus spoke about the future sacrament even before his passion, but this could be a hint only as to what was going to happen later. Whatever this mysterious chapter may mean, it cannot be the source of our knowledge about what the Sacrament of the Altar is. Here Luther was in absolute disagreement with Zwingli. It is interesting to observe that at least once Luther applies John 6:54 to the Eucharist when, like Irenaeus, he speaks of the connection of the Eucharist with the resurrection of our bodies (WA 23, 232, 31 ff). See p 148 ff with the references from *Sol. Decl. VIII.*

[118] WA 26, 374, 9 ff.

Otherwise, the Incarnation would be useless. John 6:63 is directed against the Capernaitic misunderstanding that the flesh of Christ could be eaten like ordinary meat. The flesh of Christ, although it is real flesh, is at the same time something spiritual.

> His flesh is not contrary to the Spirit, but it is rather born of the Holy Spirit and filled with the Holy Spirit.[119]

The eating of this flesh must, therefore, be distinguished, on the one hand, from the Capernaitic misunderstanding, and, on the other hand, from the *manducatio spiritualis,* which is nothing else than belief in Christ crucified.[120] This sacramental eating of the body of Christ, which is the characteristic feature of all Catholic and all Lutheran churches, has been unknown to all Reformed theologians and churches since the days of Zwingli, and was rejected even during the Middle Ages by spiritualists like Wyclif.

But, once we accept Luther's doctrine on the sacramental eating of the body, the question remains which Zwingli puts to Luther time and again: What is the use of such eating? Luther's answer is: It is not

---

[119]WA 26, 375, 4 ff.

[120]The *Formula of Concord, Sol. Decl. VII, 61-63,* gives the final dogmatical definition: 'There is, therefore, a twofold eating of the flesh of Christ, one **spiritual**, of which Christ treats especially in John 6:54, which occurs in no other way than with the Spirit and faith . . . and by itself is useful and salutary, and necessary at all times for salvation to all Christians. . . The other eating of the body of Christ is **oral** or **sacramental**, when the true essential body and blood of Christ are also orally received and partaken of . . . by all who eat and drink the consecrated bread and wine in the Supper — by the believing as a certain pledge and assurance that their sins are surely forgiven them, and Christ dwells and is efficacious in them, but by the unbelieving for their judgment and condemnation . . .' (Trigl. 995). The main reason why Luther applied John 6 to the spiritual communion only is to be found in verses 53, 54 with the doctrine on the necessity of the eating. The question whether or not the sacramental eating is necessary for salvation has been discussed throughout the centuries. Luther and the Lutheran church follow the view which was finally established in the Western church by Thomas Aquinas (*Summa theol. III, Q. 65, Art. 4*). The custom of giving Holy Communion even to infants right after baptism shows that there was a time when the whole of Christendom followed the view of the Eastern Fathers, who on the basis of John 6:54 taught the absolute necessity of the sacramental manducation. Even Augustine could say, contradicting the Pelagians: 'No one may hope for salvation or eternal life without baptism and the body and blood of the Lord. Without these it is promised in vain to infants' (MPL 44, 129). Zwingli distinguished between a spiritual eating and a sacramental eating in a different way: spiritual eating is believing in Christ; sacramental eating is believing in Christ on the occasion of receiving the bread and wine. The question of the necessity of Holy Communion is one of the great issues of present-day Roman theology. The most elaborate discussion is to be found in the great work of the French theologian M. de la Taille, *Mysterium Fidei,* Thesis 49.

our business to ask and to answer such questions. If Christ instituted the Sacrament and told us, 'This is my body', we are to obey his commandment and believe his words. What distinguishes Luther from later theologians is his reluctance to put forward any theory about the necessity of the Sacrament and how God works through it. The question of why Christ instituted Sacraments in addition to his Gospel in the Word cannot be answered. We must leave that to the inscrutable wisdom of God. Just as human reason cannot answer the question: *Cur Deus homo?*, so we cannot know why God instituted the Sacrament through which we receive the same grace that is given us through the Scriptures. Why God has so many ways to give us forgiveness of sins, no man can know. Luther always refused to answer such questions as, for example, why we should receive forgiveness of sins in the Sacrament of the Altar after we have received it in absolution; God knows what we need and why we need it. Thus, Luther repeats in the years of the Great Controversy with Zwingli what he earlier had taught about forgiveness of sins as being the great gift of the Sacrament. However, there is now a strong tendency to connect forgiveness with the body and the blood, instead of regarding these only as seals and signs attached to the Word:

> Therefore, he who drinks of this cup, truly drinks the true blood of Christ and the forgiveness of sins or the Spirit of Christ which is received in and with the cup. Here not a mere figure or sign of the New Testament or of the blood of Christ is received, as it would befit the Jews in the Old Testament.[121]

Here, as in other passages, the emphasis on the Real Presence leads to a conception of the Sacrament in which the Word and the body and blood of Christ have become really one, so that it is impossible to understand the Sacrament as a mere sign of grace.

Another trend in Luther's thinking on the Sacrament during these years is a new stress on the personal presence of Christ, not only of his body and blood, which is perhaps a result of his doctrine on the ubiquity of Christ.[122] Furthermore, the consequences of forgiveness are emphasized, especially in the *Small* and the *Large Catechism,* which are very important sources of our knowledge of Luther's

---

[121]*Large Confession,* WA 26, 468, 39 ff. Compare H. Grass, *Die Abendmahlslehre bei Luther und Calvin* (1940), 95 ff.

[122]The idea that Christ should be adored in the Lord's Supper should certainly have prevented older dogmaticians like Quenstedt, and modern scholars like H. Gollwitzer in *Coena Domini* (1937), from limiting the presence, as Luther believed it, to the body and blood of Christ. Even when he later rejects the doctrine on concomitance (see above, 78 f), Luther never doubts that Christ himself gives us his body and blood in the Sacrament.

theology on the Sacrament during these years because they present the doctrine without polemics.

> Where there is forgiveness of sins, there is also life and salvation.

This famous statement from the *Small Catechism* shows in the simplest way the nature of these consequences. In describing them in detail, Luther makes use of the traditional thoughts of the earlier church, which regarded the Sacrament of the Altar as food and as medicine.

> It is indeed called a food of souls, which nourishes and strengthens the new man. For by Baptism we are first born anew; but . . . there still remains, besides, the old vicious nature of flesh and blood in man, and there are so many hindrances and temptations of the devil and of the world that we often become weary and faint, and sometimes also stumble. Therefore it is given for a daily pasture and sustenance, that faith may refresh and strengthen itself so as not to fall back in such a battle, but become ever stronger and stronger. For the new life must be so regulated that it continually increase and progress . . . [123]

Here the old Catholic idea of the Eucharist as nourishment, refreshment,[124] and means of strengthening the inner life in its fight against sin,[125] has been translated into an evangelical understanding. The new life as fruit of forgiveness, and strength of the soul as strength of faith: this is the Lutheran version of that old idea of the fruit of the Sacrament.

The second idea is the idea of the Sacrament as medicine. Again we quote from the *Large Catechism* in order to show that this doctrine does not have its origin in polemics:

> Those who are sensible of their weakness, desire to be rid of it and long for help, should regard and use it only as a precious antidote against the poison which they have in them. For here in the Sacrament you are to receive from the lips of Christ forgiveness of sin, which contains and brings with it the grace of God and the Spirit with all his gifts, protection, shelter, and power against death and the devil and all misfortune.[126]

Here we have the much-debated 'medicine for immortality, antidote

---

[123] *Large Catechism,* V, 23 (Trigl. 757, 759). See also the subsequent paragraphs on page 759.

[124] Compare Thomas Aquinas: *'Sacramentum Eucharistiae, quod est spirituale alimentum'* (*Summa theol. Q. 73, Art 1*); *'ad spiritualem refectionem'* (*Art 2*); *'perceptio baptismi est necessaria ad inchoandam spiritualem vitam, perceptio autem Eucharistiae est necessaria ad consummandam ipsam'* (*Art. 3*).

[125] Thomas, *loc. cit., Q. 79, 6,* describes the effects of the Sacrament as preservation from death insofar as it is 'food' and 'medicine' and as armament against *exteriores impugnationes.* The Eucharist strengthens the spiritual life (*'roborat spiritualem vitam'*). Luther, of course, is independent from Thomas. It is the heritage of the Ancient Church that both have preserved.

[126] *Large Catechism,* V, 69 (Trigl. 769).

against death' which Ignatius already at the beginning of the second century quoted from the liturgy of Antioch,[127] and which played such a great role for the Greek Fathers. It is true that the idea is to be found especially in Luther's writings against Zwingli of 1527 and 1528; he had special reasons to emphasize it then over against the spiritualistic understanding which his adversaries had of the Lord's Supper. But the *Large Catechism*, and the *Formula of Concord* (which in the article on the Person of Christ, referring to John 6:48-58 and to the Council of Ephesus, twice speaks of the flesh of Christ as *vivificus cibus*) prove that the doctrine in question is not a private theory of Luther only, but has become a doctrine of the Lutheran church.[128]

Here we are confronted with the famous question whether, according to Luther, the Sacrament of the Altar — the same would apply to the Sacrament of Baptism — can have, and has, effects on the human body. It is quite clear that, in the passage just quoted from the *Large Catechism*, everything depends on the forgiveness of sins. This forgiveness leads to a strengthening of the inner life; it gives the Holy Spirit, who brings life eternal. However, since forgiveness and Spirit are inherent in the body and blood of Christ, and since the bodily and the spiritual eating in the reception of the Sacrament by the believer are one action, the whole man is influenced by the body of Christ.[129]

---

[127]'*pharmakon athanasias, antidotos tou me apothanein, alla zēn en Jēsu Christo dia pantos'*, Ign. *ad. Eph. 20:2*. For the liturgical origin of the formula, see Hans Lietzmann, *Messe und Herrenmahl* (1926), 257. This idea cannot be regarded as a 'product of the Hellenistic mind' (H. Grass, *op. cit.*, 102). It is a product of the unhellenistic eschatology of the Bible and of Jesus himself, as we shall see.

[128]'Thus in John 6:48-58 the flesh of Christ is a quickening food; as also the Council of Ephesus concluded from this [statement of the evangelist and apostle] that the flesh of Christ has power to quicken; and as many other glorious testimonies of the ancient orthodox church concerning this article are cited elsewhere', *Sol.Decl. VIII, 59* (Trigl. 1035). 'On account of this personal union . . . there is ascribed to Christ according to the flesh what His flesh, according to its nature and essence, cannot be of itself, and, apart from this union, cannot have, namely, that His flesh is a truly quickening food and His blood a truly quickening drink, as the two hundred Fathers of the Council of Ephesus have testified, *carnem Christi esse vivificam seu vivificatricem', Sol. Decl. VIII, 76* (Trigl. 1043). See the quotations in the *Catalogus Testimoniorum,* especially can. 11, of the Council of Ephesus (AD 431): '*Si quis non confitetur, carnem Domini esse vivificam, propterea quod propria facta est Verbi, quod omnia vivificat, anathema sit'* (Trigl. 1128). It is very remarkable how John 6 in the Article on the Person of Christ is understood according to the view of the Greek Fathers, and not according to Augustine's *Tractatus* on John 6, as in the article on the Lord's Supper.

[129]E. Sommerlath, *Der Sinn des Abendmahls nach Luthers Gedanken über das Abendmahl 1527-29* (1930), 82. See the entire context.

> For God is in this flesh, it is God's flesh, the flesh of the Spirit. It is in God, and God is in it. Therefore it is living and gives to all who eat it [that is, worthily], to their bodies and their souls.[130]

This is not an unimportant, incidental thought, a by-product of Luther's fight against Zwingli. The idea that the Sacrament is meant for the whole man, body and soul, is, rather, one of the fundamental elements of Luther's doctrine on the Sacrament. We find it also with regard to Baptism in the *Large Catechism*.[131] It is closely connected with the doctrine on the Incarnation, just as it was for the Greek Fathers.

No single element of Luther's doctrine on the Sacrament has met with such criticism as this idea. Not only Zwingli, Calvin, and the later Reformed churches have rejected it, but also modern Lutheranism (with the noteworthy exception of some theologians, like Sommerlath,[132] and Elert[133]) has regarded the idea that a bodily eating and drinking could give an eternal blessing to the soul, and that the grace of God even affects our body, as a remnant of non-Christian religion.[134] It must not, however, be forgotten that Luther could appeal not only to the Ancient Fathers but also to the New Testament. It is not accidental that John 6 appears here as the scriptural proof.[135] There is a connection between the Sacrament and the Last Things. Baptism looks to the resurrection of the body, and so does the Sacrament of the Altar. That the Sacraments of Baptism and the Lord's Supper are anticipations of the future, of our resurrection and the complete union with Christ, is the doctrine of

---

[130]WA 23, 244, 1 f (*Dass diese Worte . . .*).

[131]'For that is the reason why these two things are done in Baptism, namely, that the body, which can apprehend nothing but the water, is sprinkled, and, in addition, the Word is spoken for the soul to apprehend. Now, since both, the water and the Word, are one Baptism, therefore body and soul must be saved and live for ever.' *Large Catechism*, IV, 44 f (Trigl. 743).

[132]*Loc. cit.*

[133]*Morphologie des Luthertums I*, 263-80; *Der christl. Glaube*, 2nd ed., 464-476.

[134]It seems that the majority of modern Lutherans would hold this view, as the textbooks on dogmatics show, such as Althaus and Aulen.

[135]WA 23, 233, 31 ff. '*Wir sehen, wie die alten Lehrer haben auf die Weise vom Sakrament geredet, dass es dem Leibe auch gebe ein unsterblich Wesen, doch verborgen im Glauben und Hoffnung bis an den Jüngsten Tag*' (WA 23, 233, 23 ff). Luther accepts that view, referring to the immortality of the body of Christ, which we receive in the Sacrament: '*Das kann ja nicht* [*ein anderer Leib*] *sein denn der Leib Christi, da er von redet Joh. 6: "Mein Fleisch ist eine rechte Speise, wer mein Fleisch isset, der lebet ewiglich".*'

the New Testament.[136] **How** the Sacrament can have such effects, the Bible does not tell us. That is the reason why Luther never attempted to answer this question, which was discussed also by the schoolmen.[137] He was satisfied to know that a connection does exist between our receiving Christ's body and blood and our future glory. Whatever human reason might think of such a connection, Luther knew that according to Holy Scripture not only the human soul, but also the human body, is the object of God's redemption. Over against the Platonic separation of body and soul, he defended biblical anthropology against Zwingli. Jesus was not only the Saviour of souls, but also the good physician. His miracles of healing are part-and-parcel of his activity as Saviour of the world. They accompanied his preaching, just as the preaching of the church is accompanied by the Sacraments. Like the Sacraments, they have an eschatological meaning insofar as they are an anticipation of the future redemption of the whole man, body and soul (Matt. 11:5; Luke 4:18; 1 Cor. 15: 42 ff; Rev. 21:4). And the apostles knew that not only our glorified bodies after our resurrection, but also our present bodies, despite all weakness and sinfulness, are 'members of Christ' (1 Cor. 6:15), 'the temple of the Holy Ghost' (v 19). It was this great New Testament truth that Luther defended against Zwingli's idealism when he maintained in the Great Controversy that our bodies, too, participate in the grace that Christ gives through his Sacraments.

---

[136]Rom 6:3 ff; John 6:54 ff. This passage would be a sufficient proof, even if it dealt only with the *manducatio spiritualis.*

[137]Aquinas in his discussion of the effects of the Eucharist (*Summa theol. III, Q.79*) raises the question whether or not grace can be given not only to the soul, but also to the body. His answer is that, though the body cannot be the immediate recipient of grace, the grace given to the soul may indirectly affect the body. This has remained the view of Roman Catholic theology, until in more recent times the growing interest in the Greek Fathers has caused doubts as to the finality of the answer given by Thomas.

CHAPTER V

The Marburg Colloquy

1. Preparation

With his *Large Confession* of 1528 Luther regarded his discussion with Zwingli as finished. He did not intend to write on that subject any more, and did not answer the critical replies of Zwingli and Oecolampadius.[1] This book, in spite of the inevitable weakness of a polemical writing, is one of the greatest works on the Sacrament of the Altar ever written, full of exegetical, theological, and even philosophical insights — for Luther was also a philosopher in his own right — and, like every great theological work, a real confession. This character is underlined by its concluding part, which contains a complete confession of Luther's faith, a forerunner of the *Schwabach Articles* of 1529, and thus one of the sources of the doctrinal articles of the *Augsburg Confession.*[2]

> Since I see that . . . sects and errors increase, and that there is no end to the rage and fury of Satan, in order that henceforth during my life or after my death some of them may not, in future, support themselves by me, and falsely quote my writings to strengthen their error as the Sacramentarians and Anabaptists begin to do, I mean by this writing to confess my faith, point by point, before God and all the world, in which I intend to abide until my death, and therein (so help me God!) to depart from this world and to appear before the judgment-seat of Jesus Christ.[3]

This seems a very bold statement to our contemporaries, most of whom do not realize that, according to the New Testament, to be a confessor means more than to express a religious or theological conviction. (We shall have to add another statement later on the nature of a confession in the sense of the New Testament.[4] Suffice it

---

[1]See above, 115. The text of these replies is also to be found in St Louis XX, col. 1228-1473.

[2]WA 26, 499-509.

[3]WA 26, 499, 1 ff; quoted in *Form. Conc., Sol. Decl. VII, 29* (Trigl. 981).

[4]See below, 284, 285.

to state here that a real confession of faith is always made 'before God and all the world',[5] and that therefore it bears an eschatological character.) When a confession is demanded of us — and it is demanded by Christ himself of all who meet him, believers (Matt. 16:15) as well as unbelievers (Matt. 22:42) — nothing less is at stake than life and death for time and eternity (Matt. 10:28-33). One must always remember this biblical concept of a confession in order to understand the nature of the Lutheran confession with its seriousness and finality. The question has often been raised whether it is possible, in view of human frailty and fallibility, to speak with such bold confidence, and whether Luther himself would not later have changed his views. Here is the reply of the Reformer himself:

> If after my death anyone should say: If Dr Luther were living now, he would teach and hold this or that article differently, for he did not sufficiently consider it, against this I say now as then, and then as now, that, by God's grace, I have most diligently compared all these articles with the Scriptures time and again, and often have gone over them, and would defend them as confidently as I have now defended the Sacrament of the Altar. I am not drunk nor thoughtless; I know what I say; I am also sensible of what it means for me at the coming of the Lord Christ at the final judgment. Therefore I want no one to regard this as a jest or mere idle talk; it is a serious matter to me; for by God's grace I know Satan a good deal; if he can pervert or confuse God's Word, what will he do with my words?[6]

The assurance with which Luther confesses his faith is not that false *securitas* which he criticized time and again, but rather the *certitudo,* the genuine certitude of faith, based on the Word of God. Not a subjective conviction, based on 'private judgment' as to what a biblical passage may or may not mean, but the objective doctrine of Scripture, contained in the clear words of the Bible, must be the content of a confession, in Luther's sense.

Luther's *Large Confession* of 1528 follows the three Articles of the Creed. In connection with the Second Article, it deals with the problems of Pelagianism and good works, while the doctrine on the

---

[5]'*Coram Deo et toto mundo'*, as the Latin text of the *Formula of Concord, Sol. Decl. VII, 29* renders Luther's words (Trigl. 980 ff). That this is the understanding of the Lutheran church appears from the last paragraph of the *Sol. Decl.*, where the confessors state: 'Since now, in the sight of God and of all Christendom, we wish to testify to those now living and those who shall come after us (*in conspectu igitur Dei omnipotentis et coram tota ecclesia Christi, quae nunc est et quae aliquando in posteritate erit*) that this declaration . . . is our faith, doctrine, and confession, in which we are also willing, by God's grace, to appear with intrepid hearts before the judgment-seat of Jesus Christ . . .' (Trigl. 1103).

[6]WA 26, 499, 23 ff ; *Sol. Decl. VII, 29 ff* (Trigl. 981, 983).

Sacraments is included in the Third Article. Thus, the article on the Lord's Supper is brought into connection with the entire Christian doctrine. While Zwingli and all Reformed theologians stressed the fact that the Creeds do not contain any article on the Lord's Supper (the connection between the Sacrament of the Altar and the words *sanctorum communio* in the Apostles' Creed was not realized at that time), and while they did not regard a divergence of opinion on the Lord's Supper as church-divisive, for Luther the denial of the Real Presence was heresy destructive to the church — closely related to the great heresies that threatened the existence of the church throughout the centuries. Even in 1528 it was his conviction, as he expressed it shortly before his death in his *Short Confession concerning the Blessed Sacrament* of 1544 in the words:

> How will he who refuses to believe the article on the Lord's Supper [which means, as the context shows, the article of faith contained in the Words of Institution concerning the oral eating and drinking of Christ's true body and blood] still believe the article on the humanity and divinity in the one Person of Christ?[7]

He then continues by comparing the Christian doctrine with a ring or a bell which, when damaged at one point, is entirely useless.[8] The incarnation, the true divinity and true humanity in the one Person of the God-man, the virgin birth of Christ, his bodily resurrection, his exaltation to the right hand of the Father, his advent in glory, our own resurrection: all these are linked to the Real Presence of his true body and blood in such a way that the denial of this Presence is either the cause or the consequence of the denial of the other articles. The firm stand that Luther took, not only against Rome, but also against the enthusiasts and the 'sacramentarians', can be understood only if we are aware of his conviction that the very existence of Christ's Church was endangered by the inroads of the old evil foe 'in these last days', in which the Church always lives. With the eyes of a prophet,

---

[7]WA 54, 157, 25.

[8]WA 54, 159, 1 ff. The same idea that all articles of faith belong together is expressed in WA 50, 269, 13 ff (*Of the Three Symbols*, 1538): '*Es müssen wahrlich alle drei Stück geglaubt sein, nämlich: dass er Gott sei, item dass er Mensch sei, item dass er für uns solcher Mensch worden sei, das ist, wie das erst Symbolon sagt: empfangen vom Heiligen Geist, geboren von Maria der Jungfrauen, gelitten, gekreuzigt, gestorben und auferstanden etc. Fehlets an einem Stücklein, so fehlen alle Stück. Denn der Glaube soll und muss ganz und rund sein: ob er wohl schwach sein kann und angefochten werden, dennoch soll und muss er ganz und nicht falsch sein. Schwach sein tut den Schaden nicht, aber falsch sein, das ist der ewige Tod.*'

he saw the heresies that were bound to appear as soon as even one article of faith was abandoned:

> There will come, and there are present even now, many who would not believe that Christ is risen from the dead, that he sitteth on the right hand of God and what else is said about Christ in the Creed. *Die werden dem Fass den Boden ausstossen, und des Spiels ein Ende machen. Denn damit wird der ganze Christus untergehen; und wird die Welt nichts halten vom künftigen Leben, so ist denn Christus nichts mehr.*[9]

For Luther, Antichrist was a very present reality, just as he was for the apostles. It is characteristic of his profound understanding of the Church that he cannot confess the article on the Church in any confession without mentioning the terrific reality that accompanies the history of the church throughout the ages, an eschatological reality, just as the Church itself is an eschatological reality, God's people 'in these last days'. He sees Antichrist primarily in the papacy, but at the same time he emphasizes, especially in his *Large Confession* of 1528, that

> besides, also the Turk and all heresies, wherever they may be found, belong to that 'abomination' which will stand in the holy place, as it has been prophesied.[10]

As the articles of faith belong together in the one and indivisible Christian faith, so the manifestations of Antichrist in the great heresies are intrinsically one. In the *Smalcald Articles*, Luther shows why the papacy, the enthusiasts, and Islam belong together: they are expressions of the one great heresy, which is as old as fallen mankind; man refuses to accept the external word and the external means of grace, and develops his own religion, which places man where God alone has the right to stand; 'Ye shall be as gods'.[11] Luther knew full well that no human power could conquer the superhuman forces that threaten the existence of the Church, and that the Good Shepherd

---

[9] WA 50, 269, 21 ff. See the interpretation of this passage by P. Brunner, *Grundlegung des Abendmahlsgesprächs* (1954), 16.

[10] *Large Confession*, WA 26, 507, 1 ff.

[11] Part III, Art. VII, on Confession: ' . . . that we may be protected against the enthusiasts, i.e., spirits who boast that they have the Spirit without and before the Word, and accordingly judge Scripture or the spoken Word, and explain and stretch it at their pleasure . . . For the papacy also is nothing but sheer enthusiasm, by which the pope boasts that all rights exist in the shrine of his heart. . . In a word, enthusiasm inheres in Adam and his children from the beginning to the end of the world, having been implanted and infused into them by the old dragon, and is the origin, power, and strength of all heresy, especially of that of the papacy and Mahomet . . .' (Trigl. 495, 497). What an amazing insight into the history of religion is contained in these words. Each of these three heresies appeals to John 16:12 f. Each denies the finality of the biblical revelation.

alone can protect his little flock. But he also knew that what is required of us is the fearless confession of the eternal truth of God's Word.

This is the reason why Luther refused to continue the controversy, and why he rejected the idea of settling the question by means of a colloquy. It seems that Bucer, the great negotiator, was the first to suggest a personal meeting between the parties, in a letter to Justus Jonas in 1526. The following year, Philip of Hesse proposed a colloquy to Luther, but Luther declined.[12] This does not mean that Luther was afraid of a colloquy as such. He was, as his actions show, always prepared to discuss even highly-controversial questions with people who did not accept his every opinion. In such cases, he could, as we shall see, make the most surprising concessions — and by no means only because (as he himself on several occasions remarks) he was by nature inclined to yield in personal relations.[13] He was unyielding only where the Word of God was at stake. Just as Athanasius was not prepared to enter a discussion with Arius, but was ready to accept the Cappadocian interpretation of *homōousios* as meaning 'of *equal* substance' instead of 'of *one* substance', so Luther never demanded that his adversaries accept his doctrine on 'ubiquity', or his philosophical arguments concerning the possibility of the presence of Christ's true body and blood. He demanded only that the words of Christ should not be made a matter of doubt, compromise, or distortion. He could never admit that the meaning of these words should be regarded as a minor issue on which several opinions could, and ought to, be tolerated, as Zwingli thought. Luther always distinguished, as Athanasius and all great teachers of the church have done, between questions on which a discussion is impossible, and others that can be discussed on the basis

---

[12]'*Ante duos annos denegaram . . .*' said Luther at Marburg, according to Hedio (WA 30, III, 110, 4, see our text below, 185). Capito wrote from Strasburg about this refusal of Luther: '*colloqium refugit*' (Sept. 21, 1527, quoted from *Zwingli's Letters* by Th. Kolde, *Martin Luther, II,* 588). This was the Zwinglian version of the incident.

[13]'In private struggles I am the weaker one and you the more stalwart; contrariwise in public struggles I am like you are in private ones.' Thus Luther characterizes himself in comparison to Melanchthon in a letter written to Melanchthon in the crucial days of the Augsburg Diet (June 30, 1530, WA BR 5, 412; No. 1611, 19 f). K. Holl in his great essay, '*Luthers Urteile über sich selbst*' in *Gesammelte Aufsätze zur Kirchengeschichte, I: Luther* (2nd and 3rd edition, 1923), 381-419, deals with the natural shyness of Luther, and gives more examples, e.g. p.411, Luther's regret about his modest speaking at Worms (Letter to Spalatin of September 9, 1521, WA BR 2, No. 429; lines 22 f; Enders 3, 229 32 f).

of certain common presuppositions.[14] The article on the Real Presence was such an undebatable article for Luther, as was the article of the true divinity of Christ for Athanasius. Errors can be removed by a thorough discussion. Heresies must be refuted and avoided, as had already been indicated by Paul (Rom. 16:17; Titus 3:10) and John (2 John 10, 11). Modern Christendom, even modern Lutheranism, seems to have forgotten this fundamental rule, as is sufficiently proved by the endless and fruitless ecumenical discussions that are not carried out on a firm basis on articles concerning which 'there is no contention or dispute'. Here lies the deeper reason why even Lutherans no longer understand Luther's attitude toward the proposed colloquy, and the stand he took at the colloquy itself.

How, then, did the colloquy come about in spite of Luther's refusal of 1527? Several factors are to be taken into consideration. If we today look back at the critical years between the Diet of Worms and the Diet of Augsburg, we observe a development which was still hidden from contemporaries (as is the case in all historical developments). We see what no one was able to realize at the time, namely, that, with the bull *Exsurge Domine* of 1520, the unity of the Western church had finally been destroyed. A reformation of the whole church had become impossible. The terrifying *irreformabilis* of the Vatican Council was now a reality.[15] Certainly, there could be a reformation of the moral and religious life of clergy and laity, such as the *Decrees on Reformation* of Trent later tried to bring about. There could also still be a reformation of the Canon Law, though never in the sense of the conciliarist ideas of the early 15th century. The general council as supreme authority could never be restored, not only because the supremacy of the pope had been re-established at the Fifth Lateran Council which ended in 1517, on the eve of Luther's Reformation, but also because this institution had become obsolete. What, after all, is an 'ecumenical council'? Has it ever been more than a great idea? In what sense were Nicaea or Constantinople 'ecumenical', or any other of the ancient synods that were regarded as normative, to say nothing of the medieval synods that were never recognized by the East? As it would be quite impossible today to summon an ecumenical synod that would be recognized even by the

---

[14]See the division of the articles in the *Smalcald Articles*.

[15]*'Romani Pontificis definitiones ex sese, non autem ex consensu Ecclesiae, irreformabiles esse'*, Denz, 1839.

Catholic churches, Eastern and Western, either side having its own idea about what constitutes such a synod, so already at the time of the Reformation the hope that a council could settle the issues at stake and restore the unity of Christendom was sheer romanticism. Luther had stated that quite clearly in the preface of the *Smalcald Articles* when the Council had been summoned to Mantua. How right he was appears from the fact that the Council, when it eventually met at Trent in 1545, had the task of extirpating the heresy that had already been condemned 25 years before. Nothing is more significant in indicating the obsolescence of the venerable institution of a general council than the fact that Trent was completely dominated by the papacy, and also that the Roman church could do without another council for 300 years, until the *Vaticanum* finally surrendered to the pope all powers that had once been vested in the ecumenical council, so much so that even the decrees of such synods are proclaimed as the decrees of the pope.

Here lies one of the reasons why all attempts to find a solution to the urgent problems of the church in the years between the Diets of Worms and Augsburg were bound to fail. The old ecclesiastical offices and institutions no longer functioned, or, at least, were unable to cope with the situation. Hence the secular authorities had to act. Just as, during the decay of the Roman Empire when the secular authorities had been destroyed, the bishops and the rising papacy stepped into the empty places and fulfilled the duties of judges and magistrates for the Latin-speaking people, so the decay of the medieval papacy and its ecclesiastical means of government created the authority of the civil governments in the church after the year 1300. It is not true that the Reformers created this authority. Statements like: 'The Duke of Cleve is pope in his territory', were very common in the 15th century. At the end of the Middle Ages, city councils like those of Nuremberg or Zurich would not allow the bishop to appoint a minister to their churches; it was their right to call their priests. This confusion of ecclesiastical and secular authority had been inherited by the Reformation from medieval society, that *corpus Christianum* which was at the same time church and state. It was quite inevitable that the authority of secular government, be it exercised by princes or by city councils, would increase within the church. From the point of view of modern Christians, Protestant as well as Catholic, who have learned not only to distinguish between temporal and spiritual power, but also, at least in theory, to separate them, the growing influence of the state in ecclesiastical affairs in the Reformation period may be regretted. It should not, however, be forgotten that at least Luther and Calvin were anything but Erastians.[16] Catholics who criticize the political aspect of the Reformation should remember that the ecumenical synods of the Ancient Church were summoned by Christian emperors, and that their doctrinal decisions were regarded as public laws. Even the Vatican Council could finish the doctrine on the papacy only because a French army protected Rome from being taken by Italian troops. As soon as the French forces had to be withdrawn, the Council was bound to collapse.

Thus, if the fate of the Reformation movement was, humanly speaking, in the hands of the political powers, it must be admitted that this was not yet the time of the absolute state, in which religion all too often became a means of political ends. As the Emperor was still aware of his great responsibility as the *advocatus ecclesiae,* and rather resigned from his office than to grant freedom to what he could not but regard as heresy, so the princes and city councils also took their responsibility toward the church very seriously. Whether they had accepted or rejected the Reformation or tried to remain neutral, they all wanted to be Christians within the one Catholic church, notwithstanding their various views on the Gospel, the Sacraments, the Ministry of the church. Nothing could be more misleading than to read into the history of that eventful decade the state of things which later developed when various confessional churches stood side by side. The 'Protestants' of 1529 were Catholics according to their own understanding, and the Diet of Augsburg

[16]How seriously Luther took the clear distinction between the offices as a matter of faith appears from the fact that he included his doctrine on the three orders (*ordo ecclesiasticus, oeconomicus, politicus*) in his *Confession* of 1528. His view on the relationship between the ecclesiastical and the political orders always remained the same as in his book *Von weltlicher Obrigkeit, wie weit man ihr Gehorsam schuldig sei* of 1523 (WA 11, 229 ff ; Philad. 3, 223 ff) and it became the official doctrine of the Lutheran church in *Aug. Conf.* 28, 12: 'The power of the Church and the civil power must not be confounded' (Trigl. 85). In contrast to Zwingli, who as a matter of principle left the government of the church to the Christian magistrate, Luther always denied to the secular authority the government, or even a share in it, of the church. When he asked his Elector to arrange for church visitation, he appealed to him as a prominent member of the church, not as the secular ruler, as he made clear from the outset. That the princes later claimed this right as belonging to their office was against Luther's intention, and met with his strong protest. However, he was not able to stop a development that took place even in Calvinistic countries against the doctrine of their confessions. It should also be borne in mind that it was not the pope, but the king, who brought the Reformation to a standstill in France, and that in turn the Roman church had to recognize the ecclesiastical rights of the crown.

was — for the participants as for the onlookers — an event that took place within the one church of the one Holy Empire. The *Augsburg Confession* was quite serious when it expressed the hope that

> the dissension, by God's help, may be done away and brought back to one true accordant religion; for as we all are under one Christ and do battle under Him, we ought to confess the one Christ,[17]

though the last Article does envisage the possibility of a final breach.[18] To us this seems to be an incredible optimism, especially on the part of Luther and his adherents, while Zwingli and others were more sceptical. But actually no one at that time had given up the hope that somehow the unity of Christendom would be preserved or restored. The aim of all Reformers was to reform the church, not to build a new church, or even several churches.

The question, therefore, with which the adherents of the Reformation were confronted was how the achievements of the Reformation could be preserved, and the plans of the adversaries frustrated. The answers to this question differed according to varying religious convictions. Political necessities had led to the formation of alliances in Germany as well as in Switzerland. The issue in Germany was whether or not the Edict of Worms should and could be carried out in the absence of the Emperor (who right after the Diet of Worms had to leave Germany for his wars against Francis, to return only in 1530 before the Diet of Augsburg). After the anti-Lutheran princes of southern Germany and northern Germany had established political federations, at Regensburg in 1524, and at Dessau in 1525, respectively, for the purpose of suppressing the Reformation, several Lutheran territories under the leadership of John, Elector of Saxony, and Philip of Hesse formed a defensive alliance at Gotha and Torgau in 1526, shortly before the first Diet of Spires had to leave it to the conscience of each territorial authority how to deal with the Edict of Worms. This decision, caused by the outbreak of a new war between Charles V and Francis I, gave the Reformation a breathing-space, at least for a few years.

A similar development took place in Switzerland, which after the turn of the century was practically independent of the Empire. Here, too, the adversaries of the Reformation became politically active after the year 1524. Within a few years, the Swiss Federation

---

[17]AC Preface (Trigl. 41).

[18]AC, Article 28, last words.

(*Eidgenossenschaft*), which consisted of tiny cantons, was divided. The centre of the resistance against Zwingli's Reformation lay in the old, conservative cantons around Lake Lucerne (where the fight for freedom from the yoke of Habsburg had started); Zurich was the stronghold of the Reformation, soon to be followed by Berne (in 1528) and Basle (in 1529). The religious split was the more dangerous as it threatened not only the unity of the small groups, but even the very existence of independent Switzerland. Zwingli, who in 1524 had resigned from his office at the Great Minster to become the leader of the Reformation in the service of the state, must have suffered from a real 'nightmare of coalitions', to use Bismarck's words. For the coalition of the old Catholic cantons of 1524 was extended to other cantons in 1527. Negotiations with Ferdinand, the brother and substitute of the emperor, continued. North of the Swiss border, Wuerttemberg had been put under the administration of Ferdinand after Duke Ulrich had been forced to resign. Thus, not only the cause of the Reformation was at stake but also the freedom of Switzerland.

We must always keep this in mind in order to understand Zwingli's politics. He had to look for allies outside his own country. The free cities of south-western Germany, which had formed a loose federation after 1524 under the able leadership of Strasburg, had to be won for a coalition. Strong relationships had already been formed, since culturally Switzerland was still a part of south-western Germany. This part of Germany stood between the reformations of Wittenberg and Zurich, always open to influences from either side. The borderline between Lutheranism and Zwinglianism was still fluctuating, and Strasburg, under the theological leadership of Bucer, seemed to become the centre of a new type of reformation, which later spread to Calvin's Geneva under the strong influence of Bucer's theology. It is not surprising, then, that Strasburg was the birthplace of what today is called 'Protestantism', as something transcending Lutheranism and Zwinglianism, and that the same city brought together Zwingli and Philip of Hesse, the two champions of a noble attempt to save the cause of the Reformation by political action.

In 1524, at the age of twenty, Philip had accepted the Lutheran Reformation for himself and his territory. In 1526 he became the leading figure of the Gotha-Torgau federation of the Lutheran princes, a promising and far-sighted politician. He had become a Lutheran by conviction. In 1526 he still expressed himself very strongly against what at that time he called the error of Zwingli concerning the Sacrament. He soon began to waver in his Lutheran convictions under the influence of Strasburg and of the Swiss reformers, but he never gave up his Christian faith (though he later abstained for years from Holy Communion, in view of his sinful life which had brought so much shame on the Lutheran church). His cousin, Ulrich of Wuerttemberg, had made friends with Oecolampadius in Basle, where he lived in exile before he went to live with the Landgrave (one of the witnesses, by the way, of the Marburg Colloquy). Thus, Philip began to appreciate the *via media* of Strasburg, and soon he accepted it. From Bucer he learned that the difference between Luther and Zwingli was not insuperable, and that it should be possible to find a *syncretismus* on the basis of a common study of the Bible. This theological development went hand in hand with a new understanding of the political situation. Philip accepted the view of Zwingli and the politicians and theologians of Strasburg that nothing short of a federation of all Protestant territories could save the cause of the Reformation.

All alliances made in those critical years after 1524 were based on common religious convictions, if not yet on formulated confessions. The doctrinal basis for the Catholic alliances in Germany and Switzerland was clear. The Gotha-Torgau alliance was based on the common understanding of the Gospel reached by the theologians of Franconia (Ansbach and Nuremberg) and Wittenberg in 1525.[19] It was a real consensus, though not yet expressed in a common confession. This consensus was to be strengthened during the following years especially by the appearance of the writings prepared for the great church visitation in Saxony (specifically Melanchthon's *Instruction for Visitors* and Luther's *Catechisms*), as well as by Luther's books against the enthusiasts and 'sacramentarians'. The question for Philip was whether it would be possible to create a broader confessional basis that would allow the inclusion of the cities of south-western Germany and Reformed Switzerland. The means for attaining such doctrinal agreement was to be the religious colloquy, which had replaced the synod in settling religious controversies.[20]

———

[19]See the opinion (*Bedenken*) of Luther, Jonas, Bugenhagen, Melanchthon in a letter to the Elector of September 6, 1525, concerning a confession which had been drafted at Ansbach in Franconia in 1524, WA BR 3, 918.

[20]It should be borne in mind what an important role the long range of religious colloquies played in the 16th and 17th centuries: those between Lutherans and Catholics (Leipzig 1519, Hagenau and Worms 1540, Regensburg 1541); Zwinglians

Thus, the arrangement of a colloquy was planned by Philip in 1527, as we have seen. Henceforth it was his aim to overcome the resistance of Luther — he declared he would bring together Oecolampadius, Luther, and their adherents for a colloquy even if it should cost him 6,000 guilders — and to win the Lutheran princes for his political plan of a pan-evangelical alliance based on an agreement to be reached at that colloquy. The task became more and more difficult as the Great Controversy proceeded, and the gulf between the parties widened. At the same time, it became more and more urgent, as the political developments after the year 1528 seemed to lead to a catastrophe. Already in 1528, Germany was on the brink of a religious war, which at the last moment was avoided. The tension in Switzerland was growing, and a war seemed inevitable, since the Catholic cantons had reached an agreement with Ferdinand. The Turks stood at the gates of Vienna. The Emperor had defeated Francis, and was expected to return to Germany in the near future. How Luther felt at that time can be seen from his hymn 'A Mighty Fortress is Our God', which appeared in the critical days of 1528:

> *Mit unserer Macht ist nichts getan / Wir sind gar bald verloren / Es streit für uns der rechte Mann / Den Gott selbst hat erkoren.*

This was Luther's answer to the question as to how the cause of the Reformation could be saved. But was this sufficient? What ought **we** to do in that desperate situation of the church? was the question which Philip of Hesse and Zwingli asked themselves and tried to answer.

Before we continue reviewing the events of the fateful months preceding the Marburg Colloquy, we shall try to understand the theological problems that had to be decided. The first problem was the relationship between **confession** and **federation**. Federal action does not, of course, presuppose a common confession if only secular

---

and Catholics (Zurich 1523, Baden 1527, Berne 1528); Lutherans and Zwinglians (Marburg 1529); Lutherans and Calvinists (Montbéliard 1584, Leipzig 1631); Gnesio-Lutherans and Philippists (Weimar 1560); Catholics, Calvinists, and Lutherans (Thorn 1645); not to mention others. An outgrowth of academic disputation, the colloquy becomes the most important way of discussing doctrinal matters. Presided over by princes, as the ecumenical synods were by emperors, or in Zurich by the city council, colloquies were regarded by the people as great events. It was by no means pleasure in this sort of fight that made people of all walks of life interested in them. Behind this interest there lies, rather, a deep longing for religious truth, such as is unknown to the present age. This is true even if almost all colloquies had a political aspect or were caused by political interests.

matters are involved. Luther would never have objected to a common action of Catholic and Protestant states against the Turk — if we may use these terms in the modern sense. On the contrary, he was very much in favour of it, though he never would share the Catholic view that such a war was a crusade. A federation, however, with the purpose of defending the Gospel against its enemies was something quite different. We shall later quote some utterances by Luther in which he rejects every political alliance meant to defend the Gospel, because Christ alone can do that. However, he recognized the practical necessity of an alliance like that of Gotha-Torgau as an answer to the alliances of the adversaries. How could the evangelical princes fulfil their duties toward their people if they did not act harmoniously at the Diet and on other occasions?

The question of waging war was a different matter. If it was a defensive war to protect the country against aggression, no serious objection could be raised, while a war to defend the Gospel was quite impossible, according to Luther. Common political action in defending the Reformation by peaceful and lawful means presupposed a common understanding of the Gospel. The difference between the Lutheran theologians and princes, on the one hand, and Philip of Hesse, the politicians and theologians of Strasburg, and Zwingli, on the other hand, consisted only in the measure of agreement required on either side. While, for Luther, the doctrine on the Sacrament of the Altar was to be included in such an agreement, Bucer and Zwingli were convinced that this was not an article of faith in the strict sense, and that a broad formula that would leave freedom of interpretation could be accepted by either side. Even Zwingli would not have considered a federation with the Anabaptists possible. Thus, there seemed to be a certain amount of agreement on the problem of 'confession and federation'.

On closer inspection, however, it becomes evident that the broadmindedness of Zwingli, Bucer, and their political friends was not only a consequence of their understanding of the Sacrament. Luther's doctrine on the Real Presence was unacceptable to them, because it was regarded as a remnant of papal errors. To tolerate it would be an inconsistency, in view of everything Zwingli had said about this doctrine, behind which he could not but see the Antichrist.[21] The latitudinarianism of this side actually meant a

---

[21]This was at the beginning of the *Amica exegesis*. The apparent self-contradiction may be partly explained by the assumption that Zwingli made use of a traditional

subordination of the 'confession' to the 'federation', and of doctrine to politics. It was politics if Philip and Zwingli demanded a federation irrespective of the grave difference concerning the Sacrament. One must appreciate their point of view in order to understand the events immediately preceding Marburg and the colloquy itself.

The question raised by Zwingli and Philip was the problem of the relationship between **church** and **politics**, which accompanies the entire history of the church. Can the Christian church live in this world, as it is, without entering the field of politics? Was it possible during the years of the Reformation? Is it possible today? Is it not unrealistic to expect Christ to protect his Church without our own endeavours? This is a matter of principle, quite apart from the persons engaged in the discussions and negotiations of those years. This question, which has gained such reality in modern times, when the activism of the Reformed churches of the West clashed with what is called 'Lutheran passivity', can be answered only in this way: As Christians, of course, we ought to act; the question is only **what** to do.

Luther was one of the busiest men of his age, and an amazing amount of work was done by the old Lutheran church especially during periods when its cause seemed to be lost. Just as the Early Church did not attempt to save its existence either by trying to make a concordat with Nero, Domitian, and Decius, or by stirring up a revolution against these tyrants, or by making an alliance with the Persian Empire, but simply by confessing the truth of the Gospel and building up a truly confessing church whose members were prepared to die for the faith, so Luther and the early Lutheran church confined themselves to do what the Church, according to its nature as an ordinance of God, can and ought to be doing. Her sword is not a temporal one (Matt. 26:52), but 'the sword of the Spirit, which is the word of God' (Eph. 6:17).

When speaking of Zwingli, we have seen that for him such separation between church and politics was quite impossible. It is characteristic that his monument at Zurich shows him holding the Bible in his right hand, and supporting it with a sword in his left hand. To be a preacher and a politician at the same time belongs to

---

polemic against the Roman doctrine of transubstantiation as an 'invention of Antichrist' (Wyclif, see above, 45) or a 'satanic invention' (Honius, see above, 99) without realizing that if Luther's understanding of the Real Presence came under the same verdict it could not possibly be tolerated.

his very nature, as it also is characteristic of the Reformation at Zurich that the decisive disputation of 1523 between the theologians was held in the presence of the people, the open Bible lying on a table, while the city council decided whose doctrine was the truly biblical one. Under such conditions as prevailed in Switzerland, and to a certain degree at Strasburg, the Reformation was necessarily an ecclesiastical, and at the same time a political, affair. It was, perhaps, practically impossible to separate the two. Hence, for Zwingli, the use of political means, even alliances of a merely political nature (and wars, if necessary), were means not only to save the Reformation from its enemies, but even to further the Gospel in the world. It can easily be understood that this man became the friend of Philip of Hesse, who shared his view. Both were *Realpolitiker,* though as Christians they were deeply convinced that the Christian church on earth must be defended also by earthly means. Both had to learn, Zwingli at Kappel, and Philip in the Smalcald War, where such alleged 'political realism' leads to.

The time for the Landgrave to act came when the second Diet of Spires in April 1529 by a vast majority voted to withdraw the concessions made by the Diet of 1526 under pressure exerted by Ferdinand. The new decision led to the famous *Protestation* which later gave rise to the words 'Protestant' and 'Protestantism'.[22] The courageous signatories of this bold document, six princes and fourteen cities, claimed that the decree of the previous Diet (which contained the express statement that it had been adopted unanimously) could not be legally annulled except by a unanimous vote.

> Furthermore, because in matters pertaining to the glory of God and the salvation of our souls, every man must himself give an answer for his conduct, so

[22]It has already been pointed out how misleading it would be to expect to find our modern ideas of 'Protestantism' at that time. Even if the beginnings of a feeling of solidarity between the various shades of the Reformation movement from Wittenberg to Zurich were already present, the mere thought of demanding toleration also for the 'enthusiasts' and Anabaptists was inconceivable to them. The *Protestation* refers constantly to the 'pure and unadulterated Word of God', the 'Divine Scriptures' as the authority which the confessors follow. How, then, could they, without giving up their claim and denying their faith, fight for the freedom to reject this final authority, as the enthusiasts did? How could they recognize the Anabaptists, who with the denial of that Baptism which the church had practised for 1,500 years sought to destroy the Catholic church, whose faithful members the 'Protestants' of 1529 claimed to be?

> that in this respect no man can conceal himself behind other people's acts or behind majority resolutions.[23]

It was a small minority which in those decisive days fought for that Protestantism, the nature of which is not the protest **against** what usually is called Catholicism, nor what modern man calls the right of 'private judgment' in contrast to religious authority, but rather the stand **for** the inalienable freedom of a Christian man to follow his conscience as it is **bound by God's Word**.

It is quite natural that the common action of the protesting states at the Diet at once raised the question whether a closer alliance of a permanent nature was not possible. Thus far, Lutheran territories had been federated in the Gotha-Torgau alliance, while the cities of south-west Germany, under the leadership of Strasburg, had formed a loose federation that tried to keep in touch with the definitely-Lutheran states as well as with the Zwinglian cantons of Switzerland. The theological *via media,* as represented by the Strasburg theologians Bucer and Capito with their strong leanings toward Zwingli, had its political counterpart in the policy of Jacob Sturm, the leader of Strasburg's foreign politics, who wholeheartedly supported the plan of the Landgrave for a wider alliance.[24] Now, Lutheran territories had 'protested' — and that means 'confessed' — not only with the cities of Bucer's persuasion, but even with St Gallen (at that time still a free city of Germany, which had accepted Zwingli's Reformation). If ever Philip's plan was feasible, it was in that hour of emergency and confession. Within three days after the 'Protestation', Philip, indeed, succeeded in concluding a secret pact of defence with Saxony, Nuremberg, Strasburg, and Ulm. When Melanchthon, on his return to Wittenberg, told Luther about this, the Reformer wrote twice to his

---

[23]Quoted from the translation of the *Protestation* by J. Bodensieck in the outstanding book by Michael Reu, *The Augsburg Confession. A Collection of Sources with an Historical Introduction* (Wartburg Publishing House, 1930), 487 ff (the quoted passage, 489). The attention of the reader is called to this highly-important collection of sources in English translation and to Reu's excellent Introduction.

[24]Sturm, the representative of Strasburg at the two Diets of Spires and at that of Augsburg as well as at other meetings, took part also in the Marburg Colloquy. He was one of the most farsighted and broadminded politicians of German Protestantism, one of the founders of the Smalcald League in 1531. In the question of the Sacrament he supported Bucer and Philip of Hesse. For years he did not go to Holy Communion, being deeply distressed about the disunity of the theologians.

Elector expressing a grave warning against this alliance.[25] He questioned the political wisdom of the alliance, since it would only provoke the adversaries to make another alliance.

> Moreover the fear is only too well grounded . . . that the Landgrave . . . will find some occasion, not only for self-defence, but for aggression.[26]

How right Luther was in anticipating that self-defence could mean a preventive war became obvious a few weeks later, on June 8, when Zurich, on the advice of Zwingli, declared war against the Catholic cantons of central Switzerland. This war had been prepared and strategically planned by Zwingli, who accompanied the troops, a chaplain on horseback with a halberd on his shoulder. This time bloodshed was avoided. But the peace which was made on June 26 did not satisfy Zwingli. The first of his conditions was that

> the five cantons should allow God's Word to be preached according to the New and Old Testaments,[27]

but this aim was not reached because the people did not like to employ violence in a matter concerning the Word of God.[28] Zwingli foresaw that this would lead to another war, which actually did break out two years later, bringing about Zwingli's death on the battlefield.

Precisely during the weeks of Zwingli's preventive war for the Gospel, Luther wrote his letters against the pact of defence:

> It is certain that such an alliance is not of God and does not come from trust in Him, but is a device of human wits . . . In the Old Testament God always condemns leagues for human help, as, for instance, in Isaiah 7, 8, and 30. He says, 'If ye remain quiet and trust, ye shall be helped'. We ought to be God's children of faith, in true confidence. But if we are to have a league, He will send us one without our seeking it or worrying about it, as He promises in Matthew 6, 'Have no care; all this will come to you if you seek first the kingdom of God'; and St Peter says, 'Cast your care upon Him, for He careth for you'; and Isaiah, 'Who art thou that fearest mortal men?'.[29]

---

[25]Letter of May 22, WA BR 5, 75f, No. 1424; English translation in *Luther's Correspondence and Other Contemporary Letters* by Preserved Smith and Charles Jacobs, Vol. II, 478 ff. Luther's opinion (*Bedenken*) of July or August, WA BR 5, 78 ff.

[26]This and the following quotations from the letters are taken from Smith-Jacobs, 478 ff.

[27]W. Koehler, *Huldrych Zwingli*, 195. Koehler (172) quotes the characteristic saying of Zwingli that federations are made 'primarily to the honour of God and in order to pave the way for His Blessed Word'.

[28]W. Koehler, *op. cit.*, 196.

[29]Smith-Jacobs, 479 f; WA BR 5, 76 f, No. 1424.

When the alliance was interpreted as a lawful and necessary defence against a political aggressor, Luther replied than an aggression would in this case be made only on account of the doctrine. The Gospel, however, cannot be defended except by Christ himself. Since Luther did not approve of any religious war, any crusade, he could not recognize a political alliance as a proper means to defend the church, especially when this alliance comprised people of various religious convictions. How can the Gospel be confessed and defended by such a league, most of whose members

> are those who strive against God and the Sacrament, and are wilful enemies of God and His Word? By making league with them we take upon ourselves the burden of all their wickedness and blasphemy.[30]

Not even the most desperate situation of the church can, in Luther's opinion, justify such an alliance. Is not the situation of the Gospel and the Church of the Gospel in this world always desperate? And must not the alliance with those who do not accept the truth of the Gospel lead to federations in which the quest for truth is completely neglected? It is a most remarkable fact that the same Zwingli who wanted to promote the cause of the Reformation by political and even military means, when he arrived a few days before the colloquy at Marburg, submitted to the Landgrave a political plan which included an alliance with anti-Habsburg enemies of the Gospel like the king of France; in fact, both Zwingli and Philip, in the years that followed, tried to bring about a great coalition in which all anti-Habsburg powers of Europe, including the Turk, would fight for the Gospel by fighting against the Emperor.

It was this political thinking in matters of faith that Luther successfully fought at that time. His Elector followed his advice. In June, or a little later, a strictly-Lutheran confession was written, which was intended as a basis for a future federation.[31] With this confession Luther went to Marburg. It became the basis of the *Marburg Articles.* After the colloquy it was accepted by the Lutheran territories at Schwabach near Nuremberg. The following year these *Schwabach Articles* became the basis of the first part of the

---

[30]Smith-Jacobs, 479; WA BR 5, 77, No. 1424, lines 35 ff.

[31]Hans von Schubert, *Bekenntnisbildung und Religionspolitik* (1910), has definitely proved that the *Schwabach Articles* were written in the summer of 1529 before the Marburg Colloquy. For details, see M. Reu, *The Augsburg Confession,* Introduction, especially 12 ff, and Walther Koehler, *Zwingli und Luther, II,* 46. Koehler thinks of September as the time of their origin.

Augsburg Confession, the 'Chief Articles of Faith'. The Lutheran, anti-Zwinglian character of the *Schwabach Articles* appears in Article 10 on the Lord's Supper, in which it is stated

> that there is truly present in the bread and in the wine the true body and blood of Christ according to the sound of the words: 'This is my body, this is my blood', and that it is not only bread and wine, as even now the other side asserts.[32]

It is significant that the two lines, of theological thought and political action, went side by side. On October 3, the last day of the Marburg Colloquy, a meeting was begun at Schleiz between John, the Elector of Saxony, George, Margrave of Brandenburg-Ansbach, and councillors sent by Philip of Hesse to consider the future politics. The participants could not possibly know the result of Marburg. It was clear even then that the Articles adopted at Schwabach in October, rather than the *Marburg Articles,* would be the basis of the alliance of the Lutherans. They were accepted as a matter of deep conviction by Saxony, Brandenburg-Ansbach, and Nuremberg, and for political reasons by the Landgrave, but were rejected by Strasburg and Ulm. This meant that the 'Protestants' would not appear at the Diet of Augsburg as a united front; the 'confession' was to prevail over the 'federation'. The Marburg Colloquy, which tried to subordinate theology and confession of faith to political necessities, was bound to be a failure.

And yet, the attempt had to be made to find out whether or not a broader basis might be found for a federation of the evangelical states. As an experiment to find out whether a colloquy would produce better results than the literary controversy, the plan of the Landgrave, in spite of its being primarily a political enterprise, was of great theological and ecclesiastical importance.[33]

---

[32]Quoted from the translation by H. E. Jacobs in M. Reu, *The Augsburg Confession,* 43. The German text is to be found in the Goettingen edition of *Die Bekenntnisschriften der evangelisch-lutherischen Kirche,* 65. Koehler, *op. cit.,* 47 f, has rightly observed that the formulation is less strict than that of the *Large Confession,* insofar as the *manducatio oralis* and the *manducatio impiorum* are not directly mentioned. However, neither the omission of these logical consequences from the presence of body and blood 'in' the elements, nor the failure to mention the strengthening of faith in the believing communicants as a fruit of the Sacrament can be interpreted as a weakening of the Lutheran doctrine. There may have been the hope, as Koehler thinks, that Strasburg and Ulm also would accept this expression of Lutheran doctrine, but it cannot be regarded as *Unionsbekenntnis* (48).

[33]'*Das Marburger Religionsgespräch ist eine politische Aktion gewesen, hervorgerufen durch die aus dem Speyrer Reichstag 1529 geschaffene Notwendigkeit des Zusammenschlusses der Evangelischen*' (W. Koehler, *op. cit.,* 62).

The political character of Philip's endeavour appears from the fact that the first step toward the realization of his old plan was made at Spires on April 22 — the very day that he succeeded in bringing about that secret alliance with Saxony, Ulm, and Strasburg. And, again, it is significant that the first letter written with regard to that matter was addressed to Zwingli:

> We are endeavouring to bring together at some suitable place Luther and Melanchthon and some of those who hold your view of the Sacrament, so that, if a merciful God grants us His favour, they may come to some **scriptural agreement** about that doctrine and live in **harmony, as becomes Christians**. For at this Diet the papists were unable to assign any other reason for clinging to their perverse life and customs except to say that **we who profess the entire and clear Word of God do not agree among ourselves** on the doctrine of our religion. If this were not the case it would be easy to remedy matters, so that these childish things could quickly be changed (*emphasis mine*).[34]

This is the letter of a politician whose understanding of the religious situation of Christendom is surprisingly poor. The split between the 'Protestants' is regarded as the great hindrance to the progress of the Reformation. If this were healed, the papists would have no excuse for remaining what they are. It can be healed, for Lutherans and Zwinglians profess the entire and clear Word of God. Hence 'some scriptural agreement' can and must be found, and this would end the shame of the division which does not become Christians.

The theological ideas expressed in this letter from a prince who wanted to be a Lutheran are those of Zwingli and Bucer. Zwingli, as we have seen, never regarded the doctrinal difference as church-divisive. He was prepared to tolerate Luther's doctrine though he was convinced that it was against the clear doctrine of Scripture, but he was enough of a politician to overlook this difference and to regard Luther as a Christian brother, provided Luther would take the same attitude toward him. Bucer, the man of the *via media*, believed in the possibility not only of mutual toleration, but of finding a scriptural formula that could satisfy both parties; all that was required was a careful study of the Scriptures. He had emphasized the common biblical basis, especially in his commentary on *Zephaniah* (1528). We should always keep in mind that Bucer was one of the fathers of that biblicism which we later find in the pietistic movements. The study of the Bible would show, this was his conviction, what really was essential in the Christian faith, and what not. We shall discuss his eucharistic doctrine later;[35] suffice it here to state that at the time of the Great Controversy and at Marburg he, together with Zwingli,

---

[34]Quoted from Smith-Jacobs, II, 474 (No. 826).

[35]See below, 244 ff.

rejected the literal meaning of the *est*, while, on the other hand, in disagreement with Zwingli, he taught a spiritual presence of the body of Christ in the Sacrament. These ideas of Zwingli and Bucer seemed to the Landgrave to offer a basis for an agreement, or rather a compromise. As a matter of fact, neither he nor Zwingli expected the colloquy to produce any real settlement of the theological problem. Both were looking for a practical compromise that could form the basis for a common political action by all 'Protestants' against the Emperor and the papal church.

It was this political aspect of the whole matter which had caused Luther to decline the first invitation in 1527, and which made him utterly suspicious of the colloquy that was now being prepared. Even Melanchthon, who had been persuaded at Spires to agree to the plan of a personal discussion between Oecolampadius and Luther (Zwingli's name was not even mentioned by the Landgrave to the Lutherans in these negotiations, though the Reformer of Zurich had been the first to get an invitation), soon became very doubtful as to the wisdom of arranging a colloquy, at least at this juncture. He knew that, after the unsuccessful literary discussions of all these years, in which all possible arguments had been brought forward, there could not be the slightest hope for reaching a doctrinal agreement by way of a brief personal debate. And a more-or-less political compromise was out of the question for the Lutherans. At Wittenberg Luther and his colleagues could not but see in the proposed colloquy a clever move by the Landgrave in support of his political aims. And were they not right? It was on the journey to Marburg that they first heard unofficially about the invitation that had been extended to and accepted by Zwingli. Why had Philip employed such secret diplomacy instead of frankly appealing to their Christian duty to do the utmost in order to save the true unity of the church? Was it really the unity of the church that the Landgrave had in mind?

All this explains the attempts made by Luther and his colleagues to persuade the Elector to reject Philip's plan. One measure suggested was that he should refuse them leave of absence from the university. In case the colloquy should be held, Melanchthon, and later also Luther himself, suggested that 'two honest papists' should be invited.[36] This suggestion, curious as it may seem to us, shows first of

[36]Melanchthon to Elector John, May 16 (CR I, 1066, compare EA 54, 86, where the memorandum is ascribed to Luther). The Elector accepted the proposal in a letter of May 19 to Melanchthon (CR I, 1072), but the Landgrave rejected the suggestion. Luther wrote about it to Brenz on August 29 (WA BR 5, 141, No. 1470, lines 17 f).

all that the Lutherans were still hoping for a preservation or restoration of the unity of Christendom. Besides, the presence of some Roman theologians would have made it impossible for the Landgrave to make political capital out of a serious theological discussion. It was only at the urgent request of his Elector that Luther accepted the invitation for a colloquy to be held at Michaelmas at Marburg. From Luther's reply to the Elector, who had transmitted the preliminary invitation by the Landgrave, it may be concluded that Philip now strongly emphasized the Christian aspect of his plan, and that the Elector assured Luther that he was not prepared to sacrifice the confession of truth to the expediency of politics. The articles of faith drawn up by the theologians of Wittenberg, which Luther took to Marburg and which we have already come to know as the *Schwabach Articles*, are closely connected with the consent of Luther to go to Marburg.

The carefully-styled and courteous letter that Luther wrote at the end of June to the Landgrave expressed his grateful acceptance of the invitation, but states at the same time, quite frankly, Luther's misgivings concerning the possible results:

> I thoroughly believe that Your Grace is altogether serious about this matter and really means it well, and therefore I, too, am willingly inclined to render Your Grace's Christian project what I fear is a vain, and for us, possibly, a dangerous service. For I, too, heartily delight in peace.[37]

Luther continues, frankly voicing his fear

> that our opponents are seeking to use Your Grace's diligence . . . that they may hereafter be able to boast that it was not their fault; that they had gotten so great a prince to move, etc. Thus they will use Your Grace's name to accuse us of harshness . . . as though we had no desire for peace and truth.

He then asks the Landgrave to

> inquire of the other side whether they are inclined to yield their opinion, so that the trouble may not become worse than ever. For ... all conferences are wasted and all meetings are in vain if both parties come to them with no intention of yielding anything. It has been my past experience that they will insist on their own ideas after our arguments have been fairly presented; that I cannot yield after their arguments have been presented, I know as certainly as I know they are in error.

If, as the Landgrave intimated, bloodshed might result from a failure to reach unity about the question of the Sacrament,

———

[37]WA BR 5, No. 1438. Our quotations are taken from Smith-Jacobs, II, 483 f, No. 837.

> Your Grace must also know that if this should result (which God forbid) we shall be altogether guiltless of it. It is nothing new that turbulent spirits cause bloodshed. They have proved it before by Francis von Sickingen, and by Carlstadt and Muenzer, and afterwards, by God's grace, we were found entirely innocent. But may Christ our Lord tread Satan under His feet and ours.[38]

It was with this attitude toward the colloquy that Luther consented to go to Marburg. Modern Protestants will be inclined to accuse him of stubbornness and implacability. He could see a real result only if his opponent would yield. What about himself? As we shall see, he, too, was prepared to yield. But he was never prepared to deny, or even to compromise, what he had recognized to be the clear doctrine of Holy Scripture.

Thus, Luther went to Marburg, not as a negotiator, but as a confessor — not as a confessor of some private opinion, but of the Word of God. This Word was for him *extra controversiam.* If the opponents could show that this doctrine was not in accordance with the Word of God, he would, of course, have to yield and to revoke his confession of 1528.[39] But the Great Controversy of the previous years had convinced him that they were unable to refute him from Scripture. So he went to the colloquy without any hope for what the world would have called success, and yet prepared to do this best. And had he not learnt during the twelve years since 1517 that a faithful minister of the Word can do nothing but confess the truth of this Word, leaving it to God as to what the outcome may be?

2. The Colloquy

On Thursday, September 30, Luther arrived at Marburg, accompanied by Melanchthon, Justus Jonas, Cruciger, Roerer (and, perhaps, Veit Dietrich) from Wittenberg; Fr Myconius from Gotha; Justus Menius and a layman, Captain E. von der Thann, from Eisenach. The Lutherans from southern Germany: Osiander from Nuremberg, Stephen Agricola from Augsburg, and Brenz from Schwäbisch-Hall, arrived on Saturday afternoon during the second session of the colloquy. Zwingli, with the delegates from Zurich, Basle and Strasburg, had already reached Marburg on Monday,

---

[38]This means: Luther had been held responsible for the revolutionary actions of the lower nobility under Sickingen's leadership and for the Peasant's War and other riots. Meanwhile, all sensible persons had seen that the doctrine and practice of these men were contrary to Luther's understanding of the Gospel.

[39]In this sense only, H. Gollwitzer, *Theol. Aufsätze für K. Barth,* 290, is right in stating that for Luther the Colloquy was decided before it began.

September 27.[40] He represented Zurich, together with his friend Rudolph Collin, Professor of Greek, and Councillor Funk, a political official. From Basle Oecolampadius had come with Rudolph Frey as a political representative. The Swiss delegates had travelled via Strasburg, where they had stayed for ten days. This offered an opportunity not only to prepare themselves with the theologians of Strasburg for the theological discussion, but also to discuss the political situation with the authorities.

During those very days it was learned that a peace treaty had been signed between the emperor and the pope (who had been the ally of Francis), which made the situation of Protestantism all the more serious. On their departure from Marburg they were joined by the delegates from Strasburg, namely, the theologians Bucer and Hedio, and the eminent politician Jacob Sturm, whom we have already mentioned. During the days of waiting at Marburg, Oecolampadius, Hedio, and Zwingli were invited to preach in the presence of the Landgrave.

Otherwise, these days were devoted to political discussions, especially between Philip and Zwingli. Even if the colloquy should remain more or less unsuccessful, the result of this exchange of views on the political situation, and on the measures to be taken against the emperor, was very probably a real success for Zwingli. Th. Kolde says about these negotiations:

> Zwingli had already obtained what was most important for him, even before the delegates from Saxony had appeared.[41]

Even if this might be regarded as an overstatement in view of future developments, for the moment the coordination of the plans of the two great protagonists for an all-Protestant political union was of utmost importance.

When Luther and his party arrived on the appointed day, they were greeted in a friendly manner, and, like all delegates, were well received as guests of the Landgrave. The courtesy and diplomatic skill of the host helped to create that friendly atmosphere which prevailed during the entire colloquy, despite some serious moments during the discussions. Though nothing was done, or could be done, to conceal the deep contrast between the theological views held by the two sides, a Christian attitude was shown by everyone. In this

---

[40] W. Koehler, *Huldrych Zwingli,* 199 f.

[41] *Martin Luther* (1893), II, 312.

respect, the Marburg Colloquy compares favourably with other meetings and synods. It was far more peaceful, in spite of the profound differences that led to the final breach between the Lutheran and the Reformed church, than, for example, the Vatican Council.

The first day was given exclusively to personal meetings among the delegates, who thus far had known each other only from their writings. Luther had a friendly talk with Oecolampadius. He greeted Bucer half-seriously and half-jokingly with the words: 'You are a naughty boy'.[42] Zwingli he did not meet on that day, so it seems. The following day, Friday, October 1, was devoted to preliminary discussions between Luther and Oecolampadius on the one hand, and Zwingli and Melanchthon on the other. On Saturday morning at six o'clock, the colloquy proper began. It lasted throughout the day, with a break for lunch, and was continued on Sunday with a morning and an afternoon session. On Sunday evening, some very important private negotiations were held regarding a formula for union suggested by Luther after the colloquy had come to a close. It is significant that Luther, despite the obvious failure of the discussions, made a last-minute attempt to redeem the situation by proposing a formula which, though expressing the doctrine of the Real Presence, avoided everything that could offend the other side.

When this attempt, too, had failed, the Landgrave, who wanted some action taken, requested that new private discussions be held on Monday morning for the purpose of reaching at least a practical compromise. Eventually the Landgrave asked Luther to draft articles on the doctrines in which agreement had been reached. Luther obliged, and, on the basis of the *Schwabach Articles*, wrote the fifteen *Marburg Articles* which, after a brief discussion, were adopted and signed by the theological delegates on the Lutheran side, and by those from Switzerland and from Strasburg.

The hurry in which the negotiations were concluded, and the haste of the departure of the participants on Tuesday (the Landgrave left in the morning, Luther and his party in the afternoon, the Swiss and the Strasburgers probably on the same day) is said to have been due to the *sudor Anglicus*, a very dangerous epidemic, which some

[42]'*Tu es nequam*'. Luther had no real confidence in Bucer after the affair that Luther could only regard as a forgery of Bugenhagen's and his own writings. See above, 113. See also the words spoken to Bucer and the Strasburgers at the end of the colloquy, below, 213, 214.

months before had spread throughout Germany, and had now suddenly broken out in Marburg.[43]

The question has sometimes been asked whether and how far a *communicatio in sacris* had been practised between the participants at Marburg.[44] In answering that question we must keep in mind that at that time there was no 'Lutheran' or 'Reformed' churches in the later sense of those designations. All participants were 'Catholic' Christians who wanted the Catholic church reformed, even if they differed as to the way of such reformation. Consequently, the modern problem of altar-, pulpit-, and church-fellowship among churches did not yet exist. It can be said that there was no common celebration of the Sacrament. The sermons preached before Luther arrived have been mentioned. Luther himself preached a sermon on 'The great, noble article of faith, called Forgiveness of Sins', probably not on Sunday but on the day of departure.[45] In his *Table Talk* there is an indication that he heard two sermons at Marburg, one preached by Zwingli and another one by Bucer.[46] The program on Sunday, October 3, would have left room for a very early service only. The common meals, of course, began with a prayer. Hedio relates that on Monday Luther 'blessed the food'.[47] As was the

[43]It is mentioned in Luther's letter written to his wife on Oct. 4 (WA BR 5, No. 1476, 24 f. Since it is found in the postscript only, it is missing in the translation by Smith-Jacobs, II, 496, No. 851). Luther mentions the panic caused by the sudden outbreak of the disease, which proved to be very mild at Marburg, where only one case occurred (and that not a fatal one). In a letter addressed to Camerarius on the following day, Melanchthon gives this as the reason why the Landgrave hurried to dismiss the convention (CR I, 1098) which originally was planned for about a week. — The 'English Sweat' had first appeared in England in 1485; more outbreaks occurred until 1551. The worst epidemic was that of 1529 when it spread via Hamburg to the Continent and caused considerable anxiety. Wittenberg was — needlessly — panic stricken, to the great dismay of Luther, before he left for the colloquy. He, as well as Zwingli, and their parties, had to pass through infected areas on their way to Marburg. The nauseous disease which killed its victims within 24 hours was regarded by pious monks as a punishment of God for the apostasy from the church until the virus proved to be neutral in religious matters. Medical history is full of references, after the humanist physician John Caius in 1552 wrote on this disease and its treatment.

[44]A. Brux raised the problem in America in *Christian Prayer-Fellowship and Unionism* (1935).

[45]WA 29, 562 ff. Luther does not mention the question of the Lord's Supper, nor does he enter into any controversy. He emphasizes the importance of the external Word. When emphasizing the concord existing in this matter with 'your preachers', he thinks of the Church of Hesse.

[46]WA TR 4, No. 5005.

[47]Quoted from Hedio's *Itinerarium* by W. Koehler, *Das Marburger Religionsgespräch 1529, Versuch einer Rekonstruktion,* 138.

custom at that time at the meals of noblemen, some poor boys present said the prayers or the responsories, for which they later got their meal. When the Lord's Prayer was said, probably in the old way, with the liturgist beginning and the 'choir' joining in with the Fourth Petition, Luther added to 'Hallowed be Thy name' the words: 'condemned be our name more than a thousand devils'.[48] This little incident shows that, at least on that occasion, Luther could pray together with, or at least in the presence of, people with whom he was negotiating, before he had to deny them full fellowship as Christian brethren.[49]

It had been Zwingli's desire that the colloquy should be held as publicly as possible. Luther, however, preferred a disputation in a smaller circle, and the Landgrave, who by all means wanted a favourable conclusion, agreed. Only invited guests were admitted: besides theologians and other scholars, members of the court, and representatives of other estates. Carlstadt and one of his Anabaptist disciples were not allowed to be present. According to Zwingli, 24 persons were assembled, but, according to Brenz who arrived later, there were from 50 to 60.

The sessions were held not in the hall of the castle, but in a large living-room, where the four disputants — Luther, Melanchthon, Zwingli, and Oecolampadius — were seated at a special table. Zwingli, who feared that his Swiss dialect might not be understood, had suggested that the language should be Latin. But the Landgrave (who listened during the whole colloquy with the greatest attention) and other laymen present would not have been able to follow a Latin disputation. Another suggestion made by Zwingli was also rejected, to the great distress of later historians: no official minutes were kept. Zwingli wished for wide publicity in this respect also. The Landgrave was convinced that if a complete agreement on doctrine could not be reached, at least a practical *modus vivendi*, a mutual recognition as brethren, could be found. This aim, however, could be attained in a private and confidential discussion only.

Despite the lack of official minutes, private notes taken during the meetings, and reports written immediately or soon after the colloquy, make it possible to reconstruct not only the course of the

---

[48]'*Dass unser Name für tausend Teufel verdammt werde*'.

[49]What Luther's attitude was toward this problem can be learned from the way pulpit- and altar-fellowship was practised after the Wittenberg Concord had been signed; see below, 249, 250. Cf letter from Fr. Myconius to Veit Dietrich, St Louis, XVII, col. 2090 ff. See also below, 235.

discussion, but also the essential content of what the disputants said (in many cases, even the very words they spoke), though sometimes we are not quite sure where a certain word belongs.These notes are the main sources. They are supplemented by letters,[50] and by statements made by the participants on other occasions.[51]

THE PRIMARY SOURCES

The primary sources are sometimes contained in the first historical works on the Reformation. Thus, the *History of the Reformation* (1563-74), by **Bullinger** (***Bull*** in further references), Zwingli's successor, contained a report in German,[52] which is mainly based on the authentic Latin report of **Rudolf Collin** (***Coll*** in further references), a friend of Zwingli who had accompanied him from Zurich to Marburg.[53] Collin's notes must have been very popular in Switzerland; they were incorporated in the great work by Rudolph Hospinian, *Historia Sacramentaria* (1598-1602), together with Zwingli's notes on his discussion with Melanchthon on October 1, and a short report in German which Hospinian ascribes to Zwingli, but which actually is the report of **H. Utinger** (***Ut*** in further references), the manuscript of which was rediscovered in the 19th century.[54] A report from the Lutheran side in Latin was first published by J. Wigand in 1574 in one of his writings on the Sacrament in connection with the Crypto-Calvinistic controversy. The unknown author must have been one of the companions of Luther.[55] This **Anonymous** (***Anon*** in further references), besides Collin and the alleged *notae Zwinglii* (actually Utinger), were for two

---

[50] *Luther and Melanchthon* to the Landgrave, Oct. 4, WA BR 5, No. 1478; *Luther* to his wife, Oct 4, No. 1476; to N. Gerbel, Oct. 4, No. 1477; to Joh. Agricola, Oct. 12, No. 1479; to Jac. Probst, June 1, 1530, No. 1577 (all contained in Enders Vol. 7); *Melanchthon* to Elector John and to Duke Henry, Oct. 5, CR I, No. 637 and No. 638; to Joh. Agricola, Oct. 12, CR I, No. 640; *Justus Jonas* to W. Reifenstein, Oct. 4, CR I, No. 634; for the letters of Zwingli and his friends, see Koehler, *Das Marburger Religionsgespräch 1529*, 5. The Lutheran correspondence is also included in St Louis, XVII, col. 1932 ff.

[51] Bucer, Preface to the second edition (1530) of his Commentary on the Synoptic Gospels, reprinted in A. Lang, *Der Evangelienkommentar Martin Butzers* (1900), 386 ff, partly quoted by Hospinianus, *Hist. Sacr., II,* 138 ff.

[52] For the relationship between Bullinger and Collin, see Koehler, *op. cit.*, 4, where WA 30, Part III, 101, is corrected.

[53] Compare Koehler, *op. cit.*, 4, and WA, *loc. cit.*, 100.

[54] It has been overlooked by Koehler and WA that Utinger had been printed already by Hospinian, *Hist. Sacr.*, II, 127, from a manuscript ascribed to Zwingli. This work is quoted here from the new edition: Geneva, 1681.

[55] Koehler, *op. cit.*, 3, thinks it was Roerer or Myconius.

centuries the primary sources available to the historians, apart from the correspondence of the Reformers.

This becomes evident from the careful enumeration of all sources and literature on the colloquy given by Valentine Ernst Loescher in his *Historia Motuum*.[56] As in other parts of this work, which describes the controversies between Lutherans and Reformed from the Reformation to the beginning of the 18th century, the author, an orthodox Lutheran, proves to be a real historian. His chapter on the Marburg Colloquy is the first critical study of our subject, and as such deserves to be mentioned here. He is unacquainted with the report in German to the Council of Nuremberg by **Osiander** (***Os*** in further references), which was not published until 1765 (and which is therefore missing in the Walch and St Louis editions of *Luther's Works*). Though Osiander did not arrive before Saturday afternoon, and could report on the first part of the discussions only from hear-say, this source is of great importance especially for the later sessions.[57]

The 19th century brought more discoveries. A Latin manuscript entitled ***Rhapsodie Colloquii ad Marburgum*** (***Rhaps*** in further references), copied by Veit Dietrich and originally intended for Spalatin, gives a report by an unknown Lutheran witness.[58] Three minor reports by **Brenz** were published in Latin and German,[59] and the *Itinerarium* of **Hedio** (***Hed*** in further references), the Strasburg delegate, in Latin. The latter is the most important of all sources with regard to completeness and reliability.[60]

All these sources are now easily accessible in the *Weimar Edition* (XXX, Part 3) — where Hedio, Anonymous, and Collin are printed synoptically, while Osiander, Brenz, the *Rhapsodie*, and Utinger follow separately — and in the second part of Koehler's *Das Marburger Religionsgespräch*.[61]

Attempts to reconstruct the colloquy by combining the various sources have been made subsequent to Bullinger and A. Scultetus.[62]

---

[56]Second Edition, Part I (1723); cap. 6 on the Marburg Colloquy, 143-58.

[57]Koehler, *op. cit.*, 3; cf WA, *loc. cit.*, 100.

[58]Not by Luther himself. See Koehler and WA, *loc. cit. Rhapsodie* should be understood as plural: *Rhapsodiae*.

[59]WA has only two; see Koehler, 3 f.

[60]WA, 99; Koehler, 2.

[61]See 39-141.

[62]*Annales,* a history of the Reformation (Heidelberg 1618-20), where the Marburg Colloquy is rendered 'from two manuscripts', probably ***An*** and ***Coll;*** compare WA, 101; Loescher, *loc. cit.*, 147.

A popular reconstruction, in the form of a dialogue based mainly on Collin, was presented by R. Christoffel in his biography of Zwingli.[63] Martin Rade published his *Protokoll des Marburger Religionsgesprächs* in 1927.[64] The most recent attempt to reconstruct the colloquy is that of Walther Koehler.[65] It is based on a thorough examination of all sources. The original German wording, however, had to be guessed at in many cases, since most of the source material is in Latin. In order to restore the freshness of the original dialogue, all is given in direct speech,[66] although the sources use both direct, and indirect speech, sometimes Latin and sometimes German, and in many cases incomplete sentences. It would be impossible to retain this variety in an English text. Our text is based on the sources as found in the *Weimar Edition* (WA) and in Koehler. The German reconstruction by Koehler has proved to be a valuable guide and commentary. The text presented on the following pages cannot be a 'reconstruction' in the sense of Koehler's admirable attempt to restore, as far as possible, the original German dialogue. It only tries to put into English what, according to reliable sources, was said during those decisive days at Marburg.

THE TEXTS

PRELIMINARY DISCUSSIONS

Friday, October 1

Melanchthon, in a letter written soon after the colloquy to John, the Elector of Saxony, gives the following information on the preliminary discussions held privately between Luther and Oecolampadius, and at the same time between Melanchthon and Zwingli.[67]

---

[63] *Huldreich Zwingli* (Elberfeld, 1857), 308-317.

[64] *Die Christliche Welt* (1927).

[65] *Das Marburger Religionsgespräch 1529, Versuch einer Rekonstruktion* (1929), 7-38; cited in footnotes of this chapter as 'Koehler'.

[66] At the fourth centenary in 1929, the Colloquy was re-enacted by students who read Koehler's text. It was a very impressive commemoration.

[67] CR 1, 1099; St. Louis, XVII, col. 1943; Koehler, 45.

Both Oecolampadius and Zwingli were told

> that we find many other articles (besides the one on the Lord's Supper)which they also teach wrongly. Such articles, therefore, must also be dealt with in the colloquy. Zwingli, for instance, has written that there is no original sin, but that sin consists only of outward evil works and actions, while original sin denotes only innate impurity and lusts of the heart.[68] He also teaches that it is not sin if by nature we do not fear God and believe in him. This indicates clearly that Zwingli does not know much about true Christian holiness, because he finds sin in outward deeds only, like the Pelagians and all papists and philosophers. Secondly, they err gravely concerning the ministry of the Word, and concerning the use of the Sacraments. For they teach that the Holy Ghost is not given through the Word and the Sacrament, but rather without the Word and the Sacrament. This is what Muenzer taught, and what caused him to fall back on his own ideas. For that is the necessary consequence if one claims to receive the Holy Ghost without the Word.[69]
>
> Thirdly, it has been reported that people in Strasburg do not believe correctly concerning the blessed Trinity. We want to hear their opinion about that, for we have learned that some of them speak about the Godhead as the Jews do, as if Christ were not true, essential God.[70]
>
> Fourthly, they do not speak and write correctly about how man is justified before God. They do not stress sufficiently the doctrine of faith, but rather speak about it as though the works which follow faith were our righteousness. They also teach falsely how man can attain faith. Now, they were instructed by us concerning this article on that occasion, as far as it could be done in so short a time. The more they heard about it, the more they liked it. They yielded in all these points, though earlier they had written otherwise.

LUTHER AND OECOLAMPADIUS

No detailed record has been preserved of the discussion between Luther and Oecolampadius. Apart from what Melanchthon wrote in the letter quoted, there are only a few remarks in the letters of Zwingli, Luther, Melanchthon, and Bucer, and these yield nothing of importance.[71] Bucer's letter, addressed to A. Blarer, mentions that Luther in his private discussion with Oecolampadius used the same argument as in the public colloquy: 'God said, "This is my body". God is omnipotent. Consequently the body is in the

---

[68]See footnote 77.

[69]For the Lutheran doctrine, see *AC Article 5*, with the express condemnation of 'the Anabaptists and others who think that the Holy Ghost comes to men without the external Word . . . ' (Trigl. 45), and Luther's great rejection of the 'enthusiasts', *Smalc. Art., III, 8,* especially: ' . . . we must firmly hold that God grants His Spirit or grace to no one, except through or with the preceding outward Word' (Trigl. 495).

[70]According to a letter from Melanchthon addressed to Duke Heinrich of Saxony (CR I, 1103), Zwingli put the blame for this heresy on the Anabaptist L. Haetzer, one of the first Antitrinitarians of the 16th century. It seems, however, that Haetzer's ideas were discussed in Strasburg where he had stayed from 1526-28.

[71]Quoted by Koehler, 48.

bread'.[72] Koehler assumes that one of the three reports given by Brenz on the colloquy (WA XXX, I, 153 ff) might contain remnants of that private discussion.[73] Some arguments of Luther's are preserved there which are not mentioned in the other reports, and therefore may originally not belong to the colloquy proper, for example, the idea that, as a thousand years are as one moment with God, so a thousand places must be one place or even less with God.[74]

ZWINGLI AND MELANCHTHON

(Sources: Zwingli's personal notes, which have been confirmed by Melanchthon, *Hospinian II,* 122 f; *Zwingli's Works*, ed. Schuler-Schulthess, IV, 173; Koehler, 40 f.)[75]

Melanchthon admits that words have no other power than to signify.[76]

Melanchthon and *Zwingli* agree that the Holy Spirit effects in us justification by means of the Word. The Word, however, is not to be understood as material sound, but rather as the Word preached and comprehended, which means that it is the core of the audible word (*medulla verbi*) as it is understood by our mind.

Zwingli admits: We believe that original sin is a disease contracted by all descendants of Adam. This disease has the effect that we love ourselves above all things, and not God. Where there is no law, there is no transgression. In [the case of] infants there is no [transgression of the] Law. Yet they are under the punishment [which follows transgression] of the Law. Their state is such an evil or sin as to condemn.[77]

---

[72]Quoted by Koehler, *loc. cit.*

[73]Koehler, 4; *Zwingli und Luther, II,* 77.

[74]WA 30, I, 154, 5 ff.

[75]We give a translation which in some cases must be free, especially where only incoherent words are used. Explanatory words are given in parentheses. 'Philippus' in the source is replaced by 'Melanchthon'.

[76]The point is whether the external Word gives the Holy Spirit, as Luther maintained against the 'enthusiasts', who separated the Spirit from the external Word. Zwingli tries to find a middle way, though he could never accept Luther's view, according to which the Spirit is always bound up with the Word.

[77]These short notes should be understood in the light of Zwingli's *Fidei Ratio*, the confession he transmitted to the Emperor on the occasion of the Diet at Augsburg in 1530. There, in Art. 4, he explains his doctrine on original sin. While Adam's sin is 'truly sin' (*vere peccatum*), original sin in the children of Adam is 'not sin in the proper sense' (*non proprie peccatum*), but a disease and a condition which we with Paul call sin (*peccatum*). Sin in the proper sense is the transgression of the Law, like the sin of Adam or our transgression. Such transgression involves guilt. Infants have contracted that disease and condition, which makes them enemies of God and leads to

As to the Sacrament of the Eucharist, we do not disagree concerning the spiritual eating, namely that eating [Christ] is believing [in Christ].

Melanchthon states that, even if Augustine had said that the body of Christ must necessarily be in one place only, he would not accept it.

As to the passage 'It is the spirit that quickeneth; the flesh profiteth nothing' (John 6:63), it must be understood in this way: The Jews had understood the preceding words as if they were to lacerate and devour the flesh of Jesus. When Christ heard them murmuring about this, he noticed that they had mistakenly understood it as a carnal laceration. Melanchthon admits that 'The flesh profiteth nothing' if it is lacerated as the Jews understood it. For the rest, he states that the sentence 'The flesh profiteth nothing' speaks quite generally of carnal understanding, carnal judgment, etc. Melanchthon adds: Christ did not put himself into the mouth of the disciples in a circumscriptive way, as the Jews understood it as a sort of laceration, and yet meanwhile he gave his body to be eaten as a food in a hidden way.

Zwingli denies that such hidden way can be proved from the Scriptures.

---

transgressions. However, the guilt connected with the inherited condition is Adam's. It is obviously the rationalistic, humanist element in Zwingli's theology that prevents him from acknowledging the mystery that original sin is *vere peccatum*, as Art. 2 of the *Augsburg Confession* teaches. According to Luther and the Lutheran Confession, 'this hereditary sin is so deep and horrible a corruption of nature that no reason can understand it, but it must be believed from the revelation of Scriptures', *Smalc. Art. III, 1* (Trigl. 477); see *Form. Concord, Art 1.* Zwingli has great difficulty reconciling his denial of original sin as guilt with the fact that even infants have to suffer the punishment that follows transgression of divine law. He interprets Romans 5 as meaning that the condition in which Adam was after the Fall (mortality, etc.) is inherited by his descendants, as the condition of slavery is inherited by the children of a slave. Therefore infants need to be saved by the grace of Christ. This grace is not forgiveness, but rather restitution to life (*vitae restituimur*). It is not given through Baptism, which is not a means of grace, and therefore not necessary for salvation. The children of Christian parents are members of the church, as the children of the Israelites were members of the people of God (*Fidei Ratio, Art. 5*); 'By baptism the Church receives publicly him who has been received previously by grace. Baptism does not give grace . . .' (*Art. 7*). Here it becomes evident that the difference between Luther and Zwingli with reference to the means of grace is connected with a different understanding of sin and grace. For Luther the real sin of the children of Adam is original sin as guilt. 'The fruits of this sin are afterwards evil deeds' or transgressions (*Smalc. Art., loc. cit.*). In Reformed theology, Calvin rediscovered, on the basis of Augustine's understanding of Paul, that original sin is really guilt (*Inst. II, 1, 8*). But he would not, of course, admit that Baptism is more than a sign of forgiveness (*Inst. IV, 15-16*). See *Marburg Article 5* below, 217, and our remarks on 'The Result', 223, 224.

Melanchthon quotes as proof the words 'This is my body', stating that we must not, without the clear testimony of Scripture, deviate from the proper meaning of the words.

Zwingli calls this 'begging the question (*petitio principii*)'.

Melanchthon refuses with determination to admit that the body of Christ must be in one place in such a way that it cannot at the same time be anywhere else. He quotes as proof-texts the passages 'This is my body', and 'He ascended . . . that he might fill all things' (Eph. 4:10). And even if he did approve of Zwingli's sentence on the Sacrament, he would deny what Zwingli affirms, namely, that the body of Christ must be in one place. For by no means is reason able to understand and to say *how* the body of Christ is in any one place.

Zwingli replies that the body of Christ cannot be in many places [simultaneously], not because he would in any way minimize the divine power, but rather because it does not become evident from Scripture that this body should ever be in several places at the same time. For [the expression] 'that he might fill all things' means nothing else than that he was to fulfil all things that he had to accomplish [according to the will of his Father]. Furthermore, in Hebrews it is stated that he was to become 'in all things . . . like unto his brethren' (2:17), 'yet without sin' (4:15). This refers to our human nature, and this nature is finite. Christ's humanity is similar to ours, therefore it is finite.

(*After a break for lunch the discussion continues*).

Melanchthon: Most of the sentences quoted from Augustine seem to be favourable to Zwingli, but almost all the quotations from the other Fathers obviously support the doctrine of Luther.

Zwingli quotes the words of Christ: 'It is expedient for you that I go away' (John 16:7); 'Yet a little while I am with you . . . I leave the world' (John 13:33; 16:28); 'I am no more in the world' (John 17:11); 'Then if any man shall say unto you, Lo, here is Christ, or there; believe it not' (Matt. 24:23). From these passages the conclusion is to be drawn that he cannot possibly be in the world in a bodily way. For he cannot lie; God is veracious.

Zwingli comes to this agreement with *Melanchthon:* The Word is taken as the expression of the mind of God. This mind is the will of God, garbed in human words. The human mind grasps this expression of the divine will, when it is drawn by the Father.[78]

---

[78] This refers to the first question: Zwingli would never admit that the external Word is the Word of God, but he was prepared to concede that the latter is 'garbed' in the human Word.

FIRST SESSION

Saturday, October 2, 6 am.

Chancellor Feige ***(Bull, Hed, Anon)*** *opens the colloquy on behalf of the Landgrave, and admonishes the parties to lay aside all mutual animosity, to speak without passion, and to seek nothing but the glory of Christ, the well-being of Christendom, and brotherly unity. He thanks all and sundry, first of all Dr Luther, for having come at the bidding of the prince. He asks Luther to begin.*

Luther ***(Hed, Anon)***: Most illustrious prince, my gracious lord! I do not doubt that this colloquy has been planned and arranged with good intentions. Two years ago I rejected it, knowing that enough had been written on either side, and that no new argument could be presented. As for me, my opinion was firmly established, and I desire to adhere to it until the end of my life. Nor had I the intention to write on the subject any more. When, however, my gracious prince and lord, Landgrave Philip, at the Diet of Spires proposed such a colloquy, I agreed, feeling unable to disobey the pious desire of this good prince.[79] I am prepared, then, to take part in a debate. Not as if I were desirous of changing my conviction, which, on the contrary, is absolutely firm. Still, I want to present the foundation of my faith and show where the others err. However, before we start with the Lord's Supper, I must ask my opponents to explain their views on some other chapters of Christian doctrine, since pamphlets published seem to reveal opinions existing in Zurich, Basle, and Strasburg which, if really held, would constitute errors. I have been informed by letter that some people at Strasburg say that Arius — as his writings would show if we only had them — taught the doctrine of the Trinity more correctly than St Augustine or other Fathers.

Secondly, there seems to be an error concerning the two natures of Christ, which some distinguish in such a way that they appear to teach two persons in Christ.

Thirdly, as to original sin some deny that it is damnatory.

Fourthly, on Baptism some teach that it is not the seal of faith, but the sign of external association with the church only.

Fifthly, justification is attributed not only to faith in Christ, but partly also to our own abilities.

———

[79]Luther was, of course, not present at Spires.

Sixthly, there seem to be errors as to the oral word and the ministry of the Word.

Seventhly, they think that I do not teach correctly on purgatory, and there is perhaps disagreement on some other parts of Christian doctrine. Unless we first make sure that we agree in all these things, we should in vain deal with the real dignity of the Eucharist.[80]

Oecolampadius ***(Anon)***: I am not aware of ever having taught, in the articles mentioned, anything contrary to Dr Luther's doctrine. The present colloquy has been called in order that we may discuss our opinions on the Eucharist. Accordingly, this should be the first subject to be debated. If, however, it should really have happened that certain people somewhere else have not taught correctly, I hold that each person should answer for himself.

Zwingli ***(Anon, Hed)***: I am of the same opinion, especially since I have discussed these things with Master Philip. What I teach on justification has been made public in my pamphlet *On the Clarity and Certainty of God's Word*.[81] Now, therefore, the discussion should deal with the Lord's Supper. After having finished that, we can readily discuss all the rest.

Luther ***(Hed, Anon, Coll,*** supported by ***Brenz)***: I am prepared to accept this way of procedure. But I testify publicly that I do not agree with the writings of these people with reference to the articles mentioned. I want to state this clearly lest people at home may say later that I did not have the opportunity here to speak frankly. As to the Lord's Supper, your fundamental principles are these: (1) You want to prove your case by way of logical conclusions; (2) you hold that a body cannot be in two places at the same time, and you put forward the argument that a body cannot be without limitation; (3) you appeal to natural human reason.

I for one cannot admit that such clear words present a [hermeneutical] problem (*quaestio*). I do not ask how Christ can be God and man, and how his natures could be united. For God is able to act far beyond our imagination. To the Word of God one must yield. It is up to you to prove that the body of Christ is not there when

---

[80] Most of these questions had been discussed in the preliminary discussion on Oct. 1. They are dealt with in the *Schwabach Articles*, which Luther had brought along to Marburg and which later became the basis of the *Marburg Articles*. Thus, it is evident, then, that these points had been regarded as vital issues between Luther and his opponents for a long time. As regards purgatory, Zwingli had misunderstood a passage of Luther's; see Koehler, *Zwingli und Luther*, I, 687; II, 85.

[81] Zwingli (CR) I, 338 ff.

Christ himself says, 'This is my body'. I do not want to hear what reason says. I completely reject carnal or geometrical arguments, as, for example, that a large body could not fill a small space. **God is above and beyond all mathematics**, and his words are to be adored and observed with awe. God, however, commands: 'Take, eat; this is my body'. I request, therefore, a valid proof from Holy Writ that these words do not mean what they say.

(*Luther* (***Coll**, supported by **Os***) *writes the words 'This is my body' on the table with chalk and covers them with the velvet tablecloth.*[82])

Oecolampadius ***(Hed, Coll, Anon)***: It is the sixth chapter of St John that explains the other passages of Scripture. There Christ [when speaking of his flesh] does not speak of a local presence. He even says: 'The flesh profiteth nothing' (John 6:63). I am not desirous of appealing to reason or geometry — I do not deny the power of God — but, possessing the sum total of faith, I speak of that. For Christ is risen [and sitteth at the right hand of the Father; consequently his body is not here on earth]. Our opinion is neither new nor profane. It rests upon faith and Holy Scripture. One must proceed from carnal to spiritual eating. The Holy Scriptures frequently employ figurative speech, metaphors, metonymies, and the like. In such cases words have a meaning different from what they say. Thus, the words 'This is my body' may also be figurative speech, as in the expressions: 'John . . . is Elijah' (Matt. 11:14 RSV); 'That Rock was Christ' (1 Cor. 10:4); 'I am the true vine' (John 15:1); 'The seed is the word of God' (Luke 8:11).

Luther ***(Hed, Coll)***: Oecolampadius has quoted many modes of speech in Holy Scripture, such as, 'I am the vine'. He then admonishes us to understand the eating spiritually, and says: 'The Fathers are on our side'. To this I reply briefly, for it is not necessary to say very much about that. There are indeed many metaphors in Holy Scripture. But you have to prove that here, in the words 'This is my body', a metaphor is contained. Do not talk about things which we have known already for a long time. If Christ should say by way of a *demonstratio* (description) 'I am the vine', I would believe that, too. A general sentence admits a metaphor. Here, however, we have a

---

[82]By so doing Luther wanted to have before him not only the *thema probandum*, but his last and unrefutable argument. Luther liked to chalk important words, also on other occasions, in order to have them before him.

demonstrative (descriptive) sentence.[83] Therefore you must prove that it has to be understood metaphorically. So far no one has been willing to do this. Moreover, it should also be proved that spiritual eating (*manducatio spiritualis*) excludes bodily eating (*manducatio corporalis*), so that there should be no bodily eating at all. I concede that the Fathers are partly on your side if we accept your interpretation of them. But what does that matter unless you prove that 'body' here is used instead of 'figure of body'? I ask you to speak to the point without ambiguity.

Oecolampadius ***(Hed, Coll)***: 'I am the vine' is also a demonstrative (descriptive) sentence. At least, it may be.

Luther ***(Hed, Coll, Anon, Rhaps)***: I do not deny that there are cases of figurative speech in the Scriptures. Still, you have to prove that this is such a case. It is not enough that these words 'This is my body' **can** be understood in that way. What you have to prove is that they **must** be understood figuratively. Your argumentation is based on a preconceived opinion. It is a begging of the question (*petitio principii*) to conclude from John 6 where Christ speaks of a spiritual eating that there is no bodily eating at all. You want me to build the faith of my heart on this foundation. That means you are unwilling to produce any proof at all. Thus my faith is strengthened by your failure to give a proof. **I have a clear and powerful text**. Do justice to that text. What I have been waiting for all the time is that you prove what you ought to prove.

Oecolampadius ***(Coll, Anon, Hed)*** *reads from the sixth chapter of St John, and continues:* That the words must be understood figuratively is evident from this chapter. Christ speaks of the eating of his body and of the drinking of his blood to the Jews and also to his disciples. When they, understanding it as a carnal eating and drinking, shuddered, he answered, 'It is the spirit that quickeneth; the flesh profiteth nothing'. This indicates that he declined once and for all the carnal eating of his body. It should follow that he neither would, nor could, later institute what he had once rejected.

———

[83]By 'demonstrative sentence' Luther understands a sentence that establishes a fact in plain words. In this sense, 'This is my body' is a demonstrative sentence. On the other hand, 'I am the true vine' is, according to Luther's explanation of John 15, WA 45, 63, '. . . *ein sehr tröstlich Bild und ein feine, liebliche Prosopeia, damit er vor die Augen stellt, nicht einen unnützen, unfruchtbaren Baum, sondern den lieben Weinstock . . . .'* Here a metaphor is used, but the trope is not in the verb 'am', but rather in the word 'vine'. John 15:1 does not mean: 'I signify the vine'. Thus, even the use of a metaphor does not justify the understanding of *est* as *significat*, as Luther points out (WA 26, 271; 3 ff; see above, 118).

Luther **(Coll, Hed)**, *after having repeated the quotation from John 6*: You think that Christ by spiritual eating rejects bodily eating. To this I reply: He wanted to teach the Jews, the Capernaites, that he would not be eaten like bread and meat on a dish, or like roast pork. If I eat Christ bodily in the bread, this does not imply that it is something ordinary or common, but rather a benefit of the Holy Spirit. Therefore it is not common and rejectable, but a sublime manducation, for man can trust those words that here is the body of Christ.

Oecolampadius **(Anon, Coll)**: Referring to your distinction of a twofold meaning, I suggest that there is a difference between a low and carnal understanding of the divine words and a sublime and spiritual one. It is the low understanding of the eating of the flesh of Christ, repudiated by Christ himself, that Luther insists on. Christ, however, has commanded to accept the sublime and spiritual meaning, which we teach.

Luther **(Anon)**: I hear a great deal of the distinction between a twofold understanding of the words of the Supper, without testimony or authority of Holy Scripture. However carnal they may seem to you, they are, nevertheless, as no one can deny, the **words and deeds of the highest majesty** and, therefore, by no means carnal and inferior,since **forgiveness of sins, eternal life, and the kingdom of heaven are, by the Word of God, attached to these low and, as it would seem, carnal things**. Therefore, they should by no means be made void, or held in contempt as something inferior. But rather they should be held in high esteem and regarded as sublime and spiritual.

Oecolampadius **(Hed,** *supported by* **Coll)**: You regard the assumption of Christ's being in the bread to be a belief. It is an opinion not a belief. **It is wrong to attribute too much to the element.** Listen to what Augustine says (*he reads a passage from De doctrina christiana, lib. 3, cap. 9, where Augustine, commenting on 2 Cor. 3:6, 'The letter killeth, but the spirit giveth life', says*): 'When a word that is meant figuratively is accepted literally, it is understood in a carnal way'.

Luther **(Hed, Coll, Rhaps)**: I go back to the words of the Lord's Supper. If I speak of the 'body which is given for us', then this is no base understanding of Scripture. If we had to deal with the bread only, even this would still not be a 'low understanding of Scripture'. Indeed, to lift a straw at the bidding of the Lord would be something spiritual.[84] We baptize with simple water. You must not look so much upon what is said, but rather who says it. **Since God speaks thus, you must embrace the Word.** Take, as an example, a prince who gives orders to shoe a horse. The horseshoe is a very lowly thing; however, it gets a certain dignity by the command of the prince. To be hungry is also a very lowly thing [yet the Word of God says 'Blessed are they that hunger']. If we are commanded to baptize with water, we ascribe the real washing not to the water, but to the Holy Spirit. As to the element itself, we are all in agreement. We do not ascribe dignity to the bread, but to the Word, and to him who deals with us through the Word. Just as, in the case of a prince who sends his servant to shoe his horse, the piece of iron is made worthy [of being in the service of the prince]. Give due honour to the cross. God often acts in a miraculous way, employing lowly things. God acted in this way when he commanded Abraham to sacrifice his son, or when he forbade Adam to eat of the tree. When God speaks, it is for us men to listen. When he commands, the world must obey. As often as we speak of the body of Christ, we speak of the body that is at the right hand of the Father. We would readily accept your opinion, but we cannot do so since your interpretation of Scripture is vague.

(*Addressing the Landgrave:*) I beg Your Highness's pardon, but the words 'This is my body' have captured me. Even if Augustine or any other doctors would interpret the words symbolically, they should take their place behind Christ and accept his interpretation. If they do that, we will follow them. If not, the doctors will have to be disregarded, for Christ must be trusted.

But we cannot follow you on the authority of the doctors. Now it is for you to speak.

*Oecolampadius **(Hed)***: I accept the example that you have brought forward [concerning the command of the prince]. Your idea is that the Word brings the body of Christ into the bread.

*Luther **(Hed)***: This is correct. (*He again explains the simile of the prince at whose command the horse is shod, whereby a piece of ordinary iron attains a new dignity.*)

*Oecolampadius **(Coll)***: As you have the spiritual eating, **why should there be any need for bodily eating?**

---

[84]The same thought occurs in the *Sermon for Septuagesima* 1525, WA 17, Part II, 132, 18 ff: *'Und wenn er mich heisse einen Strohhalm aufheben, so wäre alsbald an dem Strohhalm geistliche Speise und Trank, nicht um des Strohhalms willen, sondern um des Worts und Zeichens willen göttlicher Wahrheit und Gegenwärtigkeit'.*

Luther ***(Hed, Anon, Coll)***: Your argument implies this idea: Since we have the spiritual eating (*manducatio spiritualis*), there is no need of a bodily eating (*manducatio corporalis*). To this I reply: We do not deny the spiritual eating; on the contrary, we teach and believe it to be necessary. But from this it does not follow that the bodily eating is either useless or unnecessary. It is not our business to judge whether it is useful or not. We have the command 'Take, eat; this is my body'. Christ gives himself to us in many ways: first, in the preaching of the Word; secondly, in Baptism; thirdly, in brotherly consolation; fourthly, in the Sacrament as often as the body of Christ is eaten, because he himself commands us to do so. If he ordered me to eat dung, I would do it. **Let not the servant inquire about the will of the Lord. We ought to close our eyes.**[85]

Oecolampadius ***(Hed)***: **Doctor, where is it written that we should go through the Scriptures with closed eyes?**

Luther ***(Hed)***: If we continued our discussion for a hundred years, still nothing would be proved. If you can do away with the text, I am satisfied. He who spoke the word of John 6 has also spoken the words 'This is my body'.

Oecolampadius ***(Coll, Hed)***: In John 6 we read: 'The flesh profiteth nothing' (v 63). If the flesh, when eaten, does not profit anything, but the Spirit only, then we have to look for that which does profit, and we will have to contemplate the will of God. We should deal with Scripture in a clear way, and compare passage with passage. That is what Augustine does. Thus I maintain that the spiritual eating is sufficient.

Luther ***(Hed, Coll)***: **And I abide by my text.**

* * *

Zwingli ***(Hed, Coll)***: It is prejudice if you, Dr Luther, will not give up your opinion. You are not ready to give up unless a passage is quoted which proves that in the Lord's Supper the body is spoken of metaphorically. This is the prejudice of the heretics, for example, of Helvidius, who denied that Jesus was the only son of Mary

---

[85]Compare the description of Abraham's faith in the lecture on Genesis 17: 'With closed eyes he hid himself in the darkness of faith, and there he found eternal light (*clausis igitur oculis abdidit se in tenebras fidei, in quibus invenit aeternam lucem*)' WA 42, 655, 4 f.

because Scripture speaks clearly of 'brothers' of Jesus.[86] It is therefore necessary to compare Scripture passage with Scripture passage. Thus, even if we do not have a passage that says, 'This is the figure of my body', we do have a passage in which Christ leads us away from bodily eating. It is the purpose of our meeting here to look into the passages, and we ought to take into consideration the passage in John 6 (v 63) because it leads away from bodily eating. From the words 'It is the spirit that quickeneth; the flesh profiteth nothing' it follows that he did not give his own body in the Supper. In fact, you yourself recognize that the spiritual eating gives comfort. Since we are unanimous in this main point, for the sake of Christ's love I beg you not to accuse anyone of heresy on account of this dissension. **The ancient Fathers, even when in disagreement, did not condemn one another in such a way**. Coming back to John 6 (v 63), 'It is the spirit that quickeneth; the flesh profiteth nothing', I do not understand this passage as meaning that the humanity of Christ profiteth nothing. For in this humanity Christ has redeemed us, and this is indeed a most consoling thought. As often as I consider that Christ had flesh like my flesh, I am immensely comforted. Your interpretation does not correspond to the intentions of the evangelist. You err when speaking in an unusual manner of tearing apart and lacerating. I read it in the Greek, lest my memory should deceive me: '*Pōs dynatai hēmin houtos dounai tēn sarka phagein?*' (John 6:52). The text speaks of eating — *esthein, edere, comedere, manducare* — not of tearing apart or lacerating. 'If I shall have ascended into heaven', then at least you will see, as Augustine comments on these words (John 6:62), that the body of Christ is not eaten essentially, really, and in a carnal way (*essentialiter, realiter, carnaliter*). In the words 'It is the spirit that quickeneth; the flesh profiteth nothing', spirit is the antithesis of flesh. You have spoken of a base understanding of Scripture. Some of your words pleased me, others not, because they seemed to be pretty childish, as, for example, 'If God ordered me to eat dung'. The works which God commands he

---

[86] Helvidius rejected (in Rome c. AD 385) the doctrine of the perpetual virginity of Mary. Refuting him, Jerome wrote *On the Perpetual Virginity of the Blessed Virgin Mary* (MPL 23, 181), which established the doctrine for the Middle Ages. The tradition was so strong that even Zwingli and Luther still accepted it. It has even crept into the Lutheran Confessions where the (unofficial) Latin text of the *Smalcald Articles,* I, 4, reads *'semper virgo'* (Trigl. 460), and *Sol. Decl. VIII, 24* (Trigl. 1022) has it even in the German text. It cannot be regarded as dogma because no real proof from Scripture can be given.

commands for our benefit. **God is truth, and he is light. He gives light and does not lead us into darkness**. Therefore he does not say, 'This is my body essentially, really, carnally', since Scripture contradicts that. The oracles of the demons are obscure, not the words of Christ. The soul 'eats' spirit, and therefore it does not eat flesh. That is not the way in which God acts. **Spirit eats spirit**. I beg you not to be angry with me; I like to see your faces, Dr Luther and Master Philip.

Luther ***(Hed, Coll)***: I promise not to yield to any passion for the sake of God and the prince. What is lost, let it be lost. Let us hope for the future. Even if we cannot come to a complete agreement, we may at the end of this colloquy discuss the question whether or not we are still able to regard one another as brethren.

As to the argument of Helvidius: It can be proved from Scripture that the word 'brother' may be used for 'cousin'. But it cannot be proved that '*hoc est corpus meum*' is a trope. What you call eating may do away with all eating. If God told me to eat a crab-apple, I should eat spiritually. For wherever the Word of God is, there is spiritual eating. Whenever God speaks to us, faith is required, and such faith means 'eating'. If, however, he adds bodily eating to that, we are bound to obey. In faith we eat this body which is given for us. While the mouth receives the body of Christ, the soul believes the words when eating the body. Furthermore, **if you say that God does not propose to us anything incomprehensible, I would not admit that**. Consider the virginity of Mary, the remission of sins, and many similar matters. In the same way 'This is my body' is also incomprehensible. 'Thy way is in the sea, and thy path in the great waters, and thy footsteps are not known' (Psalm 77:19). If we know his ways, he would not be incomprehensible, he who is to be adored in his miracles.

Zwingli ***(Hed, Coll, Anon)***: From Scripture it can be proved that the thing that is signified is [often] used for the sign. Ezekiel (5:1 ff) is ordered to shave his head. Then it [the passage] continues: 'This is Jerusalem', that is, that will happen to Jerusalem. God's passing over the houses of the Israelites (Exodus 12:27) 'is the passover'— according to the analogy, a figure of Jesus Christ. Luther does not acknowledge that such a mode of speech, as occurs in other passages, is to be found here in the Lord's Supper, although there are many texts that do not allow a literal understanding. Such a passage is Isaiah 9:14, 15: 'The Lord will cut off from Israel head and tail . . . the ancient and honourable, he is the head; and the prophet that teaches lies, he is the tail'. The prophets were wont to speak in that way. Thus, in Isaiah we find 'is (*est*)' for 'signifies (*significat*)'. Therefore, comparison of Scripture with Scripture necessitates the acceptance of *est* for *significat*. Here you, Dr Luther, employ all possible means of rhetorical extenuations. Thus, you put forward strong arguments: 'If God commanded' — of course, we know that he commands; 'If God commanded to eat his body in remembrance of him, etc.' — we know that it is God's pleasure that we do so. Luther, however, does not look upon the internal Word [the interior meaning of the word], but upon the external Word [the mere outward letter], which only signifies the will of God.[87] We say it is impossible to understand the words of the Lord's Supper literally because God has forbidden us to eat his flesh bodily. Otherwise we make the Word of God ambiguous. Luther thinks that the Word, when uttered, adds something to bread and wine. Melanchthon agrees with me that spoken words have only a significative character. It is the core of the word which carries something with it. Take an example: A papist hearing the words 'The death of Christ is our justification' does not believe these words because he fails to catch their core. The sole purpose of the words of the Sacrament is to make known the will of the Father. You reject our interpretation; we reject yours. 'Me ye have not always' Christ says in John 12:8, thus excluding a bodily presence. It is not true that God puts before us many incomprehensible things. That Christ is true God and true man is not unknown to the faithful. When Mary asked, 'How shall this be?' she received the answer: 'The Holy Ghost shall come upon thee'. She was satisfied, hearing that God's power was at work. In John 6, however, when the disciples were doubtful concerning the carnal eating, Christ spoke to them of the spiritual eating — still he taught nothing of a bodily eating. As to your words: Where the Word of God is, there is the eating, my answer is that the pope has the Word likewise. That eating takes place, not where the words are spoken, but where they are believed. As for me, I believe in those words as being efficacious, if they are accepted in faith. Augustine is right in saying 'The Word may be added to the element, and thus a sacrament comes into being'. Which word? If the papist speaks the word, no sacrament is there, although the word is added to the element.[88] The spoken words, therefore, must be comprehended by my faith. Hence, the Sacrament is 'something with an inner meaning, a sign which is used in an action'. It must be given

---

[87]See the preliminary discussion between Zwingli and Melanchthon, above, 182-184.

[88]Compare Wyclif's doctrine above, 47 and 60.

to the brethren, who testify by receiving it that Christ has died for them. I marvel how you can say that the body is eaten orally. If he is present, he is present for the comfort not of the body, but of the soul. Would he ever join disparate things? What I say you will not refute by philosophy or rhetoric. Melanchthon has admitted that the Jews did not understand the answer of Jesus (John 6:53 ff) spiritually. Christ gave an answer that he might heal them, for lack of understanding was the disease from which they were suffering. I am, therefore, speaking of the spiritual meaning of the words of the Lord's Supper. If Luther gives an ambiguous interpretation, he does violence to the words of Holy Scripture. The passage 'The words that I speak unto you, they are spirit, and they are life' (John 6:63) does not refer to words spoken by men.

*Luther **(Hed, Coll)***: You deviate from our path. You accuse me of using rhetorical means, and you reject my simile of the straw that I would lift at God's command. Ezekiel 5 and the 'passover' in Exodus 12 are allegories. There are, however, many passages in which 'is' is used demonstratively. In such cases you cannot use the art of allegorical interpretation. As to [the efficacy of] the word I want to state briefly: We do not say that the body is produced by our own words; we are rather speaking of the institution of the Lord. Take as an example the case of a servant who is leading horses to pasture at the bidding of his master. If I said on my own behalf, 'This is my body', the idea would be that the bread becomes the body of Luther, the proper place for which would be the gallows. 'Do this' (Luke 22:19): this word causes the hand of the priest to become the hand of Christ. The mouth is not mine, nor is the tongue mine, for both are Christ's. This is true even though I were a knave or a rascal. The same needs to be said also of Baptism. 'Go ye . . . baptizing' (Matt. 28:19): This works is not mine, but God's. Let me use another simile. We speak of a prince who beats another prince. In that case, the fists of all the soldiers are the fists of the prince. We do not regard these words as idle talk. Christ says 'If ye . . . shall say unto this mountain, Remove hence to yonder place; and it shall remove' (Matt. 17:20). I do not discuss the 'is', but I am satisfied that Christ says it. Even the devil is powerless over against these words. I do not want them to be joined with my power, but rather with the power and command of Christ.

As to the soul's eating the body of Christ: where the Word of God is, there must be the spiritual eating because the Word requires faith. If men refuse to believe and to eat spiritually, what does that matter?

The real body is present by virtue of the word of Christ. The sum of faith is: **It behoves us not to call in question that which the Word of our God says, unless the literal understanding would lead to an absurdity that would contradict** [not our reason, but] **the faith or an article of faith.**

As to the Blessed Virgin: 'The Holy Ghost shall come upon thee' (Luke 1:35) is the answer to her question: 'How shall this be?' It was hope against hope, just as in the case of Abraham. I do not understand that miracle. I would lose my faith if I tried to, and I would become a fool. **If you make a trope out of the words of the Lord's Supper, why not make one out of 'He ascended into heaven'** (Mark 16:19)? Again I ask you to yield and give God the glory, for your foundations are too weak.

Zwingli ***(Hed, Coll, Bull)***: We, too, ask you to give glory to God and give up your *petitio principii.* Where do you prove your thesis (*thema probandum*)? I shall carefully examine all your words. Please do not be angry about that. I am still holding that word in John 6 where the eating and drinking of the body is clearly interpreted, which you are dealing with so lightly. You will have to change your tune.

Luther ***(Coll, Hed)***: You speak contemptuously.

Zwingli ***(Hed, Anon)***: Do you not believe that Christ wanted to help the ignorant when, in John 6, he commanded the spiritual eating and repudiated the carnal eating?

Luther ***(Hed, Coll, Bull)***: By speaking with audacity you want to win your case. 'This is a hard saying' the Jews say (John 6:60), speaking of a carnal eating, which would be impossible and absurd. The obligation to prove rests on you, not on me. But we will let that text in John 6 go, since it has no bearing on the understanding of the words of the Lord's Supper.

Zwingli ***(Hed)***: And yet it can be proved that John 6 speaks of bodily eating.

Luther ***(Hed)***: Your logic is very poor.

Zwingli ***(Hed, Coll)***: No, that passage will break your neck.

Luther ***(Hed, Coll)***: Do no be conceited. Necks do not break so easily here. You are in Hesse, not in Switzerland. Christ's body is death, poison, and devil to those who eat unworthily. Death, dungeon, and the like are evil things. If, however, the Word is added to them, they are very salutary.

(Anon) I have already confessed several times that I do not despise as useless the spiritual eating instituted and commanded by our

Lord Jesus Christ. I believe it is necessary in a particular way. What I am saying, however, is that from this it does not follow that the bodily eating instituted and commanded by Christ is useless, especially not to the faithful, who eat not only spiritually but also orally. Still less can it be concluded, yea, the conclusion is quite impossible, that the true body of Christ cannot at all be bodily in the Lord's Supper. It is there, and it is useful. For even if the spirit does not eat the body of Christ in a bodily fashion, it still believes to be eating it under bread and wine, in the word which the spirit itself hears.

*Zwingli **(Coll)***: I apologize for having used an expression common among my people.

*Landgrave Philip **(Bull)** accepts the excuse and asks Luther not to be offended as far as Zwingli's mode of speech is concerned.*

SECOND SESSION

Saturday Afternoon, October 2

*Zwingli **(Hed, Anon)**, coming back to John 6, quotes extensively from that chapter and stresses especially verse 52: 'How can this man give us his flesh to eat?' He then addresses Luther:* In your *Postil*, by the way, you admit in the Sermon for Septuagesima that Christ said of himself, 'The flesh profiteth nothing'. You say: 'Eating and drinking spiritually is nothing else than to believe in the word and sign of God, as also Christ says: "He that eateth my flesh, and drinketh my blood, dwelleth in me, and I in him" (6:56), and: "My flesh is meat indeed, and my blood is drink indeed" (v 55), etc. This means: He who believes in me will live'.[89] Melanchthon in his interpretation of St John says, 'By belief in the word Christ is eaten,

[89] *Sermon for Septuagesima* on the Epistle, 1 Cor. 9:24 - 10:4; WA 17, Part II, 126 ff. The passage quoted by Zwingli (131, 32 f): *'Essen aber und trinken geistlich ist nichts anderes, denn glauben an Gottes Wort und Zeichen . . .'* The sermon deals with the spiritual eating and drinking of the Fathers in the desert as a type of our spiritual eating and drinking. In the last part of the sermon, Luther discusses the meaning of the words: 'That Rock was Christ'. He rejects again, as in the case of John 15:1, the interpretation of 'is' as 'signifies'. The metaphor is not in the 'is'. In this connection he rejects expressly the view that in 'This is my body' 'is' could mean 'signifies', and insists on the literal understanding (see especially, 134). For the problem of Luther's hermeneutical principles, see the careful study by G. Ebeling, *Evangelische Evangelienauslegung* (1942), especially 331 ff.

not in bodily eating, nor in visible appearance, nor in the [sacramental] sign'.[90] Your interpretation contains a *digressio a particulari in universale* (that is, you proceed from that which is the particular, the flesh of Christ, to that which is general, flesh in general: a carnal mind profiteth nothing). That the body is eaten in a bodily way seems to us to be an unestablished statement. If the Fathers say that the body of Christ feeds the soul, they think of the resurrection. Luther thinks the sentence 'Christ ascended into heaven' to be just as absurd as the sentence 'This is my body'. Luther asks how this is to be understood.[91] Finally, he thinks that if the words 'This is my body' are spoken [in the celebration], then the body of Christ is there, whoever the person may be that speaks them. I beg you to beware lest the papacy be brought in in this way. This is not in conformity with Melanchthon's statement in which he admitted that the words only 'signify'. Either I have understood your words, or what you say is completely absurd.

Luther ***(Hed, Coll, Anon)***: As to my *Postil* and Melanchthon, the question is not what we write or have written. Oecolampadius and Zwingli should rather prove that the real body is not eaten in the Lord's Supper. I admit that even if I shared your belief, and regarded the body of Christ as useless, yet these words would not be refuted: 'This is my body'. All the people that have written against us write as if we spoke of the Sacrament without the Word. As to the power of the words and their alleged, mere significative character: a human word is a mere sound; Emperor Maximilian is dead.[92] When, however, something is said by 'the high majesty', by God himself, such a word does not only 'signify', but it effects and brings about that which it signifies, not through our power, but through God's. Then the words are not only the sound of a speaking man, but of God, and this sound conveys something to him who eats the bread. When God says, 'Take; do that; speak these words', then it comes to pass. He speaks, and already it is done. We must learn to distinguish between our speaking and God's commanding. Nor do I say that evil men should do this. Up to this day, however, we do not know who is a believer and who is not. Even if Peter came and celebrated mass, I would not know whether he believes. Therefore I say that the

---

[90]Melanchthon does not deny the Real Presence in this passage, but rather emphasizes the paramount necessity of faith. See Koehler, *Zwingli und Luther, I, 192*, where the text is quoted.

[91]The text is not clear. The meaning is that Zwingli does not accept this parallel.

Sacrament should be celebrated among Christians. There God founds the Sacrament upon his Word, and not upon our holiness, as the Anabaptists and Donatists do. Baptism does not rest on my faith but on these words 'Go ye . . . and baptize'. God, however, wants to make use of our ministry. We cannot prevent a bad minister from celebrating the Sacrament. Thus, we do not give to or take anything away from the papacy. The papacy is to be attacked from another angle.

Philip, now you should speak. I am really tired. When I asked today whether there could not be a trope in each of the two passages: 'He ascended into heaven' and 'This is my body', I wanted to know whether in any passage at all the [word] body is understood figuratively. It would still be easier in the case of heaven, for heaven would soon suffer a trope. However, we read: 'He was taken up; and a cloud received him out of their sight' (Acts 1:9).

Zwingli ***(Hed, Coll, Anon)***: It would be an absurdity if ungodly ministers could cause the body of Christ to be present.[93]

Luther ***(Hed, Coll, Anon)***: This also is against you that, according to your convictions, you could not receive Baptism, nor hear the Word of God, nor receive the Lord's Supper, because you cannot possibly ever know whether the minister is a godly one. Thus, Paul himself (1 Cor. 1:14 ff) was unwilling to baptize. In the Bible we find godly and ungodly people as ministers, such as, the Pharisees according to Matthew 23. Judas was a traitor, and yet he held the office of an apostle. Augustine says against the Donatists that the Ministry may be given to godly or ungodly men because its foundation is not our faith, but the Word of God. This Word is efficacious and true, whoever proclaims it, according to the word 'The scribes and Pharisees sit in Moses' seat'.

Zwingli ***(Hed)***: It makes a difference whether the Pharisees teach, or whether something is done which Christ says. The ministry of preaching is higher than the ministry of baptizing. The words 'This is my body' belong to the ministry of preaching.

Luther ***(Hed, Anon)***: Whether you accept them as words of teaching or as words of the Sacrament, these words remain: 'This is my body'. The ministry of the Word and the ministry of the Sacrament are one. He to whom is entrusted the preaching of the Word, to him is also entrusted the dispensation of the Sacraments,

---

[92]Consequently, his words are no longer powerful.

[93]Here we find another interesting parallel to Wyclif; see footnote 88.

according to 1 Cor. 1:17: 'Christ sent me not to baptize, but to preach the gospel'.

Zwingli (Anon): If the person of the officiant is not to be taken into account at all, and if, thus, the words of an ungodly person spoken in the assembly of the ungodly are nevertheless efficacious, then the consequence would be that the papacy rises again and is reaffirmed.

Luther (Anon): I do not apeak of the assembly of the ungodly, but I only say that if no one can be sure of the faith of the ministers of the church, not even in the case of pious and faithful men, then we must look to the power of the Word of God more than to the faith of the ministers. While of this faith no one can be sure, the power of the Word, however, no one can doubt.

Zwingli (Anon): *interrupting the order of discussion:* You make contradictory statements on the same matter. At one time you say the eating of the flesh of Christ profiteth, at another time, just as you please, it profiteth nothing.

Luther (Anon): I have said, and still say, that the flesh of Christ, if eaten by unbelievers, is not only unprofitable, but is even poison and death, just as the Word of God and God himself [say]. Moreover, as it is unprofitable and deadly to unbelievers, so it is profitable to the faithful, **a medicine for eternal life**.[94] But even if, in itself, it were useless and pernicious, which is not the case, it still would be salutary through the word of life connected with it.

Zwingli (Anon): I insist that there must be a trope in the Lord's Supper. This can be shown, as also the Article of the Creed demands it: 'He ascended into heaven and sitteth on the right hand of God the Father'. Otherwise, a great difficulty would arise, namely, that, while Christ says he is in heaven,we should seek him in the Supper. For **one and the same body cannot be in several places at the same time.**

Luther (Anon): Should one not rather assume a trope in the sentence 'He ascended into heaven', and leave the text of the Lord's Supper as it is? For figurative speech could much more conveniently be found in the word 'heaven', which, as is generally acknowledged, is used in Scripture in various meanings.

Zwingli (Anon): This sentence does not require a figurative understanding.

Luther (Anon): Nor does the other one.

* * *

---

[94]See above, 147, 148.

Oecolampadius ***(Hed, Coll, Anon, Bull)****, replacing Zwingli, who feels exhausted:* I am not yet satisfied with our discussion of John 6. I plead for a fair exegesis of Scripture. In John 3, Christ teaches Nicodemus that the one and only means of entering the kingdom of heaven is regeneration. Since this is sufficient, it is not necessary, and is without benefit, that the body of Christ should be eaten in the Supper in a bodily way.

Luther ***(Hed, Anon)***: You are right in demanding that nothing should be added to the Scriptures. However, you must prove that we have added something. For, concerning the Scriptures we have wrestled with the pope. God has many ways to create, support, and increase faith in us: when we hear the Word, either publicly or privately; when we are baptized; when we are fed with the body of our Lord; etc. Which of these he uses, and why he uses so many and diverse ones, we should not try to understand. He himself knows what is good and profitable for us.

Oecolampadius ***(Anon)***: We read in John 16:28: 'I came forth from the Father, and am come into the world: again I leave the world, and go to the Father'. This passage excludes the presence from the Lord's Supper, and compels us to admit a trope in the Words of Institution.

Luther ***(Anon)***: The words of Christ in Luke 24:44, 'These are the words which I spoke unto you, while I **was** yet with you', indicate what he means when he speaks of 'leaving the world'.

Oecolampadius ***(Anon, Hed)*** *proposes the passage John 16:7, It is expedient for you that I go away . . .':* Since Christ says it is expedient if he goes away, there is no doubt that his presence would be not only inexpedient, but even a hindrance, as he himself continues: 'If I go not away, the Comforter will not come unto you'. *Oecolampadius then discusses Romans 8:11, 'He that raised up Christ from the dead shall also quicken your mortal bodies'.* This hope is being taken from us if we let the bread be the body of Christ. If we let the bread be the body of Christ, our hope of resurrection corresponding to the resurrection of Christ is destroyed.

Luther ***(Anon, Hed)***: This hope is not only not taken away, or destroyed by the presence of Christ, but rather supported and confirmed. Faith looks upon the body of Christ present in the Sacrament, and upon the body which is in heaven.

Oecolampadius ***(Hed)***: Luther says the same all the time as if we had the bread without the Word of God. The church is founded upon the word 'Thou art . . . the Son of the living God' (Matt. 16:16), not upon the word 'This is my body'.

Luther ***(Hed, Coll, Anon)***: It annoys you that I always stick to the words 'This is my body'. I am not doing this without consideration. I confess that the body is in heaven, but I also confess that it is in the Sacrament. I desire to stick to these words that Christ is in heaven, and that he is in the Sacrament. I do not ask what is against nature, but only what is against the faith.

(Anon): If you regard the flesh as useless, you may do so as far as I am concerned; but we rely on God's Word. The Word says, first, that Christ has a body: that I believe. Furthermore, that even this body has ascended to heaven and sitteth on the right hand of the Father: that I also believe. The Word says in the same way that this body itself is in the Lord's Supper, and is given us to be eaten: this also I believe. For my Lord Jesus Christ can easily do it when he desires to, and in his words he testifies that he will do it. On these words I shall rely steadfastly until he himself, by another word, says something different.

Oecolampadius ***(Anon, Brenz)*** *proceeds to a discussion of circumscription and finiteness as natural properties of a body and draws the conclusion:* Each body must necessarily be in one place only. It cannot be in several places simultaneously. Thus, since the body of Christ is in heaven, it cannot be in the Sacrament on earth.

Luther ***(Anon, Rhaps, Brenz)***: **I do not want to hear mathematical distinctions in this connection**. For God, as the Aristotelian philosophers also admit, can cause one body to be either in one place only, or in several places at the same time, or outside of every place, or he is even able to bring it about that several bodies are simultaneously in one place. For the world is, indeed, the largest of all bodies, and yet, according to some physicists, it is in no place, since outside of the world there is neither space nor time. Therefore I will not anxiously discuss the mode of presence (*modus praesentiae*), whether the body of Christ be in a place or outside a place, because this is quite irrelevant. I do not, therefore, demand such arguments of reason, but clear and valid words from Scripture. If it is desired, however, I am prepared to have a discussion with you on mathematics to your heart's desire at an appointed hour. But I can predict already that by such discussions nothing can be gained in this matter. Testimonies from Scripture are required.

Oecolampadius ***(Anon, Hed)***: From Matthew 26:11, 'Ye have the poor always with you; but me ye have not always', it follows: According to his divinity, grace, and power, Christ is present to all always and everywhere. If, however, he speaks of his absence, then necessarily he will be absent as far as his humanity is concerned. Thus, in the Supper he cannot be present bodily. He has become 'in all things . . . like unto his brethren' (Heb. 2:17). As he is of one substance with the Father according to his divinity, so he is of one substance with us according to his humanity.[95] What we are agreed on is that Christ is present in heaven [according to his divinity and humanity] and in the Supper [according to his divinity].

Luther ***(Hed, Anon)***: Christ is, indeed, present until the end of the world in Baptism, in the Supper, in the preaching of the Word. Until his coming **you** may distinguish between his humanity and his divinity; this is no concern of **mine**. 'Ye have the poor always with you; **but me ye have not always'. That is the best argument you have put forward today**; it sounds fairly plausible. Christ is in the Sacrament substantially, as he was born of the Virgin. If my opponents think that the passage Matthew 26:11 contradicts the words of the Lord's Supper, why do they not look for a figurative meaning in that passage rather than in these words? In Matthew 26:11 we have the most [nearly] perfect analogy of faith. For it speaks of faith in things unseen and of faith in a promise. What Christ really meant is that he would not again be with them in such a way as to be in need of their previous services. He would rather send us the poor through whom we could serve him. The antithesis is: **Visibly** ye do not have me always, but ye have the poor. You may wash **their** feet; **me** ye shall not have always. In this sense he says also in Luke 24:44, 'These are the words which I spake unto you, while I was yet with you' (that is, while I was with you in the way of an ordinary, visible presence).

Oecolampadius ***(Anon, Rhaps)***: **You should not cling to the humanity and the flesh of Christ, but rather lift up your mind to his divinity.**

Luther ***(Rhaps, Anon):*** **I do not know of any God except him who was made flesh, nor do I want to have another.** And there is no other God who could save us, besides the God Incarnate. Therefore we shall not suffer his humanity to be underestimated or neglected.

Oecolampadius ***(Hed, Anon, Coll)***: We also say that we do not know Christ after the flesh (2 Cor. 5:16), because we know him after the Spirit also in the Sacrament. If you are not a new creature, you know Christ after the flesh only.

---

[95]According to the Creed of Chalcedon; compare the Athanasian Creed.

Melanchthon ***(Hed, Coll)***: 'Not after the flesh' means 'not after our flesh'.

Luther ***(Anon)***: Nor do we know him 'after the flesh'. To know 'after the flesh' means to know in an external way without the Spirit and without faith. We know Christ after the Spirit if we are certain by faith that Christ has come for our salvation and has done and suffered all for us.

Oecolampadius ***(Anon)***: When Christ gave us his body he, indeed, gave the body that he had. He had, however, a body that was capable of suffering and dying. If this be true, surely that body cannot be profitable for us, but rather a spiritual eating is required.

Luther ***(Anon)***: The eating of the body of Christ can be profitable because the promise of forgiveness of sins is connected with it. However, since every promise requires faith, and faith is a spiritual knowledge, therefore that bodily eating, too, if it is done in faith, should be regarded as something spiritual. It is sufficient for me that such a profitable body is given to me to be eaten. Whether that body is mortal or capable of suffering — mortality and passibility are accidentals — I do not care more about that than I would care about the garment in which Christ was dressed at the Last Supper.

Oecolampadius ***(Hed, Coll)***: You do not admit of a trope in the Words of Institution, and yet you understand them as synecdoche. Thus, you introduce a new meaning contrary to the doctors of the church universal.

Luther ***(Hed, Coll, Anon)***: May God decide that question! We do not compel anyone, but leave the matter to God. Synecdoche is a form of speech to be found not only in Holy Scripture, but also in every common language, so we cannot do without it. By synecdoche we speak of the containing vessel when we mean the content, or of the content when also including the vessel, as, for example, when we speak of the mug or of the beer, using only one of the two to denote also the other. Or, to take another example, if the king tells his servant to bring his sword, he tacitly includes the sheath. Such understanding is required by the text. The metaphor does away with the content, such as when you understand the 'body' as 'figure of the body'. That the synecdoche does not do. We admit the synecdoche in order to satisfy the sophists. In Holy Scripture you find it in John 1:33: 'Upon whom thou shalt see the Spirit descending'. The Baptist saw the dove in which the Holy Spirit was. Figurative speech removes the core and leaves the shell only. Synecdoche is not a comparison, but it rather says: 'That is there, and it is contained in it'.

There is no better example of a synecdoche than 'This is my body'.

Philip, you answer. I am tired of talking.

Oecolampadius ***(Coll)*** *tries to show that John 1:33 could be understood in support of his view.*

Zwingli ***(Hed, Anon)***: Something has been said already of Christ's body in heaven, but the following passages are to be taken into consideration: 'God sending his own Son in the likeness of sinful flesh' (Rom. 8:3; ***Hed*** *quotes, instead, 8:29*). 'Who, being in the form of God . . . took upon him the form of a servant, and was made in the likeness of men: and being found in fashion as a man . . .' (Phil. 2:6 ff). 'God sending his own Son in the likeness of sinful flesh' (Rom. 8:3). 'Wherefore in all things it behoved him to be made like unto his brethren' (Heb. 2:17). '[He] was in all points tempted like as we are, yet without sin' (Heb. 4:15). 'As in the earthy, such are they also that are earthy; and as is the heavenly, such are they also that are heavenly' (1 Cor. 15:48). I will not allow these passages to be passed over. They show that the humanity of Jesus was finite like ours. '**If Christ's body is above, it must be in one place**', as Augustine says, supported by Fulgentius. Luther, however, makes it to be everywhere (*ubique*) as something infinite (*infinitum*). As our body is in one place, so also his body cannot be in two places; or as our bodies, after having been transformed into his image, would be without a place or in several places simultaneously.

Luther ***(Hed, Coll, Anon, Os, Rhaps, Bull)***: As to the Fathers, we shall find out whether you can boast of them. You speak for your party, we for ours. Your conclusion from the 'conformity' or 'similarity' between Christ's body and our future bodies is not cogent. It is an *argumentum ab accidente ad substantiam*. Even if it were valid it would prove nothing except that the **form** of our future bodies would be similar to [that of] Christ's body. It would by no means follow that also with regard to **power** we [our bodies] should be similar to his body, but for a special dispensation of God. As to the second argument, based on 'in all things made like unto [us]' (Heb. 2:17), which again is an *argumentum ab accidente ad substantiam,* this would lead to statements like those that Christ had dark eyes, a wife, a home in Germany, and so on. I cannot admit mathematical similarities here. In my book I have written about mathematical similarities.[96] You have read that, but you did not understand it. I do

[96] *Large Confession*, WA 26, 326, 29 ff. Quoted in *Form. Conc., Sol. Decl. VII, 93 ff* (Trigl. 1004 ff).

not like to dispute any longer on mathematics. Let us not try to inquire **how** Christ's body is in the Lord's Supper. In Holy Scripture I do not admit mathematical dimensions. **God is higher than all mathematicians**. Christ can keep his body without space at a certain place. **He is in the Sacrament [but] not as in a place.**

Zwingli ***(Coll, Hed)*** *reads from the Greek New Testament: 'Hos en morphē theou hyparchōn . . . morphēn doulou labōn'* (Phil. 2:6,7).

Luther ***(Hed)***: Read German, or Latin, not Greek.[97]

Zwingli ***(Hed, Coll, Bull)***: I beg your pardon for having used the Greek New Testament. I have been using it for twelve years. The Latin Testament I have read only once. The word *morphē* in Philippians 2 has these two meanings (divine infinite form, and human finite form). Christ is finite, as we are finite.

Luther ***(Coll, Hed)***: I admit that. But God can cause the body of Christ to be either not in a place, or in a place.

Zwingli ***(Anon):*** We, too, speak of a sacramental presence of the body of Christ, which means that the body of Christ is in the Supper representatively (*repraesentative*).[98]

Luther ***(Anon)***: You want to speak of a permanent presence of the body of Christ in such a way that you take away from the bread the substance of the body, leaving us only the empty shell, while the words of Christ sound differently: 'This is my body'.

Zwingli and Oecolampadius ***(Anon, Os, Rhaps)*** *admit:* God certainly **can** make it possible for one body to be in different places at the same time. We, however, demand proof that he does so in the Lord's Supper. He does not do this, as appears from the fact that Holy Scripture shows us Christ always in a particular place, as in the manger, in the temple, in the desert, on the cross, in the sepulchre, at the right hand of the Father. From this it follows that Christ's body must always be in a particular place.

Osiander ***(Os)***: To this I reply: Such Scripture passages do not prove more than that Christ at certain times was in particular places. They do by no means prove, however, that he always and for ever has been, or must be, in one place, and that he cannot be, naturally, or supernaturally, in no place or in several places simultaneously, as you think.

[97]Luther regarded this as the vanity of a humanist, especially since most of those present could not understand Greek. Zwingli had a better knowledge of Greek than Luther, who from his monastic days was accustomed to the Vulgate.

[98]This means that he is mentally present to the unbelieving communicant. See W. Koehler, *Zwingli und Luther, II,* 106.

Zwingli ***(Os)***: I have proved that Christ was in one place. It is up to you to prove that he is in no place or in many places.

Luther ***(Os)***: At the beginning of our colloquy, you promised to prove that this would be impossible, and that our understanding is wrong. It is your duty to give that proof, and not to demand a proof from us. For we do not owe you a proof.

Zwingli ***(Os)***: It would be a shame to hold, teach, and defend such an important article without being able or willing to give a proof from Scripture.

Luther ***(Os, Rhaps, Anon.***[99]***)*** *lifts the tablecloth and reads the passage which he had written with chalk on the table: 'Hoc est corpus meum'.* This is our Scripture passage. You have not yet taken it from us, as you promised to do. 'This is my body.' **I cannot pass over the text of my Lord Jesus Christ, but I must confess and believe that the body of Christ is there.**

Zwingli ***(Anon)***, *jumping to his feet:* Thus you, also, Doctor, assume that the body is in the Supper locally. For you say, The body of Christ must be **there. There! There! This is certainly an adverb of space!**

Luther ***(Anon)***: I have simply quoted the words of Christ, and I was not prepared for such a conclusion. If we want to deal cunningly with one another, then I testify that **I have nothing whatever to do with mathematical reasons,** and that **I exclude and reject completely from the words of the Lord's Supper the adverb of space**. The words are: '**This** is my body', not: '**There** is my body'. Whether it is there locally or not locally, I do not want to know. For God has not yet revealed anything with reference to that, and no mortal man can prove it one way or the other.

Zwingli ***(Coll)***: Should, then, everything go according to your will?

THIRD SESSION

Sunday Morning, October 3

Zwingli ***(Anon, Hed)***: The words *morphē* [form] and *schēma* [fashion] indicate that the body of Christ must occupy a certain space, and must exist locally.

Luther ***(Hed, Coll, Anon, Os)***: I have told you already: the body of Christ may be in space, and it may not be in space. God can even

———

[99] According to ***Anon*** this dramatic scene took place on Sunday morning.

cause my body not to be in space. This text does not contain mathematics. What space is is taught by mathematics. The schoolmen have held that one body can be in many places, or many bodies in one place, or that a body can be in no place at all. They say that God can do the same with all bodies, let alone with the body of Christ. Who am I to measure the power of God? He maintains the largest organism existing, the universe, without space. Therefore the world does not have a place where it exists.

Zwingli ***(Hed, Coll, Anon, Bull)***: You draw conclusions from that-which-may-be to that-which-is. What I say to be true of space should be true, also, of the adverb of space. Do not take refuge with the schoolmen. Prove, I pray, that the body of Christ can be in many places.

Luther ***(Coll, Anon, Bull)***: 'This is my body'.

Zwingli ***(Anon)***: We are not the authors of the doctrine we teach, but the oldest doctors of the church have already taught it, such as Augustine when he said 'Whatever exists in a certain place is a body'.

Luther ***(Anon)***: It is, indeed, true that whatever is contained in a place is a body. However, that which is a body must not always be contained in a place.

Zwingli ***(Anon)***: Augustine says again, 'Take away space from bodies, and you will have taken away the bodies'.

Luther ***(Anon)***: According to the general rule it is true, indeed, that bodies are contained in space, but God can easily preserve bodies outside of any space.

Zwingli ***(Hed, Coll, Rhaps, Anon, Os, Bull)***: There is a passage in Fulgentius which says that the body of Christ is in one place: 'Since one and the same Son of God, true God, born of God the Father, has become true man for us from human seed — for he is of the seed of David according to the flesh — he has a true divine, and a true human nature. He has not lost the marks of true divinity, and he has accepted the marks of true humanity. He is one and the same who was born after the flesh of his mother in time, and who remains after his divinity from the Father eternal. He is one and the same person who is a man locally circumscribed according to his human origin, and who is immeasurable God according to his divine origin'.[100] I

[100] *Ad Thrasamundum* (MPL 65, 264). It is not known where Zwingli stopped. The continuation is: 'He is one and the same who according to his human substance was absent from heaven when he was on earth, and left the earth when he ascended into heaven, and who according to his immeasurable divine substance did not leave heaven when he descended from heaven, nor left the earth when he ascended into heaven'.

object to your assertions that, first, 'everything is full of Christ', and secondly, 'if the divinity had not suffered in Christ, it would not be Luther's Christ'.[101]

Luther **(Hed, Anon)**: I am prepared to listen to the Fathers. But the passage from Fulgentius does not deal with the Lord's Supper. It was directed against the Manichaeans and other heretics who denied the humanity of Christ. To refute them, Fulgentius intended to prove that Christ had a real body. He tried to prove that by showing that Christ was a human person, locally circumscribed, this local existence proving that he had a real body. What Fulgentius thought about the Lord's Supper can be seen from another passage in which this Father states that the body and blood of our Lord are offered in the Supper: 'Know, therefore, what happens when the sacrifices are offered, in order that you may understand why the coming of the Spirit is necessary. For that is fulfilled in the offering of the sacrifices, which according to the witness of the blessed apostle, our Saviour himself has commanded: "The Lord Jesus the same night in which he was betrayed took bread: and when he had given thanks, he brake it, and said, Take, eat: This is my body, which is broken for you" '.[101A]

Zwingli **(Hed, Coll, Anon, Bull, Rhaps)**: This quotation from Fulgentius is correct. It is well known. The word 'offer (*offerendi vocabulum*)', however, ought to be understood in a figurative way as meaning 'to celebrate the remembrance' ('*memoria oblationis*' in **Hed, Coll;** '*figurative pro memoriam agere*' in **Anon;** '*ein Wiedergedächtnis des Opfers*' in **Bull**), as Augustine interprets it in a letter to Boniface.[102] Thus, also, the words 'body' and 'blood' should be accepted in a figurative way, as we are accustomed to say by way of a metonymy: 'Tommorow will be Ascension', which means nothing more than 'remembrance of Ascension'.

Luther **(Hed, Coll)**: These are not proofs, but exaggerations. I do not accept 'oblation' for 'remembrance of oblation'.

Zwingli **(Anon, Coll)**: In that case you re-establish the sacrifice of the mass, and that means to revoke all your pious and learned writings against that sacrifice.

Osiander **(Hed)**: How is it if the Fathers erred in speaking of the sacrifice?

---

[101] *Large Confession,* WA 26, 319 ff.

[101A] MPL 65, 785.

[102] MPL 33, 363. The passage is quoted by Koehler, 113.

Luther (according to ***Coll****, Luther dismisses the word sacrifice;* ***Coll, Anon, Bull)***: I am bound and held captive by the words of the Lord, spoken at the institution, and therefore cannot accede to your opinion on the basis of your remarks. The words 'This is my body' prove that the body of Christ can be in many places simultaneously. For these words prove the presence of the body in the bread.

Zwingli ***(Coll)***: If, then, the body is in the bread, it has to be there as in a place.[103] There I have caught you, Doctor.

Luther ***(Coll)***: I leave it to God whether or not the body of Christ is in a place (*in loco*). For me this is enough: 'This is my body'.

Zwingli ***(Coll)***: You are begging the question. In the same way, a quarrelsome person could say, 'John was the son of Mary', for Christ said 'Behold thy son', and he would persistently repeat, 'Behold thy son, behold thy son'.

Luther ***(Hed, Coll, Anon)***: You charge me with begging the question, and you beg the question yourself. We do not need a *petitio principii,* for **every article of faith is a principle in itself and does not need to be proved by another article.**

Oecolampadius ***(Anon)*** *reads some passages from Augustine on the words in John 6:32: 'Moses gave you not that bread from heaven . . .' and concludes:* The body of Christ in which he rose from the dead must be in one place.

Luther ***(Hed, Anon, Brenz, Os)***: I reply to the passage from Augustine as I did in the case of Fulgentius: this passage again has nothing to do with the Lord's Supper. In his letter to Januarius, Augustine emphasizes that the body of Christ is eaten orally.[104] In another letter, Augustine establishes the rule that his writings should always be measured by the standard of Holy Scripture. Wherever he would seem to contradict Scripture, his doctrine would have to be interpreted according to the canonical books or, if that be impossible, rejected.

Zwingli ***(Coll)***: Scripture passages ought to be compared with one another and to be explained by themselves. Tell me, is the body of Christ in a place?

---

[103]In a letter to his wife dated Oct. 4 (WA BR 5, No. 1476), Luther writes that the best argument of Zwingli was: '*corpus non potest sine loco, ergo Christi corpus non est in pane'*.

[104]Luther does not give the quotation literally. Augustine (MPL 33, 203) refers to the custom of fasting before Holy Communion: ' . . . *placuit Spiritui sancto, ut in honorem tanti sacramenti* ***in os*** *Christiani prius* ***dominicum corpus*** *intravit, quam caeteri cibi'*.

Brenz ***(Coll)***: It is without place.

Zwingli ***(Coll, Bull)***: Augustine says the body of Christ must be in one place; if it were not in a place, it would not be a body.

Luther ***(Hed, Coll, Bull)***: 'It must be in one place': This word of Augustine does not speak of the Lord's Supper. In the Sacrament the body is not as in a place.

Oecolampadius ***(Hed)***: Then the body of Christ is not really in the Sacrament *sōmatikos*, bodily, that is, with a true body.

FOURTH SESSION

Sunday Afternoon, October 3

Oecolampadius ***(Coll, Hed)***: You have admitted that the body of Christ is not in the Sacrament as in a place. Now I ask in all sincerity: How, then, can there be a body? (*He reads from Fulgentius and Augustine.*)

Luther ***(Hed, Coll)***: In the beginning of our discussion we took as our basis the Holy Scriptures. They are not against us. Then you appealed to the Fathers. Among them you have Augustine and Fulgentius on your side. The rest are against you.

Oecolampadius ***(Coll)***: Bring forth the Fathers who are on your side.

Luther ***(Hed, Coll)***: I do not know of any doctor of the church who would create agreement among us. I am wondering why we quarrel about the 'place', it being agreed by the whole of Christendom that God can exist outside of space or in a specific place. **Let us find means by which we can come to an agreement, lest there be uproar among the people, and in order to remove this very bad dissension.** I admit that the Sacrament is called a sign of a holy thing (*sacramentum sacrae rei signum*).[105] **I admit that the sacraments are sacred symbols** and that, as such, they signify something which is beyond them, and which transcends our intellect. It is childish if a person, seeing the bread, says: I have seen the Lord. We must lift up our mind. But **to speak of a mere sign, that I cannot bear. There is a difference between natural signs and signs instituted by God.** As to that, we are one.

Oecolampadius ***(Hed, Anon)*** *quotes some passages from Augustine* (*De doctrina christiana IV, 21 and Quaestiones in Heptateuchum, MPL 34, 701 ff*) *with the quotations, 'The soul is the*

---

[105]Augustine, MPL 41, 282.

blood' (Lev. 17:11-14), and 'That Rock was Christ' (1 Cor. 10:4): **I admit that the sacrament is not only a sign, but that in the Lord's Supper there is the true body of Christ through faith.**

Luther ***(Hed, Coll)***: Augustine was a young man when he wrote the *Quaestiones* against the Manichaeans, and he had no sure text to prove his opinion. Again I say: **It is necessary to subordinate the doctors of the church to Christ.**

Oecolampadius ***(Hed, Coll, Os, Oecolampadius)***: We quote the ancient doctors in order that every one may see that we do not have a new doctrine. **We do not build on them, but on the Word of God** Everyone knows who Augustine was and that he taught and confessed not his private opinion only, but rather that of the entire church of his day.

Luther ***(Hed, Anon, Os):*** I have already answered your argument sufficiently. If you have stronger arguments, put them forward. From those that you have submitted, we cannot be moved to alter our understanding of the words of the Lord's Supper.

Oecolampadius ***(Hed, Anon, Os, Rhaps)***: As you are not moved by our text, we are not moved by your expositions. In vain would we produce a thousand sermons of the Fathers. **It seems to me, therefore, to be better to cease the discussion.**

Luther ***(Os)***: Now you have proved nothing, as your own conscience will tell you.

Chancellor Feige ***(Os)*** *interrupts the discussion, admonishing the parties to seek means and ways of coming to an agreement.*

Luther ***(Os, Hed)***: **I do not know of any other means but to give due honour to the Word of God and to believe with us. I remain in my faith.** I cannot give in.

Zwingli or Oecolampadius ***(Coll)***: **We can neither comprehend nor believe that the body of Christ is there.**

Luther ***(Hed, Brenz, Os, Bull, Rhaps)***: **I commend you to God and his judgment**. *(Luther then thanks Oecolampadius for having made plain his views in a friendly manner and without bitterness. He also thanks Zwingli although he had spoken in a more bitter way. He asks that his own bitter words, if he, yielding to his own flesh and blood, had spoken such, might be forgiven.)* Let there be a mutual pardoning.

Oecolampadius ***(Hed)*** *asks for God's sake that the poor church should be taken into consideration.*

Zwingli ***(Hed, Os)*** *asks Luther to pardon his bitterness. He goes on, almost weeping:* **It has always been my eager wish to have you as a friend**, and I still ask for that. There are no men, not even in Italy and France, whom I would like to see more than you.

Luther ***(Hed, Brenz)***: Ask God that you may be enlightened.

Oecolampadius ***(Hed, Os)***: You, too, should ask for that. You need it not less.

* * *

Jacob Sturm ***(Hed, Os, Brenz)***: Most illustrous prince, my gracious lord, I left Strasburg with the idea that only one article was in controversy and was to be discussed here. Dr Luther, however, at the beginning of this colloquy said something which might be used to the disadvantage of my city, namely, as if the Trinity and other doctrines were not taught correctly by us. If I remained silent, this might lead to the assumption that these things have not been settled here. Being sent here, together with two of our preachers, by the City Council of Strasburg, I would thus bring home two quarrels instead of one. I therefore beg Your Highness to allow Master Bucer to destroy the suspicion and answer the objections.

(After a short deliberation, permission to speak is given to Bucer.)

Bucer ***(Hed, Brenz, Os)*** *speaks on the doctrines of the Trinity, the Person of Christ, original sin, Baptism, justification, the ministry of the Word as they are taught in Strasburg, rejecting especially the suspicion of Arianism. In conclusion* ***he asks Luther to testify that this doctrine is orthodox.***

Luther ***(Hed, Os)***: No, I cannot do that. I am neither your Lord nor your judge. You reject me as well as my doctrine. Thus, I cannot regard you as my disciples. We were well aware that you desire to spread your doctrine under our name. I have now heard you, but I do not know whether or not you teach the same at home. Therefore I refuse to give you a testimony. Nor do you need it. For everywhere you boast that you have not learned from us. It is evident that you have not learned from us. I do not want to be your teacher. As to our teaching, you have my writings and my confession.

Bucer ***(Hed, Os)***: Will you recognize me as a brother, or will you show me my errors that I may overcome them?

Luther ***(Os)***: I am neither your Lord, nor your judge, nor your teacher. Your spirit and our spirit cannot go together. Indeed, **it is**

quite obvious that we do not have the same spirit.[106] For there cannot be one and the same spirit where, on one side, the words of Christ are accepted in sincere faith, and, on the other side, this faith is criticized, attacked, denied, and spoken of with frivolous blasphemies. Therefore, as I have told you, we commend you to the judgment of God. Teach as you think you can defend it in the sight of God.

* * *

Chancellor Feige ***(Os, Brenz)*** *expresses the thanks of the prince to all who have accepted his invitation to take part in the colloquy. For the present they are dismissed, but they are to stay in their rooms and be prepared to accept the summons of the Landgrave, either together or individually, for he wants to take counsel with them before they leave.*

FINAL NEGOTIATIONS

Sunday Night, October 3

On Sunday night the Landgrave took counsel with individual participants in the colloquy concerning the question whether, despite the failure of the discussions, some agreement might not be found. The result of these conversations was a formula suggested by the Lutherans.

Luther's Suggestion

'We confess that, **by virtue of the words "This is my body, this is my blood"**, the body and blood are truly[107] — *hoc est: substantive et essentialiter, non autem quantitative vel qualitative vel localiter*[108] —

[106] In his letter to J. Probst at Bremen dated June 1, 1530 (WA BR 5, No. 1577, 340, 54) Luther quotes the words from memory: 'You have another spirit than we (*Vos habetis alium spiritum quam nos*)'. It is noteworthy that this famous word was addressed to Bucer, not to Zwingli.

[107] The text was preserved by Oecolampadius and is confirmed by later quotations. See Koehler, 131 ff. The original is German, with Latin words to explain the *wahrhaftiglich*.

[108] The formula maintains the Lutheran doctrine of the Real Presence without mentioning the question of the *manducatio impiorum*. The real body and the real

present and distributed in the Lord's Supper. Since we so far have held the opinion that our dear sirs and brethren, Oecolampadius, Zwingli, and their adherents, totally reject the Real Presence of this body and blood, but now in a friendly colloquy have found it to be otherwise, we now declare and state that the arguments and reasons found in our books concerning the Sacrament are not directed against and do not apply to Oecolampadius, Zwingli, and their adherents, but against those who totally reject the presence of the body in the Supper.'

While this was to be signed by the Lutherans, the version for the Zwinglians contained the corresponding declaration:

'Since we so far have held the opinion that our dear sirs and brethren, Martin Luther, and Melanchthon, and their adherents, hold and teach that the body and blood of Christ are in the Supper *quantitative vel qualitative vel localiter*, according to carnal thinking, but now in a friendly colloquy have found it to be otherwise, . . . [as above, *mutatis mutandis*] . . ., but against those who put Christ's body and blood in a gross and carnal way into the bread and wine'.[109]

---

blood are present 'substantively and essentially'. What is meant by these words may be understood from the hymn *'Gott sei gelobet und gebenedeiet'*, the first stanza of which Luther took over from the Middle Ages as a document of the pure doctrine still preserved by the medieval church: *'Herr, durch deinen heiligen Leichnam / Der von deiner Mutter Maria kam / Und das heilige Blut / Hilf uns . . .'* This popular German hymn, which was sung at Corpus Christi based on the Latin *'Lauda, Sion, salvatorem'* expresses the simple belief in the Real Presence which Luther shared with the church before him, and which he regarded as a necessary article of faith. The negative statement 'not quantitatively or qualitatively or locally' corresponds to the scholastic doctrine that body and blood are present, not according to their quality (the qualities which body and blood otherwise have), not according to quantity (extension, etc.), nor locally (see above, 35). The difference between Luther and the schoolmen on this point is that he uses these words, not to give any theory as to the *how* of the presence, but only to reject the 'geometrical' (as he calls it; we would say 'physical') understanding of the presence.

[109]Osiander (WA, 150) simplifies the matter by relating from the point of view of the Lutherans:'If the other side would confess that the body of Christ is present in the Supper, and not in the memory of men only, then we would abstain from all further questions and not ask whether it is there in a bodily or spiritual way, in a natural or supernatural way, locally or not locally, and we could accept them again as brethren'. (See also Koehler, 132.) On the basis of this suggestion by the Lutherans, not only Osiander, but also modern scholars (v. Schubert, E. Seeberg) have put the blame for the failure of Marburg on Zwingli. W. Koehler, *Zwingli und Luther*, II, 115 ff, shows why the formula which contained Luther's doctrine on the Real Presence was not acceptable to Zwingli.

As Zwingli rejected this suggestion, which in 1534 became the basis for an agreement in Wuerttemberg, and later a union between Wittenberg and the cities of south-western Germany, the attempt of Sunday night to reach a union was bound to fail.

Monday, October 4.

At the request of the Landgrave, who did not want the colloquy to end in a complete failure, discussions within smaller groups were held on Monday morning. The main subject seems to have been whether or not, despite existing differences, altar- and church-fellowship could be practised. It was the opinion of the Landgrave, who was convinced that the controversy was about words only, that a certain *syncretismus* should be possible.[110] This, however, was rejected by the Lutherans 'for great and Christian reasons'.[111] Finally, the Landgrave, in order to get at least one result, asked Luther to draft articles in which that measure of agreement which had been found to exist was to be expressed. Thus, Luther formulated fifteen articles, based on the articles which he had brought from Wittenberg and which later were called the *Schwabach Articles.*[112] These *Marburg Articles* were discussed, and with few alterations were accepted, to the surprise of Luther, who did not think that Zwingli would accept statements that were not in line with his previous doctrine. It appears that the Landgrave, who himself seems to have taken part in formulating Article 15, removed existing obstacles.[113]

THE MARBURG ARTICLES

Article 1

That we on both sides unanimously believe and hold that there is only one true natural God, Maker of all creatures, and that this same

---

[110]This word was used in the 16th and 17th centuries for what we now call 'union'.

[111]Osiander, WA, 151.

[112]In the Wittenberg Edition of *Luther's Works*, Article 14 on infant baptism was accidentally omitted, and Article 15 became Article 14. This mistake is still to be found in the editions preceding Walch, and, consequently, St Louis, XVII, col. 1940 ff. Even EA 65, 88 ff (published in 1855) gives only 14 articles, while Walch XXIII, 35 has corrected the old mistake. G. J. Beto follows that text of St Louis, XVII without taking into account the correction, col. 1942, footnote. Hospinian has the 15 articles; Loescher mentions only 14.

[113]W. Koehler, *Huldrych Zwingli*, 212.

God is one in essence and nature, and triune in the persons, namely Father, Son, and Holy Spirit, as it was decreed in the Council of Nicaea, and is sung and read in the Nicene Creed by the entire Christian Church throughout the world.

Article 2

We believe that not the Father, nor the Holy Spirit, but the Son of God the Father, true and natural God himself, became man through the working of the Holy Spirit, without the agency of male seed, born of the pure Virgin Mary, complete in body and soul as another man, but without sin.

Article 3

That this Son of God and Mary, undivided in person, Jesus Christ, was crucified for us, died, was buried, rose from the dead, ascended into heaven, sits at the right hand of God, Lord over all creatures, and will come to judge the living and the dead.

Article 4

We believe that original sin is innate, and inherited by us from Adam, and is such a sin as condemns all men. And if Jesus Christ had not come to help us by his death and life, we would of necessity have died eternally and could not have entered God's kingdom and salvation.

Article 5

We believe that we are saved from this sin, and from all other sins, as well as from eternal death, if we believe in this Son of God, Jesus Christ, who died for us, and that beyond this faith no works, station, or order can make us free from any sin.

Article 6

That this faith is a gift of God which we cannot obtain by any preceding works or merits, nor acquire by our own strength, but the Holy Spirit gives and creates this faith in our hearts, as it pleases him, when we hear the Gospel or Word of Christ.

Article 7

That this faith is our righteousness before God, on account of which God reckons and regards us as righteous, godly, and holy, without all works and merit, and thereby delivers us from sin, death, and hell, and receives us into grace and saves us, for the sake of his Son, in whom we accordingly believe and thereby enjoy and partake of righteousness, life, and all possessions. Therefore, all monastic life and vows, when they are reckoned as aids to salvation, are altogether condemned.

Article 8

That the Holy Spirit normally gives this faith or his gift to no one without preaching, or the oral Word, or the Gospel of Christ preceding, but by and with such oral Word he works and creates faith where and in whom it pleases him (Rom. 10:17).[114]

Article 9

That Holy Baptism is a sacrament that has been instituted by God as an aid to such faith, and because God's command 'Go ye, baptize', and God's promise 'He that believes' are therein, it is not a mere empty sign or watchword among Christians, but rather a sign and work of God by which our faith grows,[115] and through which we are regenerated to eternal life.

Article 10

That such faith, when we have been reckoned and made righteous and holy by it,[116] by the efficacy of the Holy Spirit, exercises good works through us, namely, to love our neighbour, to pray to God, and to suffer all persecution.

Article 11

That confession or the seeking of counsel from one's pastor or neighbour should, indeed, be unconstrained and free, but nevertheless is very helpful to consciences that are distressed,

---

[114]The emphasis of Article 6 and 8 on the external Word as means of grace is noticeable; compare AC Article 5.

[115]The old prints vary between *'fordern'* and *'foddern'*. Both can mean either 'require' or 'make grow' ('further'). A decision is impossible. Zwingli understood 'require'. See the note to Article 9 in WA, 165 f.

[116]Notice here how the original Lutheran doctrine is expressed, according to which *iustificari* means at the same time *iustum effici*. The believing sinner is absolved, and this makes him righteous in the eyes of God, though his righteousness is hidden to the sinner and to others. Thus, he is *peccator simul et iustus*.

troubled, or burdened with sins, or that have fallen into error, especially on account of the absolution or consolation of the Gospel, which is the true absolution.

Article 12

That all magistrates and secular laws, courts and ordinances, wherever they are, are a truly good estate, and are not forbidden, as some papists and Anabaptists teach and hold. On the contrary, that a Christian who is born or called thereto, can certainly be saved through faith in Christ, just as in the estate of father or mother, husband or wife, etc.

Article 13

What is called tradition or human ordinances in spiritual or ecclesiastical matters, provided they do not obviously contradict God's Word, may freely be kept or abolished according to [the needs of] the people with whom we deal, in order to prevent unnecessary offence in practising love toward the weak, and to preserve peace. Also that the doctrine forbidding marriage to priests is a doctrine of the devil (1 Tim. 4:1 f).

Article 14

That baptism of infants is right, and that they are thereby received into God's grace and into Christendom.

Article 15

We all believe and hold concerning the Supper of our dear Lord Jesus Christ that both species should be used according to the institution of Christ; also that the mass is not a work whereby one obtains grace for another, dead or living; also that the Sacrament of the Altar is a sacrament of the true body and blood of Jesus Christ, and that the spiritual partaking of this body and blood is especially necessary for every true Christian. In like manner, that the use of the Sacrament, like the Word, is given and ordained by almighty God in order that weak consciences may thereby be excited to faith by the Holy Spirit. And although at present we are not agreed as to whether the true body and blood are bodily present in the bread and wine, nevertheless each party should show Christian love to the other, so far as conscience can permit, and both should fervently pray Almighty God that he, by his Spirit, would confirm us in the right understanding. Amen.

Martin Luther
Justus Jonas
Philip Melanchthon
Andreas Osiander
Stephen Agricola
Johann Brenz

Johann Oecolampadius
Ulrich Zwingli
Martin Bucer
Caspar Hedio[117]

3. The Result

It belongs to the very nature of a great historic event that its true significance is hidden from its witnesses and contemporaries. This rule applies also to the four eventful days in the autumn of 1529 at Marburg. Neither Luther nor Zwingli, neither Bucer nor Philip of Hesse, nor any one of the theologians and politicians who witnessed the discussions were able to estimate the importance of what had happened — hence the divergence in their opinions as to the result.[118] A kind of uncertainty may even be observed in the utterances of the individual participants. The generous hospitality of the Landgrave, the community life of the participants at the castle, the fact that men who had known one another from writings only — and polemical ones at that — had now become personally acquainted: all this helped to remove old prejudices. Each side promised in the future to write in a more friendly way on questions that were still controversial.

Luther, writing to his wife on October 4, called the colloquy a friendly one.[119] On the same day he wrote to Nicholas Gerbel in Strasburg, who had sent greetings to him through the Strasburg delegates:

---

[117]Translated from the text, WA, 160 ff. The English translations by J. Bodensieck (Reu, *The Augsburg Confession*, Part II, Sources, 44 ff) and G.J. Beto (*Concordia Theol. Monthly*, XVI, No. 2, February 1945, 91 ff) have been consulted and made use of as far as possible. The WA gives very valuable commenting notes, especially from the *notae* that Zwingli added to the edition which appeared at Zurich, after the first prints in the form of tables had been made at Marburg.

[118]W. Koehler, *Zwingli und Luther, II,* 139, gives an illuminating review of the utterances by the participants.

[119]'*Wisset, dass unser freundlich Gespräch zu Marburg ein Ende hat, und sind fast in allen Stücken eins . . . .*' (WA BR 5, No. 1476, line 3 f).

> It seems to me that a good deal of that scandal is being removed, since public strife in writings and disputations is to cease; indeed, we did not expect to accomplish as much as we did. Would to God that also the stumbling-block which still remains might at last be removed through Christ.[120]

In the same letter, Luther makes it clear what the conditions of a real union would be:

> As we have forcefully defended our position, and the other side has yielded much of theirs, and remained stubborn in the one article on the Sacrament of the Altar only, they were dismissed in peace... Charity and peace we owe even to our enemies. They were told, to be sure, that in case they should fail to come to their senses concerning this article, they might enjoy our charity, but could not be regarded by us as brethren and members of Christ.

These passages show clearly what Luther thought at the end of the colloquy about its result. In the first sermon which he preached at Wittenberg on his return, he gave a report that expressed the same view:

> Things look rather hopeful. I do not say that we have attained brotherly unity, but a kindly and friendly concord, so that they seek from us in a friendly way what they are lacking, and we, on the other hand, assist them. If you will pray diligently, the concord may become a brotherly one.[121]

Stronger expressions were used by Luther in a letter written on October 12 to John Agricola,[122] where he states that the opponents had humbled themselves beyond measure, asking for peace, and that they were unfit for a disputation.[123]

Melanchthon, Osiander, and J. Jonas, in their reports and letters, did not speak in an offensive way, though it is quite natural that the other side resented every hint at their having yielded.[124] Zwingli seems to have been the first to speak of 'victory' and 'defeat':

> We are certain that our actions were right in the sight of God. Posterity will testify to that. Truth has prevailed so manifestly that, if ever a person has been defeated, it is the impudent (*impudens*) and stubborn (*contumax*) Luther.[125]

---

[120]WA BR 5, No. 1477.

[121]The report is contained, as a digression, in the Sermon on Deut. 6 (WA 28, 668 f).

[122]WA BR 5, No. 1479.

[123]*Loc. cit.*, lines 7 and 12 ('*inepti et imperiti ad disputandum*').

[124]Melanchthon and Jonas in CR I and St Louis, XVII; Osiander, WA 30, part 3, 144 f.

[125]Quoted from R. Christoffel, *Huldreich Zwingli, Leben und ausgewählte Schriften* (1857), I, 324; compare W. Koehler *Huldrych Zwingli*, 215. *'Es kann gegenwärtig als allgemein anerkannt gelten, dass von einem Starrsinn, einer eigensinnigen Versteifung auf den Bibelbuchstaben bei Luther nicht geredet werden darf.'* W. Koehler, *Zwingli und Luther, II,* 133.

It is only after such utterances had become known, and in the completely-changed situation of the summer of 1530, that Luther, too, spoke of his opponents as having been defeated.[126] This difference of opinion concerning the result at Marburg shows already how little actually had been achieved.

The lack of a real result was at first hidden by the *Marburg Articles,* which were understood by each side in a different way. For Luther and the Lutherans, they were the beginning of a real union, a theological document which proved that Zwingli was able to yield in important matters, and thus justified the hope that he would eventually accept that last point on which agreement had not been reached. For Zwingli and his friends, this document was the utmost that they could concede. It was for them a success insofar as it now was no longer possible for the papists to claim Luther as their ally; at the same time, it was a sufficient basis for common political action and eventual fellowship of all Protestants. Hence, it had not only theological, but also great political significance.

For the Landgrave it was a highly-important, political and ecclesiastical document. The *Marburg Articles* are, indeed, a monument to the diplomatic skill of this great church politician. It was a masterpiece of diplomacy to persuade Luther, after the colloquy had failed, to draft this set of theses, and to persuade Zwingli to accept them. Only a political genius could change an obvious failure into a seeming success. With Luther and Zwingli agreeing on fourteen out of fifteen articles, and even expressing their agreement concerning the Lord's Supper on five out of six points in Article 15, not only the participants (even Luther), but also the contemporaries on either side could cherish the hope that a full union was not very far off. For more than four centuries, the clever diplomacy of Philip of Hesse, and the wishful thinking of all friends of a Protestant union, were able to deceive Christendom as to the real outcome of the days of Marburg.[127]

When Luther, after his own suggestion for a union had been rejected, agreed to formulate articles on which there was agreement, he made use of the articles that had been drafted some months before

---

[126]WA BR 5, No. 1577, line 39: '. . . *cum victi essent etiam in coena Domini*', preceded by the statement that the 'sacramentarians' claimed that Luther had been vanquished ('*me esse victum*') at Marburg.

[127]Even W. Koehler, *Zwingli und Luther, II,* 127, states: '*Die Marburger Artikel sind im besten Wortsinne eine Konkordie*'. Actually, they are a *concordia discors.*

as a basis for an alliance of the Lutheran territories, and which later were called the *Schwabach Articles*, as we have seen. Hans von Schubert, in his book mentioned earler, not only destroyed the opinion (generally held up to 1910) that Luther immediately after Marburg changed the *Marburg Articles* with their peaceful tendency into the anti-Zwinglian *Schwabach Articles* (which always had been regarded as proving Luther's irreconcilableness), but he also made it clear how closely the *Marburg Articles* follow the articles that Luther had brought from Wittenberg, and which also played a role in the preliminary discussions.

How it was possible for Zwingli to accept *Marburg Articles* 4 on original sin, 8 on the Word as means of grace, 9 on Baptism, 10 on confession, and 14 on infant baptism, remains a mystery. For even if the formulation was obliging, so that in some cases either side could find its opinion expressed, as in the article on original sin, the man who the following year was to submit his *Fidei Ratio* to the Emperor, and soon after his *Exposition of the Christian Faith* to the King of France, could not possibly with a good conscience accept the articles on the Word and on Baptism. How could he declare with Article 9 that Baptism

> is not a mere empty sign or symbol among Christians, but a sign and work of God,

and in Article 14 that in Baptism children

> are received into God's grace and into Christendom,

while in the *Fidei Ratio* (Art. 7) he pointed out that the Sacraments do not convey grace or even contribute to the reception of grace, and that

> by Baptism the Church publicly receives him who previously has been received by grace?[128]

How could he reconcile the doctrine that the Holy Spirit gives faith and his gifts through the oral Word (*Marburg Art. 8*) with the view, expressed in *Fidei Ratio* (Art. 7), that the Holy Spirit does not need any vehicle, as the wind blows where it wills? Though this passage deals with the Sacraments as alleged means of grace, it includes the rejection of the external Word as a necessary means of grace. For the

---

[128]E. F. K. Müller, *Bekenntnisschriften,* 87, 11. Zwingli continues: 'Therefore baptism does not confer grace, but the Church testifies that grace has been given him to whom baptism is given'. An English translation of this confession of Zwingli's is to be found in *Huldrych Zwingli* by S. M. Jackson (1903), 452 ff.

invisible and imperceptible way, in which 'every man that cometh into the world' is enlightened, is sufficient for salvation. Also, those who never have heard the Word of God can be saved, as Zwingli points out to the King of France when describing the bliss of heaven:

> You may hope to see there the communion of all saintly, wise, faithful, constant, courageous, and virtuous men who lived from the beginning of the world; the two Adams — the first who was saved, and the second who saved him — Abel, Enoch, Noah, Abraham, Isaac, Jacob, Juda, Moses, Joshua, Gideon, Samuel, Elijah, Elisha, Isaiah and the Mother of God of whom he prophesied,[129] David, Hezekiah, Josiah, John the Baptist; furthermore, Hercules, Theseus, Socrates, Aristides, Antigonus, Numa, Camillus, the Catos, the Scipios. . . In short, no virtuous man has ever lived, no saintly, no believing soul has ever lived . . . whom you would not meet before God. Or for what purpose would we strive with all efforts of our souls, except for our attaining the prize of such life?[130]

We have quoted this passage in order to show that the unity which was believed to have been established by the *Marburg Articles* was an illusion.

Luther was rightly shocked when this *Exposition of the Christian Faith* was published after Zwingli's death:

> Tell me, whosoever wants to be a Christian, why do we need Baptism, the Sacrament, Christ, the Gospel, the prophets and the Holy Scriptures, if such ungodly pagans as Socrates, Aristides, and even the horrible Numa (who, as Augustine writes in *De civitate Dei,*[131] founded all idolatry in Rome by the revelation from the devil[132]), and Scipio the Epicurean, are blessed and saints along with the patriarchs, prophets, and apostles in heaven, though they knew nothing of God, Scripture, Gospel, Christ, Baptism, Sacrament, or the Christian faith?[133]

Luther can explain this only by assuming that Zwingli either had broken the agreement of Marburg, or that he had never believed what he then had confessed.[134]

---

[129]Like the medieval exegetes, Zwingli still believed that Isaiah 11:1 referred to Mary.

[130]Quoted from Christoffel, II, 296 (where the whole *Expositio* is given in German). Zwingli's idea is that all truth found with pagans goes back to a special revelation of God or rather to the influence of the Holy Spirit that 'blows where he wills'. The difference, in contrast to Luther, is that for Zwingli 'the Spirit is not bound to the Word'. See G.W. Locher, *Die Theologie Huldrych Zwinglis, I* (1952), 54 f.

[131]VII, 34 f.

[132]Augustine, *loc. cit.,* calls it revelation by demons.

[133]*Short Confession,* WA 54, 143, 27 ff.

[134]'Since now in this booklet Zwingli has not only broken our agreement at Marburg, indeed he has not taken it seriously . . .' (WA 54, 144,7); ' . . . it is certain that in every respect he acted insincerely with us at Marburg' (*ibidem*, 143, 10 ff).

The deep disappointment which Luther expresses in these words from his *Short Confession of the Blessed Sacrament* of 1544 reveals the tragedy of Marburg. This tragedy does not consist in the fact that a union proved to be impossible, but rather in the inability of either side to fathom the gulf that separated Luther and Zwingli. There is hardly one among the 14 Articles of agreement which was understood by either side in the same way. It may be admitted that Luther was wrong when he later accused Zwingli of dishonesty. The difference with regard to such Articles was that for Luther they were articles of faith, which had to be taken quite seriously, while Zwingli regarded them as welcome political means to an end. What mattered to him was the end, namely, the union of all Protestants, which he regarded as possible in spite of the existing differences; the means by which this end could be reached were for him of minor importance. It was Luther's fault, which can be partly understood, but not excused merely because the articles had to be hurriedly drafted and accepted. How could he ever accept such an ambiguous statement as that of Article 11:

> That ***confession***, or the ***seeking of counsel*** from one's pastor or neighbour, should indeed be unconstrained and free, but nevertheless is very useful to consciences . . . on account of the ***absolution*** or ***consolation of the Gospel,*** which is the true absolution (*emphasis mine*).[135]

He ought to have known, or at least found out, that Zwingli rejected private confession, and abhorred the idea that a pastor could forgive sins in the name of God. Zwingli and all his adherents interpreted this Article as speaking of spiritual counsel and proclamation of the Gospel, while Luther and the Lutherans found therein their doctrine of the Office of the Keys. It seems that in this, as perhaps in all the *Marburg Articles,* there was an anticipation of the great art of modern ecumenical theologians of formulating theses of agreement and disagreement which everyone is free to interpret according to his pleasure.

This theological inadequacy of the *Marburg Articles* is the reason why they have not played any part in attempts to formulate an evangelical confession. They were published by Luther together with his *Large Confession* of 1528, and by Zwingli with his comments. In Hesse, and in some small territories of western Germany, they gained

———

[135]See W. Koehler, *Zwingli und Luther, II,* 124. By the Office of the Keys, Zwingli understood only the exercise of church discipline. *Commentarius de vera et falsa religione, Hauptschriften I,* 173 f.

a certain authority.[136] They were praised by all later advocates of a union between the Lutheran and the Reformed churches, and Luther was blamed for not having adhered to them.[137] However, they had already been practically forgotten when the Diet of Augsburg met and the Lutherans handed over their *Augsburg Confession*, Zwingli his *Fidei Ratio*, and four cities of south-west Germany their *Confessio Tetrapolitana* written by Bucer. Nothing shows more clearly the futility of the attempt made in the *Marburg Articles* to find a common basis for a pan-Protestant alliance against Rome. It was a sort of local patriotism when the Faculty of Marburg and the Church of Hesse in 1929 arranged a celebration of the fourth centenary of the Colloquy for the purpose of bringing together all Protestants, including the Baptists (whose ancestors had not been admitted in 1529), and other religious communities which call themselves Protestants, into one great organization.[138]

The *Marburg Articles* are not, and never have been, the confession of the doctrines that are common to Protestants with the exception of the doctrine on the Lord's Supper. Even Article 15, which tries to state the points of agreement and the one point of disagreement concerning this Sacrament, is useless on account of its ambiguity. For, the alleged agreement, 'that the Sacrament of the Altar is a sacrament of the true body and blood of Jesus Christ', was understood differently by either side. This is indicated in the note which Zwingli added to his edition of the Articles:

> The Sacrament is the sign of the true body, etc., consequently it is not the true body.[139]

---

[136]W. Koehler, *Huldrych Zwingli,* 214.

[137]Carl Immanuel Nitzsch, *Urkundenbuch der Evangelischen Union* (1853), 1 ff; W. Koehler, *Zwingli und Luther, II,* 127. See also the interesting book by H. Hermelink, quoted in the following note.

[138]This remarkable celebration, which, however, was without any result, is described in the official report by Heinrich Hermelink, *Das Marburger Religionsgespräch 1529/1929, Zum vierhundertjährigen Gedächtnis* (Gotha, 1930). It was a futile attempt to show theologically and practically that there is a unity in Protestantism despite the variety of Protestant churches and confessions, and to promote a closer cooperation among the Protestant churches. Some valuable speeches were given, the most outstanding of which is that by Emil Brunner (38 f), which will be mentioned later. The practical suggestions made, especially by Rudolf Otto, were not carried out, as the ecumenical conferences of Stockholm (1925) and Lausanne (1927) had already gone far beyond the plan of a pan-Protestant alliance. A common celebration of the Lord's Supper was impossible, just as it had been 400 years earlier.

[139]'*Sacramentum signum est veri corporis etc., non est igitur verum corpus.*' WA 30, part 3, 170 f (note to Art. 15). Also other comments of Zwingli are to be found in WA, *loc cit.*

Thus, here, too, the disagreement is already concealed in what was proclaimed as a statement of agreement.

Nothing shows more clearly than the *Marburg Articles* that the doctrinal difference concerning the Lord's Supper is not, as Zwingli and his friends believed, a difference in one point of doctrine only — and a minor one at that — since it is not an article of the Creed. Luther was right when from the very beginning he saw that, as the Words of Institution are the Gospel itself,[140] a difference in the understanding of the Sacrament must reveal nothing less than a difference in the understanding of the Gospel. If he did not realize this in the atmosphere of the last day at Marburg, the reason was that he interpreted the Articles according to his theology, and took it for granted that Zwingli, in accepting the terms, also agreed with the content. He failed to see, as many Lutherans later in their discussions and negotiations with Reformed theologians also have failed to see, that Zwingli's theology, and later that of Calvin, allowed for a far more flexible use of theological terms.

This versatility of Zwingli and his friends and successors is not, as in the case of Bucer, determined by their characters; it is rather a different understanding of Christianity. Koehler has repeatedly called our attention to the fact that the controversies on the Sacrament between the Reformers were instrumental in creating the concept of what Bucer called *ratio Christianismi*, the essence of Christianity.[141] This idea belongs to the humanist interpretation of the Christian faith. Erasmus distinguished between those vital truths of the Bible which are sufficient for Christian piety, and questions and answers which should not be discussed.[142] Erasmus connected this distinction with the interpretation of the Bible, the single passages of which are often understood differently.[143] While for Erasmus, who remained a faithful son of the Roman church, the church and ecclesiastical tradition were the final authority in defining what is essential and what not, for Zwingli this authority was, of course, Holy Scripture. For him the Word of God was clear and sufficient, provided the Holy Spirit enlightens the hearer or the reader.[144] Thus, he himself was absolutely sure about his

---

[140]WA 11, 432, 19 ff.

[141]W. Koehler, *Zwingli und Luther, I,* 829; *Huldrych Zwingli,* 183. See above,170.

[142]*De libero arbitrio* (ed. J. von Walter I, a, 8).

[143]*De libero arbitrio* (ed. J. von Walter I, b, 1 ff and 8).

[144]See chapter IV above, 115,116, and the present chapter,181,182.

understanding of John 6 as the key to the understanding of the Words of Institution, without asking whether perhaps the difficulty of a literal understanding of these words had not driven him to John 6 as a possible means of avoiding that difficulty. Whatever the more-or-less unconscious motive of always resorting to John 6:63 may have been, Zwingli was deeply convinced that he, and not Luther, followed Scripture.

How, then, is it to be explained that he was prepared to recognize Luther as a brother in the faith, in spite of what he regarded as Luther's grave error? The answer is that for him the Sacrament, and the doctrine on the Sacrament, did not belong to those essentials of the Christian faith concerning which there must be unity within the church. In contradistinction to Luther, the understanding of the Gospel on which there must be unanimity is independent of the understanding of the Lord's Supper and of the Sacraments in general. The Sacrament for Zwingli is not part and parcel of the Gospel; it is an ordinance of Christ, to be performed by Christians. This performance may have some effect on the soul of the faithful, insofar as the 'sign' makes the Word of the Gospel clearer. But the Sacraments can never be means of grace in the strict sense. They only signify the grace which has been given without them, as he puts it in Art. 7 of his *Fidei Ratio*:

> I believe, indeed, I know, that all the sacraments are so far from conferring grace that they do not even convey or distribute it.[145]

That the Sacrament is also a sign has never been denied by Luther and the Lutheran church,[146] as it is the conviction also of Roman doctrine. The question is only whether, according to Scripture, it is not more.

Here lies the deepest reason for the differing attitudes of Luther and Zwingli, not only toward the Sacrament as such, but also toward the **doctrine**, that is, the **understanding** of the Sacrament. If the Sacrament, though performed by man, is an act of God, and if this act (as other passages of the Lutheran Confessions indicate even more clearly) is more than a sign, namely, an **instrument** by which God gives something,[147] then the denial of this character of the

---

[145]E. F. K. Müller, 86; S. M. Jackson, 466.

[146]See AC Article 13 (Trigl. 49): '. . . not only to be marks of profession among men, but rather to be signs and testimonies of the will of God toward us (*signa et testimonia voluntatis Dei erga nos*)'.

[147]'. . . *per verbum et sacramenta tamquam per* ***instrumenta*** *donatur Spiritus Sanctus*' (AC Article 5).

Sacrament is nothing less than a destruction of the Sacrament. The Sacrament is either a means by which God gives his grace, or it is no sacrament at all — at least, not in the sense in which the church for 1,500 years, since the days of the apostles, had understood the Sacrament. Nothing can conceal the difference between churches for which the Sacraments are instruments of divine grace and churches which deny this.[148]

The most important result of Marburg was that the difference became unmistakably clear. For Luther the right understanding of the Sacrament as a means of grace, the understanding of the Words of Institution in their simple, literal sense, was an essential article of the Christian faith. He never demanded the acceptance of a theological theory. His doctrine on the ubiquity of the body of Christ, or any other theological attempt to explain the mystery, was not even mentioned. The suggestion which he made after the colloquy, and which was meant to settle the controversy, shows what he regarded as essential and what not, namely, the confession that

> the body and blood are truly, that is, substantively and essentially — though not quantitatively, or qualitatively, or locally — present, and are given.[149]

What this meant he made clear in his letter to the Christians at Frankfurt in 1533, warning them against pastors who taught openly, or held secretly, the Zwinglian view that the communicants receive orally nothing but bread and wine. The communicant

> is not satisfied if he is being told: 'Believe the body which Christ thinks of and enquire no further'. No, dear friend, this he believes even before he comes, and even if he does not go to the Sacrament. He rather asks, and this is his reason for coming, whether he receives orally mere bread and wine. He does not ask what he should believe concerning Christ and his body, but what it is that the pastor gives him with his hands . . .[150] One must frankly and soberly declare

---

[148]In his most important dogmatical work, *Commentarius de vera et falsa religione* (1525), Zwingli criticizes the unbiblical term, not only because it is an unbiblical word, which was done occasionally also by Luther in his early years, but because it caused the erroneous concept that an external thing could bring forth internal effects. Compare W. Koehler, *Zwingli und Luther, I,* 81, and F. Kattenbusch, art. *'Sakrament'*, PRE 17, 374, 46.

[149]See 214, 215.

[150]Here follow the untranslatable words: '*Hie gilts nicht den Brei im Maul wälzen, und mumm mumm sagen. Man muss ihn nicht lehren: glaube den Leib, den Christus meint, sondern den Brei ausspeien und das Mummen lassen, frei und durre sagen, ob er mit dem Munde eitel Brot und Wein empfahe*' (561, 3 ff). We quote this passage to show that for Luther 'Zwinglians' were not only people who held Zwingli's view of the Sacrament as a memorial feast, but also those who spoke of a Real Presence in an ambiguous way.

> whether he receives orally mere bread and wine. . . . Therefore, it is my honest advice, which before God I owe you who are at Frankfurt and whoever else may be in need of it: If anyone knows that his pastor teaches the Zwinglian way publicly, he ought to avoid him. He should rather abstain from the Sacrament all his life, than to receive it from him, and even die and suffer all things. If, however, his pastor should be an equivocator who pretends that in the Sacrament Christ's body and blood are truly present, and must yet be suspected . . . of meaning something different than what the words imply, he should unhesitatingly go or send word to him asking for a clear statement of what he gives you with his hands and what you receive orally.[151]

This, and nothing else, is what Luther meant with his offer at Marburg, the simple and unambiguous acceptance of the literal meaning of the Words of Institution without any theological theory about the *how* of the Presence. This is the point of disagreement stated in Article 15.

The disagreement concerning this question caused Luther to refuse the fraternal handshake and recognition as a brother in the faith to Zwingli at the end of the colloquy. He did not do it lightheartedly, as is shown by his attempts to save the union after the breakdown of the discussions. He had to take this stand because nothing less was at stake than the Word of God, the Sacrament of Christ, and thereby the existence of the Church. Not the existence of a Lutheran church; Luther was never interested in that. Denominations in the modern sense had not yet come into existence at the time, except as names given to certain groups in Christendom. Only by and by, confessional churches came into existence after the unity of Western Christendom had failed.[152] The question for Luther was whether or not the Sacraments, as means of grace, and whether the Sacrament of the Altar, as the Sacrament of the true body and blood of Christ, were rooted in the Gospel and therefore essential for the Church. He could not but answer this question in the affirmative. A church without the Sacrament as real means of grace was for him a church without Christ, who had instituted Baptism as a washing of regeneration and the Supper as the Sacrament of his true body and

---

[151] WA 30, part 3, 560, 33 ff.

[152] What we call the 'Lutheran' church was designated in the 16th and 17th centuries as the 'Evangelical' church or the 'Church of the Augsburg Confession'. The churches of the *Formula of Concord* also speak of themselves as 'our reformed churches' (as in Trigl. 851). The *Apology* Article 15 (Trigl. 327) is the only passage where the word 'Lutheran' occurs in the *Book of Concord*. It is a complaint made against the papists: 'This blessed doctrine, the precious holy Gospel, they call Lutheran'. This, of course, is no objection to the present name of the Church of the Augsburg Confession.

blood. This is the reason why he could not recognize Zwingli as a brother in the faith.

While some of the delegates, especially Bucer, were prepared to accept the formula proposed by Luther on Sunday night, Zwingli rejected it. He could not return to Zurich, as Koehler points out,[153] with a formula which, considering all he had taught during the previous years, could not be understood by the people otherwise than as a relapse into Romanism. Any doctrine that implied the Real Presence of the true body and blood in, with, and under the elements was for Zwingli fundamentally Catholic and papist, no matter what safeguards against a materialistic understanding of the presence might be attached to it. How could the common people of Zurich understand that a presence of the body of Christ in the bread should not be a local one? How could they be expected to distinguish between Luther's and the pope's *sub duabus speciebus*?[154] Luther, of course, would have answered that he did not expect Christians to understand theological theories, but to accept in simple faith the unspeakable mystery of the words: 'This is my body'. He would regard the Roman doctrine a lesser heresy than Zwingli's denials of the Real Presence and of the nature of the Sacraments as 'instruments' of God's grace. We must understand that it was simply impossible for Zwingli to accept such a doctrine. Had he agreed to Luther's suggestion, a new controversy would soon have arisen. Neither political nor other practical considerations made it impossible for him to accept Luther's view, even in its mildest form, but rather his understanding of Scripture, which was determined by the assumption that 'God does not propose to us anything incomprehensible',[155] and that 'Spirit eats spirit'.[156]

Whether such assumptions are necessary presuppositions for an understanding of the Word of God, as Zwingli believed, or whether they are philosophical prejudices which prevent the true understanding of God's Word, as Luther was convinced, that is the

---

[153]See W. Koehler *Huldrych Zwingli*, 211. Koehler thinks that Zwingli himself could have accepted the formula in the sense 'substantially present in the heart', but this would not have been the understanding of Luther. Koehler adds: 'It was good that his regard for the people made it impossible for Zwingli to accept ambiguous formulas'.

[154]*'Sub duabus speciebus / Signis tantum et non rebus / Latent res eximiae'* (Aquinas); *'Unter der Gestalt des Brots und Weins'* (AC Article 10).

[155]See 193.

[156]See 193.

question which at that time divided the two Reformers and their followers. It is a question which cannot be answered by a compromise. This was seen quite clearly, not only by Luther, but also by Zwingli. There is no *via media* between *est* and *significat*. It shows the greatness of Zwingli in contrast to Bucer, Calvin, and all prophets of a middle road between Wittenberg and Zurich. Whatever shortcomings he may have had, he was a clear thinker. The issue between Luther and Zwingli was a question of faith and, therefore, a question of conscience. While, in other points, as the *Marburg Articles* show, he could yield in a way which seems to indicate that either he did not fully realize the seriousness of the questions involved, or he acted as a politician, here the point was reached where he could not give in. It is of no avail to ask who is responsible for the failure of the colloquy, which Luther had anticipated from the outset. As believing Christians we shall have our personal convictions as to who was right and who was wrong. The church historian can only state the fact that each one was bound in conscience to follow his understanding of the Word of God.

How it is possible for Christians who really want to obey this Word, and seriously ask the Holy Spirit to enlighten them, to arrive at contradicting conclusions as to the meaning of a certain passage, no one can know. The reason is not, as the Catholic churches claim, the lack of an infallible teaching office which through the unfailing enlightenment of the Holy Spirit is able to decide authoritatively which exegesis is right and which is wrong. Otherwise, one should expect that the churches which reject the *sola Scriptura*, the church of Rome and the Eastern churches, would agree which that infallible teaching office is. The reason is rather to be found in the nature of God's revelation. God's Word always comes to us hidden in human words, as Christ's divinity was hidden in his humanity. Thus, not by our own reason, but rather by the grace of the Holy Spirit, can we perceive the divine truth in faith. This applies also to the understanding of God's Word by the Reformers. They are fallible like us. There is profound truth in the words which Emil Brunner, a delegate from Zurich, spoke at the fourth centenary of Marburg in 1929:

> Let us not offer excuses for our Reformers, but let us be grateful to them for having taken so desperately seriously the questions of faith, the quest for the truth of their doctrines. For this very earnestness represents the real fount of strength of the Reformation. Had they taken their doctrines less seriously, had they been willing to make compromises for the sake of unity, had they been more afraid of the reputation of being stubborn than of the inner reproach of

having been unfaithful to God's commission, then also the break with Rome and the Reformation would never have occurred.[157]

If the attempts to find an agreement between Luther and Zwingli on the doctrine of the Sacrament were bound to fail, why was it not at least possible to reach a mutual recognition as Christian brethren that would establish a *modus vivendi* between the Protestants in that dangerous hour when the existence of the Reformation was at stake? This is what Philip of Hesse was hoping for, and what also Zwingli desired. It was in all sincerity that Zwingli at the end of the colloquy asked tearfully for Luther's friendship.[158] Why did Luther have to refuse the right hand of fellowship and recognition as brethren in the faith? When Zwingli asked him not to accuse anyone of heresy on account of the dissension concerning the bodily eating, provided the spiritual eating was recognized, and when he referred to the Ancient Fathers who did not always condemn one another when they were in disagreement, Luther answered:

Let us hope for the future. Even if we cannot come to a complete agreement we may at the end of this colloquy discuss the question whether or not we are still able to regard one another as brethren.[159]

It is remarkable that, according to Bucer, at the end of the colloquy Luther had already expressed his preparedness to recognize the other side as brethren, when Melanchthon 'who was well disposed toward the Emperor and Ferdinand' kept him from making this concession.[160] This story corresponds to what Luther wrote to Melanchthon during the Diet of Augsburg about his own weakness in public struggles.[161] It is, at the same time, in agreement with

---

[157]H. Hermelink, *op. cit.,* 39.

[158]See above, 213.

[159]See above, 193.

[160]Letter from Bucer to Ambrose Blarer, October 18, 1529, quoted by Koehler, 139 f: *'Sic finem accepit disputatio, et coepit princeps urgere Lutherum et suos, ut nos fratres agnoscerent, sicut nos agnoscimus illos, sed . . . frustra.* ***Lutherum autem semel consensisse****, sed mox a Philippo retractum. Philippus bene vult Caesari et Ferdinando.* ***Utinam vidisses, quem candorem, quam simplicitatem, quam veritatem Christianismi exhibuerunt utrique.****'* Koehler, *Zwingli und Luther, II*, 118, thinks this statement by Bucer should not be overestimated in view of what Luther wrote on that same October 4 to his wife (WA BR 5, No. 1476, line 6 ff). He reports that the Landgrave tried to persuade Luther to recognize the other side as brethren and members of Christ. 'We did not like this fraternizing, though we wanted to be peaceful and amicable.'

[161]WA BR 5, No. 1611, line 19 ff; cited above, 155.

Melanchthon's hope for a union, not of the Protestants only, but of all Christendom. For it must always be kept in mind that the hope for a complete reunion of all Christians was a greater power in the 16th (and even in the 17th) century than we modern Christians are inclined to think. Not only the controversies between Catholics, Lutherans, and Reformed at the time of the Reformation, but also the discussions between the theologians of the Age of Orthodoxy, must be understood against the background of this hope.

There was, indeed, a marked difference between the Lutheran and the Reformed churches in this respect. While, ever since the days of Zwingli and Calvin, the Reformed church understood all Protestant churches as a great unity against the papal church, in spite of existing differences in theology, liturgy, and polity, the Lutherans regarded this as a simplification of the real situation. They saw not only the borderline which separated the church of the Gospel from the church in which the Roman Antichrist was still ruling, but at the same time also the borderline that existed between the church of the pure Sacrament and the churches that had lost, together with the Real Presence, the Sacrament of Christ. What to Zwingli and his friends was the difference of theological schools of thought, which might be tolerated within one and the same church, was for Luther the difference between church and heresy. Even if at Marburg he had been doubtful for a moment as to the possibility of recognizing Zwingli as a brother, this doubt had soon been removed.

We have already quoted Luther's admonition to the Christians at Frankfurt in 1533,[162] and his *Short Confession* of 1544.[163] Both make it clear beyond a doubt that he regards those who deny that the body of Christ is given with the hand, and received orally, as heretics with whom there can be no church fellowship. It is not accidental that he often compares this heresy, as far as its seriousness is concerned, with Arianism.[164] He finds this similarity especially in the way in which the representatives of these two heresies hide their true thoughts behind orthodox-sounding phrases. Just as the Arians believed Christ to be a mere creature, but called him God before unlearned Christians, with the secret understanding that he had only the **name** of God, so the new heretics maintained before the people that the body and

[162]See above, 229.

[163]See above, 153, 154.

[164]*Admonition to the Frankfurters.* WA 30, Part 3, 559, 17 ff: *Short Confession,* WA 54, 159, 5 ff.

blood of the Lord are really present in the Sacrament with the secret understanding that he is present spiritually only and is received, not orally, but spiritually by faith.[165] And just as there could not be a mutual recognition as brethren between the Orthodox and the Arians in the fourth century, no church- and altar-fellowship, so impossible was it for Luther to recognize the deniers of the Real Presence as full brethren in the faith and to have altar- and church-fellowship with them.

He was prepared to extend them the Christian love that a Christian owes to everyone, even to his enemies. He would have agreed with the statement made in the *Book of Concord*, and repeated by all orthodox theologians, that the

> condemnations, censure, and rejections of godless doctrines, and especially of that which has arisen concerning the Lord's Supper [are not meant] to condemn those men who err from a certain simplicity of mind, but are not blasphemers against the truth of the heavenly doctrine, much less, indeed, entire churches, which are either under the Roman empire of the German nation or elsewhere,

but such condemnations refer only to

> the fanatical opinions and their obstinate and blasphemous teachers . . . because these errors conflict with the express Word of God.[166]

The recognition, however, that also in a heretical communion there are still at least remnants of the means of grace, true believers, and consequently something of the true church of Christ, does not imply that there can be *communicatio in sacris*, i.e. church- and altar-fellowship, with such communion or its individual members. In this respect Luther and the Lutheran church have followed the example of the Ancient Church, which from the time of the apostles throughout the centuries refused admission to the Sacrament of the Altar to all who were regarded as heterodox or schismatic.[167] The

---

[165]WA 30, Part 3, 559, 6 ff.

[166]AC Preface (Trigl. 19).

[167]W. Elert, *Abendmahl und Kirchengemeinschaft in der alten Kirche hauptsächlich des Ostens* (1954), has proved this fact about the Ancient Church on the basis of an overwhelming amount of source-material. It is noteworthy that the Lord's Supper from the very beginning was what today is called 'closed communion'. As the doors were literally closed before the celebration, so all liturgies since the oldest liturgical formulas of the New Testament (1 Cor. 16: 20 ff; Rom. 16: 16,17, cf *Didache* 10, 6) contain warnings to people who could not be admitted. One of the reasons given for the refusal of church- and altar-fellowship is false doctrine (Rom. 16:17). Whenever the holy kiss is mentioned in the New Testament, a reference to Holy Communion must be assumed. The kiss of peace (*'pax'*) is given at the beginning of the

idea that people could be admitted to Holy Communion with whom there is no perfect peace, no unity of faith, and consequently no church-fellowship, is a modern idea which was absolutely foreign to the churches in the 16th century.

This principle that altar-fellowship is church-fellowship was even recognized by the old Reformed churches. Under no circumstances would Zwingli have admitted Baptists to Holy Communion. When Strasburg in 1536 accepted the Lutheran doctrine by agreeing to the *Wittenberg Concord*, the church of Zurich strictly forbade her students to receive Holy Communion there.[168] Those who at present favour what they call 'open communion' have no right to appeal to Zwingli. Such open communion, according to the conviction of the church of all ages up to the modern world, is no communion at all, no sacrament to be justified by New Testament practice and doctrine.

The issue between Luther and Zwingli, between the Lutheran and the Reformed churches of the 16th century, was solely whether the two doctrines on the Sacrament were theological opinions which could and should be tolerated in one and the same church, or whether they had to regard one another as heretics, which made altar- and church-fellowship impossible. While Zwingli regarded Luther's view as wrong, he was prepared to tolerate it because, in his opinion, the question of the Sacrament did not belong to the essentials of the Christian faith. He found, in this respect, many followers in the Reformed churches; however, in the 16th century, as a consequence of the bitter controversies, other Reformed theologians denied the possibility of such intercommunion.[169] Luther, on the other hand,

---

Sacrament, which expresses and constitutes the 'communion of the body of Christ' in the twofold sense of the sacramental and the mystical body. The *'pax'*, however, which signifies the complete unity of the church, is inseparably connected with the *anathema* which 'excommunicates' those who are not included in that unity.

[168] V.E. Loescher, *Historia Motuum*, I, 235, quotes from a letter of Bullinger: *'Qui sacramentis nobiscum communicant, ipsa communicatione profitentur, se eandem habere nobiscum de Sacramentis fidem; atqui juvenes nostri non eandem vobiscum fidem habent'*. The principle is quite clear: altar-fellowship presupposes a common faith concerning the Sacrament. — Loescher *op. cit.*, II, 10, reports that Calvin took a similar attitude toward the Lutherans after the controversy with Westphal had begun.

[169] For instance, Beza. In the 17th century some theologians, like Turretini (d 1687), held the opinion: 'Between those who are not united in the fundament of faith there can be no church-fellowship' (quoted from E. S. Cyprian, *Unterricht von kirchlicher Vereinigung der Protestanten* (1726), preface, 8). This corrresponds exactly to the doctrine of the Lutherans. The Reformed Church of France was the first to declare at its National Synod at Charenton in 1631 that Lutherans should be admitted to the Sacrament.

never had any doubt that the denial of bodily presence and bodily eating in the Sacrament was a heresy that made intercommunion impossible. As he left Marburg, hoping that the other side would eventually see this heresy, and accept the Real Presence in the sense of his last suggestion, so during the following decade he left nothing undone to win over as many as possible of those who in the days of Marburg had stood against him. However, when he saw that all his attempts were in vain, and that the old heresy appeared in new forms, he had to repeat his 'no' of Marburg, as he did in his *Short Confession* shortly before his death:

> I rate as one concoction, namely as sacramentarians and fanatics, which they also are, all who will not believe that the Lord's bread in the Supper is his true natural body, which the godless or Judas received with the mouth, as well as did St Peter and all [other] saints; ***he who will not believe this*** (I say) ***should let me alone and hope for no fellowship with me;*** this is not going to be altered *(emphasis mine)*.[170]

Thus, at the end of his life, being aware of his forthcoming death and the Last Judgment, he reaffirmed the attitude which he had taken in the *Large Confession* of 1528, in the *Catechisms,* in the *Smalcald Articles*, not to mention numerous other writings. It was the attitude he had forcefully defended at Marburg, even though prepared to yield wherever God's Word would allow. The world regards this firmness as

> stubborn determination to sacrifice everything on the altar of dogma.[171]

That is the judgment, not only of politicians and historians, but also of theologians of all denominations, in spite of the fact that all modern scholars who have really studied the sources, among them outstanding historians like Hans von Schubert and Walther Koehler,[172] have unanimously arrived at the conclusion that it is impossible to explain Luther's stand at Marburg as stubbornness and obstinate insistence on the letter of the Bible, when actually his whole understanding of divine revelation was at stake.

Such legendary simplifications of historical facts — another is the view that it was Luther who commenced the controversy on the Sacrament — are due not only to a lack of real knowledge and to

---

[170]WA 54, 155, 29 ff; quoted in *Form. Conc., Sol. Decl. VII,* 33 (Trigl. 983).

[171]*The Cambridge Modern History, Vol. II: The Reformation* (1907), 209. We quote this passage on Luther's stand at Marburg as an example of the average view of modern historians.

[172]See the quotation from W. Koehler above, 221, footnote 125.

the regrettable influence of average textbooks (which in many cases present second- or third-hand material rather than facts established by research), but also to the fact that modern Protestantism is hardly able to appreciate a real confessor, and to understand that there is an eternal truth which must not be compromised. Already at the Diet of Augsburg, Luther's confession became the confession of the rising Lutheran church. The man who stood alone in his confession at Worms was not allowed to take part in the Diet of 1530. Instead, churches confessed the same faith, which included the faith in the Real Presence. Whatever discussions and controversies were bound to follow, whatever new attempts would be made to solve the problem, the Lutheran church would reaffirm Luther's doctrine on the Real Presence in the *Formula of Concord.* Knowing that the existence of the Church on earth depends on the Sacraments of Christ, she would believe, teach, and confess that the words of the Sacrament must be understood in their simple, literal sense, as Luther had written them on the table at the beginning of the Marburg Colloquy: '*Hoc est corpus meum*'.

CHAPTER VI

The Aftermath

1. The Continuation of the Controversy

It seems very difficult, if not impossible, for those who are involved in a great historic decision to recognize its irrevocability. This is especially true of the doctrinal decisions made in the history of the church. It took two generations and long theological and ecclesiastical controversies before the decision on the *homoousion* doctrine adopted at Nicaea in 325 was repeated and confirmed by the Second Ecumenical Council in 381. In a similar way, two generations had to continue the theological work and the ecclesiastical controversies on the Lord's Supper in the 16th century before the *Formula of Concord* in 1577 reaffirmed the decision of Marburg as far as the Lutheran church is concerned, and thus definitely decided that there is no middle road between Luther and Zwingli, but only the choice between the *est* and the *significat*. Even these decision did not find general acceptance, and today, 400 years later, attempts are still being made to solve a problem which Marburg has already proved to be insoluble.

The only approach which at times became popular during these four centuries — for it seemed to offer at least a practical solution — was the idea of Zwingli, Bucer, Philip of Hesse, and other politicians: If a doctrinal agreement cannot be reached, there can at least be a mutual recognition and a common celebration of the Sacrament. The history of the unions, however, shows that this apparently-practical solution is no solution at all. For, apart from the fact that a common celebration presupposes a common liturgy in which, if it is a real liturgy, the doctrinal differences are bound to appear in a different form, such practical intercommunion leads to a destruction of the Sacrament. For a sacrament which is a mere rite performed without the necessity of believing a divine interpretation, may be a more-or-less impressive, mysterious action, but it is not the

Sacrament of Christ, which is always constituted by the Word — as even the Roman church has not quite forgotten. Here lies the deeper reason why in all union churches — we must include also many Lutheran churches that for practical purposes have accepted the union — the disintegration of the Sacrament is inevitable.

What is still more surprising than the blindness of theologians as regards the definiteness of the decision of Marburg is the fact that even eminent historians do not realize that the controversies which followed Marburg were an aftermath only. There is a widespread conviction, even among serious students of the Lutheran Reformation, that the controversy between Luther and Zwingli was only the prelude to the real discussion that began when the notable mediators, first Bucer, and later Calvin, entered the scene. This view which, even in the case of historians, actually goes back to Reformed convictions concerning the Sacrament, is supported by the fact that, after all, Reformed Christianity is not Zwinglianism, but Calvinism. The immense tragedy of Zwingli's life; his early death in 1531, which was immediately followed by the death of Oecolampadius; the fact that the Reformation in German Switzerland had to be taken over at the time of its worst crisis by men of minor stature, while in Geneva Calvin began to shine as a star of the first magnitude: all this contributed to an underestimation of Zwingli. It seems that not until today does the Reformer of Zurich come into his own again, after the noteworthy editions of his works by Koehler, Farner, and others have inaugurated a new study of Zwingli's theology.[1]

This statement is, of course, not meant to minimize the significance of Calvin as a theologian, and as one of the most distinguished churchmen of all ages. Eminent as he may have been as a systematic theologian — he was more of a reproductive and systematizing mind than an original thinker — his doctrine on the Sacraments could be understood, as we shall see, by the Lutherans as only another version of Zwinglianism. It was not, as the common opinion is, a misunderstanding on the part of the Lutherans if they rejected it as a new, and even more dangerous, form of Zwingli's doctrine. There is no question that Calvin wanted to give more than

---

[1]In addition to the various books on W. Koehler, some new monographs seem to have opened new perspectives, e.g. Arthur Rich, *Die Anfänge der Theologie Huldrych Zwinglis* (1949); G. F. Locher, *Die Theologie Huldrych Zwinglis im Lichte seiner Christologie, I: Die Gotteslehre.* However, nothing new has been discovered concerning Zwingli's doctrine on the Sacraments. In this respect his own writings are clear.

Zwingli, being deeply convinced that he was closer to Luther, and that he had found the true *via media* between the two. This personal feeling, however, can never abolish the fact that even the most conscientious among Lutheran theologians, men who had a very clear picture of what had happened since Zwingli's death in the field of eucharistic doctrine within the Reformed churches, could not find any essential difference between Zwingli and Calvin. We must never forget that Calvinistic influences had meanwhile pervaded the Lutheran churches, and that many Lutherans had sympathized with Calvin. And yet his doctrine was rejected by the vast majority of Lutherans. No one can read the report on the colloquy held in 1586 at Montbéliard (a German enclave in France at that time) at the request of the Duke of Wuerttemberg between Beza from Geneva and Jacob Andreae from Tuebingen, and their colleagues, without feeling that either party knew exactly what the other taught.[2] No serious and unprejudiced historian can deny that, rather than misunderstandings, it was conflicting concepts of the Sacrament, as they had become evident already at Marburg, that caused the negotiations and discussions of the next two generations to end in the same inevitable failure as at Marburg. Thus, the hopeless controversy was destined to continue, much to the distress of pious souls, and with the most harmful consequences for the churches involved.

The Marburg Colloquy had been an attempt to reach agreement on the Lord's Supper between various schools of theological thought in the interest of a common political action by the evangelical states. How utterly this attempt had failed became evident during the following months when the Diet of Augsburg was prepared. The *Marburg Articles* were practically forgotten. The confession to which the future was to belong in Germany was the *Augsburg Confession,* the doctrinal contents of which go back via the *Schwabach Articles* to Luther's *Large Confession* of 1528. The significance of the *Augsburg Confession* lies in the fact that it was more than the statement of a theological school, and more than a mere political document. It was the first confession of a church arising out of the Reformation movement.

---

[2]Also in this case, official minutes were not published. Both sides, however, handed in their statements, and these have been published, together with a narrative of the colloquy by the theologians of Tuebingen: *Acta Colloquii Montis Belligartensis* (1587). Beza challenged their correctness and wrote a *responsio* the same year. The result of this colloquy was a rise in the tension between the parties. The situation was worse than after Marburg.

The signatories declare expressly in the preface, addressing the Emperor:

> We offer . . . the Confession of our preachers and of ourselves, showing what manner of doctrine based on divine, Holy Scripture has been up to this time set forth in our lands, dukedoms, dominions, and cities, and taught in our churches.[3]

Princes and cities are speaking, but what they express is primarily the faith of the churches which 'by common consent' teach what is contained in the Articles that follow.[4] By common consent these churches accepted as their belief and doctrine what Luther and Melanchthon had confessed at Marburg concerning the Sacrament. Attempts have been made time and again to read another doctrine into Article 10 of the *Augsburg Confession.* The short formulation of the Latin text:

> *De coena Domini docent, quod corpus et sanguis Christi vere adsint et distribuantur vescentibus in coena Domini*

has been interpreted as containing Melanchthon's later view that the Presence is not to be found in the elements, but in the action, *'in coena Domini'*.[5] Apart from the fact that we possess a letter written from Augsburg by Melanchthon to Veit Dietrich, in which the author of the *Augsburg Confession* confirms that the Article on the Lord's Supper was formulated according to the doctrine of Luther,[6]

---

[3]Trigl. 38, following the German ('. . . *übergeben wir unserer Pfarrherren, Prediger und ihrer Lehren, auch unsers Glaubens Bekenntnis, was . . . sie aus Grund göttlicher Heiliger Schrift . . . predigen, lehrer, halten und Unterricht tun'*) and the Latin (*'in ecclesiis tractaverint'*). The princes share this faith as members of their churches, and they speak for them because no one else could do it.

[4]The question has been debated as to what is meant by the 'churches' that confess the articles of the *Augsburg Confession*, whether local congregations (which did not exist at that time), or territorial churches in the later sense. The latter is impossible because in the *Formula of Concord* 'churches and schools' are regarded as the subject of the confession. As a matter of fact, we find here the old usage of 'church', according to which 'church' and 'churches' are interchangeable because the church exists and becomes manifest in the 'churches' (cf Acts 9:31, Gal 1:2 and the seven 'churches' of Rev. 2 and 3, which represent the 'church' of Asia).

[5]The most recent attempt was made by Helmut Gollwitzer, *Coena Domini* (1937), 72. There is no real difference between '***in*** the bread' as Marburg Art. 15 puts it, which had the approval of Melanchthon, and '***under*** the species of bread and wine' of AC 10, especially as there was general agreement among the Lutherans — as among the Catholics — that the presence is not a local one. It is significant that Melanchthon took no exception to the statement of the *Smalc. Art. III,* 6 'that bread and wine in the Supper are the true body and blood of Christ' (Trigl. 493), which is the best expression of Luther's doctrine. Regarding Melanchthon's development, see below, 252 ff.

the German text (which is no less official than the Latin one) teaches expressly the *unio sacramentalis* when it states:

> *Dass wahrer Leib und Blut Christi* ***wahrhaftiglich unter der Gestalt des Brots und Weins*** *im Abendmahl gegenwärtig sei und da ausgeteilt und genommen wird (emphasis mine).*

'Under the species of bread and wine distributed and taken': can anything be clearer? Much has also been made of the fact that the rejection of those that teach otherwise is expressed in the Latin text by '*improbant* (they disapprove)' instead of the stronger *damnant*. Here again, the German text is the official and normative commentary. It uses the same word '*verwerfen* (reject, condemn)' with which *damnant* is elsewhere rendered. If the text of the *Augsburg Confession* should leave room for doubt as to whether or not Luther's doctrine is contained in that article, the *Apology* with its strong emphasis on the 'bodily presence', which the church of the Augsburg Confession has in common not only with the Roman, but also with the Greek church, would at once dispel any doubts.[7] Besides, it must not be forgotten that not only did Zwingli transmit *Fidei Ratio* to the Emperor, but Strasburg also, with three other cities, delivered the *Confessio Tetrapolitana*, with an article 'On the sacrament of the body and blood of Christ' which expressed Bucer's doctrine. All of these facts prove sufficiently that it was the genuine Lutheran doctrine, which the Lutheran church has confessed ever since its first confession.

The discussions and controversies that followed the decision of Marburg and Augsburg are determined by three factors, each connected with the name of an important theologian. The first is the attempt to bring about a union between the adherents of the *Augustana* and the *Tetrapolitana*. These endeavours, which were necessitated by the political situation after the Diet, found their theological leader in the person of **Martin Bucer**. He succeeded in bringing about the Wittenberg Concord of 1536. His plans, however, reached further. Having established a union between Wittenberg and Strasburg, he also wanted to win German Switzerland for this union. This utopian enterprise was bound to fail. The hope that an understanding concerning the Sacrament was possible, and that, thus, the decision of Marburg could be revoked, was nourished by

---

[6]Letter of June 26 (the day after the AC had been solemnly transmitted and read), CR II, 142.

[7]*Apology*, Art. 10 (Trigl. 246 f).

the position of **Melanchthon** who, as in other important doctrines, had moved further and further away from the stand he had taken at Marburg and Augsburg. The development in Melanchthon's views is again closely related to **Calvin's** appearance in the history of the Reformation in Germany. We do not intend to give an account of the events in which these three men, directly or indirectly, played important roles. We must rather confine ourselves to a brief discussion of the contribution made by each of them to the great question of the Sacrament, and of the answer which the Lutheran church had to give to their doctrines in the final decision of the *Formula of Concord.*[8]

2. Martin Bucer and the Wittenberg Concord

Martin Bucer belongs to those characters in the history of the Reformation whose destiny it was to live in the shadow of greater and more successful men. Actually, he represents a type that can be identified neither with Lutheranism nor with Zwinglianism. As a theologian, he became the teacher of Calvin. Much of what is regarded as genuine Calvinistic doctrine, in fact, goes back to Bucer. As a churchman he was in his way a great organizer, in Strasburg as well as in Hesse. It was a new type of church that he organized, based on the idea of church discipline as an essential mark of the church. Confirmation, as it was understood and practised in the Lutheran church after the Pietistic Movement took a hold on Lutheranism

---

[8]As in our chapter on the Great Controversy, we must confine ourselves to the main characters in these debates. Since we cannot deal with such men as Brenz, Bugenhagen, and Osiander within the framework of this book, we must also abstain from discussing the doctrine of Schwenckfeld, whom Luther regarded as one of the most dangerous 'sacramentarians'. He exercised a powerful influence in two of the leading cities of south-west Germany: in Strasburg after 1530, and in Ulm from 1535 to 1540. The *Formula of Concord* does not deal with him in the article on the Lord's Supper, but rejects his doctrines in Article 12,'Of other factions and sects' (Trigl.1101), especially the doctrine 'that the flesh of Christ belongs to the essence of the Holy Trinity'. Philippists have put this doctrine on the same level as Luther's doctrine on ubiquity. But this mixture of docetism and monophysitism has nothing to do with Luther's Christology. Schwenckfeld was an enthusiast who never accepted the Lutheran doctrine on the means of grace. He did not regard bread and wine as means by which the body and blood of Christ were distributed. The gift of Holy Communion is the spiritual participation in the deified 'flesh' on the part of the believer. There is a possibility that Schwenckfeld had an indirect influence on the way Calvin later thought of the participation of Christ's body, as W. Koehler thinks (RGG, V col. 355). Some illuminating pages from *An Answer to Luther's Malediction by Caspar Schwenckfeld* (1544) are now easily accessible in *The Library of Christian Classics,* XXV, 161 - 181.

toward the end of the 17th century, was introduced by Bucer in Hesse, but it was not introduced in Wittenberg until the *cathedra Lutheri* became a victim of the Prussian Union. Each of those questionable confirmation vows which are a cause of distress and concern to every conscientious Lutheran pastor is a monument to Bucer's understanding of Christianity. Modern scholarship has discovered that he is not only the father of the conventicles which later became so popular with the Pietists,[9] but, after going to Cambridge, he also became one of the fathers of English Puritanism.[10] Whatever the influence of Luther meant to him and to his theology (after the young Dominican with his strong humanist leanings met the famous Augustinian at the Heidelberg Disputation of 1518), he belongs, as one of his biographers remarks, to the 'Fathers of the Reformed Church',[11] representing a more-or-less independent type of Reformed Christianity. By nature he was a diplomat, a mediator, and a negotiator. As he negotiated the marriage of his friend and colleague Capito by writing a beautiful letter, so he was later the negotiator between his friend, Philip of Hesse, and Luther and Melanchthon in the sad and fateful affair of the Landgrave's bigamy. It was not only on this occasion that he transgressed the limits to be observed by a faithful mediator. Not only did Justus Jonas find in him what he called a 'foxlike cleverness',[12] but his friends were also sometimes disappointed when they observed the

---

[9]W. Bellardi, *Die Geschichte der 'Christlichen Gemeinschaft' in Strassburg* (1546-50). *Der Versuch einer zweiten Reformation* (1934) in *Quellen und Forschungen zur Reformationsgeschichte, XVIII.*

[10]A. Lang, *Puritanismus und Pietismus. Studien zu ihrer Entwicklung von M. Butzer bis zum Methodismus. Beiträge zur Geschichte und Lehre der Reformierten Kirche, VI* (1941). This book is a very important supplement to the same author's first work, *Der Evangelienkommentar Martin Butzers* (1900). Lang has definitely shown the dependence of Calvin on Bucer, as G. Anrich formulated it: 'Just as Calvin introduced the liturgy of Strasburg in Geneva, so his doctrine on the Lord's Supper and on predestination, and his theory on church discipline and on the office of the elders are based on what Bucer taught. Calvin also praises Bucer's exegetical works as samples and foundation of his own works' (*Die Religion in Geschichte und Gegenwart*, 2nd ed. I, 1297).

[11]G. Anrich, *loc. cit.*, and in his biography of Bucer (1914). An older biography of the two Strasburg Reformers, Capito and Bucer, by J.M. Baum appeared in 1860 in the collection *Leben und ausgewählte Schriften der Väter und Begründer der Reformierten Kirche.*

[12]See W. Koehler *Zwingli und Luther, I,* 730 f; II, 146. A similar judgment by Brenz is mentioned later (see 248). For Bucer's doctrine on the Sacrament, see A. Lang, *Der Evangelienkommentar Martin Butzers* (1900), 287-88, with the texts, 433 ff and 446 ff.

negative side of Bucer's great diplomatic ability, for example, in the case of the alterations which he made in Bugenhagen's *Exposition of the Psalms* and in Luther's *Postil.* We must mention this side of Bucer's character here, because it explains much of his attitude in the controversies on the Sacrament. It was natural for him to underestimate the contrast existing between Luther and Zwingli, and to overestimate his own ability to reconcile what actually could not be reconciled. His was, therefore, the destiny of many a mediator, who not only causes grave disappointments to others, but, still more, experiences the failure of his own life-work.

As to the Sacrament of the Altar, Bucer from the beginning represents a type of doctrine which is meant to overcome the antagonism between the Lutheran and the Zwinglian doctrines, though on all important questions he sides with Zwingli against Luther (just as Strasburg, too, in the years of the Great Controversy was politically closer to Zurich than to Wittenberg and the Lutheran territories). What draws him to Zwingli is the conviction that man's salvation can be brought about by spiritual means only. The Word of God and man's faith work salvation, even in the Sacrament. Nothing material can help the soul. He was as far as Zwingli from assuming that God gives his grace and his Spirit through external means. Just as it is not external Baptism, but the Spirit that works our regeneration,[13] so also it is not the eating of bread and the drinking of wine, but faith in Christ that constitutes the eating of the body and the drinking of the blood of Christ. Bucer readily accepts Zwingli's understanding of *edere* as *credere.* He, too, could have spoken the words of Zwingli at Marburg: 'Spirit eats spirit'. As he rejects the idea of instruments and means of grace,[14] so he rejects as nonsense (*deliramentum*) Luther's assumption that in a miraculous way the bread is the body, the wine is the blood. Like Zwingli he had accepted the figurative understanding of the Words of Institution from

[13]Bucer explains Titus 3: '*Per lavacrum quidem ait, regenerationis, id autem cum nequaquam sit, externus Baptismus, Spiritu enim renovamur, satis aperte indicatur, Apostolum hic totum ordinem salutis et renovationis, quo, ut externum eius signum, locum aliquem et baptismus aquae obtinet enumerare*' (Lang, *loc. cit.*, 416). The *signum* of external Baptism, then, has its place in the *ordo salutis* (this term goes back to Bucer), but is not the means by which the Spirit is given. The passage was written in 1527.

[14]'*Sophistarum est ista de instrumentis et mediis spiritus et gratiae Dei philosophia, non Christianorum*' — from Bucer's *Exposition of St John* (1528), quoted by W. Koehler, *Zwingli und Luther,* I, 733.

Honius. Like Zwingli, he regarded John 6 as the passage from which the Sacrament had to be understood. It was with these views that he entered the Great Controversy and went to Marburg.

And yet, he was not merely a Zwinglian. Where does the difference lie? The characteristic feature of his doctrine on the Sacrament of the Altar is to be found in the fact that he, unlike Zwingli, had never given up the Erasmian assumption of a spiritual presence of Christ and a spiritual eating and drinking of the body and blood which were not simply identical with belief in Christ. Like Erasmus, he believed in an inscrutable, mysterious presence, the nature of which cannot be defined except by saying that a 'materialistic' understanding is impossible. Bucer was sure that he could easily convince Luther and the Wittenbergers, by way of a colloquy on the basis of the Bible, that at the Last Supper Jesus could not have given his body (in which he stood before his disciples) in the twelve pieces of bread; and that after his ascension his body was in heaven, and consequently, since it was a true body, it could not be simultaneously on earth.[15] And yet, there is in the celebration of the Lord's Supper a real communion between the believer and the body of Christ. While we receive the bread outwardly, our spirit or inward man receives the body of Christ by faith. As the material food and drink nourishes and strengthens our body, so the inward man is nourished and strengthened by the communion with the body of Christ.[16] In this sense Bucer is able to speak not only of a presence or real presence of Christ, but he can use the formula *unio sacramentalis*. This expression meant for Luther the close connection between the bread and body, the wine and the blood, so that to receive the elements meant at the same time to receive the body and blood. The difference becomes clear if we realize that Bucer was unable to accept the *manducatio oralis* as well as the *manducatio impiorum*. It was in this sense only that Bucer was prepared to accept Luther's suggestion at Marburg.[17] This is also the meaning of his words in the *Tetrapolitana* of 1530:

> That the Lord, as in His Last Supper, so also today, in this Sacrament gives to His disciples and to the faithful, when they celebrate His Holy Supper, His true body and true blood truly to eat and to drink, according to His words:

---

[15]Koehler, *op. cit.*, 734.

[16]Lang, *Der Evangelienkommentar Martin Butzers*, 246, and the texts, 433 ff. The liturgy of Strasburg teaches accordingly in the admonition to the communicants that they were about to eat and drink spiritually the true body and blood of Christ (Lang, 247).

[17]See above, 214, 215.

'Take, eat, this is my body, etc.', 'drink all of it, this is my blood, etc.', as food for their souls and for eternal life, that they may remain in Him and He in them.[18]

Bucer was always convinced that this was the doctrine of the New Testament and the *via media* on which Luther and Zwingli could meet. Like Zwingli, he rejected the literal understanding of the Words of Institution and the *deliramentum* of the synecdoche, as well as Luther's understanding of the *unio sacramentalis,* together with the *manducatio oralis* and the *manducatio impiorum.* Unlike Zwingli, he maintained that the symbols and signs in the Sacrament are by no means empty, but bring the true believer into contact with the true body and blood of Christ. The question remains whether, not only in the *Tetrapolitana,* but also in the liturgy of Strasburg, the variance with the Lutheran understanding of the Real Presence should not have been drawn more clearly so as to avoid any misunderstanding on the part of the Christian laity. Brenz regarded this article of the *Tetrapolitana* as 'fox-like and cunning (*füchsisch und verschlagen*)'. We may look to Bucer for the origin of the custom of theologians to speak of a 'real presence' when the Real Presence is not actually meant, to speak of the reception of the 'true' body of Christ when honesty would demand that the congregation be informed (as the 'Black Rubric' does in the 1662 *Book of Common Prayer*[19]) that what they orally receive is bread only, and that the true body of Christ is in heaven and not here. He is responsible for that ambiguity which in the later period of the controversies of the 16th century did more damage than any clearly-outspoken error.

We cannot follow up the development of Bucer and the historical events which ensued from the Diet of Augsburg. The only question to be answered is how it was possible for Luther and Bucer to agree on the *Wittenberg Concord* of 1536 and what this *Concord* means. Three factors should be taken into consideration. First, there was a strong desire on the part of the south-German cities to reach an

---

[18]E. F. K. Müller, *Die Bekenntnisschriften der Reformierten Kirche,* 72, 17 ff.

[19]In this rubric the custom of kneeling is explained: 'That thereby no adoration is intended or ought to be done, either to the sacramental Bread and Wine there bodily received, or unto any Corporal Presence of Christ's natural Flesh and Blood. For the Sacramental Bread and Wine still remain in their very natural substance, and therefore may not be adored (for that were idolatry, to be abhorred by all faithful Christians); and the natural Body and Blood of our Savior Christ are in heaven, and not here; it being against the truth of Christ's natural body to be at one time in more places than one'. An earlier form appeared in the Book of 1552. See below, .

agreement with the Lutheran territories. This was not caused only by the political situation, which made it advisable for all Protestant estates in Germany to join the Smalcald League; it seems that, in the years following Zwingli's death, the attractive power of his understanding of the Sacrament was diminishing. Even in German Switzerland a type of doctrine began to appear which in some respects was closer to Bucer than to Zwingli. Thus, the *Confessio Helvetica Prior* of 1536 emphasizes that the sacred symbols of bread and wine are received by the faithful as food for spiritual and eternal life. While rejecting any bodily presence, the Confession maintains that with these symbols the communion of the body and blood of Christ is offered.[20] Furthermore, Bucer himself develops his doctrine during these years toward a more realistic understanding of the Presence. Though never giving up his protest against any theory which would, more or less, identify the elements with the body and blood, the distance between the earthly and the heavenly gifts, so to speak, becomes smaller. It is obvious in the negotiations of these years that he can say that the body is given 'with the bread (*cum pane*)'. This *with* does not mean the same as Luther's *with*, because it is not interchangeable with 'under' or 'in'. Finally, Luther's last suggestion at Marburg, which had been unacceptable to Zwingli, proved to be fruitful in 1534 when it became the basis of a concord between Wuerttemberg and the cities of south-west Germany.[21] However, Bucer, who had been prepared to accept the formula at Marburg, now found that one should not say that the body of Christ is present 'by virtue of the words', but rather 'according to the words'.

Luther's readiness to be satisfied with a mild formulation of the Real Presence was the greatest help in all these negotiations, though he was inexorable when he suspected that something was read into his words which would make it possible to deny the Real Presence which he had defended at Marburg. When, during the last days of 1534, negotiations were held in Kassel at the request of the Landgrave, Luther gave Melanchthon some instructions which could not leave the slightest doubt as to what for him remained as the minimum requirement for a possible agreement.

---

[20]E. F. K. Müller, *Die Bekenntnisschriften der Reform. Kirche,* 107, 13 ff.

[21]For this and the following, see the valuable studies by Ernst Bizer, *Studien zur Geschichte des Abendmahlsstreits im 16. Jahrhundert* (1940), 65 ff, and Walther Koehler, *Zwingli und Luther,* II, 320 ff, especially 337 f where Bucer's political use of the document is criticized. The current overestimation of Bucer (Bizer, Torrance) is corrected by Koehler's objective evaluation.

> Our opinion is that the body is in such a way with or in the bread that it is truly received with the bread. Whatever the bread suffers or does is also true of the body. Thus, it is rightly said of the body of Christ that it is carried, given, received, eaten, when the bread is carried, given, received, eaten. That is the meaning of 'This is my body'.[22]

This, and nothing else, was Luther's understanding of the *unio sacramentalis* which he never could give up. Where this was admitted, however, he was always prepared to establish church-fellowship. He never made the *how* of the Real Presence a dogma of the church, and the question of ubiquity was never mentioned in all these negotiations.

The *Wittenberg Concord* is to be understood on the basis of these facts. It is no misunderstanding that this document was incorporated into the *Formula of Concord* as one of the many Lutheran confessions on the Lord's Supper. It is a Lutheran confession, and we can only wonder how Bucer could accept it, especially since its acceptance included the acceptance of the *Augsburg Confession.* First of all, it is a declaration on the part of Luther and his colleagues, stating what Bucer and his companions confessed, and what is regarded as a sufficient basis for the establishment of church-fellowship. It is not a common confession. What did Bucer admit?

> They concede that through the sacramental union the bread is the body of Christ.[23]

This passage can only be understood in the Lutheran sense of the *unio sacramentalis* if the words are meant seriously that

> according to the words of Irenaeus [concerning the two things present in this Sacrament] . . . they hold and teach that with the bread and wine the body and blood of Christ are truly and essentially present, offered, and received.

These words, at the same time, contain the *manducatio oralis*, for what else could 'offered, and received' mean? If Bucer did not understand them in that way, he should have demanded another formulation, as he did in the case of the *manducatio impiorum.*

---

[22]Bizer, *op. cit.,* 72 ff. The words 'and are crushed with the teeth' are a later addition, as Bizer shows on page 75. It should not, however, be said that this does not mean a real alteration. There is a difference of opinion as regards the words of Melanchthon that he was a messenger of a foreign opinion ('*nuntius alienae sententiae*'). While O. Ritschl, *Dogmengeschichte des Protestantismus,* IV (1927), 18, footnote 75, and others, agreeing with V. E. Loescher, *Historia Motuum,* II, 32, deny that this refers to Luther's instruction, Bizer (*op. cit.,* 72) and W. Koehler (*op. cit.,* 377) again hold the opinion that Melanchthon's famous word in his letter to Camerarius (CR II, 822) indicates a dissension from Luther.

[23]This and the following quotations are taken from Trigl. 977.

And what did Luther concede? It was no concession if he admitted that there is

> no transubstantiation, that is, an essential transformation of the bread and wine into the body and blood of Christ,

no local inclusion, nor any permanent union apart from the *usus sacramenti* which would justify the papistic misuses, for he had never taught anything like that, as everyone knew. His only concession was that he, following a suggestion by Bugenhagen, permitted the expression *manducatio indignorum* instead of *impiorum.* He could not very well refuse this biblical term, but, obviously, here the difference between Luther and Bucer is to be found. Bucer understood by 'unworthy' people (*indigni*) those who, though believing the words of Christ, do not have the real, saving faith, while the 'godless' (*impii*) are people who do not have even the *fides historica.*[24] Luther, indeed, had no interest in the question as to what Jews or Turks or other non-Christians might receive, because Holy Scripture does not say anything about this. For him the *impii* are the 'hypocrites and evil persons' (*hypocritae et mali*) who in this life are mingled with the true believers (AC Article 8). *Impii*, according to the Lutheran Confessions (AC Article 20, Trigl. 54; *Apology*, Article 4, Trigl. 204), are people who, like the devils, have the *fides historica*, but do not really believe in Christ as their Saviour. Thus, the artificial distinction which Bucer makes collapses; the *indigni* to whom he ascribes the mere *fides historica* are identical with what Luther calls *impii.* The concession which Luther made is, therefore, only a terminological one. Luther was satisfied with this terminology, which is based on the text of 1 Cor. 11. It is impossible, however, to understand the *Wittenberg Concord* in any other way except that Luther, as in his suggestion at Marburg, was satisfied with this mild formulation of his doctrine. It is quite incorrect for E. Bizer in his book (which is otherwise quite valuable) to interpret the *Wittenberg Concord* as a real union between two views, and to recommend it as a pattern for a real evangelical union in our time.[25]

Koehler seems to be right in regarding the Concord as a self-deception by both sides.

> Both were united on the basis of a biblical formula which had been accepted

---

[24]For the following see Bizer, *op. cit.*, 124 and W. Koehler, *op. cit.*, 445 ff. The main sources are available in St Louis, XVII, col. 2084-2140.

[25]See the Introduction with its practical aspects, 1-9.

> because it was a biblical word. But they were not one as regards the interpretation.[26]

The negotiations, as well as the result, prove how Luther was prepared to concede whatever he could with a good conscience. He was not so unyielding as many of his critics believed him to be. It was a great moment in his life when the document was signed on May 26, and, perhaps, an even-greater moment when on the following Sunday pulpit- and altar-fellowship could be practised, Bucer receiving the Sacrament from Bugenhagen, the pastor of the *Stadtkirche*, after he himself had preached the sermon for that occasion. The *Wittenberg Concord* proved a success in that it brought south-German Protestantism into the Lutheran church—especially since the acceptance of the Concord included the acceptance of the *Augsburg Confession*. It was a failure in that Bucer's hope for a larger union was not fulfilled. The indefatigable negotiator tried in vain to win the Swiss churches for the *Wittenberg Concord*, and thus to revise the decision of Marburg. The only result was that he lost the confidence of both sides.

There was, and there is, no middle road between the *est* and the *significat*. Not to have seen this in time, and to have overestimated his ability to reconcile views which are irreconcilable: this was the tragedy of Bucer.

3. Melanchthon's Defection from Lutheran Doctrine

One of the most touching scenes in the history of the Reformation occurred in June 1540 at Weimar when Melanchthon, on his way to the colloquy that was to be held at Hagenau between Protestants and Catholics, suffered a complete breakdown, partly caused by the excitement to which he was exposed in connection with the bigamy of Philip of Hesse. He was a dying man when Luther arrived and saved him from imminent death through fervent prayer.

We must keep this incident in mind to understand Luther's relationship toward his old co-worker, the patience he showed him even when everyone expected a breach between the two men to be inevitable. This was more than a friendship; it was a spiritual relationship that could not possibly be destroyed, even by the worst forebodings that Luther had in the last years of his life. It is a remarkable fact that the year 1540 became the definite turning-point

---

[26] W. Koehler, *op. cit.*, 449.

in Melanchthon's views on the Sacrament, as if the man who had been prayed back to life had undergone a profound shock that had changed him. This change, which was a gradual departure from Luther's doctrine, had, indeed, begun years before. But now the deviations from the doctrine which he himself had confessed at Marburg and Augsburg became so serious, and after Luther's death so dangerous to the Lutheran church, that the whole existence of Lutheranism was at stake.

Melanchthon came to Wittenberg as a humanist, and remained a humanist throughout his life. He developed into one of the greatest educators of his century, and devoted his life to the performance of an amazing amount of work on two Faculties, as a professor of languages and as a theologian, as an organizer of higher education in Germany and as a man of the church. This eminent humanist scholar became a genuine Lutheran theologian under Luther's strong influence, as the first edition of his *Loci* shows. But he never ceased to be a humanist, and in the course of time the humanist tendencies of his theology came forth again. This did not matter as long as he remained faithful to Lutheran dogma; in every living church there must be room for a variety of theological thinkers, provided they are in agreement as to the dogma of the church. Thus, a difference of interest in, or emphasis on, certain points of doctrine, and even a difference of expression, could well be tolerated. Luther always felt that he and his learned friend supplemented each other. As Melanchthon had learned from him, so he had learned from Melanchthon. It has great significance for the Lutheran church that its Confessions were not written by Luther alone. As Melanchthon's *Augsburg Confessions, Apology,* and *Tractatus* are happily supplemented by Luther's *Smalcald Articles* and *Catechisms,* so even the *Formula of Concord* was written by disciples of Melanchthon and of Luther. This variety in expression of one and the same truth gave the Lutheran Confessions a richness which the confessions of other churches do not possess. Nothing is more significant for the Lutheran church's independence of human authority than the fact that Luther approved of the *Augsburg Confession* although he clearly stated that he would have written it in a totally different way. It is the doctrine of the Gospel that matters, and not human theology.

The theological difference between Luther and Melanchthon was bound to develop into a crisis, as soon as the Gospel itself was at stake. This became evident in the second edition of the *Loci* in 1535, where the synergistic doctrine of the three causes of conversion appeared: the Word of God, the Holy Spirit, and the human will insofar as it does not reject the grace offered. Here Melanchthon opened the door to the *liberum arbitrium* of Erasmus without realizing that danger. It is well known what trouble this and other mistakes caused the next generation. Here we are concerned only with Melanchthon's deviation from the Lutheran doctrine on the Sacrament of the Altar, which he had defended so forcefully at Marburg, and also confessed in the *Augsburg Confession* and in the *Apology*.

What was the reason for his change of mind? It is true that he always had laid special emphasis on the celebration as such, and that he had never shared Luther's doctrine on the ubiquity of the body of Christ. But he never had any doubt concerning the Real Presence up to the Diet of Augsburg in 1530. On the contrary, in some respects he criticized Zwingli's doctrine even more strongly than Luther did. A closer examination, however, reveals a characteristic difference between him and Luther. The one and only reason why Luther could not give up his understanding of the Real Presence was the Word of the Lord. Melanchthon, too, was convinced that Luther's doctrine was the biblical one. But for him, as for all humanists, the understanding of the Bible was also a philological problem, and philologists are accustomed to asking for human authorities. His opposition to Zwingli and Oecolampadius was largely determined by his conviction that their doctrine was contrary to that of the Ancient Church, the *erudita antiquitas* of the Church Fathers. He was afraid, as he wrote to Oecolampadius in April 1529, of becoming the author or defender of a new doctrine.[27] This was his main argument against the Swiss Reformers.

Early in 1530 he published *Sentences from Some Ancient Writers on the Lord's Supper*, a collection of patristic passages in support of the realistic view of the Sacrament. In this booklet he stated that,

---

[27]*'Ego enim nolim alicuius novi dogmatis in ecclesia vel auctor vel defensor existere'* (CR I, col. 1048). The same argument he used in a letter to Brenz in 1535(CR II, col. 824). It is most significant that thirty years later he criticized the strict Lutheran doctrine on the Sacrament which Hesshusius in Heidelberg defended with the same argument, doubting *'an recentioribus licuerit novum dogma invehere in Ecclesiam'* (Opinion of November 1, 1559, CR IX, 963). Now he considered Luther's doctrine an innovation, contradicting Clement of Alexandria, Origen, Tertullian, Augustine, and others.

although faith depended solely on the Word of God, the opinion of the Church Fathers should nevertheless be consulted, because this opinion had always been the common conviction of the church, and it would not be safe to disagree with the common doctrine of the Ancient Church.[28] When at the Diet of Augsburg he received the *Dialogus* in which Oecolampadius — as he had already done at Marburg — quoted passages from the Fathers which seemed to favour the opposite view, Melanchthon was not, at first, very much impressed. However, in subsequent years, his former view on the unanimity of the Church Fathers was shaken. The consequence was that Melanchthon gradually became more broadminded, and accepted Bucer's practical view that several opinions concerning the Sacrament could be tolerated within the church, as had been the case in the Ancient Church, provided the Real Presence of the body and blood of Christ was generally accepted. Melanchthon never accepted Bucer's understanding of the Sacrament, and he always regarded Zwingli's doctrine as wrong, but he shared Bucer's hope that an agreement would eventually be possible after the *Wittenberg Concord* had been accepted by the Protestants of southern Germany and the *Confessio Helvetica Prior* of 1536 seemed to many to indicate that the Swiss were abandoning the strictly-Zwinglian position. Consequently, he was able to work together with Bucer in establishing a union on the basis of the *Wittenberg Concord*.

In order to understand his development with regard to this doctrine, we must keep in mind that Melanchthon had never shared Luther's profound, vital interest in the Sacrament. While Luther could not live without the Sacrament, Melanchthon would have been able to do without it, like all humanists, had it not been an ordinance of Christ. In this respect he is very close to the Reformed church. This great schoolmaster was quite unable to understand the liturgy. This becomes evident from his preface to Lucas Lossius's *Psalmodia* (1553), an impressive collection of the great liturgical canticles and hymns of the Middle Ages, adapted for the Lutheran mass. As he even says in the *Augsburg Confession*, Article 24, such hymns are meant 'to teach the people'. Would he ever have been able to coin a sentence like Luther's: 'This Sacrament is the Gospel'? Though in

[28]'*Neque vero tutum est, a communi sententia veteris ecclesiae discedere*' (CR II, 30 f).

Article 5 of the *Augsburg Confession* he could teach with a good conscience that

> through the Word and Sacraments, as through instruments, the Holy Ghost is given,

the Sacraments remained for him essentially **signs** of grace, though effective signs.[29] Their efficacy rests upon the will of God to accompany the signs with his grace. He has ordained that in the Lord's Supper we are to receive the body of Christ when the bread is exhibited.[30]

What distinguishes Melanchthon from Zwingli, Bucer, and Calvin is this: though he confesses with Augustine that the body of Christ is in one place in heaven, he does not assume that Christ's body can be in one place **only**. He admits that it can be in several places at the same time in a mysterious way, in which several places are like one point to the person of Christ — an idea which he seems to have learned from Luther.[31] The difference over against Luther lies in the fact that, under the influence of Bucer, he more and more sees the danger that Luther's doctrine may again lead to an *artolatreia,* an adoration of the host, and thus to a materialistic view of the Real Presence. He fears the 'materialism' of Luther's doctrine. In this

---

[29]The first edition of the *Loci* deals with the Sacraments in general under the title '*De signis*' (ed. Plitt-Kolde, 4th edition, 224). The Lord's Supper is also defined as a sign (241). Still AC 13 defines the sacraments as 'not only . . . marks and professions among men', but rather as 'signs and testimonies of the will of God'. The definition of a sacrament as a sign is generally accepted by all Western churches on the authority of Augstine. The difference arises when the question is asked what this sign effects.

[30]Melanchthon makes use of the Scotist idea of a *pactum* which makes the Sacrament efficacious (see the quotations given by Gollwitzer, *op, cit.,* 72, especially CR II, 315: '*ex pacto efficientes*'). Peter Lombard's statement: 'The sacraments of the New Testament effect that which they signify' (*Sent. IV, Part 1, Q. 4*) posed the question: What is an effectual sign? can a ***sign*** be the ***cause*** of grace? This was maintained by Aquinas, *S. th. III, Q. 62, Art. 1,* while the Franciscans began to find the cause in the will of God in a tacit pact with the church to add his grace to the sign in each particular case. This doctrine, discussed by Bonaventura, was definitely established for his school by Duns Scotus, *Opus Oxoniense,* in *Sent. IV, Part 1.* This doctrine was bound to destroy the Sacrament as a means of grace, as soon as the will of God in the Sacrament was subordinated to the will of God in predestination (Wyclif, Calvin). For the Lutheran church, the firm Word of God in the Sacrament, the never-failing promise of Christ, is the cause of its efficacy.

[31]See Gollwitzer (*op. cit.,* 70), who quotes from *Iudicium de Zwinglii doctrina* (CR II, 222): '*Nos enim dicimus, quod non sit* ***necesse*** *corpus Christi in uno loco esse*'. The additional statement that *'arcano modo, quo diversa loca personae Christi simul, tamquam unum punctum, praesentia sunt'* corresponds exactly to the statement made by Luther in his discussion with Oecolampadius mentioned in chaper V, 181 f.

respect he was the ally of all who wanted to retain the pure spirituality of the Sacrament, without realizing that such spiritualization destroyed the reality of the Incarnation. This is the reason Melanchthon more and more emphasizes the Presence in the celebration, in the action, instead of in the elements, although these retain their importance as signs. The great difficulty in his doctrine is its lack of clarity. It is inconceivable how the same man, who already in 1534 regarded Luther's doctrine as an *aliena sententia*, could accept the *Smalcald Articles* of 1537. Even in his later writings, we find passages in which he seems to confirm the doctrine that he held at Marburg and Augsburg. This lack of clarity is the reason why many did not realize his deviation from Luther, and why everyone claimed him: the Lutherans as well as Bucer and Calvin.

His deviation from the old doctrine was not even realized when the *Augustana Variata* appeared, a new edition which Melanchthon had made for the colloquy to be held between Protestants and Catholics at Worms, after the failure of the Colloquy of Hagenau, where Cruciger had been the substitute for his sick friend.[32] Melanchthon left for Worms in October 1540. The alterations made in the Latin text of the *Augsburg Confession* were not taken very seriously at that time, not even by Luther, especially since our modern view of the absolute accuracy and reliability of such a reprint did not exist in the 16th century. They were intended by the author to facilitate the negotiations, and to make it easier for the Protestants to present a united front at a moment when even Catholics were very hopeful with regard to a positive result of the colloquy. Only later did the Lutherans discover that the alterations were not as harmless as they had at first seemed to be, and then they realized that it was not permissible to treat a confession which expressed the *magnus consensus* existing between churches as a private book like the *Loci*. Although some churches of Reformed and union character later regarded the *Variata* as a confession, it must not be forgotten that the alterations were made only in the Latin text; no one thought of making the corresponding alterations in the German text, the authority of which remained unquestioned.

---

[32]The text is to be found in CR 26, where the title does not give the slightest hint at the variation. According to V.E. Loescher, *Historia Motuum,* II, 37, the book appeared at the end of 1540. Some of the major deviations are to be found in the Göttingen edition of the *Bekenntnisschriften*.

The *Variata* clearly reveals what changes had taken place in Melanchthon's understanding of the Sacrament. Article 10 reads: 'Concerning the Supper of the Lord they [our churches] teach that with the bread and wine the body and blood of Christ are offered to those who eat in the Lord's Supper'.[33] The word 'with (*cum*)' had also been used in the *Wittenberg Concord.* It can mean the same as 'in' or 'under'; it can, however, also be understood in a different way, namely, as *simul cum* (simultaneously with). In this sense it was understood by Calvin, who was present at Worms, and who accepted the *Variata.* The word which we have translated as 'offered' replaces the 'distributed' of the *Invariata.*[34] It occurs also in the *Wittenberg Concord*, where the corresponding passage reads:

> with the bread and wine the body and blood of Christ are truly and substantially present, offered, and received.[35]

The words 'truly and substantially present' are not to be found in the *Variata*; likewise, the rejection of 'those who teach otherwise' (which is an essential part of the article in the *Invariata* of 1530) has been omitted. That these alterations were not made for practical purposes only, but are rather indicative of a profound change that had taken place in Melanchthon's theology since 1530, becomes evident if we compare the alterations made in other articles, especially in Article 5. There the relationship between the means of grace and the gift of the Holy Spirit is described by the ambiguous *simul*:

> For the Holy Ghost is given and is effective through the Word of God and through the Sacraments. When we hear the Gospel and meditate on it, or receive the Sacraments, and find consolation by faith, the Holy Ghost is at the same time (*simul*) effective according to the word of Paul (Gal. 3:22): 'that the promise by faith of Jesus Christ might be given to them that believe'.

The understanding of the means of grace as 'instruments', which had become so important to Luther in the Great Controversy, and which was clearly expressed in the *Invariata*, had disappeared. It is not surprising that Calvin readily signed the *Variata*, and regarded himself henceforth as in substantial agreement with the church that

---

[33]'*Die coena Domini docent, quod* ***cum*** *pane et vino vere* ***exhibeantur*** *corpus et sanguis Christi vescentibus in coena Domini*'. Cf. *Apology,* 10, 1.

[34]'. . . ***distribuantur*** *vescentibus in coena Domini'*; German text: '. . . *wahrer Leib und Blut Christi wahrhaftiglich unter der Gestalt des Brots und Weins gegenwärtig sei und da ausgeteilt und genommen werde*' (Trigl. 46).

[35]See above, 250. The original German text reads: '. . . *wahrhaftig und wesentlich zugegen sei und dargereicht und empfangen werde*' (Bizer, *op. cit.,* 118). The Latin text quoted in *Form. Conc., Sol. Decl. VII, 14* (Trigl. 976) reads: '. . . *cum pane et vino vere et substantialiter adesse, exhiberi et sumi . . .*'

Melanchthon represented, the true Church of the Augsburg Confession. With the *unio sacramentalis* in Luther's sense, Melanchthon had, without ever admitting it frankly, practically given up the *manducatio oralis* and the *manducatio impiorum*. This development became more and more apparent in the following years.

But the breach between Luther and Melanchthon which had been expected by many, even by Melanchthon himself, never occurred. When Luther's *Short Confession* appeared at the end of September 1544, not even Bucer's name was mentioned in it, though Luther had lost all confidence in him after Bucer, together with Melanchthon, had in the preceding year written a church-order for the proposed Reformation of Cologne which taught the Sacrament of the Altar in the sense of the *Tetrapolitana*. Luther expressed his deep disappointment in Bucer's character, but he did not officially sever the bond of fellowship.[36] This, and the fact that he did not openly reject Melanchthon, can be explained from a human point of view only. He knew death was at hand for him. He would not give up the hope that what had been achieved at Wittenberg in 1536 might bear fruit. It is not permissible, however, to conclude from the tolerance which Luther practised in these cases that Luther's and Melanchthon's view on the Lord's Supper are of equal value in the Lutheran church.[37] Otherwise, Melanchthon's synergism would also have to be tolerated. A new controversy on the Lord's Supper was

---

[36]'*Das Klappermaul, den Bucer*' (WA BR 10, No. 4014, 24).

[37]This is the constant assertion of all adherents of a union in Germany and elsewhere. They go even so far as to ascribe to Luther a practical or even a verbal retraction of his views. There is a tradition according to which Luther before starting on his last journey to Eisleben called for Melanchthon and told him: 'Dear Philip, I must confess, we have gone too far in the matter of the Lord's Supper (*Lieber Philippe, ich muss bekennen, der Sache vom Abendmahl ist viel zu viel getan*)', whereupon Melanchthon suggested writing another pamphlet which would help bring about a reconciliation. Luther is said to have answered that he had thought of that often himself, but this would make suspect the whole doctrine; he would commend the matter to God; 'You should also do something after my death (*Tut ihr auch etwas nach meinem Tode*)'. The story goes back to Hardenberg of Bremen, who claims to have it from Melanchthon himself. In view of the *Short Confession* of 1544, which contains Luther's testament in this respect, it cannot mean a retraction of what he wrote there. Actually, the words of Luther and the whole conversation, as it really took place, refer to the deletion of certain strong words used against Bucer in *Dass diese Worte noch feststehen* of 1527 from the new edition of the 2nd volume of *Luther's Works*. This has been shown by J. Hausleiter in *Neue Kirchliche Zeitschrift*, IX, 381 ff and X, 455 ff (1898 and 1899), contradicting the book by Th. Diestelmann, *Die letzte Unterredung Luthers mit Melanchthon über den Abendmahlsstreit*, 174. See also E. Bizer, *op. cit.*, 244.

bound to come. The clouds of an approaching new thunderstorm darkened Luther's last years. But, just as he had hesitated to enter the Great Controversy with Zwingli, and at Marburg went to the limit in making concessions which he could make with a good conscience, so he sought unto the end to stay by the peace established by the *Wittenberg Concord*. It was the next generation that had to fight for Luther's doctrine against the fruits which grew out of Bucer's and Melanchthon's views as expressed in the theology of Calvin.

4. Calvin's Attempt to Solve the Problem of the Sacrament

Regret has often been expressed that Luther and Calvin never met. During the years of his exile at Strasburg (1538-41), Calvin enjoyed the friendship and the theological influence of Bucer. And for more than 20 years after they first met at the Colloquy at Worms, Calvin and Melanchthon kept in touch with each other through personal friendship and correspondence. But between Luther and Calvin there was no personal contact. Luther never wrote to Calvin, and the only letter which Calvin wrote to Luther was never delivered by the cautious Melanchthon. How much Luther knew of Calvin is not known. The few utterances which have been preserved (as far as they are not apocryphal, like the alleged favourable words of Luther on Calvin's *Treatise on the Lord's Supper* of 1541) do not give a clear picture, and Luther probably had no clear idea of Calvin and his doctrine.[38]

This lack of a definite conception on Luther's part regarding the Reformer of Geneva has made all kinds of conjectures possible. While strict Lutherans were inclined to believe that in Luther's evaluation Calvin would have been only another Zwingli, others speak of him as if he were the only true Lutheran in the 16th century after Luther.[39] Either view, of course, is untenable; on the other hand, there is some truth in both. Calvin began his work as Reformer as a 'Lutheran'. He wanted to be Luther's disciple, and felt himself far closer to him than

———

[38]The few passages where Luther mentions Calvin had been collected and carefully interpreted by Hans Grass, *Die Abendmahlslehre bei Luther und Calvin* (1940), 170-172. It seems that Luther at first had a favourable opinion, but became doubtful as to Calvin's understanding of the Sacrament in connection with the teachings of Bucer and Melanchthon. Joh. von Walter, *Christentum und Frömmigkeit, Gesammelte Vorträge und Aufsätze* (1941), 261, thinks that the famous passage of Luther's *Lectures on Genesis* (WA 43, 463) about the misuse which would later be made of his utterances on predestination refers to Calvin's *Institutio*.

[39]This is, more or less, the view of such outstanding theologians as Tholuck in the 19th and Karl Holl in the 20th century, to say nothing of minor authorities.

to Zwingli and Oecolampadius. As a Lutheran he wrote the first edition of his *Institutio religionis christianae*, following the train of thought of Luther's *Catechism*. His 'Lutheranism', however, was limited by the fact that he knew only such works by Luther as were written in (or translated into) Latin.[40] Consequently, the most important writings of Luther on the Sacrament were unknown to him, and he was unable to follow the Great Controversy between Luther and Zwingli which was in progress while he was being converted from Catholic humanism to what at that time in France was called 'Lutheranism'. It seems that Zwingli, whose *Commentarius de vera et falsa religione* he had read, exercised a greater influence on him than he realized.[41] But, above all, it was Bucer who helped to shape his theology, first by his writings, especially his *Commentary on the Gospels*, and later during the years of their association at Strasburg.[42] 'Bucer was the spiritual father of Calvin', says A. Lang,[43] referring mainly to the two doctrines that are of special importance for Calvin: the doctrine on predestination, and the doctrine on the Sacraments. The connection with Bucer and Strasburg as regards the Lord's Supper is indicated also by the fact that the liturgy of Geneva had its origin in Strasburg.[44] In comparing Bucer and Calvin, we have the impression that Calvin elaborated with French clarity on what he had learned from Bucer.

In his doctrine on the Lord's Supper, Calvin tries to find the *via media* between Luther and Zwingli. Already in the first edition of the *Institutio*, which appeared in the year of the *Wittenberg Concord*, his doctrine was almost complete. Without mentioning names, he rejects the understanding of the Words of Institution held by Luther on the one hand, and by Zwingli and Oecolampadius on the other hand.

---

[40]As to the Lord's Supper he had to rely on *De captivitate Babylonica, Sermon on the Sacrament of the Body and Blood of Christ,* which had been translated into Latin in 1527, and Luther's letter to Herwagen (see above, 113). For the whole problem, see W. Niesel, *Calvins Lehre vom Abendmahl* (1935), 22 ff.

[41]Karl Holl, *Joh. Calvin, Ges. Aufsätze, III, 256 f* has shown that Calvin read Zwingli even during the latter's lifetime (of course, the Latin works only). For more details see Niesel, *op. cit.,* 30 f. How far Zwingli influenced Calvin, directly or indirectly through Bucer, is still open to debate.

[42]Calvin lived at Strasburg from 1538 till 1541.

[43]August Lang, *Zwingli und Calvin* (1913), 108. Lang has definitely proved the dependence of Calvin on Bucer in his great work *Der Evangelienkommentar Martin Butzers and die Grundzüge seiner Theologie* (1900).

[44]W.D. Maxwell, *The Liturgical Portions of the Genevan Service Book* (1941) with valuable texts which show how the influence from Strasburg went via Geneva to Scotland. See below, 264.

Neither is the bread the body or the body is the bread, nor is the bread a mere sign or figure of the body. In the Sacrament 'we are spiritually fed',[45] that is, our souls are fed with the body and blood of the Lord.[46] There is no Real Presence of the body of Christ in the Sacrament, as Luther believes, for the body of Christ exists, locally circumscribed, in heaven. To believe that this body could be at the same time in heaven and in the Sacrament would mean to revive Marcion's docetism.[47] Nor is it permissible to understand the body as glorified, for in the first Supper the body was not yet glorified. Not the true and natural body or the substance of the body is given in the Sacrament, but the benefits which Christ has gained for us through his body.

> This is the presence of the body which is required by the nature of the Sacrament.[48]

To this doctrine in the first edition of the *Institutio* Calvin always adhered, though in his later writings he developed and improved it.

The first progress is to be found in the *Confession of Faith concerning the Eucharist* written in the following year in preparation for negotiations to be held at Berne. In this short confession, which he had written in conjunction with Farel and Viret, and which also had been signed by Bucer and Capito — one year after the *Wittenberg Concord* — Calvin explains how the body of Christ, which is in heaven, and therefore cannot be in the Sacrament, can become food for our souls:

> While we as long as we sojourn in this mortal life cannot be included or contained in the same place with Him, the efficacy of His Spirit is not limited by boundaries of space and therefore is able to bring together and to connect what is separated by local distance (*locorum spatiis . . . disiuncta*). Thus we recognize that His Spirit is the bond of our participation of Him. The Spirit feeds us with the substance of the flesh and blood of our Lord for immortality.[49]

This idea assumed great importance for Calvin. It is the Holy Spirit that bridges the immense gap between the Sacrament on earth and

[45] '*Spiritualiter pascimur*' CR (Calvin) I, 118.

[46] 'The sacrament is something spiritual through which our Lord wanted to feed not our bellies but our souls (*non ventres nostros, sed animas pascere voluit*)', *loc. cit.*, 121.

[47] *ibidem*, 121; the argument of Marcionitism stems from Zwingli.

[48] '*. . . dicimus vere et efficaciter exhiberi, non autem naturaliter. Quo scilicet significamus non substantiam ipsam corporis, seu verum et naturale corpus illic dari, sed omnia quae in suo corpore nobis Christus praestitit. Ea est corporis praesentia quam sacramenti ratio postulat*' (*ibidem*, 123).

[49] CR (Calvin) IX, 711 f: '*Ergo Spiritum eius vinculum esse cum ipso participationis agnoscimus, sed ita ut nos ille carnis et sanguinis Domini substantia . . . pascat*'. English translation by J. K. S. Reid in *Calvin: Theological Treatises* in *The Library of Christian Classics, XXII* (London, 1954), 168 f.

the body of Christ in heaven, which is, as it was for Zwingli, a local distance that cannot be understood as a metaphysical distance between our world and the world of God — as is sometimes done by modern Reformed theologians.[50] Another answer to the question as to how we can receive the body, which is in heaven, is to be found in the *Small Treatise on the Holy Supper* of 1541, and in all later writings of Calvin on that subject. At the end of the *Small Treatise,* Calvin criticizes the two parties in the controversy on the Sacrament for having failed to have patience to listen to each other. He is looking forward to an agreement to be reached in the near future, and states:

> There is not yet any published formula in which agreement has been framed. But this will happen when God is pleased to bring into one place all those who are to draw it up.

Calvin's confidence is noteworthy: Nothing more is required than a conference to accept the formula, which, obviously, is ready in the mind of Calvin. He continues:

> Meanwhile it must content us that there is brotherliness and communion between the churches, and that all agree in what is necessary for meeting together, according to the command of God. We all confess, then, with one mouth that in receiving the Sacrament in faith, according to the ordinance of the Lord, we are truly made partakers of the real substance of the body and blood of Jesus Christ. How this is done, some may deduce better and explain more clearly than others. But be this as it may, on the one hand we must, to shut out all carnal fancies, raise our hearts on high to heaven, not thinking that our Lord Jesus Christ is so abased as to be enclosed under any corruptible elements. On the other hand, not to diminish the efficacy of this sacred mystery, we must hold that it is accomplished by the secret and miraculous virtue of God, and that the Spirit of God is the bond of participation, for which reason it is called spiritual.[51]

This passage, perhaps the most perfect expression of Calvin's doctrine, contains the idea that we must lift up our hearts to partake

[50]As by Wilhelm Niesel, whose great knowledge of Calvin is unfortunately limited by a tendency to modernize or 'Barthianize' the Reformer of Geneva; see *Calvins Lehre vom Abendmahl* (1935), 92: 'There is an immense distance between Him and us, not a distance in the ordinary local sense, but such a distance as exists between our world and the world of God'. Hans Grass, in his excellent presentation of Calvin's doctrine, *Die Abendmahlslehre bei Luther und Calvin* (1940) 212, raises the objection that Calvin unmistakably speaks of a local distance. Like Zwingli, Calvin would indeed never have been able to accept Luther's assertion: 'The right hand of God is everywhere'.

[51]CR (Calvin) V, 460. Here quoted from the English translation by J. K. S. Reid in the book cited in footnote 49.

of the body of Christ, which is in heaven. We find it also in the old liturgy of Geneva in the exhortation addressed to the communicants:

> . . . the only way to dispose our souls to receive nourishment, relief, and quickening of his substance, is to lift up our minds by faith above all things worldly and sensible, and thereby enter into heaven, that we may find and receive Christ where he dwelleth, undoubtedly very God and very man, in the incomprehensible glory of God the Father . . .[52]

This passage from the old liturgy shows what the origin of the idea is. It is the *sursum corda* of the mass, though the idea occurs also in Oecolampadius' words spoken to Luther at Marburg, that he should not stick to the humanity of the flesh of Christ, but rather lift up his mind to his divinity.[53] The origin of the idea of the Holy Spirit as the *transporteur* who brings the body of Christ to us is unknown. Perhaps Calvin was influenced in this respect by one of the Greek Fathers for whom the invocation of the Holy Spirit effects the Real Presence. In the liturgy of Geneva there is no trace of an invocation of the Spirit.

These two ideas, especially the *sursum corda*, made it possible for Calvin to speak of a real participation of the body and blood of Christ. Now he even speaks of the 'substance' of the body, which he expressly rejected in the *Institutio* of 1536. It is astonishing how realistic his terminology becomes during the following years. We receive the 'substance' of the body. We receive the body 'really', 'truly', 'essentially', 'substantially'. His language in this respect has become almost as strong as Luther's. Small wonder that the question was soon raised what Calvin really meant. In order to understand his attitude, we must consider that he was honestly convinced that he had found the solution to the problem. He wanted to do justice to Zwingli and Oecolampadius, whose figurative understanding of the Words of Institution he had accepted. On the other hand, he felt himself to be closer to Luther, with whom he shared the conviction that the body of Christ is received 'substantially'. Melanchthon, who had become his friend, seemed to him to be the man who could bring about the reconciliation.

[52]We quote from the old English translation (in modern orthography) used by the English refugees at Geneva at the time of Mary. John Knox, the minister of the congregation, brought this liturgy to Scotland, where it was in use for some generations, one of the finest specimens of classical Calvinistic piety. The text with interesting notes has been published by W. D. Maxwell, *The Liturgical Portions of the Genevan Service Book* (1931). The passage quoted is on page 124 in English and Latin. Calvin's French text is to be found on page 132.

[53]See above, 203.

The serious situation of the Protestant churches in all countries—in Germany before the Peace of Augsburg, in England at the time of Mary, in France where the Reformed church was persecuted—seemed to demand a union still more urgently than at the time of Marburg. What Bucer had failed to attain was now regarded as possible. Calvin's doctrine on the Lord's Supper seemed to be the great means of a union of all Protestants. In 1549 he had come to an agreement with Bullinger in the *Consensus Tigurinus* which meant a complete union between German- and French-speaking Switzerland, between the churches of Zwingli and those of Calvin. The text of the *Consensus* was published only in 1551, and its appearance caused the Lutheran pastor Westphal in Hamburg to criticize Calvin. Thus, the so-called Second Controversy on the Lord's Supper broke out. Calvin was disappointed beyond measure, and answered with polemical writings which were not less acrimonious, and in many respects even more scornful, than those which Luther had written against the 'sacramentarians'. This controversy had the same result as the Great Controversy of the 1520s: it proved that no understanding was possible because there is no *via media* between *est* and *significat*. It was a tragic error for Calvin to believe that he had found the solution. Nothing less than this controversy with all its bitterness could clarify the situation.

First of all, Calvin's realistic expression had to be interpreted. What is the 'substance' of the body of Christ which we receive? It cannot be what Luther understood by 'substance', namely, the true body, the crucified and glorified body of our Lord. The body cannot be 'transported', says Calvin; according to him the body is in heaven and not here, as the *Consensus Tigurinus* puts it in Article 25:

> the body of Christ, as a true human body, must be finite, and is contained in heaven as in a place; thus it is necessarily distant from us by such a local distance as separates heaven from earth.[54]

Suppose Calvin were right in his assumption that the Holy Spirit brings the body to us (there is no Scripture passage which would allow such assumption): according to Calvin's own presuppositions

[54] '. . . *corpus Christi, ut fert humani corporis natura et modus, finitum est, et coelo, ut loco, continetur; necesse est a nobis tanto locorum intervallo distare, quantum coelum abest a terra*' (E.F.K. Müller, *Bekenntnisschriften der Reform. Kirche,* 163, 18 ff). It has been pointed out that the *Consensus of Zurich* does not represent the whole doctrine of Calvin. However, it contains nothing that he could not accept. Otherwise, his signature would have been a dishonesty. Calvin was different from Bucer, who sometimes could accept things for political reasons. Thus the 'substance' of the body is actually not more than its 'power' or the 'benefits' connected with that body.

the body could not possibly be here on earth and in several places simultaneously. And from what Scripture passage could the assumption be deduced that at the Lord's Supper our soul ascends to heaven? These are hypotheses meant to make it possible to retain that sacramental realism which, as Calvin has rightly seen, belongs to the nature of this Sacrament.

No one can study Calvin seriously without feeling the deep longing of this man for the real Sacrament. There is a touching hunger and thirst for the Sacrament which expressed itself in the classical liturgies of the old Reformed churches. Calvin really wanted to retain the Sacrament. Only reluctantly did he give up the desire to have the Sacrament celebrated each Sunday. But his theology, and perhaps still more the philosophical presuppositions of this theology, made it impossible to reconcile the realistic terminology with his actual thoughts. This was seen at once by the Lutherans. For Luther the crucial question had always been: Must the word *est* be understood literally? Is there a 'sacramental union' between the elements and the body and blood, so that we receive the body together with the bread? Do we receive the body and blood of Christ orally? Do the *impii* or *indigni* receive it, or the believers only?

All these questions had to be answered by Calvin in the negative. The Words of Institution are to be understood figuratively; a literal understanding is impossible. The body of Christ is not where the consecrated bread is. Body and blood are not received orally. What the mouth receives is bread and wine only. Only the soul of the believer receives the body and blood simultaneously.[55] Consequently, there cannot be any such thing as the *manducatio indignorum* which Bucer had admitted in the *Wittenberg Concord.* What Calvin can admit is that the body and blood of Christ are offered to all who partake of the Supper, while the unbeliever receives nothing but bread and wine. How could such a view of the Sacrament claim to bridge the gulf between Zwingli and Luther, and even to be closer to Luther than to Zwingli? The great difference remains the same. The Sacrament is not a means, but a sign, of grace.

---

[55] Here lies the reason why we cannot say with Calvin and the Reformed theologians: We disagree only concerning the mode of the presence, not concerning the presence itself. The question is whether the body and blood of Christ are really present, irrespective of our belief or unbelief.

Even Wilhelm Niesel, who tries to Lutheranize Calvin's doctrine as far as possible, arrives at the conclusion:

> The communion with our exalted Lord exists also outside the celebration of the Supper. Calvin can, indeed, say all that which we have stated in this book about that communion without mentioning the Lord's Supper. Thus, for example, in a letter addressed to Petrus Martyr Vermigli he shows conclusively how we are united through faith by the Holy Spirit with Christ — and that means also with His body and blood — and how only in this way we receive the benefits of Christ.[56]

Niesel adds:

> Indeed, what we receive in the Lord's Supper, that we receive daily in hearing the sermon, in reading the Scripture, in prayer. What other communion with our Lord should be possible than that which is created by the Word and the Spirit?[57]

We need the Sacrament because it is an external sign which affirms the word of the divine promise. No Lutheran would deny the truth contained in this statement. But it is not the whole truth.

The Sacrament is a sign, but at the same time it is more. It conveys to us God's grace. That is what Luther had learned in his fight against the 'sacramentarians': only in the Real Presence of the true body and blood of Christ do we have that assurance which the Lord's Supper gives us. Luther himself never doubted this Presence. It was the silent presupposition of everything which he had said in his early writings on the Sacrament as a sign and seal attached to Christ's promise. He had seen then where the figurative understanding of the sacramental words was bound to lead. If 'This is my body', 'This is my blood' were understood figuratively, then there would be no assurance that 'given for you', 'shed for you' were to be taken literally. Then the *proprium* of this Sacrament would be lost, the eating and drinking of what Christ had sacrificed for us, and with it the Real Presence of the whole Christ, according to his divinity and humanity, in his Church on earth, here and now, as an anticipation of our eternal union with him. No one who knows Luther can assume that he would have been satisfied with Calvin's doctrine, which, in spite of all realistic language, did not admit of more than that spiritual manducation which all Reformed churches teach. This new attempt to bring about a union which had not been attained at Marburg, and which even Bucer had failed to achieve, could not be successful, to the great disappointment of Calvin and the whole Reformed church, and to

---

[56] *Calvins Lehre vom Abendmahl* (2nd ed., 1935), 96, with quotations from Calvin.
[57] *Op. cit.*, 97.

the distress of many serious Christians in the 16th century, and later, who did not realize what was at stake. The old reproaches, which once had been levelled against Luther and his stand at Marburg, were now hurled against the Lutherans who opposed Calvin, and against the authors and signatories of the *Formula of Concord,* which brought about the final decision on the controversies on the Sacrament in the 16th century.

5. The Decision of the Formula of Concord

There are only a few creeds or confessions in the history of the church which have been reviled in such a manner as the *Formula of Concord.* It is surprising that the criticism came not only from outside, but also from inside, the Lutheran church. Even modern historians, who otherwise show a remarkable ability for understanding and impartially describing peculiar concepts of the Ancient and the Medieval Church, seem to lose their patience when it comes to the *Formula of Concord.*[58] We could fill a whole book with the abuses that have been levelled against this last great confession of our church, even by people who call themselves Lutheran. There are even Lutheran theologians who wholeheartedly accept the earlier Lutheran Confessions and never would approve of such abuses, who also take the *Formula of Concord* seriously, and yet keep their distance from it.[59] In the latter instance, the reason is that the *Formula* obviously represents a later type of Lutheran theology

[58] As an example, we quote Friedrich Loofs, one of the greatest scholars in the field of the history of doctrine. In his *Leitfaden der Dogmengeschichte* (4th edition, 1906), 914-28, he deals with the *Form. Conc.: Der 7. Artikel behandelt . . . die coena domini klugerweise so, dass die* ***christologischen Ungeheuerlichkeiten,*** *die von Luthers Abendmahlslehre unabtrennbar waren (und im 8. Artikel auch zur Sprache kommen) hier möglichst nicht zur Sprache kommen'* (920, *emphasis mine*). In a similar strain the whole *Formula* is spoken of, especially Articles 7 and 8. This is not surprising if we remember that, for this great scholar of the school of Ritschl, Luther's doctrine on the Lord's Supper was '*eine der grandiosesten Verirrungen christlicher Glaubensgedanken*' (quoted from *Vom Sakrament des Altars,* ed. H. Sasse (1941), 136, where the references are given). On p 938 Loofs criticizes the broadmindedness of the Preface concerning the judgment on heresies which even a representative of the '*alleinseligmachende*' Roman church would approve. This was the understanding of the Lutheran Confessions, in which even in the first quarter of this century students at the University of Halle-Wittenberg, which claimed to continue the tradition of the *cathedra Lutheri,* were brought up.

[59] This is true even of Edmund Schlink, one of the most serious representatives of a theology which has learned to understand again the meaning of the Confessions of the Lutheran Church. See *Theologie der luth. Bekenntnisschriften* (3rd edition, 1948), 18 f and 262. This excellent work should be studied by every Lutheran pastor.

quite naturally, since it was written 40 years after the *Smalcald Articles*. This confession represents, in many respects, the transition from the Reformation period to the period of Orthodoxy. Up to this day, however, no one has been able to prove that its theology represents a defection from the Reformation.

It is noteworthy that the theological reasons which once caused a minority of Lutherans not to accept the *Book of Concord* lay entirely in the strictly-Lutheran character of the *Formula*. The critics took exception to the use of the word *damnamus* instead of *improbant* in connection with the Reformed doctrine on the Lord's Supper. This, after all, makes no real difference, since in the *Augsburg Confession* the German text uses the same word *verwerfen* in Articles 9 and 10, and since *damnare* and *rejicere* are always used synonymously in such 'condemnations'.

The second theological objection was directed against Luther's doctrine of the 'ubiquity' which should not be made a dogma of the church. Actually, this dogma is not taught by the *Formula of Concord*, as we shall see. All such objections could be raised against Luther's *Large Catechism*, too. The criticism came from the side of Philippists,[60] but disciples of Melanchthon, like Chemnitz and Selneccer, had been among the authors of the *Formula*, and the confession as a whole met with the approval of the vast majority, not only of the Lutheran princes and magistrates, but also of the pastors (about 8,000). Never had a confession at its appearance found such an overwhelming acceptance.

It is true that there are Lutheran churches which, mainly for political reasons, never accepted the *Formula of Concord*,[61] and there is a general understanding among Lutherans that a church may be regarded as Lutheran even without this confession. If this, however, should mean that a church which rejects it and teaches against it may still be regarded as a church of the Augsburg Confession, the serious question arises whether this church still holds the *Augsburg Confession* in the sense of the Fathers. This is especially

[60]Among them was a fine Christian like Martin Schalling, the author of the hymn '*Herzlich lieb hab ich dich, o Herr*'. One of the reasons for their reluctance to 'condemn' Calvinism was the fact that just at that time the Reformed Church of France had to go through a most dreadful persecution. The Lutherans who signed the *Formula of Concord* repeatedly expressed their sympathy with the Christians in France, and did not pass any judgment on the church in France, as the Preface to the *Book of Concord* shows.

[61]The most important ones in Germany are: Hesse, Anhalt, Pomerania, Holstein, Bremen, Frankfurt, Nuremberg; outside Germany: Denmark and Norway.

true if the article on the Lord's Supper is rejected under the pretext that the *improbant secus docentes* of AC Article 10 is not directed against Calvin and his adherents. It is directed against everyone who denies the Real Presence of the true body and blood of Christ in, with, and under the bread or wine, whatever his name may be. He who rejects Article 7 of the *Formula of Concord* must also reject, at least, the *Large Catechism*. But who will teach the *Small Catechism*, if he does not accept the *Large Catechism*? It seems that on this point a great dissension exists among the Lutherans of the world, which becomes evident in the crises through which all Lutheran churches are going today.

It must never be forgotten that the *Formula of Concord* was meant to settle controversies which had arisen within the churches of the Augsburg Confession after Luther's death. It is not directed against the decrees of Trent as such (though these are in the background), nor against Calvin's doctrine as such. The Council of Trent is mentioned once in the *Thorough Declaration*, the Calvinists once in the *Epitome*, but the name of Calvin does not occur.[62] The *Preface* makes it clear beyond doubt that

> the condemnations, censures, and rejection of godless doctrines, and especially of that which had arisen concerning the Lord's Supper . . . had to be expressly set forth in this our declaration,

however,

> it is in no way our design and purpose to condemn those men who err from a certain simplicity of mind, but are not blasphemers against the truth of the heavenly doctrine, much less, indeed, entire churches which are either under the Roman empire of the German nation or elsewhere.

This explanation of what the condemnations of our Confessions mean was quoted and commented on very often by the orthodox theologians of the following century. It has always been regarded as an official statement of our church (which, by the way, corresponds exactly to similar statements of the Church Fathers who always distinguished between heresies and the persons who held heretical opinions).[63] Even the strictest of the champions of Lutheran orthodoxy in the 17th century never gave up this attitude — for

[62]Melanchthon's name is never mentioned either, except in the Preface (*Bekenntnisschriften*, 752). The name of Calvin's successor, Beza, occurs once.

[63]'*Dogmata impia et ab haereticis profecta arguere et anathematizare oportet. Hominibus autem parcendum et pro salute ipsorum orandum est*', Chrysostom, *Sermo de anathema* (MPG 48, col. 952; the real title of the book is *De non*

instance, A. Calov who enjoys the bad reputation of having been the most irreconcilable among the 'confessionalists' of his time. Like all other representatives of Lutheran orthodoxy, he always emphasized that the condemnations of the *Formula of Concord* do not imply a judgment on entire churches. In his *Historia syncretistica* he points out that the Ecumenical Synods of Nicaea and Constantinople, while condemning certain heretics, did not condemn the entire churches in which these errorists taught.[64] In the same way the Lutheran church never passed judgment on the Reformed churches in France or Scotland. We reject the heresies taught in these churches, but we would never say that the true church of Christ is no longer in these churches, just as we believe that also in the church of Rome there are still true believers in Christ, and, therefore, his Church. Philip Nicolai, another of the controversialists of the orthodox period, expressly stated his belief that, even in Abyssinia or in the mission churches of the Jesuits in America, the Church of Christ still existed, inasfar as the means of grace had been preserved there. This true ecumenicity of the Lutheran church must always be kept in mind, if we want to understand the inexorable seriousness with which it has always upheld the principle that church- and altar-fellowship can be practised only where a consensus on the truth of the Gospel and on the Sacraments of Christ has been reached. To the world this seems to be a contradiction, because it thinks in terms of 'broad-mindedness' and 'narrow-mindedness'. In the church of Christ, however, such contradiction does not exist, because the quest for truth and the quest for unity are one; in our Lord's highpriestly prayer for his Church the petition 'That they all may be **one**' is inseparably connected with the preceding 'Sanctify them through thy **truth**'.

anathematandis vivis vel defunctis), quoted by Johann Gerhard, *Loci XXIII* (ed. Preuss, VI,181) in his discussion of the problem as to how the condemnation of heretics may be reconciled with Christian charity, and by A. Calov, *Historia syncretistica*, 38.

[64] 1682, here quoted from the 2nd edition, 1685, 38 and other passages. The *Historia syncretistica* is a history of the union movements from the beginning of the Reformation to 1680, written from the point of view of an orthodox Lutheran. In order to correct the current prejudices and false ideas about the spirit of this Orthodoxy, the following passage from the Preliminary Chapter may be quoted: '*Was würde das für eine herrliche Gnadengabe Gottes zu achten sein, wenn auch nur bei den drei Haufen im Okzident, der Päpstler, Lutheraner und Reformierten es zur wahren Gott wohlgefälligen Einigkeit gedeihen könnte? Und wer wollte solch ein Unchrist sein, dass er nicht, wenn's möglich solches Gut auch mit seinem eigenen Blut zu erkaufen bereit wäre? Denn sollen wir das Leben für die Brüder lassen, 1 John 3: 16, wer wollte nicht für so viel Millionen Christen sein Leben freudig lassen!*'

It is this concern for the unity of the church in the truth of the Gospel which finds its expression in the decision of the *Formula of Concord* concerning the Lord's Supper. The inclusion of such an article in the confession had been necessitated by the fact that Melanchthon's deviation from Luther in this doctrine had paved the way for the inroad which Calvin's doctrine had made into German Lutheranism. Entire territories, like the Palatinate (Heidelberg), had become Calvinistic, but, in addition to that, the Calvinistic understanding of the Sacrament had slowly penetrated into the Lutheran church and created what is called 'Crypto-Calvinism', a Calvinistic view on the Sacrament which claims to be the real doctrine of the *Augsburg Confession*, and makes use of the Lutheran terminology, so that Christian laymen, and even pastors, could not see the difference. That had happened in Saxony, and even at Wittenberg when, after Melanchthon's death, his son-in-law Peucer became the leader at the university. The intolerable situation led to a catastrophe in 1574 when the *Exegesis perspicua*, a treatise on the Lord's Supper, written by a physician in Silesia who was a disciple and friend of Melanchthon, was published anonymously at Leipzig, and was circulated and eagerly read and recommended at Wittenberg.[65] It revealed what the Philippists at that time were really thinking. They taught that in the Lord's Supper there is a *communio corporis et sanguinis Christi*, however, only in the sense that Christ is present, according to his divinity, while his body is in heaven. Eating the bread brings the partakers into unity with his (spiritual) body, the Church. There is no sacramental union, no *manducatio oralis* and no *manducatio impiorum*. Luther's Christology is definitely rejected, and put on the same level as Eutychianism (Monophysitism), which destroys the true human nature of Christ. It was this Crypto-Calvinism which made it imperative to discuss the doctrine *de coena Domini* in the new confession. Article 7 of the *Formula of Concord*, which was supplemented by Article 8 on the Person of Christ, gave the necessary answer to Crypto-Calvinism (and thus, indirectly, also to the Calvinists) of that time and also to the Crypto-Calvinists of all ages, for this disease of the Lutheran church is a chronic one.

It is a most serious question for all Lutherans why Crypto-Calvinism has accompanied our church throughout the centuries up to this very day. Perhaps the Crypto-Calvinism which caused the article of the *Formula of Concord* is nothing compared with the

[65]The author was Joachim Curaeus. The book *Exegesis perspicua et ferme integra controversiae de coena Domini* was reprinted at Marburg in 1853. The *Exegesis* was, as the sub-title says, submitted to all adherents of the Augsburg Confession who would judge it without prejudice.

Crypto-Calvinism of today, which seems to prevail in the majority of Lutheran churches, and finds its expression even in the doctrinal statements of the 'younger churches' on the mission fields which want to be Lutheran. In these cases, of course, the influence of the mother churches is responsible for the decay of the Lutheran doctrine on the Sacrament. But why does the Lutheran church time and again succumb to that disease?

If one reads the *Exegesis perspicua* and similar writings of the later 16th century, it becomes quite obvious that the same humanistic influence which finds an expression in the letter of Honius, and in the doctrine of Zwingli, and which was revived in the theology of the later Melanchthon and in Calvin's understanding of the Sacrament, asserts itself in the Melanchthonian school. This humanism helped to shape modern Western civilization. It contains a rationalistic element even where it accepts the great doctrines of Christianity. Its understanding of man is definitely idealistic and, therefore, opposed to the Lutheran concept of the Sacrament, which to modern man seems materialistic. Seen from this aspect, Crypto-Calvinism has a meaning far beyond the tragic controversy of the time following Melanchthon's death. The decision of the *Formula of Concord* becomes of utmost importance also for the Lutheran church in its fight against modern Crypto-Calvinism.

What does this decision mean? It is, briefly speaking, a reaffirmation of Luther's doctrine in view of the attempts to interpret the Lutheran formulas in a Calvinistic sense. Since the issue dealt with the correct interpretation of the Lutheran doctrine, the *Solida Declaratio*, after having stated the *status controversiae*, first gives an interpretation of the previous confessions concerning the Sacrament of the Altar: the *Augsburg Confession* and the *Apology;* the *Wittenberg Concord* of 1536, which is literally quoted and must therefore be regarded as a part of the *Formula of Concord*; the *Smalcald Articles;* and Luther's *Large Catechism*. It is shown that all these confessions contain the Lutheran doctrine and defy any other interpretation. Since Luther is regarded as 'the most distinguished teacher of the churches which confess the Augsburg Confession',[66]

[66]Art. 7, 41 (Trigl. 984): '*Dieweil denn D. Luther der vornehmste Lehrer der Kirchen, so sich zur Augsburgischen Konfession bekennen, zu halten, als dessen ganze Lehre, Summa und Inhalt in den Artikeln vielermeldeter* [often mentioned] *Augsburgischer Konfession verfasst . . . so kann und soll mehrgedachter Augsburgischer Konfession eigentlicher Verstand und Meinung aus keines andern denn aus D. Luthers Lehre und Streitschriften eigentlicher und besser genommen werden*'.

further quotations are given from his *Large Confession* of 1528,[67] and his *Short Confession* of 1544,[68] to show what his doctrine had been, and how he had foreseen that after his death his doctrine would be misinterpreted. The *Thorough Declaration* then shows what Luther and the Lutheran confessions understood by the words 'The bread is the body ', or by using the terms 'under the bread', 'with the bread', 'in the bread'. The scriptural proof is then given from the four narratives of institution (St Paul's account being understood as a special revelation) and from Paul's commentary in 1 Cor. 10 and 11: The words of Christ must be received in sincere faith, as he has not given or indicated another meaning; 1 Cor. 10 says clearly that 'the bread which we break is the distributed body of Christ'; 1 Cor. 11:27 proves the *manducatio impiorum*:

> 'Whosoever shall eat this bread and drink this cup of the Lord unworthily', sins not merely against the bread and wine, not merely against the signs or symbols and emblems of the body and blood, but 'shall be guilty of the body and blood of the Lord Jesus Christ', which, as there present, he dishonours, abuses, and disgraces . . .

The careful exegesis is followed by statements on the **spiritual** eating of the flesh of Christ which is nothing else than faith, and the **oral or sacramental** eating,

> when the true, essential body and blood of Christ are also orally received and partaken of in the Holy Supper, by all who eat and drink the consecrated bread and wine in the Supper — by the believing as a certain pledge and assurance that their sins are surely forgiven them, and Christ dwells and is efficacious in them, but by the unbelieving for their judgment and condemnation.[69]

This oral eating is to be understood,

> not in a gross, carnal, Capernaitic, but in a supernatural, incomprehensible way.[70]

Since the Crypto-Calvinists used the word 'spiritual' in a misleading way, the meaning of 'spiritual', which had caused so much misunderstanding, is made clear in a later passage:

> To the Sacramentarians this word *spiritual* means nothing else than the spiritual communion, when through faith true believers are in the Spirit incorporated into Christ, the Lord, and become true spiritual members of his body. But when Dr Luther or we employ this word *spiritual* in regard to this

---

[67]The quotations from the *Large Confession* are given above in Chapter IV where passages from Art. 7 of the *Formula of Concord* had to be quoted since they render exactly the doctrine of Luther.

[68]For the *Short Confession* see above, 224 and 237.

[69]Trigl. 993, 995.

[70]Trigl. 995.

> matter, we understand by it the spiritual, supernatural, heavenly mode, according to which Christ is present in the Holy Supper.[71]

The doctrine on the Real Presence is followed by an elaborate statement on consecration, which we have already mentioned when discussing Luther's doctrine,[72] which also in this case is faithfully rendered by the *Solida Declaratio*. Then follows Luther's answer to the philosophical objections to the possibility of the Presence of Christ's body, quoted from his *Large Confession*, with which we are already acquainted. The long article is concluded, like all articles of the *Formula of Concord*, with the rejection of errors. First, the Roman errors (transubstantiation and the adoration of the consecrated host, sacrifice of the mass, *communio sub una*), which had been confirmed by the Council of Trent, are rejected; then the various errors of the 'sacramentarians', from Zwinglianism to Calvinism. The last condemnation is directed against

> all presumptuous, frivolous, blasphemous questions and expressions which are presented in a gross, carnal, Capernaitic way regarding the supernatural, heavenly mysteries of this Supper,[73]

that is, against all speculations as to what happens to the Sacrament if it is eaten by a mouse, or similar questions that have been discussed since the Middle Ages, and which cannot be answered because God's Word has no answer to them.

The *Formula of Concord*, without any doubt, is right when it claims that the earlier confessions defy a Calvinistic interpretation and teach Luther's doctrine. It is furthermore right in asserting that it renders and reaffirms Luther's understanding of the Lord's Supper. The Reformed adversaries, however, and also Lutherans who refused to accept the *Formula*, saw that there was a difference between the new confession and the earlier ones. What is this difference? It is the insertion of certain passages from Luther's *Large Confession* of 1528, especially the long quotation (*Sol. Decl. VII,* 93-104) about the possibility of the Real Presence. First of all, the question was raised whether or not Luther's authority was exaggerated if his controversial writings were taken as a source of doctrine. This objection can easily be answered by the statement of

---

[71] Trigl. 1009.

[72] See above, 135.

[73] *Sol. Decl. VII,* 128 (Trigl. 1015); compare *Epit. VII,* 42 (Trigl. 816).

the Introduction to the *Formula*,[74] which makes it clear that the authority of Luther or any other teacher of the church, or any confession or other writing, extends only as far as the person or writing teaches God's Word. No one has the right to doubt the seriousness of the authors of the *Formula of Concord* in their confession of the *sola Scriptura*. This applies also to those passages which they took from Luther's writings apart from his *Large Catechism* and the earlier confessions.

Secondly, it has been asked whether or not the inclusion of the quotations from Luther's answer to Zwingli's denial of the possibility of the Real Presence has brought into the confessions philosophical thoughts which should have no place in a confession of the church. As we have observed, Luther was obliged to answer Zwingli's philosophical arguments against the Real Presence by showing that, even from the philosophical point of view, the possibility of other modes of the presence of a body besides the *praesentia localis* or *circumscriptiva* could not be denied. If the *Formula of Concord* accepted these passages, the intention was not to establish philosophical theories about the nature of the body. Doctrines of the church can be only what Holy Scripture teaches, as Luther himself formulated it in the Smalcald Articles:

> The rule is: The Word of God shall establish articles of faith, and no one else, not even an angel.[75]

Not every argument used by Luther and by the *Formula of Concord* is an article of faith, but only that which the confession has taken from God's Word. Hence, in this case (as the abbreviated quotation of Luther's words in the *Epitome* clearly shows,[76]) only the famous four reasons on which Luther based his doctrine against Zwingli are to be regarded as dogma of the Lutheran church: the article of the

---

[74]It is not necessary to quote the well-known serious assurances of the *Epitome, 'De compendiaria regula atque norma . . .'* (Trigl. 776 ff) where the *sola Scriptura* is firmly established. Instead, we quote from the Introduction of the *Sol. Decl. III* (Trigl. 851) concerning the authority of the *Augsburg Confession:* ' . . . since in these last times God, out of especial grace, has brought the ***truth of His Word*** to light again from the darkness of the Papacy through the faithful service of the precious man of God, Dr Luther, and since this doctrine has been collected from, and according to, God's Word into the articles and chapters of the Augsburg Confession . . . we confess also the First, Unaltered Augsburg Confession . . . ***not because it was composed by our theologians but because it has been taken from God's Word and is founded firmly and well therein'*** *(emphasis mine).*

[75]*Smalcald Articles II,* 15 (Trigl. 467).

[76]*Epitome VII,* 5 (Trigl. 811).

Christian faith that Jesus Christ is perfect God and man in one person, undivided and inseparable; that God's right hand is everywhere; that God's Word is not false, and cannot deceive; that God has and knows of various modes of being in any place, and not only the one which the philosopher calls 'local'. This, and no more, is the addition which the *Formula of Concord* made to the older confessions with regard to the article on the Lord's Supper. But all this had been the silent presupposition of all earlier doctrines on the Real Presence. It was not new, nor can it be regarded as unbiblical, for even the last of the four points is at least a correct conclusion from what Scripture says about the body of the glorified Christ.

The question may be asked, as it often has been asked, whether or not the *Formula of Concord* dogmatized the doctrine of Luther on what his adversaries have called 'ubiquity', the view that the body of Christ, being at the right hand of God, is everywhere, though we cannot find it except in the Lord's Supper.[77] We have already stated that Luther himself did not demand the acceptance of this theory.[78] What he demanded was the recognition that in the Lord's Supper the true body and blood of Christ are present. In the generation after his death, two theological views were held by Lutheran theologians, and even by theologians who prepared or formulated the *Formula of Concord*. While Brenz and Andreae, like other theologians in Wuerttemberg, retained Luther's doctrine of the omnipresence of the glorified body of Christ, Martin Chemnitz and others taught that the glorified body **can** be in many places, wherever Christ wills it. This theological difference was discussed by the adherents of both schools of thought. But it was not made a church-divisive issue, and could not be made one, as there is no Scripture passage that would allow a decision one way or the other. Thus, the *Formula of Concord*, which was drafted by men who varied on that point, like Andreae and Chemnitz, does not teach more than what is technically called 'ubivolopresence' or 'multivolopresence' in the sense believed by Chemnitz. The decision is contained in Article 8 on the Person of Christ. It is expressed in words which show the meaning of the Real Presence better than any other passage. They speak of

> the majesty . . . which Christ has received, according to His humanity, at the right hand of the majesty and power of God, namely, that also according to His assumed human nature and with the same, ***He can be, and also is, present where***

———

[77]See above, 121 ff.

[78]See above, 229.

> ***He will,*** and especially that in His Church and congregation on earth ***He is present as Mediator, Head, King, and High Priest,*** not in part, or one-half of Him only, but the ***entire person of Christ*** is present, to which both natures belong, the divine and the human; not only according to His divinity, but also according to, and with, His assumed human nature, according to which ***He is our Brother*** and ***we are flesh of His flesh and bone of His bone.*** Even as He has instituted His ***Holy Supper*** for the certain assurance and confirmation of this, that also according to that nature according to which He has flesh and blood He will be with us, and dwell, work, and be efficacious in us' (*emphasis mine*).[79]

This, then, is the meaning of the Real Presence according to the *Formula of Concord:* Christ is present, the entire Christ, God and man, our Mediator and High Priest through whom we have forgiveness of sins, our King whose glory is still hidden to human eyes, our Brother as true man, he in us and we in him, when we receive the Sacrament for the assurance and confirmation of his presence with all its blessings: forgiveness, life, and salvation.

Was it really a misunderstanding (as we are sometimes told) that the Lutheran church retained this doctrine, and rejected Calvinism in every form? Was it really so that the whole contention was about the mode of the presence (*de modo praesentiae*), not about the presence (*de praesentia*)? This has been the constant assertion of all adherents of Calvin, and all friends of a union in the sense of Bucer and Calvin, up to the German unions of the 19th century and to the 'Confessional Church' of the Barthian type in our day. The issue has never been whether Christ is present, but whether the entire Christ is present. Not the mode of presence was at stake, but the question whether or not the body of Christ is present. If this is admitted, if the *unio sacramentalis*, the *manducatio oralis*, and the *manducatio impiorum* are conceded, the question of the *how* could be left open. That was Luther's suggestion at Marburg, as it had always been his opinion.

The Lutheran church has never abandoned this attitude, not even in the *Formula of Concord.* This is true even in view of Article 8 of the *Formula* on the Person of Christ. Here the christological implications of the Lutheran doctrine on the Lord's Supper are discussed, as Luther himself had to discuss them in his *Large Confession.* The Sacrament of the Altar, as Luther understood it, demands that the classical doctrine of the church on the Two Natures and the One Person of Christ be taken seriously. Much of the criticism that Luther's eucharistic doctrine has met is the result of modern theological schools of thought, like that of Ritschl, which no

---

[79] *Sol. Decl. VIII,* 78 (Trigl. 1043, 1045).

longer understood and took seriously the classical doctrine as it was established by the first four Ecumenical Councils from Nicaea to Chalcedon, and as it is expressed in the Creeds of Ephesus and Chalcedon, which form the basis of the second part of the Athanasian Creed (*Symbolum Quicunque*) and of Article 3 of the *Augsburg Confession.* Neither Luther nor the *Formula of Concord* taught anything new when they emphasized the *unio personalis*, the true unity of the two natures of Christ in the one Person, rejecting every attempt to make this union a mere verbal one by denying that also the human nature shares the properties of the divine. The **terminology** of the doctrine of the *communicatio idiomatum* is not a dogma of the church, just as the words 'nature' and 'person' are only theological terms which we use to denote realities that transcend human reason, but which are testified to by Holy Scripture. Whether the Western Christian, in speaking of the Trinity uses the terms *una substantia, tres personae*, while the Eastern church uses *hypostasis* (which would correspond to the Latin *substantia* for what we call 'person'), does not matter at all. What matters is the doctrine itself. There can be no doubt that the Christology of Luther and of the *Formula of Concord* in discussing the reality of the union of the natures in the person of Christ, is doing full justice to the 'paradox',[80] the mystery of the God-man. And only he who acknowledges this mystery can accept the mystery of the Real Presence of the entire Christ, in his divine and in his human nature, in the Sacrament of the Altar. That is the reason why the *Formula of Concord* had to confirm Luther's Christology, as he had maintained it at Marburg, when it reaffirmed the decision of Marburg on the Lord's Supper.

---

[80]The first to use this word in this connection seems to have been Cyril of Alexandria in his *Dialogus cum Nestorio* on the question whether the Blessed Virgin is the Mother of God (MPG 76, 252). Cyril calls the Incarnation a *paradoxon.* See W. Elert, *Der christliche Glaube* (1941), 404, and the entire paragraph 394-404. The first to apply the word 'paradox' to the Eucharist seems to have been Clement Alex., *Paidagogos, I, cap. VI, 43, 1* (ed Stählin, GCS, I, 115, 24): *'ō, tou paradoxou mystēriou!'.*

CHAPTER VII

The Sacrament of the Altar and the Lutheran Church Today

1. The Question Today

Almost 400 years have elapsed since the Lutheran church made its final decision concerning the doctrine of the Lord's Supper. What does this doctrine mean today for churches that call themselves Lutheran? Is the doctrine, as it was finally proclaimed by the *Formula of Concord*, still their doctrine? Can it be, in view of the immense changes that have taken place in all fields of human life in the spheres of philosophy, science, and general culture, as well as in the spheres of religious life and theological thought? In the 17th century a decay of the sacramental life of Christendom had already become noticeable. Although the liturgies of the 16th century and the doctrines on the Sacrament were preserved in all branches of Christendom in the period of orthodox theology, the Sacraments no longer occupy the minds of Europeans as they did in the 500 years from Berengar to the *Formula of Concord.* The 18th century, the period of Pietism, Enlightenment, and Rationalism, witnessed a complete decline in the understanding of the Sacraments. Baptism and Holy Communion were no longer understood. Even the Roman church experienced the decay of the mass. Divine worship was understood more or less as a means of instruction, of imparting knowledge and moral education. The unquenchable thirst of the human soul for mysteries and for sacred rites found its satisfaction in secret societies of various kinds outside the church. But the number of communicants was rapidly decreasing. In some parts of German Lutheranism where reliable statistics are available, a decrease of up to 90 per cent took place between 1700 and 1800. This loss has never been made up for, although in the 19th century the rediscovery of the church was accompanied by a new interest in the Sacraments. This new interest in the sacramental life of the church, however, was limited to comparatively small circles.

One of the most remarkable facts of our age is the great Liturgical Movement, that originated in the Roman church of the 19th century, and after World War I began to sweep throughout Christendom irrespective of the borderlines of churches and denominations. The fact that this movement has remarkable parallels in the great political movements of our time, which for many people have become a substitute for religion, seems to indicate that a profound change is taking place in the inner life of modern man.[1] The age of pure reason seems to come to an end after the realm of the subconscious has been discovered. A trend toward the irrational, a rediscovery of the inseparable connection between body and soul, matter and spirit, can be observed everywhere. This might lead to a revival of the Sacrament in the church. The question remains, however, whether this movement would also lead to a revival of the Sacrament in the Lutheran sense. The influence exerted on the Lutheran church by the modern Liturgical Movement seems to point more to a strengthening of romanizing tendencies than to a new understanding of Luther's profound perception of the inseparable connection between the Sacrament and the Gospel. Thus, the question whether or not the Lutheran doctrine on the Sacraments is still tenable remains a serious problem, even if Christendom as a whole should experience a revival of its sacramental life. An entirely different understanding of Baptism and the Lord's Supper might be the result of such a

---

[1]It seems that the Belgian sociologist Hendrik de Man, *Zur Psychologie des Sozialismus* (2nd edition, Jena, 1927) was the first to show how socialism in Europe had developed into a substitute for religion, especially for workers who had experienced a real conversion from Catholicism to Marxism. In the homes, pictures of saints were exchanged for pictures of the prophets and martyrs of socialism; processions, new festivals like that of May 1, Karl Marx's *Das Kapital* as an inerrant bible, the *Communist Manifesto* as a new creed, the fight against heretics and modernists, etc., replaced former ecclesiastical institutions and religious ways of life. Similar observations could be made in the case of Italian Fascism, German National Socialism, and Russian Communism. In Germany, every flag of a party organization had to be consecrated by being brought into contact with the flag that was still stained by the blood of the first 'martyrs' of the movement. The large portraits of Lenin and Stalin were the icons of the new Russia, the mausoleum of Lenin at the Kremlin, where his embalmed body could be seen (a masterpiece in the art of preserving a corpse — saints do not decay) was the goal of innumerable pilgrimages just like the great sanctuaries of the old holy Russia. In contradistinction to the Masonic rites, these new cults were performed publicly.

movement even within our own church. The question appears to be twofold: the problem of the doctrine of the Lutheran confession, and the problem of the exegetical basis of this doctrine. Naturally, these belong together as two aspects of one and the same question. For practical reasons only, we discuss first the confessional problem and secondly the biblical one.

a. *The Confessional Problem*

It is a remarkable fact that all Lutheran churches today still uphold the doctrine on the Sacrament as we find it in the *Book of Concord.* This is true even of churches that for various reasons have never accepted the *Formula of Concord.* For the doctrine of its Article 7 is practically the same as that of the earlier confessions, especially the *Augsburg Confession* and Luther's *Catechisms.* Seen from the outside, no Lutheran church seems to reject or deny the classical Lutheran doctrine on the Sacrament.

This is all the more significant since the majority of the churches that have grown out of the Reformation of the 16th century have abolished their historic confessions, either practically or theoretically. If a Lutheran took issue with a Swiss theologian on the matter of the Sacrament, he would soon find that for the churches of Switzerland neither the *Confessio Helvetica Prior* or *Posterior*, nor the *Catechism of Geneva*, nor the *Consensus Tigurinus* has any binding force comparable to that of the *Augsburg Confession* in the Lutheran churches. They are regarded as historical documents only, which may be used or disregarded by the individual pastor and his congregation, the confessional obligation of the ministers being limited to the faithful interpretation of Holy Writ according to their best understanding. The same is true of almost all Reformed churches. It may seem, then, that the old adversaries of the Lutheran doctrine in Reformed Protestantism have completely disappeared. If we discuss the Sacrament with Reformed theologians we no longer have to deal with strict followers of Zwingli or even of Calvin.

A similar process has taken place in the Church of England. Every candidate on taking Holy Orders has to sign the 39 Articles. This, however, does not imply an acceptance of their doctrinal contents. When the Archbishop of Canterbury, Dr Fisher, was asked by an English newspaper to write a contribution to a series of articles by leading churchmen on the belief of their respective churches, he stated that

> the principal beliefs of the Church of England are expressed in its *Book of Common Prayer* and are summarized in the Apostles' Creed.[2]

Not one word did he say about the 'Articles of Religion', which are not a part of the Prayer Book, though they are printed among the appendices. The clergy of the Church of England are free to teach either the clearly-Reformed doctrine on the Lord's Supper contained in Article 28, or transubstantiation (as Anglo-Catholics do), or consubstantiation (as Pusey did[3]), or even a Zwinglian view. If in a discussion with Anglicans we draw their attention to the 'Black Rubric' in the *Book of Common Prayer,*[4] and in the *'Alternative Form'* of 1928, some would strongly maintain the binding character of its doctrinal content, while others would minimize it.

If we maintain that this makes the signing of the confession a mere legal formality, which should rather be omitted, we should ask ourselves in all humility whether we are not guilty of the same sin. At the Third Assembly of the Lutheran World Federation, in 1957, an expert said about the 'critical' situation of the Lutheran churches in this respect:

> We ourselves are today perhaps farther than ever removed from complete agreement on the traditional Lutheran doctrine of the Lord's Supper. Today there is at least one Lutheran church which has reached agreement on the Lord's Supper with its Calvinistic neighbour church.

He then mentions various types of intercommunion established between Lutherans and non-Lutherans, and continues:

> Some present-day Lutheran exegetes assert that the Lutheran doctrine of the Lord's Supper as stated in the Confessions does not do full justice to the biblical witness. And then there are many Lutherans who view all this as deplorable apostasy from the faith of the fathers.[4A]

Lutheranism, as a whole, is certainly more conservative concerning the confessions of the Reformation. This conservatism, however, may look very much like sheer backwardness to an outsider.

---

[2]Reprinted in Geoffrey Fisher, *Redeeming the Situation, Occasional Sermons* (1948), 40.

[3]See his book *The Doctrine of the Real Presence* (1855), written because he had been censured for deviation from the Reformed doctrine of Art. 28.

[4]See above, 248. The omission of the rubric in the Prayer Books of some Anglican Churches (Scotland, USA, South Africa, India-Burma-Ceylon) is not meant to imply any change in doctrine.

[4A]H.W. Gensichen, *Messages of the Third Assembly, Minneapolis 1957,* 48 f.

Actually, perhaps all Protestant churches are going through the same process of losing their old confessional standards, the difference lying solely in the rate of progression.

Thus, it might seem that both the entire discussion about the Sacraments of the 16th century, and its result, which we find in the various confessions, have become obsolete. The churches which once were involved in these discussions seem to exist no longer. And yet it would be quite wrong to underestimate the vital power of the old confessions. First, it must not be forgotten that even if all doctrines of the confessions of the Reformation were abandoned by the Lutheran and Reformed churches, there would be at least one church which would keep its confession of the 16th century, and would be bound to stay by it until the end of the world. That is the Roman church with the decrees of Trent and the *Professio Fidei Tridentina*. Even if we should forget or abandon the doctrines of our confessional writings, these doctrines would remain at least in the *canones*, the formulas of rejection attached to every doctrinal decree of Trent. Thus, they would at least remain as a constant reminder of what was taught by our Reformers and by the church of our fathers. At the same time these doctrinal statements of Rome would be a permanent question addressed to our church. They would require an answer, perhaps a new answer. But to abstain from answering them, as the Anglicans suggest, would be impossible.

This leads to the second point to be stressed. A confession solemnly made by a church, and even by an individual Christian, has an amazing power of survival. If even the great heresies of the past reappear time and again, either openly or in disguise, how much more is this true of the great truths confessed by the church of Christ! There will be old and new forms of Arianism, of Pelagianism, of the denial of the Real Presence in the Lord's Supper — to mention only a few great heresies — until the Last Judgment. But there will also be confessors of the *homōousios*, of the *sola gratia* and *sola fide*, of the Real Presence, until the Last Day. The true confession is never man-made.[5] It was our Lord himself who asked his adversaries the question: 'What think ye of Christ? whose son is he?' It was he himself who put the question to his disciples: 'Who say ye that I am?' It is he

[5]For the following, compare what was said above, 151 f, about Luther's confession. According to the New Testament, confession of faith is closely connected with confession of sin (as in Luke 5:8) and with confession as praise of God (Phil. 2:10). In his writing of 1538 on the three Symbols (WA 51, 262 ff) Luther regards the *Te Deum* ('*Te Deum laudamus, te Dominum* ***confitemur***') as one of the Christian Symbols.

who demands the confession of faith. Wherever the Gospel is preached, the question arises out of this Gospel: Who is he? The confession is the answer to the question contained in God's Word. This confession may be a merely human theory. It may be wrong. It may, if given by alleged Christians, be a heretical statement. But it may also, like that of Peter, be given by God, as Jesus said to this first confessor of the church: 'Flesh and blood hath not revealed it unto thee, but my Father which is in heaven'. At any rate, the confession remains. It follows the confessors into eternity, and will be answered by Christ himself: 'Whosoever . . . shall confess me before men, him will I confess before my Father which is in heaven'. And the same is true of a wrong confession, of a denial of Christ: 'Whosoever shall deny me before men, him will I also deny before my Father which is in heaven'. This eschatological character of a confession, as Luther and the Lutheran church understood it when they always confessed in view of the Last Judgment, explains that a confession shares the timelessness of the Word of God.

Here lies the reason for the fact that confessions are never dead issues. They may be forgotten for a time. They may be denied or legally abolished. But their contents remain a living reality, and time and again they are revived in the history of the church. This is true also of the great dogmatic decision of the *Formula of Concord* concerning the Sacrament of the Altar. It remains a living reality even after 400 years. This may be the deeper reason why thus far no Lutheran church has dared to abolish it, even though it may be neglected and practically denied.

b. *The Biblical Problem*

The confessional problem is closely connected with the question whether the dogmatic decision of the Lutheran Reformation can be upheld in view of the indubitable advancement of biblical studies that has taken place during the last four centuries. We should cease to be Lutherans if we refused to face this question quite frankly. Luther was a professor of biblical exegesis. His discovery of the *sola fide* was the result of serious biblical research. The Lutheran Reformation was born in the study and in the lecture room of a biblical scholar. The Lutheran doctrine on the Sacraments, and particularly on the *sacramentum sacramentorum*, was based, as we have seen, not on an ecclesiastical tradition, not on the ideas of a theological school, but solely on what Luther could not but recognize as the clear doctrine of the Bible. Even the critics and adversaries of his understanding of the

Words of Institution must admit that sound and solid exegetical work is behind each and all of his writings on the Sacrament. We must believe him when he repeatedly assures us that he was well aware of the difficulties presented by a literal understanding, and how much easier it would be for human reason to accept Zwingli's view. 'But the text is too strong for me.'[6] Thus, the final decision on the question whether the Lutheran church today can, and must, stand by the doctrine of Luther as it was accepted by the Lutheran Confessions must fall in the field of exegesis.

Wherein does the progress of biblical scholarship since the days of Luther consist? We need only compare a modern dictionary on the New Testament with the corresponding tools available to the scholar of the 16th century in order to gauge the advancement made in our understanding of the language and terminology of the Bible. Serious historical research has revealed the Jewish and Hellenistic background of the New Testament. We know far better than any one could possibly know in the 16th and 17th centuries the Jewish background of the Lord's Supper. Thus, new light has been shed on many passages.

Few today would defend the statement of Paul in 1 Cor. 11:23: 'I have received of the Lord that which also I delivered unto you' as referring to a special revelation given to the apostle of the Lord, as Luther believed, in agreement with the Fathers and with his contemporaries.[7] As the parallel use of the words 'receive' and 'deliver' in 1 Cor. 15:3 shows, Paul refers to an oral tradition that goes back to the Last Supper and to the words spoken by the Lord himself. The terminology he uses is exactly the same as that used in the synagogue in which he had been educated. This tradition is essentially in accordance with what we find in Mark — the interpreter of Peter — whom Matthew follows. Luke, Paul's disciple, combines the two traditions, following the principles set forth at the beginning of the Gospel. The slight differences between the four accounts, and especially between the two oldest ones, Paul's and Mark's, are partly due to the fact that they were not originally preserved as historical documents, but as liturgical texts. Thus, for liturgical use it no longer seemed to be of any avail to mention the fact, still preserved by Paul, that the cup was given, not together with the bread, but 'after they had supped', though most of the later

[6] WA 15, 394, 19 f; see above, 64, 65.
[7] *FC, Sol. Decl. VII, 52* (Trigl. 990).

liturgies restored this feature on the authority of Paul and Luke.[8] On the other hand, Paul's account already seems to have been influenced by the liturgical character of the tradition. Careful linguistic investigations have shown that the original words spoken by Jesus at the institution of the Sacrament, and underlying all the four narratives, seem to be identical with the words found in Mark.[9] We are mentioning these facts in order to show where the difference lies between the approach of the modern exegete and the exegesis of the Reformers. For us the historical approach is necessary, because the historicity of such an event as the institution of the Lord's Supper by Jesus has been questioned in a way that was completely unthinkable in the 16th century.

At the same time, the historical elucidation of the text gives us a far more vivid picture of the events related in the New Testament. The discovery of the individual character of the various Gospels, their language, their way of relating events and words, has made it possible to understand a chapter like John 6 in a new way. We understand, better than any of the Reformers could possibly realize, the mysterious character of such a text, which reveals profound truths by hinting at them rather than by making them plain to the mind of the average man. There are sayings of Jesus in the Gospels which could be, and were meant to be, understood by anyone. There are other words that could be understood by those only who had 'ears to hear', that is, those to whom God had given the right understanding. There are events and words that must be understood against the background of the Old Testament. Although God's Word comes to

---

[8]Compare the words of the *Qui pridie* of the Roman *Canon Missae* ('*Simili modo* ***postquam coenatum est*** . . .') and all Western liturgies. Of the Eastern liturgies only a few, like that of the 8th book of the *Apostolic Constitutions*, Theodore of Mopsuestia, and the Nestorians leave out 'after they had supped'. The whole problem was carefully examined by the Roman Catholic scholar Fritz Hamm, *Die liturgischen Einsetzungsberichte* (Münster, 1928).

[9]This is the conclusion reached by Joachim Jeremias, *The Eucharistic Words of Jesus* (English translation, 1955); see especially 115: 'This means — and this result surprised me very much — that the earliest text of the Words of Institution which can be established by comparison of the texts is identical with the text of Mark'. The Aramaic words were probably, according to J. Jeremias, '*den bisri*' and '*den idhmi*' (not '*guphi*' for 'my body', as G. Dalman and others have assumed). '*Bisri*' would then correspond to 'my flesh' in John 6. The book of Jeremias is one of the most important ever written on the Lord's Supper. Unfortunately, the author has added to the scholarly historical investigation of the facts an interpretation of his own which makes the Last Supper a mere parabolic action by Jesus. See also: Julius Schniewind and Ernst Sommerlath, *Abendmahlsgespräch*, ed. by E. Schlink (1952), and the present author's '*Das Abendmahl im Neuen Testament*' in *Vom Sakrament des Altars* (1941).

us in human language and makes use of human logic, there are passages that transcend human logic because they speak of things which transcend our reason.[10]

For example, in the great discourses of Jesus preserved in the Fourth Gospel, the sequence of thoughts is not like a straight line, but rather like a spiral: the same thought repeated on a higher level and in a different context. It is therefore neither necessary nor even possible to find in John 6 the words 'bread' and 'eating' always used in the same sense. In the first part of the discourse (6:32 ff) Jesus can speak of himself as the bread from heaven, the true manna. There the 'eating' is a spiritual one, and a sacramental eating is being hinted at. The two lines of thought belong together, as may be seen also in 1 Cor. 10,where Paul describes the manna as a spiritual food, a type of the sacramental bread. Hence, it is impossible to read such a discourse or dialogue like a discourse of Cicero or a Platonic dialogue.[11] Luther had a profound understanding of the difference between the Synoptic Gospels and St John. He knew that the constant repetition of the same thought was used to indicate the mystery and incomprehensibility of the truth concerned.[12] But he also frankly admitted that he himself was not able to explain fully the Gospel that he liked so much because he considered it the most apostolic one.[13] Though at present no exegete would claim to give an exhaustive explanation of the Fourth Gospel, we have, nevertheless, learned something about the language and style of such a text which must have been written in a state of inspiration different from the inspiration which we believe to have moved the other evangelists. It is not by accident that the Church has always regarded John as the 'divine', the *theologos*, which means the liturgist, whose way of speaking of God, of Christ, of the divine mysteries, reminds us of the language of the liturgy rather than of the plain speech of ordinary life.

---

[10] We may think of Luther's words in his explanation of Rom. 12:2; WA 56, 446, 31 ff, quoted above, 93, 94.

[11] See above, 143 f. Excellent studies of the style of John are to be found in the commentaries by E. C. Hoskyns (1947) and C. H. Dodd (1953).

[12] '*Evangelium Johannis saepe repetit quasi loquax. Per hoc indicat* ***mysterium*** *discipulis et* ***incomprehensibilem rem*** *esse naturae, quod Christus abeat . . .*' WA 20, 376, 21 f (*Sermon for Jubilate* 1526).

[13] '*Johannes est evangelista ad quem exponendum pertinet alius quam ego. Ipsemet deberet praedicare'*. WA 29, 366, 14 f (*Sermon on Whitmonday* 1529). For further information see G. Ebeling, *Evangelische Evangelienauslegung. Eine Untersuchung zu Luthers Hermeneutik* (1942), 211-20, especially 216 f; W. von Leowenich, *Luther und das Johanneische Christentum* (1935).

We confine ourselves to these brief remarks which may indicate in what direction a real progress of New Testament scholarship beyond that of the 16th century may be found, as far as the Lord's Supper is concerned. Two facts, however, remain unchanged.

The first is the historicity of the institution of the Sacrament by Jesus, in spite of minor divergencies of the narratives concerning the circumstances. The attempts to explain the Sacament as a product of the early Hellenistic church, under the influence of pagan mystery-religions, have completely failed. Apart from the fact that it would be quite inconceivable that the pagan world, which had so many communion rites, could raise any serious objections to the religious 'cannibalism' of the Christians, the Jewish background of the Lord's Supper is generally recognized. On the other hand, it is quite impossible to explain the Christian Sacrament by referring to the Jewish custom of blessing bread and the cup of wine on the occasion of solemn meals, or to the rites connected with the Passover. For no Jew could ever have conceived the idea of drinking blood (even in a figurative sense) which was strictly forbidden by the Law. Such an act could be instituted only by the Lord of the Law. It is also impossible to understand the Last Supper as something that was originally not meant to be repeated. Even if the command 'This do in remembrance of me' does not occur expressly in the text of Mark and Matthew, there can be no doubt that these texts presuppose the celebration of the Sacrament by the church. No sound historical scholarship today will deny that Jesus himself instituted the Sacrament of the Altar, and spoke the words: 'This is my body', 'This is my blood of the covenant shed for many'.[14]

The second fact is that all attempts to overcome the old controversy over the meaning of 'This **is** my body' have utterly failed. The objection that *estin* could not have been spoken in Aramaic was answered in the 16th century. In the sentence *den bisri* (This is my body), the copula *is* is contained in the predicate, and the Greek translation (which, by the way, is our normative text) is perfectly correct. What Jesus said in his mother tongue is exactly what we express in the words 'This is my body'. Since the time of David

---

[14]See J. Jeremias, *op. cit.*, 115. The question as to how the Pauline version ('This cup is the new testament in my blood') is to be explained may remain open here. It cannot be retranslated into Aramaic. Obviously, the meaning is quite the same as the version of Mark and Matthew: The cup contains the blood shed as the sacrifice for the establishment of the New Covenant.

Friedrich Strauss's famous *Das Leben Jesu* (1835), the whole controversy has frequently been declared obsolete under the pretext that the alternative between a literal and a figurative understanding did not exist for the people of the ancient world, to whom a symbol was never a mere sign only but always something containing a reality. But how could the Early Church be accused of cannibalism if the bread was regarded as a symbol in that sense only? Furthermore, the very ancient distinction between the *eucharistia* and the *eulogiai* (the consecrated bread which is the body of Christ, and the bread which has been blessed by prayer) proves that the Early Church already recognized the difference between the bread that was blessed by prayer in the Jewish way at the love feast, the *agapē*, and the consecrated bread of the Eucharist, which was the body of Christ. Although, as far as we can see, the term *eulogia* in this sense does not occur before Hippolytus's *Church Order,*[15] Paul also had to combat those who could not distinguish between the Eucharist and the *agapē,* and, therefore, not between ordinary food and the body of the Lord (cf 1 Cor. 11:20 ff with verse 29). This distinction is to be found even where the consecrated bread is still called a *figura, typos,* or *antitypon* of the body of Christ, as Cyril of Jerusalem did in the Fifth of his *Mystagogical Catecheses*, when he calls the Eucharist an '*antitypon* of the body and blood of Christ',[16] while in the Third of these *Catecheses* he makes it quite plain that before the consecration (which for him is the *epiclēsis*) the bread is bread, and after the *epiclēsis* it is the body of Christ.[17] The same distinction is being made by all Eastern Fathers. Therefore it is not permissible to assume that the Early Church did not know the difference between what later was called the 'symbolic' and the 'realistic' understanding of the Words of Institution.

In a similar way, all attempts have failed to settle the old controversy by finding a new meaning for 'body'. It has been

[15]See the Ethiopian text with German translation by H. Duensing, *Abhandlungen der Akademie der Wissenschaften in Göttingen, Phil. Hist. Klasse, III,* 32 (1946), XVII-XIX, 69. Here the nature of *eulogia* is explained: The bread of the *agape* is 'bread of blessing, not "offering" like the body of the Lord'. The catechumens, who are not permitted to take part in the Eucharist, are allowed to participate in the blessed bread and the cup of blessing. This *agapē* is the continuation of Jewish meals as they are still in use today. Later the *eulogiai* became the substitute for the consecrated bread for those who attended the liturgy without receiving Holy Communion. This is still customary in the Eastern churches where the worshippers receive the *eulogiai* before leaving church. The usage is found also sometimes in Roman churches.

[16]*Cat. 23, 20,* MPG 33, col. 1123.

[17]*Cat. 21, 3,* MPG 33, col. 1091.

suggested that the Greek *sōma* can mean 'person'. But, apart from the fact that Jesus probably spoke of his *sarx* (*basar,* flesh), what then would be the meaning of *haima* (blood)? Moreover, the assumption that the Aramaic 'flesh and blood' ought to be understood in Old Testament terms as meaning the whole man is untenable, because originally 'flesh' and 'blood' were not given simultaneously. All attempts, then, to find a new understanding of the words of the Sacrament which would supersede the old controversy have been in vain.

Whatever modern scholarship may have contributed toward a better understanding of the Lord's Supper in the New Testament, the old issue remains the same. Literal and figurative interpretations are opposed to one another, just as in the five centuries from Berengar to the *Formula of Concord*. The question of the *est* remains the same as it was at Marburg. The indubitable fact that the majority of modern Protestant scholars still take sides with Zwingli and Calvin, although a growing number of them admit that Paul at least has a realistic understanding, is not a result of biblical scholarship, but, rather, of the fact that modern Protestants are still so much under the spell of a rationalistic view of the world that they are not prepared to accept the miracle that is bound up with the literal understanding of the Words of Institution, especially since they cannot see why such a miracle should be necessary. Thus, the Lutheran church, like all of Christendom, is today still confronted with the same question that occupied the minds of the Christians in centuries past. No new answer has been found.

2. The Answer Today

a. *This Is My Body*

If the Lutheran church today retains, with the Confessions of the 16th century, the literal understanding of the Words of Institution, she knows, as did the Reformer, that this doctrine gives the greatest offence to human reason, and, therefore, must meet with the strongest contradiction by the world. While this can be said of all doctrines of the church — especially of such fundamental doctrines as those of the Trinity, the divine-human Person of Christ, and the justification of the sinner by faith alone — the doctrine of the Real Presence is especially repulsive to large sections of Christendom, although it must be admitted that the vast majority of Christians throughout the world, Eastern Orthodox as well as Roman

Catholics, to mention only these two, still accept it as a fundamental article of the Christian faith.

It has a deep significance that we hear of the first great apostasy from Christ at the end of that great chapter of John which begins with the miracles of the feeding of the 5,000 and of Jesus walking on the water, and which then continues with the great discourse on the bread of life and the mystery of Christ's body and blood. Not only the Jews of Capernaum were offended. 'Many . . . of his disciples, when they heard this, said, 'This is an hard saying; who can hear it? . . . From that time many of his disciples went back, and walked no more with him.' (John 6:60, 66). When John wrote his Gospel, the theme of which was 'The Word was made flesh', a great apostasy had already begun which led many Christians in such countries as Syria and Egypt — in fact, the majority of the members of the church — into the gnostic sects that denied both the Incarnation and the Real Presence. 'They do not believe that the Eucharist is the flesh of our Saviour Jesus Christ', says Ignatius.[18] From John,as from Ignatius, it

---

[18] *Ad Smyrn. VII, 1.* It was probably this docetism that caused John to replace the Pauline 'body' (*sōma*) by 'flesh' (*sarx,* corresponding to the Old Testament *basar*), because 'flesh' defies a docetic interpretation. 'Flesh' means here 'true body', as Paul also had in mind. The Apostles' Creed, then, confesses ***'carnis** resurrectionem'* (following ***'sarkos anastasin'*** of the old Roman baptismal creed). For the same reason the Lutheran formula of distribution says: 'This is the ***true*** body . . .' in order to avoid all ambiguity. The 'true' (or substantial) body for Luther and the Lutheran church is always the body born of Mary which hung on the cross, was resurrected, ascended into heaven, and sits at the right hand of the Father. The question whether the crucified or the risen and exalted body is meant is meaningless because it is always the same body. It is this body and nothing else that is meant by 'This is my body'. This must be maintained because modern forms of docetism make their appearance, speaking of the body — or even of the true body and blood of Christ — without making it clear what the body actually is, and thus leaving the way open for a more-or-less figurative understanding. For example, the statement made by the South India United Church and the Federation of the Evangelical Lutheran Churches of India (published in *Lutheran World* II, No. 1, 1955, 74 ff) on the question of Holy Communion, admits the *unio sacramentalis* (we receive the body and blood of the Lord with the elements) and even the *manducatio impiorum*. Great as this concession to the Lutheran doctrine may be, the really crucial question as to what we receive remains unanswered: 'We must, on the one hand, ***deny that in this sacrament we eat the material flesh of Jesus of Nazareth;*** on the other hand, we must deny that Christ's presence in the sacrament depends upon our faith, or that in it we receive the body and blood of Christ spiritually, apart from eating and drinking the bread and the wine. We believe that as we receive the bread and wine according to His commandment, we receive the body and blood of Christ in a spiritual manner because of the sacramental union which He has established by His word' (75). What is the difference between the 'material flesh of Jesus of Nazareth' and what here is called 'body and blood of Christ'? According to Luther they are identical, though the 'blessed body that came from Thy Mother Mary

becomes evident that, as the doctrines on the Incarnation and on the Real Presence belong together, the denial of one must needs lead to the denial of the other. When Jesus asked the Twelve, 'Will ye also go away?' (John 6:67), Peter answered with the confession which at the same time is a reaffirmation of his belief in the Incarnation and of his acceptance of the 'hard saying' of Jesus concerning the eating of his body and drinking of his blood: 'Lord, to whom shall we go? thou hast the words of eternal life. And we believe and are sure that thou art that Christ, the Son of the living God'. Just as in this first crisis of the Christian faith the apostles rely solely on the words of Christ as the last authority and the rock on which they ground their faith, so the Lutheran church today, like Luther in his time, has no other reason for the belief in the Real Presence than the *ipsissima verba* of our Lord. We have already quoted the touching words from Luther's *Large Confession* about how a Christian who has retained his faith in the simple words of Christ can speak of his Saviour in his last hour.[19] This is the attitude of the Lutheran church.

Just as Luther had to assert that the adversaries of the Real Presence were unanimous only in their denial, but differed in the positive answers as to what the Words of Institution meant, so we must maintain that thus far no real alternative to the literal meaning has been offered. The great majority of modern Protestant theologians would assert that the words must be understood figuratively, and that the action of Jesus was his last parable, a twofold parable, such as Jesus frequently used (the parables of the grain of mustard and of the leaven, of the lost sheep and the lost coin), or, rather, a parabolic action like those of the prophets. But they cannot agree as to what the meaning should be. What is the *tertium comparationis*? Some would say: As the bread is broken and this wine is shed, so my body will be broken and my blood will be shed. Others would give the explanation: As I give you this bread and

---

and the blessed blood' are now glorified. It seems that the authors regard Luther's realism as 'Capernaiticism'. How can the Christians of South India with Anglican and Reformed background be expected to understand the doctrine for which the Lutheran church stands, if the representative of the church of the Sweden Mission 'most emphatically' maintained 'that the old Lutheran doctrine of oral partaking of the Body and Blood of Christ is quite untenable' (*loc. cit.*)? The older generation of Leipzig missionaries saw quite clearly that India with her pseudo-incarnations badly needs the message of the real Incarnation which is bound up with the Real Presence. (See Richard Frölich, *'Mission und Abendmahlsgemeinschaft'* in *Vom Sakrament des Altars* (1941), 257-269.)

[19]See above, 87.

wine, so I shall give my body and blood for you. Some representatives of this interpretation would emphasize that flesh and blood together should mean his whole person; others again (such as Althaus) would find in the separate giving of bread and wine a symbol of the separation of body and blood in death. Jeremias reminds us of the fact that the two actions did not take place together, so that the *tertium comparationis* in the case of the bread would be the fact that it is broken; in the case of the wine, its red colour. E. Lohmeyer in his commentary on Mark offers a new explanation. He would understand *touto* not as subject, but rather as predicate, *estin* being understood not as 'signifies', but rather as 'is', expressing the identity existing between bread and body in the sense that, as his 'body', his person, was so far the centre of the community of his disciples, from now on the eating and drinking of bread and wine would be that centre. Where this meal was to be celebrated, he would be in the midst of them.[20] We quote this view because it shows that even some modern exegetes realize that *est* cannot in this connection mean *significat*, while, on the other hand, they try to escape the necessity of taking the words in the old sense.

This inability of modern exegetes to reach agreement on the meaning of the alleged parable is sufficient proof of the fact that the Last Supper was more than a parabolic action. A parable is usually introduced as such, with such words as: 'The kingdom of heaven is like . . .' The parabolic actions of the prophets are unmistakably interpreted in clear words, as, for example, Ezekiel 4 and 5,[21] or Acts 21:11 where Agabus explains his action: 'So shall the Jews of Jerusalem bind the man that owneth this girdle'. The objection that Jesus gave an explanation of this action can be answered in this way only: A parabolic action cannot be explained by another parable. If the words are to be taken as an explanation of what Jesus did or gave, they must be taken literally. Either Jesus meant what he said, or he

---

[20] *Das Evangelium des Markus (Meyers Kommentar)* (1937), 306 f.

[21] Such an action may be an *oth* ('token' or 'sign') in the Old Testament sense ('This shall be a sign to the house of Israel', Ezek. 4:3), where, according to Oriental thinking, that which signifies and that which is signified are seen in a close relationship (which, however, can never be identity). Thus, 'This is my body' can never be explained, as has been done by Rudolf Otto and others, from 'This is Jerusalem', Ezek. 5:5, which must be understood in the context of chapters 4 and 5, where the parabolic actions of the prophet are described and clearly explained for what they are: proclamations of the divine message in the form of symbolic actions; *verbum visibile*. (See the discussion on Ezekiel 4 and 5 at Marburg, 193 and 195.

proposed a puzzle which so far no one has been able to solve.[22]

But, even if Jesus had proposed such a puzzle, if the Lord's Supper could actually not be understood from his words — a merely theoretical assumption which no one could venture to make — where would we have to look for an authentic commentary? Most certainly, in the New Testament itself! Such a commentary has been given by St Paul. It is worth noting that the first explanation of the Lord's Supper is older than our Gospels, and was necessitated by the first misunderstanding and the first abuses of the Sacrament of the Altar, which occurred in the church already in the early apostolic age. Unprejudiced scholarship cannot but admit that, according to 1 Cor. 10:16,17, not our faith, not the celebration as an act, but the bread and the wine (as the content of the cup) constitute the communion or participation of the body and blood of Christ: 'The cup of blessing which we bless, is it not a participation in the blood of Christ? The bread which we break, is it not a participation in the body of Christ? Because there is one bread [loaf], we who are many are one body, for we all partake of the same bread [loaf]' (RSV). This understanding is confirmed by 1 Cor. 11:27: 'Wherefore whosoever shall eat this bread and drink this cup of the Lord, unworthily, shall be guilty of the body and blood of the Lord'. Such passages lose their meaning, as Luther clearly pointed out to Zwingli, if it is not true that the bread **is** the body and that the content of the cup **is** the blood. He who participates unworthily in the bread and the wine sins against the body and blood of Christ.

If it must be admitted that this is Paul's understanding, as is being done by an overwhelming majority of modern critical scholars, two questions must be answered. First, we must ask whether it is conceivable that Paul's understanding of the Lord's Supper was essentially different from what Jesus meant when he instituted the Sacrament? There is not the slightest trace of any objection raised by the other apostles to the doctrine of Paul. And even the adversaries of the Apostle to the Gentiles, who rejected his understanding of the Gospel, seem to have found no fault with his doctrine on the

---

[22]The main reason for the failure of modern exegetes to reach an understanding of the sacramental words lies in the fact that they all try to understand psychologically what Jesus did and said that night. Who would dare to say what the God-man on his way to Calvary must or must not have felt? We have only his words. The soul of Christ is inaccessible to human psychology, which can understand sinful men only. This must always be kept in mind in any discussion of the Sacraments. They also defy psychological explanation.

Sacrament. Who, then, would have had the authority to alter the original meaning of the Last Supper, and to create a new version of the Sacrament as it was understood and celebrated throughout the centuries?

Secondly, it must be seriously asked what understanding of Holy Scripture lies behind the idea that an apostolic commentary on the Lord's Supper is not binding on the church? In the years after 1945, when German Protestant theologians from various churches and with various convictions met for a discussion of the Sacrament of the Altar, with the purpose of overcoming, if possible, the old confessional differences through the findings of modern New Testament research, it appeared that almost every biblical scholar found the realistic concept of the Lord's Supper somewhere in the New Testament. Some found it in John 6, others in 1 Corinthians 10 and 11, others even in the Synoptic Gospels. But what becomes of the authority of the New Testament if I find the realistic understanding in Paul's writings, and reject it because I do not find it in the Gospels? If there is no doctrine of the New Testament, but only a doctrine of Paul, of John, of the Synoptists, then the unity of the New Testament is destroyed. We know, of course, that there are in the New Testament a variety of theological expressions, but all are expressions of one and the same truth. If we forget this, we abandon the New Testament, and with it the authority of the Bible to the catholic churches. Was not Luther right, after all, when he saw that a false interpretation of the Words of Institution must necessarily lead to a destruction of the Word of God? Here lies the strongest reason why the Lutheran church for centuries has so seriously maintained the doctrine of the Real Presence. As Luther's attitude at Marburg was not determined by obstinacy and stubbornness, but by respect for the words of Christ, so the attitude of the Lutheran church toward the Sacrament of the Altar is not to be understood as mere conservatism or traditionalism, but as an expression of the belief that the Word of God cannot be maintained when the Sacrament is abandoned.

Thus, the Lutheran church, when asked today why she still upholds the doctrine of the Real Presence, can give no other answer than that given by Luther and by the Lutheran Confessions: Since Christ has given no other explanation, we are bound by his words. Obedience to the Word of God, and nothing else, is the firm foundation of our belief. In this respect we are in quite the same situation as Luther was at Marburg. If we are told that the literal understanding of the *est* leads to absurdities — Christ standing before his disciples and giving them his body and blood to eat and drink; his body being in heaven and in many places on earth simultaneously in all celebrations of the Sacrament — if our contemporaries repeat Zwingli's objection that God does no propose to us incomprehensible things, we can only answer with Luther that all miracles and mysteries of God are incomprehensible to our reason.

And yet, it must be admitted that the realistic understanding of the Sacrament of the Altar contains still another difficulty. The mystery of the Real Presence, the miracle which occurs in every celebration of the Sacrament, is not more incomprehensible than the mysteries of the Trinity, the true divinity and true humanity of Christ, the virgin birth, the empty grave. The particular difficulty presented by the Lord's Supper lies in the eating and drinking. It is not so much the question as to what the use of a bodily eating and drinking should be — this question has been answered sufficiently by Luther — but rather the idea of eating the body and drinking the blood of our Saviour. Does not this idea belong to the sphere of pre-Christian, primitive religions?

The similarity existing between the Christian sacraments and old pagan rites was recognized by the Apostolic and the Early Church.[23]

———

[23]Justin (*Apol. I, 62*) explains the fact that the pagans practised holy washings comparable to Christian Baptism as an imitation of the Christian sacrament by the demons who in this way tried to prevent people from receiving the true Baptism. In the same way he explained the similarity between the Christian Eucharist and the communion celebrated in the cult of Mithra. No lesser an authority than St Paul himself recognized the similarity between the sacrifices and sacred meals of the pagans and the Lord's Supper. 'I would not that ye should have fellowship with devils. Ye cannot drink the cup of the Lord, and the cup of devils; ye cannot be partakers of the Lord's table, and of the table of devils'(1 Cor. 10:20 f). In speaking thus of having fellowship (*koinōnos*) or partaking (*metechein*) with demons, he even admits that there is a demonic reality behind these pagan rites, and that taking part in such ceremonies establishes a 'communion' with demonic powers. The most striking parallels have been discussed by J. Frazer in *The Golden Bough*, 3rd edition, V: 'Spirits of the Corn and of the Wild', (Vol. II, 1912) 86 ff ; cf Abridged Edition, 488 ff). Frazer describes the ceremonies, on the basis of the narrative of the Spanish historian Acosta: 'The custom of eating bread sacramentally as the body of a god was practised by the Aztecs before the discovery and conquest of Mexico by the Spaniards'. Acosta emphasizes the reverence and veneration with which men, women, and children, received the pieces 'as it was an admirable thing, saying that they did eat the flesh and bones of God'. The bread was then also carried to the sick. It is an overstatement when the great English scholar goes on to say that 'the ancient Mexicans, even before the arrival of Christian missionaries, were fully acquainted with the doctrine of transubstantiation and acted upon it in the solemn rites of their

Such similarities do not prove more than the parallels found between the Christian doctrine on the Trinity and the Hindu 'trinity' of Brahma, Vishnu, and Siwa, or other *vestigia trinitatis* in pagan religions. 'Every dogma is as old as the world.' Just as the cult of dying and rising saviour-gods in ancient mystery-religions proves nothing but the profound longing of the human soul for the true Saviour (who is not merely a mythological figure, but whose death and resurrection are historical facts), so all sacred meals and 'communions', the 'eating of the god' and 'drinking his blood', are expressions of that longing for the true Sacrament of Christ which seems to be rooted in the subconscious depth of the soul of man. To accept the words of Christ in simple, childlike faith is not more difficult than to accept the words about his sacrificial death. For, the idea of Christ as the Lamb of God that was slain for our sins also leads back to a very old period in the history of mankind when bloody sacrifices were brought for the sins of men. It is even possible that ancient paganism, which believed bloody sacrifices to be necessary for the forgiveness of sins, was closer to the truth than modern Protestantism which has demythologized 'the Lamb slain from the foundation of the world', and thus is no longer able to understand even the *Agnus Dei* of the liturgy: 'Lamb of God, that takest away the sins of the world, have mercy upon us . . . give us thy peace'.

b. *The Meaning of the Real Presence*

In spite of every assertion we may make that it is the Word of God, and this Word only, that compels us to accept the doctrine of the Real Presence, modern Protestantism will not cease to ask the question which has been put to our church since the days of Zwingli: Is it really the Word of God only, or are there, perhaps, some other reasons, too, which make you believe this inconceivable doctrine? John Henry Newman, in the last chapter of his *Apologia pro vita sua* has some words about the difficulties presented to human reason by the doctrine of transubstantiation, which may be applied, *mutatis mutandis*, to the Lutheran doctrine of the Real Presence: 'It is difficult, impossible to **imagine**, I grant', he says, 'but how is it

religion'. This alleged magical conversion of bread into the flesh of the god cannot be described as 'transubstantiation', though this word is sometimes used in a rather careless way even by English theologians. Similar rites were practised in India, as Frazer reports. Nowhere, however, has the parallel 'flesh and blood' been found.

difficult to **believe**?' He then refers to Macaulay, who at first could not understand how men could resist (as Macaulay puts it) 'the overwhelming force of argument against it', until he came to understand the firm belief of Thomas More: 'The doctrine of transubstantiation is a kind of proof charge. A faith which stands that test, will stand any test'. The same is true, perhaps more true, of the Lutheran belief in the Real Presence.

It was for Luther, and it is still today, the great test whether we are able to found our faith on the Word of our Lord alone, or whether we still have need of some support from human sources. Therefore we must examine ourselves whether our faith is a purely-biblical faith, or whether it is perhaps influenced, if not determined, by a theology or philosophy which we like to label 'Lutheranism'. For that reason we can only be thankful to those who ask us questions like these: What is the rationale of your doctrine on the Real Presence? Why are you not satisfied with that presence which our Lord promised in the words: 'Where two or three are gathered together in my name, there am I in the midst of them'? All Christians believe that this presence takes place in the celebration of the Lord's Supper. All churches could pray in the words of the eucharistic prayer of the old Mozarabic liturgy:

> Be with us, be with us, Jesus, good High Priest, in our midst as Thou wert in the midst of Thy disciples.[24]

Why should there be in the Lord's Supper, in addition to this presence, the Real Presence of Christ's body and blood, a presence which no one is able to imagine, and the necessity of which defies explanation? What can a *manducatio oralis* mean if the Sacrament is food for our souls,[25] to say nothing of a *manducatio impiorum?* What can the sacramental eating and drinking give in addition to what we receive through the Word of God? Do we not have everything Christ can give us in the Word of his Gospel? What else did the sinners whom Christ pardoned need but his word of absolution: 'Thy sins are forgiven thee'; 'Today shalt thou be with me in paradise'? If it is true that the spiritual eating and drinking of the body and blood of Christ by faith in him is necessary and sufficient for salvation, as all Western churches agree, what, then, is the

---

[24] '*Adesto, adesto, Jesu bone pontifex, in medio nostri: sicut fuisti in medio discipulorum tuorum*' (MPL 85, 116). The prayer continues: '*sanctifica hanc oblationem, ut sanctificata sumamus . . .*' Then follows the consecration by the Words of Institution, which clearly indicates that this liturgy also recognized another presence.

[25] cf '*praesta meae **menti** de te vivere*' in '*Adoro te devote*' and the Lutheran hymns.

particular gift we receive through the sacramental eating and drinking? The Lutheran church has to face these questions again in every century. It cannot be satisfied with simply repeating what former generations have answered. Maybe our contemporaries will be at a loss to understand our answer, just as Zwingli and Calvin were. But we have to answer them.

In trying to give our answer to the questions of this century, we must, however, clearly distinguish between questions that can be answered and others that cannot. Christian theology is always tempted to appear to know more than it possibly can know, to be wiser than Holy Scripture is. This is especially true of the theology of the Sacraments. Theological and philosophical speculations have been employed to answer questions that the Word of God does not answer. The most notable example is the doctrine of transubstantiation, but Lutheran theologians are by no means immune to similar dangers. If the old rule should apply anywhere, that theology has to speak where God's Word speaks, and to be silent where God's Word is silent, then surely it applies in the doctrine on the Sacraments. This does not, of course, mean that theology need only repeat the words of the Bible. Nor does it mean that we are forbidden to draw conclusions from the biblical statements, provided such conclusions remain within the analogy of faith. It means solely that the **source of all doctrine** can be nothing but Holy Scripture. Following these rules, what have we to say about the meaning of the Real Presence?

(1) *'Word and Sacrament'*

Very often the attempt has been made to understand the Lord's Supper and the meaning of the Real Presence by defining the nature of the Sacraments in general, and applying the definition thus reached to the Sacrament of the Altar. In discussing Augustine's doctrine on the Sacrament,[26] which has so deeply influenced all churches of the West, we noted that, in contrast to all other churches, the Lutheran church, though in Christian freedom making use of Augustine's theory and formulas, never developed a **dogma** on the nature and the number of sacraments, the reason being that there is no scriptural basis for such a doctrine.

The Lutheran way of dealing with 'the sacraments' is rather to start from the individual Sacrament, as the *Augsburg Confession* does when it deals first with Baptism, then with the Lord's Supper, then

[26]See above, 19, 20.

with confession and penance, and finally with the 'use of the sacraments'. This way only can lead to a real understanding of the nature of each sacrament, because this nature is to be found in the *proprium* of the individual sacrament rather than in what they all have in common. This becomes evident as soon as we realize the various ways in which they were instituted. It belongs to the very nature of the Sacrament of the Altar that the sacramental words contain an exact statement on the time, the historic moment of the institution: 'in the night in which he was betrayed'. This is not the case in the baptismal formula, and the church has never been quite sure about the time of the institution of Baptism. While some have found it in the moment when the risen Lord gave the baptismal command, there are strong reasons for distinguishing between the institution of Baptism and the command to practise it generally in connection with the preaching of the Gospel to all nations. According to John 3:22 and 4:1, 2, Jesus (or rather, his disciples) performed baptism at the same time as John the Baptist. There seems to have been a development, not only of the baptismal formula (compare Acts 2:38; 10:48; 1 Cor. 1:13-15; Matt. 28:19 with the reading of Eusebius), but also of the ways of administering this Sacrament (which, being a bath, could not be performed at church).

The main difference between the two Sacraments is to be found in the fact that the sacramental words in the Lord's Supper are the words which Christ spoke at the institution, and which he speaks at all times through his ministers, words of him who is God himself and who is, therefore, able to effect what they say. They are words of consecration which effect the Real Presence of the body and blood of Christ. There is, then, no real parallel between the sacramental words in these two Sacraments, though the desire to understand them from the concept 'sacrament' has led to attempts to assimilate one to the other. Thus, a benediction of the baptismal water has been introduced. Such blessing by prayer is possible, but it is not a consecration comparable to that of the Lord's Supper. The Presence of Christ is different in the two sacraments. It is also a mistake to argue: If the Sacrament of Baptism performed by a heretic is valid, provided it has been performed with the proper element and the proper baptismal formula, then the Sacrament of the Altar must also be valid in heretical communities, provided the proper elements are used and the Words of Institution are spoken. Though Luther and the Lutheran church have always rejected the doctrine that the validity of the sacrament depends on the minister's 'intention' (at least, to do what the church does), Luther bluntly denied that the body and the blood of Christ are given and received in churches where the minister does not wish to give, and the communicants do not wish to receive, the true body and blood. Such a celebration he could not regard as the Sacrament as Christ instituted it.[27] The Lutheran church has never decided the question — because it cannot be decided — as to what God may give to pious Reformed Christians who in a bona fide manner celebrate the Lord's Supper according to their convictions. We would not deny that in such a case at least a spiritual communion may take place. But we cannot regard the *verba testamenti* as being on the same level with the formula of Baptism in which the minister says what he does at the command of Christ. For in those words Christ himself speaks, and the minister would not speak *ex persona Christi* if he did not speak the Words of Institution as Christ understood them and wanted them to be understood. This is the reason why the Lutheran church, like all other churches except the Baptists, recognizes a baptism performed in another church, but has never recognized the Sacrament of the Altar in those communities which deny the Real Presence, and, consequently, does not allow anyone, even in a case of emergency or *in articulo mortis*, to receive Holy Communion in such churches.[28]

---

[27]See above, 228 ff , and 236 ff.

[28]Peter Brunner, *Grundlegung des Abendmahlsgesprächs* (1954), 28-33, gives some very well-considered theses on the possibility of a renewed colloquy between Lutherans and Reformed on the basis of modern biblical and historical theology in both churches. He rejects the superficial unionism of former times which did not realize the depth of the issues, and the seriousness of the authority of Holy Scripture. As a Lutheran theologian in a union church (Brunner is professor at Heidelberg), he leaves open the possibility that Lutherans may admit that in a congregation which follows the *Heidelberg Catechism* the body and blood of Christ may be received, because this Catechism teaches a presence of the body and blood, though in the sense of Calvin (according to question 79, 'we partake of His true body and blood through the power of the Holy Ghost as certainly as we receive the holy signs — i.e., bread and wine — orally'). However, Brunner, as a clear and sincere thinker, adds in a footnote (p 32) that Luther, had he known the *Heidelberg Catechism*, would not have agreed with Brunner's view. The author himself admits that he could not recognize the Sacrament as valid where the Real Presence was completely denied: '*Darin hat Luther doch wohl recht gesehen, dass dort wo eine Präsenz des Leibes und Blutes Jesu Christi bestritten wird, die Substanz des Sakraments selbst zerstört wird'*. He also agrees with Luther in admitting that such heresy would be worse than the Roman doctrine on transubstantiation. This means that while the sacrament of the Zwinglians cannot be recognized, it is possible to recognize that of the Calvinists. This is the view of the Lutherans within union churches, otherwise they could not be members of such churches. Peter Brunner himself must admit that Luther would not share his view. The

All this must be kept in mind if we want to know why it is impossible to understand an individual sacrament like the Lord's Supper from a general concept of a sacrament. It is not even possible to draw a clear line of demarcation between 'Word' and 'Sacrament', or even between churches of the Word and churches of the Sacrament. Claus Harms, in one of his famous theses of 1817, found the nature of the Roman church in the emphasis on the Sacrament, the nature of the Reformed church in the emphasis on the Word, and the nature of the Lutheran church in the equal emphasis on Word and Sacrament. Though there is a certain truth in that statement, it is an oversimplification of the facts. In the Roman church the preaching of the Word is always subordinate to the administration of the Sacraments, as is indicated by the simple fact that a Catholic priest can be a priest in good standing without ever having preached, while he is obliged to celebrate mass daily, if possible. Yet, an eminent, modern Catholic dogmatician has claimed:

> The Church is not only Church of the Word [Protestantism], and not only Church of the Sacrament [the danger of the Eastern Church], but rather Church of the Word and the Sacrament.[29]

Even in the most 'sacramental' churches, the Word is always regarded as that which constitutes the Sacrament. The element or *materia* is always inferior to the Word as the *forma*. What Luther expresses in his words on Baptism is a general conviction of all churches:

> Without the Word of God the water is simply water and no baptism. But with the Word of God it is baptism.

This must be emphasized to contradict certain attempts by modern liturgical movements to understand the Sacrament more or less, from the aspect of the element, as if certain mysterious natural qualities of water, or of bread and wine, or certain human actions, like washing or submerging, eating and drinking, revealed the essence of the Sacraments.[30] Such attempts must be rejected from the outset. They lead unavoidably back to a pagan mystery-religion in which nature and the powers of nature are deified, and the creature is

---

question whether a Lutheran in danger of death could receive the Sacrament from a Reformed minister was denied by Luther and all dogmaticians, as was also the case in the pastoral advice given in the books on *casus conscientiae*, e.g., Balduin, *Tractatus de casibus conscientiae*, edition of 1654, 345, where it is made clear that the Lord's Supper must not be received from a minister who is known to be a Calvinist.

[29] Michael Schmaus, *Katholische Dogmatik, III,* Part 2 (1934), 17.

[30] Such attempts appear as early as in the 19th century under the influence of Schelling's philosophy of nature, and of theosophical ideas, even in outstanding

worshipped instead of the Creator. Baptismal rites, communion feasts, and other expressions of what the world would call 'sacramental' religion, are to be found in many religions. What distinguishes the Christian Sacraments from such rites is not earthly elements or the human actions, but the Word of God, the institution of Christ. Thus, Word and Sacrament belong together, and the Sacrament may well be called *verbum visibile*,[31] provided it is not regarded as a mere sign, but as a real means of grace.

It is the same grace that is given through the Word and the Sacrament. The question as to why the church needs both cannot be answered because there is no answer to be found in Holy Scripture. Thus, all speculations on the nature and the necessity of the Sacraments should be dropped. Scripture tells us that God has many ways of dealing with us and conveying his grace to us. Christ comes to us in the written Word of Holy Scripture, in the preaching of the Gospel, in Baptism, in the absolution of the penitent sinner, in Holy Communion. He is present in all these means of grace, but not in each of them in the same way. Why he has given us the Sacrament of the Altar, and with it the special way of his Presence which is inherent in this Sacrament, we cannot know. Instead of finding the rationale of this Presence by way of speculation, we must hear in humble faith what Christ himself said, and what Paul added by way of an authentic commentary.

(2) *'In Remembrance of Me'*

No branch of Christendom has ever forgotten that the Lord's Supper is the great memorial which Jesus Christ left as his testament to his Church on earth when he said, 'This do in remembrance of me'. All liturgies, Eastern and Western, Catholic and Protestant, seem to indicate that, at least in this one point, there is agreement among all Christians, and this is borne out by the fact that also the great

---

Lutheran theologians. Among modern theologians, Paul Tillich in *Religiöse Verwirklichung* (1930) has emphasized that the Sacraments must be understood from the elements: There is a necessary connection between Baptism and water, Holy Communion and bread and wine. The *Berneuchen Movement* in German Protestantism emphasized this idea in its earlier stage. Later, W. Stählin, the leader of the movement, became more careful, but his book *Vom göttlichen Geheimnis* (1936, English translation 1937) still contains a certain philosophy of nature, as in the sentence: *'In den Elementen, die bei dem Sakrament der christlichen Kirche dienen, ist die ganze Schöpfungswelt repräsentiert'* (132).

[31]The *Apology*, Art. 13 (Trigl. 309): '. . . Just as the Word enters the ear in order to strike our heart, so the rite itself strikes the eye, in order to move the heart. The effect of the Word and of the rite is the same, as it has been well said by Augustine that a Sacrament is a visible word . . . '

confessional churches of the 16th century, from Zurich to Wittenberg, from Rome to Geneva and Canterbury, were in undisputed agreement that this Sacrament was the *memoria*, the remembrance of the atoning death of Christ. How deeply this understanding of the Lord's Supper is rooted in the New Testament, and what a close relationship exists between remembrance and the Real Presence, must be shown.

In masterly words, though with the limitations of a purely historical approach, Oswald Spengler expressed the historical character of New Testament Christianity amid the world of religions which surrounded it:

> The incomparable thing which lifted the infant Christianity out above all religions of this rich springtime is the figure of Jesus. In all the great creations of those years there is nothing which can be set beside it. Tame and empty all the legends and holy adventures of Mithras, Attis, and Osiris must have seemed to any man reading or listening to the still recent story of Jesus' sufferings — the last journey to Jerusalem, the last anxious supper, the hours of despair in Gethsemane, and the death on the cross. . . Christianity is the one religion in the history of the world in which the fate of a man of the immediate present has become the emblem and the central point of the whole creation.[32]

This historical character of the revelation of Christ, which this revelation shares with that of the Old Testament, made the Gospel from the very beginning a 'remembrance'. As the eye-witnesses remembered Jesus, his words and the events connected with his life, death and resurrection (Acts 1:21; 10:41; 1 John 1:1, 2), so they 'delivered, handed down (*paredōkan, tradiderunt*)' what they had seen and heard to those who were to believe the Gospel, as Paul puts it when he reminds the church of Corinth (1 Cor. 15:1-5): '. . . in what terms I preached to you the gospel, which you received . . . if you hold it fast . . . for I delivered to you . . . what I also received,[33] that Christ died for our sins . . . that he was buried, that he was raised on the third day . . . and that he appeared to Cephas, then to the twelve . . .'(RSV). It is the foremost task of the church to preach the Gospel, to preserve the written record of the apostolic message which we have in the New Testament, and to explain its contents again and again to each new generation, and so to preserve the 'remembrance' of Jesus Christ.

---

[32] *The Decline of the West*, Authorized Translation by C. F. Atkinson (1947), II, 222.

[33] This does not contradict Gal. 1:12, where Paul strongly maintains that he has not received the Gospel from man, but by the revelation of Christ. From human tradition he received the formulas of the Church and the details about Jesus' life and words.

This has been done in the church of all ages and will be done until the end of the world.

Whenever a church neglected this duty to preach, and confined itself to a more-or-less solemn performance of a liturgy that was no longer understood by the people — as inevitably happens if the Sacrament is not constantly explained by the preaching of the Gospel — the remembrance of Christ was bound to become dim or to be lost. This, by the way, never occurred in the Early Church. Ambrose converted the Manichaean Augustine by his sermons, not by the liturgy, which in its simplicity may have been far less impressive than the Manichaean and other pagan liturgies. It is certainly not accidental that the most profound writings of Fathers like Augustine and Chrysostom originally were sermons which had been taken down in shorthand while being preached.

This type of remembrance, however, should not be confused with what we today call 'remembrance' when, for instance, at the 'shrine of remembrance', we call to mind soldiers fallen in war, and the battles they fought. The remembrance of the church is, of course, remembrance of a real, historical person, of events which once occurred in the past and are not repeatable. The church, like the Bible, takes historical events very seriously, perhaps more seriously than historians do. 'When Cyrenius was governor of Syria'. 'In the fifteenth year of the reign of Tiberius Caesar, Pontius Pilate being governor of Judaea'; *passus sub Pontio Pilato*: such exact dates belong to the remembrance of the events of sacred history. We find the same thing even in the Old Testament: 'In the days of Uzziah king of Judah, and in the days of Jeroboam the son of Joash king of Israel, two years before the earthquake' God spoke to Amos (1:1); 'In the year that king Uzziah died' Isaiah (6:1) was called by God to be a prophet. No religious message of any other ancient religion could contain such statements. When did Attis or Osiris die? Such a question would be absolutely meaningless to the adherents of these gods; the divine figures, and events told in connection with them, belong to the sphere of timeless myth, not in the sphere of real history. Where did Attis die? That does not matter. But it matters that Jesus died 'outside the gate' of Jerusalem (Heb. 13:12); his grave was known. Compare the touching myth of Isis searching for her dead husband with the Gospel narrative of Mary Magdalene, Mary the mother of James, and Salome searching for the dead body of Christ in the early hours of that Sunday at the well-known sepulchre, in order to see the difference between myth and history. So careful was the Early Church in delivering the message that Paul, when enumerating the witnesses of the resurrection of Christ, does not even mention the women. Otherwise, the world might have said what Renan said eighteen centuries later: 'The strong passion of a possessed woman gave to the world a resuscitated god' (whereupon it was ably answered, 'No, it only gave us a gardener').

The history that the church remembers is real history. However, like the history of the Old Testament, it is not ordinary history like the biography of Socrates or the history of the Greek people; it is sacred history in which God is at work in a way quite different from the ways in which he acts in all other human history. The remembrance of which we are speaking here is, therefore, more than recalling a history event like the Battle of Hastings or the life of Napoleon. It cannot even be compared with the remembrance of Buddha or Muhammad in the great religions that originated in their doctrines. It means, at the same time, to remember God: 'He hath made his wonderful works to be remembered. . . . He sent **redemption** unto his people; he hath commanded **his covenant** for ever: **holy and reverend is his name**', as Psalm 111 puts it. When the psalm continues: 'The fear of the Lord is the beginning of wisdom', it refers also to the wisdom (a gift of the Holy Spirit) of writing and understanding that sacred history. It was such wisdom that helped a man like St Luke, who introduces himself at the beginning of his Gospel as a historian who judges his sources, the first 'higher critic' in the church, though in the service of the Holy Spirit. The understanding of the history which the church remembers requires, indeed, more than a good memory, more than sound judgment in historical matters. It requires 'wisdom', 'fear of the Lord', faith.

The great example for such remembrance among the old people of God was the great memorial of the passover: 'This day shall be unto you for a memorial [*zikkarōn,* in LXX *mnēmosymon,* not *anamnēsis* as in the Lord's Supper]; and ye shall keep it a feast to the Lord throughout your generations; ye shall keep it a feast by an ordinance for ever' (Exod. 12:14). Though that feast could no longer be celebrated in the proper way after the destruction of Jerusalem, the slaughter of the Passover lambs being a sacrifice, it is still today, as for the Jews in the Diaspora of the ancient world, the greatest example of what remembrance could mean for the old people of God. It kept alive the remembrance of God's great saving act, the redemption of Israel from the bondage of Egypt, the miracle that constituted Israel as a people. So strong was the tradition of this festival that it lived on in the church as *Pascha* with a new meaning; in all Romantic languages (as even in the Irish *Caise* where *p* is replaced by *c*) Easter is still called by the Greek name for Passover, *Pascha*. In the Epistle for Easter Day (1 Cor. 5:7, 8), Paul (and, probably, John in his chronology of the passion) created the first Christian idea of Easter as the true Passover, first celebrated on the day of the Jewish feast to commemorate the death and resurrection of Christ as the true Passover lamb who brought about the redemption of the new people of God from the bondage of this world, from the dominion of sin, death, and devil. Soon this redemption through the resurrection of Christ was commemorated on each Sunday, and the festival of Easter became independent from the Jewish Passover. The church remembered the death and resurrection of Christ each Sunday, by celebrating the Sacrament that Christ had instituted as his Passover with the words: 'This do in remembrance of me'.

With this Sacrament, a remembrance began such as the world had never witnessed before. No person in the world has been remembered throughout the ages as Jesus Christ has been. No historical event is commemorated so often, and with such strong sentiment, as the death and resurrection of Christ. 'This do in remembrance of me.' The remembrance of Christ in the preaching of the Gospel, and the remembrance in the Sacrament, belong together. In the two cases, the way of remembering is not the same, as Zwingli believed. For the Sacrament is not only a means of helping us to recollect the past, to call to mind Jesus Christ, as a crucifix helps us to remember Christ, or a festival helps to call to mind a historic event. Even the remembrance of Christ by means of the Gospel is different from our remembering Socrates by reading Plato's *Phaedon*, because in the word of the Gospel, Christ, the Word Incarnate, speaks to us.

In the Sacrament he gives us the same as he gave to the Twelve at the Last Supper. He gives us his true body, which was sacrificed on Calvary and raised from the dead at Easter. This makes us not only contemporaneous with him, but unites us with him in a way that transcends everything that we otherwise call remembrance. The centuries that separate us from his earthly days, and from the time of his death and resurrection, disappear. The atoning death of our Lord occurred 'once for all' (*ephapax*, Rom. 6:10; Heb. 7:27; 9:12; 10:10). It cannot in any way be repeated, otherwise it would not be a historical event. Thus, it is not permissible to speak of the Sacrament of the Altar as an 'unbloody repetition', or, as the *Catechismus Romanus* does, an 'instauration' of the sacrifice of the cross.[34] Even the ambiguous word 'representation', which has become very popular with modern theologians under the influence of the Liturgical Movement, is dangerous and quite unsatisfactory, because it endangers the uniqueness, finality, and sufficiency of Christ's sacrifice on Calvary.[35] This must be said here because even Lutherans are beginning to speak of the Sacrament of the Altar as a 're-presentation' of the sacrifice of Christ in the sense that an event of the past is made present. The 'presence' in this Sacrament, however, is not the presence of an event or an action which occurred in the past (*passio Christi*, the suffering of Christ), but it is rather the Presence of Christ's body and blood, of his true humanity and true divinity (*Christus passus*, Christ who has suffered for us). It is this Real Presence of the crucified and risen Lord, who gives us his true body

———

[34] *Cat. Rom., pars II, cap. 4, q. 61.*

[35] '*Repraesentare*' is the carefully chosen substitute for *renovare* or *instaurare* in the doctrine of Trent on the sacrifice of the mass. Sessio XXII, cap. 1, states that Christ in the Last Supper instituted the mass as a '*sacrificium, quo cruentum illud* ***semel in cruce*** *peragendum* ***repraesentaretur****, eiusque* ***memoria*** *in finem saeculi permaneret, atque illius salutaris virtus in remissionem . . . peccatorum* ***applicaretur***' (Denz. 938, *emphasis mine*). Exactly what is meant here by *repraesentare* is not quite clear. The *Catechismus Romanus* understands it as instauration, but this is no official explanation since the *Catechismus* is not a dogmatic document in a strict sense. The word was introduced into terminology of the church by Tertullian, the father of ecclesiastical Latin. He understands 'representation' as 'manifestation' or 'public declaration' (G. Dix, *The Shape of the Liturgy* 255 f). Aquinas calls the celebration of the Sacrament an 'image representing the passion of Christ (*imago . . . repraesentativa passionis Christi*)', *Summa theol., III, Q. 83, Art. 1.* Neither in this nor in other passages does Thomas have in mind what certain modern theologians, especially of the Benedictine school of Maria Laach (like the late Odo Casel, *Das christliche Kultmysterium* (2nd edition, 1935) and numerous other publications), understood by *re-praesentatio*, namely, that an event of sacred history, like the passion of Christ, is present again in the Sacrament (Casel, *op. cit.*, 102). This much-debated theory rests upon the assumption that the Hellenistic mystery-cults in which certain mythical occurrences, like the death and resuscitation of a deity, are made present, 're-presented', must be regarded as 'a shadow of things to come' (Col. 2:17), namely, of the true mysteries (Sacraments) of Christ. This assumption and the whole theory must be rejected. How can the mythical experiences of non-existing deities be compared with the historical events of Christ's death and resurrection? The best criticism of this theory (*Mysterien-Theologie*) — the purpose of which seems to be the explanation of the identity of the sacrifice of the cross and the sacrifice of the mass which is taught by Trent — was given by the Catholic scholar Gottlieb Soehngen in *Symbol und Wirklichkeit im Kultmysterium* (1940). Gregory Dix has convincingly refuted the view of an essential influence of the mystery-religions upon the Christian Eucharist (*The Shape of the Liturgy,* especially 64).

and blood to eat and to drink that lends to the **remembrance** of his death a reality and actuality such as we do not find otherwise in the recollection of a historical event.

Thus, remembrance and the Real Presence belong inseparably together. The Word of the Gospel is realized; the Lamb of God, once slain on Calvary under Pontius Pilate, is here. We eat the flesh of the true Lamb of God, of whom the Passover lamb of Israel was a type. This Real Presence of what Christ has offered once for all at a certain moment of history points to that profound mystery of Christ's sacrifice which the Bible expresses when it speaks of the 'Lamb slain from the foundation of the world' (Rev. 13:8), and the 'eternal' high priest (Heb. 6:20, and others).[36] The atoning death of Christ, an event which occurred once in our earthly time, belongs also to the sphere of timeless eternity, because it is the death of the Son of God Incarnate. Just as all human history from the beginning of the world was already under the shadow of the cross of him in whom the fathers believed as the future Messiah, so the sacrifice of Calvary remains an ever-present reality until the end of the world, and in a particular way for those who partake of the true body and blood of Christ in remembrance of him.

(3) *'For the Remission of Sins'*

'This Sacrament is the Gospel.' Nowhere does the meaning of this statement of Luther become so clear as when we try to understand the words of Jesus: 'Given for you . . . shed for you . . . shed for many . . . for the remission of sins'. For the Gospel **is** the forgiveness of sins, nothing else. It is not a theory about the possibility of forgiveness, not a vague religious message that there is a merciful God. Every Muslim knows that 'Allah is merciful'. Where the Gospel is misunderstood as a religious theory, the unavoidable consequence is Albrecht Ritschl's ingenious discovery that there is no such thing as the wrath of God! Hell is closed, and eternal punishment abolished: that is the comfort modern Protestantism has to offer to poor sinners!

The Gospel of Jesus Christ, however, is something quite different. 'Thy sins are forgiven thee': that was his Gospel. To hear this message is more than comfort; it is bliss. When Christ sent his apostles into the

---

[36]Over against modern attempts to find in Hebrews the idea of a sacrificial mass, it must be emphasized that this very epistle stresses the 'once' of Christ's sacrifice (Heb. 7:27; 9:12; 9:26; 10:10, cf 1 Peter 3:18).

world to preach the Gospel to all nations, it was, again, not a theoretical message that he entrusted to them, but the power to forgive sins, which he himself had received from his heavenly Father: 'As my Father hath sent me, even so send I you. . . . Whose soever sins ye remit, they are remitted unto them; and whose soever sins ye retain, they are retained'. It is not by accident that wherever the Office of the Keys was no longer practised, where confession and absolution were neglected or abolished, the great misunderstanding of the Gospel as one of the many religious messages of mankind arose. And, again, it is not accidental that the decay of confession and absolution has always been accompanied by the decay of the Sacrament of the Altar. For the Lord's Supper also is the remission of sins to everyone that receives it in faith. We do not need to repeat what has been said about that in our discussion of Luther's doctrine.[37] Only a few words are necessary to point out what this aspect of the Sacrament means to the church today.

The church today lives in a world that has lost the sense of sin and guilt in an appalling way. Speaking of the Reformation, Claus Harms and Tholuck remarked that people of the 16th century at least spent money to get rid of their sins, while in the 19th century the sale of indulgences would be a very poor business because there were no longer any consciences troubled by sins. Our 20th century seems to have made still further progress! Who still remembers the extinction of entire Christian people in the Orient in the first quarter of this century? Who is still concerned about the killing of more than six million Jews, and the not-less-cruel eradication of other peoples? The guilt of our generation is not diminished by the fact that such cruelties have occurred throughout the history of mankind. The difference is that men in earlier ages knew that guilt must be atoned for. What a profound understanding of human sin and guilt and their consequences finds its expression in the tragedies of Aeschylus and Sophocles! Was not ancient (and even primitive) paganism, which tried to reconcile the gods by sacrifices, on a higher moral level than modern mankind, which simply forgets its sins? Even in the church there is a tendency to indulge in such happy oblivion. After the last war, theologians made the comforting discovery that there is no 'collective guilt' of nations, let alone of churches, in spite of everything the Old Testament says about God's pleading with his people, punishing his people, and in spite of everything that 'the

[37]See above, 88 ff and 146 ff.

Spirit saith unto the churches' in Revelation 2 and 3. What is wrong with modern Christendom?

We are told that the quest of the 16th century was the quest for a gracious God, while today the question is whether there is a God at all. But to ask for God, if it is a serious asking and seeking, always means to ask for a gracious God. Otherwise, the quest for God is a purely philosophical, metaphysical quest. We are told that the interest in religious problems (and even church membership) is growing. But such a change may not mean much more than a sort of intellectual conversion, a change from old-fashioned materialism and atheism of the 19th century to another metaphysical system, such as a renewed Thomism. Religion may become fashionable again in an age of uncertainty and fear. A real conversion would be a conversion of the heart, a conversion of the whole man, as he repents of his sins and asks for pardon. In such a situation, the Sacrament of the Altar is of inestimable importance. For the church it is the best means of overcoming the intellectualism that threatens her very life. A Good Friday sermon may be heard as something that appeals to our heart, or merely to our intellect. Even the Passion music of Bach, which carries the message of the Gospel so impressively to many of our contemporaries throughout the world, may be understood from a merely aesthetic point of view. The Lord's Supper, however, cannot be understood intellectually or aesthetically; it can be understood 'by faith alone'. It requires complete self-humiliation and submission to the words of Christ: 'This is my body . . . This is my blood'. Whenever we hear these words at the celebration of the Sacrament in humble faith, taking them as they sound, we know that he is present who is at the same time the eternal High Priest and the Lamb slain from the beginning of the world. We know that we receive what he has sacrificed to atone for all sins of all men — from the fall of the first man and the first fratricide to the terrific mass-murders of our time, and to all sins and inconceivable crimes which may be committed until the day of the Last Judgment. Can we receive this precious body and blood without realizing the greatness of human sin, the greatness of our own sin? And who can hear the words: 'Given for you . . . shed for you . . . for the remission of sins' without realizing the greatness of Christ's love for sinners and God's mercy toward us? Here forgiveness is received as a reality by the believer. It is the same forgiveness that we received in absolution, though in a different form.

The question has often been asked why we should receive forgiveness of sins in the Lord's Supper after we have just received it in absolution. Attempts have been made to find a difference between the assurance of forgiveness given in absolution and that given through the Sacrament. There is no such difference, for one and the same grace is given through the Gospel and the Sacrament. However, it is true that the manner in which forgiveness is imparted to us in the Sacrament points to the fact that God's grace is meant for the whole man, body and soul, and that there is a connection between the participation of the 'vivifying flesh' of our glorified Lord and the resurrection of our bodies. We discussed this problem when we tried to understand what Luther taught in this respect in his great writings against Zwingli.[38] It has been suggested that this doctrine had only transitory importance for him during the years of the Great Controversy, but this is untenable. What Luther taught on that question in his *Large Catechism* always remained his doctrine and that of the Lutheran church,[39] as indicated in the passages quoted from the *Formula of Concord*.[40] It is also impossible to explain the idea as a remnant of an ecclesiastical tradition that goes back to the Church Fathers, especially those of the East. Luther would not have preserved such thoughts, had he not seen that they are based on the New Testament. It is noteworthy that the Lutheran theologians of the 16th century fully agree with Luther in this respect, notably Matthesius, Chemnitz,[41] and Selneccer. The devotional literature of that time makes frequent use of the idea in describing the fruit of the Sacrament.[42]

———

[38]See above, 146-150.

[39]See above, 147.

[40]See above, 148.

[41]*Examen Concilii Tridentini, II, locus 4, sectio 2* (ed. Preuss, 303 ff) accepts the doctrine of the Fathers as undisputed.

[42]For instance, J. Matthesius, *Bekenntnis vom heiligen Abendmahl* (1598), quoted by Aug. Vilmar, *Kirche und Welt*, Vol. I, 331: '*Darum speiset uns der Herr Christus mit seinem eigenen Leib und Blut, dass nicht allein unser Seele und Geist, sondern auch unser Fleisch und Blut seiner Gnade, Güte, Wohltat, Herrlichkeit in alle Ewigkeit mitgeniessen solle, wie denn . . . die heiligen Patres sehr fein und tröstlich pflegen zu reden*'. In a similar way, the pastors of Mansfeld wrote in their *Grund reiner Lehre von dem hochwürdigen Sakrament* (1571), explaining Luther's doctrine on the Lord's Supper in the *Small Catechism* to the Christians in France, that the fruit of the Sacrament is not only forgiveness of sins, but also the life which follows forgiveness: '*Denn so wir seinen Leib essen und sein Blut trinken, so bleiben wir in ihm und er in uns. Und sagen die alten Lehrer, dass wir dadurch nicht allein in die Gemeinschaft seines geistlichen Leibes, welches ist die Kirche, gesetzt werden, sondern wir werden*

Still, Johann Gerhard maintains

> that this our body in which sin and death are dwelling in this life will be resuscitated from the dust of the earth to eternal life because it has been nourished with the vivifying body of Christ.[43]

Most of the orthodox theologians since the beginning of the 17th century, however, with some noteworthy exceptions like A. Calov, have more or less given up the idea of a connection between Holy Communion and the resurrection of our bodies, obviously under the influence of the renewed Aristotelian philosophy (which at one time also prevented Aquinas from accepting the idea of the Eucharist as 'medicine of immortality, the antidote against death').[44] At the end of the orthodox period, Hollaz in his great work knows only a threefold end of the Eucharist: remembrance (*recordatio,* no longer *memoria* or *commemoratio*) and proclamation of the passion and death of Christ; sealing (*obsignatio*) of the grace of the Gospel; and mutual love among the communicants.[45] It has rightly been observed that every Calvinist could accept this.[46] It is obvious that with the realistic understanding of the effects of the Sacraments, the Real Presence, though doctrinally still preserved and defended, has lost its meaning.

When the understanding of the Real Presence was renewed in the 19th century, together with the faith of the Lutheran church, some speculative theologians could not resist the temptation to learn more about the relationship existing between the Lord's Supper and our

---

auch seiner Natur teilhaftig'. Referring to Eph. 5:30, they continued: *'dass unsere Leiber . . . durch die allerheilsamste Speise des teuren Leibes und Blutes Christi also zubereitet werden, dass sie gewisse Hoffnung haben der Auferstehung von den Toten'.*

43'. . . *illud ipsum corpus nostrum in quo peccatum et mors in hac vita habitant, ex pulvere terrae ad vitam aeternam sit suscitandum, quia vivifico Christi corpore est nutritum', Loci XXI, cap. 20, par. 213* (ed. Preuss, V, 211). Gerhard quotes, among other passages, 1 Cor. 6:17; 12:13; 15:22; John 6:54, 56; 15:5, and gives the customary quotations from the Fathers which are also found in Chemnitz, *loc. cit.* (Ignatius, Irenaeus, Athanasius, Chrysostom, a.o.).

44See above, 149, 150.

45*Examen theol. Acroamat.* (1707), *III, Sect. II, Cap. V, q. 20;* ed. 1741, 1132.

46A. F. C. Vilmar, *Kirche und Welt* (1872), I, 351; cf R. Rocholl, *Die Realpräsenz* (1875), 356 ff with rich material on the doctrine of the Lutheran Fathers. Rocholl (359) calls attention to what Beza conceded at the Colloquy of Montbéliard in 1586: 'Although faith is the only instrument and organ with which Christ is received, still its fruit and use also reaches our body. For our bodies also become immortal through the communication and communion of this body'. This is even more than Hollaz says, though he would admit that this is correct. It becomes evident from the doctrine of late Orthodoxy that the Sacrament no longer had the profound meaning for the lives of the Christians that it had a hundred years earlier. This is one of the reasons why people could no longer see a real difference between the Lutheran and the Reformed churches.

resurrection than it is possible to know. They assumed, as did some Catholic thinkers, that through the Sacraments, especially through the bodily eating and drinking of Christ's body and blood, some supernatural substance is imparted to our body to make it capable of being resuscitated. Such speculations are as unbiblical as the theory of transubstantiation; they discredited the doctrine of Luther and the early Lutheran church. Our fathers never intended to give an explanation of the bodily effects of the Sacrament. Even the Fathers of the Ancient Church, like Ignatius, Justin Martyr, and Irenaeus, the main representatives of the doctrine of the 'medicine of immortality', did not think of giving an explanation of the mystery that was first proclaimed in the liturgy. We must never forget that these men wrote in the face of martyrdom. Ignatius wrote his *Epistle to the Ephesians* on his journey to Rome, where he was to be thrown to wild beasts in the circus. He knew what would happen to his body, and that he would never have a grave from which to rise. Irenaeus knew what had happened in his absence to the martyrs of Lyons, the ashes of whose bodies had been thrown into the Rhone. Although some Church Fathers, especially Athenagoras and Tertullian (but also Tatian, Cyril of Jerusalem, and Augustine), tried, in their writings on the resurrection, to give an apologetical explanation of the possibility of the resurrection of the body, in the last instance they all had to recur to the omnipotence of God, who works the miracle of resurrection as he brought about the miracle of creation.[47]

The resurrection is an eschatological event, and, therefore, inconceivable to human reason. The 'divine nature' of which we are partakers, according to 2 Peter 1:4: 'having escaped the corruption that is in the world', is not a nature comparable to anything we call 'nature' in this world. As the glorified body of our Lord is not subject to the laws of physics, chemistry, or biology (in spite of Luke 24:42), in a similar way, our bodies, after they have been 'fashioned like unto his glorious body' (Phil. 3:21), will no longer obey the laws of this present nature. We can neither say how the identity of this present body with the resurrected body is to be understood, nor can we know what the future body (which will no longer belong to the realm of nature) will be like. The church cannot, therefore, form any dogma beyond the fact of the resurrection, as it is expressed in the Creeds. As the resurrection of the body and the Real Presence of the true body

[47]The most important writings are: Athenagoras, *On the Resurrection of the Dead* (shortly after AD 177), MPG 6; Tertullian, *De carnis resurrectione* (AD 208), MPL 2 (CSEL 47).

and blood of Christ in the Lord's Supper are beyond all human imagination, so we cannot know what the relationship may be between our participation in the body and blood of Christ and our resurrection.

What we can and must say is this: As the final absolution in the Last Judgment is anticipated in the absolution, and as our death and resurrection are anticipated in Baptism, so also an eschatological gift is received even now in the Lord's Supper.[48] All of these gifts belong together. They are various aspects of one and the same salvation, which is meant for the whole man, soul and body. For, according to the anthropology of the Bible and of Luther, man does not **consist** of soul and body; he **is** soul and body. He is flesh also in the natural life of his mind and soul. Consequently, there is no redemption of the soul without redemption of the body. Each of the means of grace is meant by God to save the whole man. Therefore, it would be quite wrong to deny that the Lord's Supper has a meaning also for our mortal bodies. This is the profound insight into the mystery of God's saving grace that Luther expressed in the simple words of his *Catechism*: 'Where there is forgiveness of sins, there is also life and salvation'.

(4) *'Sanctorum Communio'*

Among the many names given to the *sacramentum sacramentorum*, none seems to be more popular with English-speaking Christendom than Holy Communion.[49] It expresses the profound interpretation of the Lord's Supper that St Paul has given in 1 Cor. 10.[50] We have seen that verses 16 and 17 can have no other meaning than that the **drinking** of the blessed cup and the **eating** of the broken bread are the 'communion of the blood of Christ' (*koinōnia tou haimatos,* Vulgate: *communicatio sanguinis Christi*) and the 'communion of the body of Christ' (*koinōnia tou sōmatos,*

---

[48]The question may be raised whether it would not be better if the old Augustinian concept of a sacrament and the definitions based on it were replaced by the view that a sacrament is an action instituted by Christ in which we receive even now, under earthly signs or actions, the gifts of our future salvation. We should at least interpret the customary 'heavenly gifts' in a strictly eschatological sense. In the sacrament the future becomes present without ceasing to be future.

[49]For the following, see also Herman A. Preus, *The Communion of Saints* (1948), 110-127.

[50]See above, 295 ff.

Vulgate: *participatio corporis*).[51] All attempts to make either the 'breaking' or the 'blessing' (that is, the action instead of the partaking of the elements) the means of communion have failed. Nor is it possible to regard faith as the means of establishing the communion with or participation of the body and blood. Paul does not speak of this. The point he makes is, as the following words on the sacrificial meals of the Jews and Gentiles prove, that the eating and drinking establishes what he calls 'communion of the blood', 'communion of the body'. Verse 17 would lose its meaning if the consecrated bread were not the body: 'Because there is one bread, we who are many are one body, for we all partake of the one bread' (RSV). Because the bread is the body, we who partake of this body are the 'body of Christ'. Paul can also say: 'We, being many, are one body in Christ' (Rom 12:5). There is obviously a distinction between the 'body of Christ' that we receive in the Sacrament, and the 'Body of Christ' that we are who partake of that sacramental body.

The church later distinguished between them as the *corpus Christi sacramentale* and the *corpus Christi mysticum*.[52] Zwingli and modern theologians have tried to understand the Pauline passages as referring to the *corpus mysticum*. Starting from this usage of the word 'body', they arrived at the conclusion that 'body' is used figuratively also in the case of the body in the Sacrament. Pope Pius XII in his encyclical *Mystici corporis* settled an old controversy among Catholic theologians concerning the question whether calling the Church the 'body of Christ' is figurative speech or not. The decision was in favour of those who regard it as a simile, suggesting that the Church is a living organism on earth. Lutheran theology has to uphold the realistic understanding of both. As the consecrated bread **is** the body of Christ, so the Church **is** the Body of Christ. We have to distinguish, of course, between these two realities. The sacramental body is a reality in the sense of our doctrine on the Real Presence. The mystical Body is also a reality, though on another level. As the Church **is** the people of God, so she **is** the Body of Christ. We are not only compared to members of Christ, we **are** — and even our bodies (1 Cor. 6:15) **are** — members of Christ. All these expressions about the Church as the Body, Christ as the head, Christ

[51] We do not know why in this passage the cup precedes the bread. In *Didachē 9* the eucharistic prayer 'concerning the cup' also precedes the prayer 'concerning the broken bread'. In 1 Cor. 10 the reason may be that St Paul in v 17 draws a conclusion from the 'one bread'.

[52] The Greek Fathers sometimes use the term 'mystical body' for 'sacramental body'.

as the bridegroom and the Church as the bride (Eph. 5:25 ff ; Rev. 19:7 ff; 22:17; compare the parables of Jesus in Matt. 25:10 and Mark 2:19, and the book of Hosea) are more than mere imagery; they point to supernatural realities. We call God 'Father' not because we compare him to an earthly father. The relationship between the eternal Father and the eternal Son is, rather, the prototype of the relationship between the earthly father and his son (Eph. 3:15). No human reason is able to fathom the depth of the idea that the Church is the Body of Christ. It is pure rationalism if we understand it in the sense of human sociology, which compares human society to a 'body' of men, and understands the Church as a living organism, as other societies can be understood as organisms.

The actual relationship between the mystical and the sacramental body of Christ no one is able to define. The Church, as the mystical Body (or, as our Lutheran Fathers sometimes put it, the spiritual body) of Christ, is constituted by the means of grace. Here, too, the rule applies that one and the same grace is given through each of the means of grace. 'For by one Spirit we were all baptized into one body . . . and all were made to **drink** of one Spirit' (1 Cor. 12:13 RSV). The unity of the Church, and the communion existing between her members, is created by all these means working together: 'There is one **body** and one **Spirit**, just as you were **called** to the one hope . . . one Lord, one faith, one **baptism** . . .' (Eph. 4:4,5 RSV.). We are **called** through the Gospel into the unity of the mystical Body of Christ; we are **baptized** into that body and made members thereof; and we are kept in the unity of that body through the participation of the **sacramental body and blood** of Christ, for the Sacrament of the Altar has always rightly been regarded as the great Sacrament of the unity of the Church.

Maybe the Pauline idea of the Church as the Body of Christ was first conceived by the apostle at the Table of the Lord. At any rate, when the churches of the New Testament gathered around the Table of the Lord and received his true body and blood, they knew that they were one in Christ and with Christ, that they were his Body, bound together by a fellowship that did not exist otherwise. Each local church was God's people, Christ's Body in that particular place. The bond of the Spirit, of the *agapē*, the foremost gift of the Spirit, the unity of the one Body of Christ, kept them together in the oneness of the *una sancta ecclesia*, even if these local churches did not know one another. This is the Church of the New Testament. This is the Church we believe to be a great reality in the world, although our eyes cannot see it. For as the body of Christ in the Sacrament is hidden to our eyes, so the mystical body is hidden to any earthly eye: '*Abscondita est ecclesia, latent sancti*', as Luther puts it.[53] And yet, in both cases, what is hidden to our perception is a great reality: This **is** my body. As the Church is not a *civitas Platonica*, but a great reality in this world — far more real than all other societies because it is eternal — so the body of Christ that we believe to be in the Sacrament is a reality, the real body of Christ. These realities condition each other. No one can understand what the Church is, if he does not understand what the Sacrament of the Altar is. It is not accidental that the decay of the Sacrament during the last centuries has led to a decay of the understanding of the Church. At the moment when the Real Presence of the body and blood of Christ in the Sacrament was no longer understood, the Church was regarded as a human society, one of the many religious societies in the world, be it the nation in its religious aspect, be it a society of pious individuals who formed a fellowship for mutual religious edification. Thus, the decay of the Sacrament in the modern world was bound to end in a decay of the Church. And any rediscovery of the Church will begin with a rediscovery of the Sacrament of the Altar.

The connection that exists between the sacramental and mystical body of Christ, between the *koinōnia* of the body and blood of Christ, and the *koinōnia* that exists within the mystical Body of Christ, is clearly expressed in 1 Cor. 10:16, 17. This scriptural truth has found an expression also in the Third Article of the Apostles' Creed:

> *Credo in Spiritum Sanctum, sanctam ecclesiam catholicam, sanctorum communionem, remissionem peccatorum, carnis resurrectionem, et vitam aeternam.*

Here we find a description of the grace that is given to us with the Holy Spirit through the means of grace, through the Gospel, through Baptism and the Sacrament of the Altar: forgiveness of sins, followed by 'life and salvation', namely, the resurrection of the flesh and life eternal. No one can read the Third Article without thinking of the Sacraments. They are not directly mentioned, as the Nicene Creed mentions 'one baptism for the remission of sins', but they are implied in the words of the Western Creeds.

---

[53] *De servo arbitrio*, WA 18, 652, 23 ; see the *Apology*, Articles 7,8, paragraphs 5, 12, 29 (Trigl. 226 ff), where it is made clear the the Church as the Body of Christ is hidden in this world.

An old problem is presented by the words *sanctorum communionem*, which are a late addition to the Creed, first found in Gaul (Faustus of Reji, fifth century) and in the Mozarabic liturgy.[54] However, since the formula is already found in an exposition of the Symbol by Niceta of Remesiana in Dacia about AD 400, it is likely that it is of Oriental origin, though the Nicene Creed does not contain a corresponding passage. The Latin text is ambiguous and can mean either 'communion of holy things (*sancta*)' or 'communion of holy persons (*sancti*)'. Both interpretations occur in the early centuries of the formula, although the understanding as 'communion of saints' prevailed and became the normative understanding in the Middle Ages and in the Reformation. 'Communion of saints' was, thus, understood as an explanation of 'holy catholic church'; this cannot be correct since the Latin Creed in contradistinction to Eastern creeds like the present form of the Nicene Creed ('God of God, Light of Light, very God of very God'), does not use repetitions or explanations, but introduces a new fact in each clause.

There can hardly be any doubt that the Greek form was *tōn hagiōn koinōnia*, which would mean the *koinōnia* or *metalēpsis* (participation) of the *hagia* (the holy things). *'Ta hagia tois hagiois'* (*sancta sanctis*, 'the holy things [the body and blood of the Lord] to the saints') was an exclamation of the Greek liturgies, still in use today. It is a warning against participation in the body and blood of Christ on the part of unholy people, people who do not belong to the church (excommunicated sinners, schismatics, heretics), the fitting answer of the congregation being: 'One is holy, one is Lord, Jesus Christ to the glory of God the Father'. To confess *sanctorum communionem* in this sense would mean to confess belief in the Real Presence, in the participation of the body and blood in Holy Communion.

---

[54]The question has been thoroughly discussed by F. Kattenbusch in his great book *Das apostolische Symbol* (2 volumes, 1894 and 1900), especially II, 927-50. The sources have been published by C.P. Caspari in his invaluable works: *Quellen zur Geschichte des Taufsymbols und der Glaubensregel* (Christiania [Oslo], 3 volumes, 1866-75), and *Kirchenhistorische Anekdota* (1883), 281-360. The most important texts of the Western Creeds are available in Hahn, *Bibliothek der Symbole und Glaubensregeln der Alten Kirche* (3rd edition, 1897). For brief information see *Bekenntnisschriften der Evangelisch-Lutherischen Kirche,* Göttingen Edition, Introduction to the Apostles' Creed. The latest and most illuminating discussion of the whole problem is to be found in Werner Elert, *Abendmahl und Kirchengemeinschaft in der alten Kirche hauptsächlich des Ostens* (1934). For Luther's doctrine on the Communion of Saints see: Paul Althaus, *Communio Sanctorum* (1929), and Herman A. Preus, *The Communion of Saints* (1948).

It may seem surprising that there is even the possibility of an ambiguity in the Creed. Should not the church know exactly what she believes and confesses? On closer examination, however, the seeming ambiguity proves to be something more than a regrettable lack of clarity. We confess a fact that exists within the holy catholic church: the existence of a *'koinōnia'*, a communion, which according to St Paul (1 Cor. 10:16, 17) is at the same time participation in the body and blood of Christ and membership in Christ's mystical body.[55] In eating the sacramental body we are members of the mystical Body, one with Christ (*syssōmos*), as Chrysostom puts it in the famous words that repeat the old imagery found in the *Didache* of the second century, and which are quoted time and again by the medieval schoolmen and the Reformers (especially by Luther in his sermons on the Sacrament of the Altar[56]):

> What is the bread? The body of Christ. And what do they become who partake of it? The body of Christ: not many bodies, but one body. For as the bread consisting of many grains is made one, so that the grains nowhere appear; they exist indeed, but their difference is not seen by reason of their conjunction; so we are conjoined both with each other and with Christ: there being not one body for thee, and another for thy neighbour to be nourished by, but the very same for all. . . Now if we are all nourished by the same and all become the same, why do we not also show forth the same love?. . . For this was the old way too in the time of our forefathers: 'for the multitude of them that believed', says the text, 'were of one heart and soul' (Acts 4:32). Not so now, however, but altogether the reverse. Many and various are the contests betwixt all, and worse than wild beasts are we affected towards each other's members.[57]

From such quotations it becomes evident that the two possible translations of *sanctorum communio* belong together, and that,

———

[55]W. Elert, *op. cit.,* 18 ff shows on the basis of rich patristic material that *koinōnia* ('communion') and *metalēpsis* ('participation') were used as synonyms. Today, *koinōnia and metalēpsis* are still among the many names given by the Eastern Orthodox church to the Sacrament of the Altar. The most elaborate exposition of 1 Cor.10:16 f is given by Chrysostom, *Hom. in 1 Cor. ad 10:16 f* (XXIV, 3 ff.; MPG 61, 199 f). The passage is examined by Elert, *op. cit.,* 27. Chrysostom feels that *koinōnia* is stronger than *metalēpsis*. Commenting on the words 'the bread which we break, is it not the communion of the body of Christ?', he asks: 'Why did he not say participation (*metalēpsis*)? Because he intended to express something more and point out how close the union (*henōsis*) was: we communicate not only by participating and partaking, but also by being united. For as that body is united with Christ, so we are also united with him by this bread' (translation from *Nicene and Post-Nicene Fathers*, ed. Ph. Schaff, XII (1889), 139 f). Contradicting Elert, we would say that, though he is right in assuming that the words are interchangeable, *koinōnia* has that stronger meaning in the New Testament (Acts 2:42; Gal. 2:9; 1 John 1:3, 7; and even Hebrews 13:16).

[56]See above, 88.

[57]*Hom. in 1 Cor. ad 10:17* (XXIV, 4: MPG 61, 200; *Nicene and Post-Nicene Fathers,* XII, 140).

therefore, the seeming ambiguity is only an expression of the mysterious fact that the partaking of the Sacrament constitutes the fellowship of the believers.

Here lies the basic reason why church fellowship has been altar-fellowship, and vice versa, ever since New Testament times. The oldest traces of Christian liturgy in the New Testament prove that even at the time of the apostles the 'holy kiss', the kiss of brotherly love (*agapē*) and peace (*pax*), was given at the beginning of the Eucharist (in the Eastern church it is still given before the Credo) or the Communion (in the Latin church).[58] Whenever we find the exhortation in the New Testament: 'Greet one another with a holy kiss' (1 Cor. 16:20; 2 Cor. 13:12; Rom. 16:16; 1 Thess. 5:26; 1 Peter 5:14), this indicates that the reading of an apostolic epistle (otherwise, a sermon) was followed by the celebration of the Lord's Supper. The greetings attached to such passages testify to the fellowship that tied the local church to churches elsewhere and to the entire 'brotherhood throughout the world' (1 Peter 5:9). Thus, Holy Communion becomes the great Sacrament of the true unity of the Church. To believe in the Real Presence implies belief in the communion of saints as a reality existing within the Church.

Like the body and blood of Christ, the communion of saints, too, is an object of faith. Even Chrysostom had to admonish his people to live according to the example of the first church, in which the true communion, the true love of Christ, kept the church together. But, obviously, the church of the New Testament was confronted with the same problem, as is indicated by the frank statements in Acts on the situation in the first church of Jerusalem (5:1 ff; 6:1 ff) and the continuous exhortations of Paul and John, to say nothing of the serious admonitions of the exalted Lord in Revelation 2 and 3. As the body of the Lord in the Sacrament is an object of belief and not of perception, so the communion of saints that exists within the church, and even the Church of which the Creed speaks, cannot be perceived but only believed.

This is all the more true since the *koinōnia* in the New Testament sense is never merely a communion among men. As this *koinōnia* is

---

[58]It is probably this custom that caused the rumours of incest committed in the secret services of the Christians (*Oidipodeioi mixeis*) which played such a great role in the early persecutions and in the Christian apologies. The custom, still preserved even in some Lutheran churches, that men and women have separate seats in the church, originated in the practice of the '*pax*' being given by men to men and by women to women.

the communion of the body of Christ in the twofold sense that we have dealt with, it is also communion with the Triune God, as St John says: 'That which we have seen and heard we proclaim also to you, so that you may have **fellowship** (*koinōnian*) with us; and our **fellowship** (*koinōnia*) is with the Father and with his Son Jesus Christ' (1 John 1:3 RSV), and as St Paul in his Trinitarian greeting (2 Cor. 13:14) speaks of 'the grace of the Lord Jesus Christ and the love of God, and the **communion** of the Holy Ghost'. Again, we find here that the same grace given through the Real Presence of the body of Christ is given by the Holy Spirit, by the whole Trinity. *Opera Trinitatis ad extra sunt indivisa.* As the works of the blessed Trinity are indivisible and inseparable, so the means of grace belong together, each of them giving one and the same grace. Thus, the communion of saints is an unearthly reality. It extends from this world into the world to come, from the *koinōnia* that connects Christians with one another and with the persons of the Trinity to the *koinōnia* that exists within the Triune God between the Father, the Son, and the Holy Spirit.

(5) 'Come, Lord Jesus!'

All we have said about the meaning of the Real Presence finds its culmination in the eschatological character of the Lord's Supper. 'With desire I have desired to eat this passover with you before I suffer: For I say unto you, I will not any more eat thereof, **until it be fulfilled in the kingdom of God'**. These words immediately precede the institution of the Sacrament in the narrative of St Luke (22:15,16). According to Mark and Matthew, the outlook into the eschatological future follows the institution: 'Verily I say unto you, I will drink no more of the fruit of the vine, **until that day** that I drink it new in the **kingdom of God'** (Mark 14:25 and Matt. 26:29). St Paul concludes his narrative of the institution with the words which we do not know whether he formulated himself or whether they belong to the tradition that he 'received' and faithfully 'handed on' to the church of Corinth and to all his congregations: 'As often as ye eat this bread, and drink this cup, ye do shew the Lord's death till he come' (1 Cor. 11:26).[59] As the Sacrament of the Altar looks back to the Last Supper, so it looks forward to the Messianic meal in heaven, the

---

[59]In some Eastern liturgies (such as that of St Basil, see Brightman, *Liturgies Eastern and Western,* 328) this verse is treated as a statement by Jesus belonging to the Words of Institution.

wedding-feast of the future, when Christ as bridegroom and the Church as his bride will be united at the 'marriage supper of the Lamb' (cf Rev. 19:9 and 19:7; 3:20 and the parables of Jesus in Matt. 22:2 ff; 25:1 ff; also Mark 2:19 and Hosea 2:21). The Lord's Supper is, at the same time, a feast of remembrance and a feast of hope — hope in the deeper sense of the New Testament, hope for the advent of Christ in glory. In celebrating this Sacrament, the Church shows forth, proclaims, the death of the Lord 'till he come'. That is, the death of our Lord and his advent in glory belong together. This Sacrament, therefore, is the remembrance of the terrific hour when the Lamb of God was slain, and at the same time it is the joyful looking forward to the day when our redemption will be accomplished at the Supper of the Lamb.

Often the question has been asked how it was possible that the Early Church survived what for many Christians must have been dreadful disappointments. The apostles had to admonish and comfort those who could not understand why the *parousia*, the advent of the Lord, was delayed: 'Where is the promise of his coming? for since the fathers fell asleep, all things continue as they were from the beginning of the creation' (2 Peter 3:4). If this question was asked even at that time, what should we answer to the world today 'that asketh a reason of the hope' that belongs to the very nature of the Christian faith? We may be quite sure that no answer we can give will ever be accepted as satisfactory. The world simply will not and cannot understand that such a hope for the advent of Christ can remain alive, accompanying the church through the centuries of history.

This can be understood in the church only, in the church which gathers around the Lord's Table. Just as the Sacrament of the Altar bridges over the centuries of the past and makes the death of Christ, that unique historical event, a very present reality, so the Second Advent of Christ is anticipated in the Sacrament. One of the oldest liturgical formulas has been preserved, in the Aramaic language of the earliest days of the church, in the *maranatha* of 1 Cor. 16:22[60] and *Didachē* 10:11: 'Our Lord, come!' We find this oldest eucharistic

---

[60] H. Lietzmann, *Messe und Herrenmahl* (1926), 229, has rightly observed that we find the first traces of a eucharistic liturgy in 1 Cor. 16:20 ff: 'Greet ye one another with an holy kiss . . . If any man love not the Lord . . . let him be anathema. Maranatha. The grace of our Lord Jesus Christ be with you'. Here we find elements of the later liturgies: the exhortation to give the ***kiss*** of brotherly love (*agapē* in the Greek liturgies before the Creed at the beginning of the mass of the faithful, *pax* in the Latin mass before

prayer, which is also the oldest invocation of our Lord in prayer, at the conclusion of Revelation in the Greek form: 'Come, Lord Jesus!' The fact that St Paul and even churches of the second century preserved it in Aramaic (like the *abba* in Mark 14:36; Rom. 8:15; Gal. 4:6) shows how important it must have been. It obviously has a twofold meaning: the church prays for the advent of her Lord in glory; at the same time she prays for his presence in the Sacrament. As he came to his disciples at Easter on the first day of the week, and as he came to them again 'after eight days', so each Sunday is the 'Lord's Day', as the day of the Messiah is called in the Old Testament (Amos 5:18). Christ's final advent (*parousia*) is anticipated in the celebration of his Sacrament, because he really comes to his Church. The petition 'Come, Lord Jesus!' is already fulfilled in his Real Presence in the Sacrament. This coming of the Lord in the Real Presence makes the Lord's Day a day of unspeakable joy, a day of praise and thanksgiving. It makes the Eucharist not only an anticipation of the blessed future, but also a participation in the eternal worship in heaven, which St John saw in the great vision he had at Patmos just

---

communion); the ***anathema***, which excludes those who cannot be admitted because they destroy the unity of the Church; the ***invocation*** of the Lord, which asks for his coming; and the ***salutation***. *Pax* and *anathema* have their parallels in Rom. 16:16 f, where mention is made, not of the schismatics, people who destroy the unity by sinning against love, but of heretics who destroy the teaching of the Gospel. The invocation and the salutation are to be found in Rev. 22:20 f in almost the same words: 'Come, Lord Jesus! The grace of the Lord Jesus be with all the saints' (RSV). The salutation in its full trinitarian form (as in 2 Cor. 13:14) still introduces the dialogue before the Preface in the Eastern masses today, while the Latin liturgy has replaced it by the simple *Dominus vobiscum*. The *anathema* and the *maranatha* we find also in the remnants of the liturgy preserved in *Didachē* 10:6· 'If any is holy, let him come: if any is not holy, let him repent. Maranatha'. The warning against unworthy communion contained in the *anathema* has the form '*Ta hagia tois hagiois*' in the Greek liturgies. The original meaning of *maranatha* was later forgotten. Since the Middle Ages it has been understood as a curse, belonging together with *anathema*. An old prayer of the Mozarabic liturgy ('*Adesto, adesto, Jesu . . .*'), which we have already mentioned (above, 299) seems to point back to the old *maranatha*. Linguistically it is possible to read *maranatha*, which would mean, 'Our Lord is coming' (present tense instead of imperative), but *marana tha* 'Our Lord, come' (*marana* is *status emphaticus* of *maran*, and *tha* is imperative) is far more likely. The question is of importance, because this invocation at the Lord's Supper seems to be the beginning of the invocation of Jesus as Lord, and that means God, in the worship of the Church. *Mar*, to be sure, does not have quite that full meaning, but as soon as it was translated into Greek with *Kyrios* the full divinity of Christ found an adequate expression. *Kyrios* is the translation in the LXX of *Yahweh*, the holy name of God, as the frequent 'I am' in the sayings of Jesus in St John also hints at the 'I am', the interpretation of *Yahweh* (Exod. 3:14). *Kyrios* is 'God in His revelation', as it is also used in the Hellenistic religions and in the cult of *Kyrios Kaisar*.

at the time when the churches of Asia assembled for their divine service (Rev. 1:10; 4:1 ff). This is the reason why the *Sanctus*, the hymn which the seraphim and all the heavenly hosts (Isa. 6:3; Rev. 4:8) sing in the presence of God (the *epinikion*, the hymn of victory, as it is called in old Greek liturgies) belongs to the eucharistic liturgy together with the *Benedictus*: 'Blessed is he who comes in the name of the Lord. Hosanna in the highest'. From the Early Church to the Fathers of the Lutheran church, a cloud of witnesses testifies to the truth that the Lord's Supper is 'heaven on earth'.[61]

It is this Sacrament that made it possible for the church to survive what in the eyes of the world must have been the greatest disappointment, the delay of his *parousia*. This Sacrament has accompanied the Church throughout the centuries, and will accompany her to the end of the world, even to the Last Day when he will come again in glory to judge the living and the dead. This Sacrament is *cibus viatorum*, food for the wayfarers, as our medieval Fathers called it. This blessed bread is eaten by the Church on her way from this world to the world to come. The flesh of the true Lamb of God is eaten, as the first Passover lamb was eaten by the people of God of old: 'Thus shall ye eat it; with your loins girded, your shoes on your feet, and your staff in your hand; and ye shall eat it in haste' (Exod. 12:11). This blessed bread is the manna, the life-giving bread from heaven. As Israel was miraculously sustained in the desert by the spiritual food of the manna and the spiritual drink of the water from the rock, so the Church, on her way from 'Egypt', the old aeon of sin and death, to the 'promised land' of the new aeon of eternal life, is sustained in the desolate desert of this world by the spiritual food and drink of the true body and blood of him who is at the same time the Passover Lamb of the New Covenant and the Bread of Life. This understanding of the Lord's Supper we find in 1 Cor. 10:1 ff and John 6. It also underlies the Epistle to the Hebrews, where the Church is described as the wandering people of God on its way from this world of suffering and death to the abiding city of God (13:14),

[61]'Heaven on earth' is the Eucharist according to the Eastern church. Thus, Sergius Bulgakow could describe the Eastern liturgy under the title '*Le ciel sur la terre*'. This calls to mind the legend of the origin of the Church in Russia, which tells how Wladimir, Prince of Kiev, sent messengers to the various religions of the East. When they attended the liturgy at the Hagia Sophia in Constantinople 'they did not know whether they were on earth or in heaven'. This, then, decided the question which religion Russia should accept. From the devotional literature of the Lutheran church, we quote from a prayer by Scriver: '*Dass dein Abendmahl mein Himmel auf Erden werde*'.

whence 'we await a Saviour, the Lord Jesus Christ, who will change our lowly body to be like his glorious body' (Phil. 3:20, 21 RSV). Then, when we shall have reached the end of our pilgrimage, we shall no longer need the Sacrament, and the Lord's Supper will be replaced by 'the Supper of the Lamb'.

Again it must be said that the Sacrament of the Altar, thus understood, is closely connected with Baptism, as Paul puts them together in 1 Cor. 10. In Baptism, also, the future is anticipated, our death and our resurrection (Rom. 6:3 ff). Both of these Sacraments must be accompanied by the preaching of the Word of God. Without that constant explanation through the preaching of the Gospel, they would be meaningless rites. Again we must state that one and the same grace is given by each of these means of grace, and yet God works in each of them in different ways. We are not allowed to emphasize one of them at the expense of the other. Nor are we allowed to neglect the spiritual meaning which each of them has. It was a great loss when during the last centuries the Lutheran church more or less neglected the Sacrament of the Altar. This failure to realize the great gift of this Sacrament has impaired the whole life of our church, the life of our congregations, as well as the spiritual life of individuals. It has also deprived the sermon of much of the power that is inherent in the proclamation of the true Gospel.

Conclusion

'This Sacrament is the Gospel.' This was Luther's great discovery. It was this insight that caused him to fight for the Sacrament of the Altar, when it was attacked, with the same seriousness with which he had to wage his great war for the Gospel. In both cases he was not the aggressor. God had led him into the fight 'like a horse whose eyes have been blinded', as he himself put it. He had to fight for the holy Gospel of the *sola gratia* and *sola fide*, and he had to fight for the Sacrament.

It is noteworthy that his two-front war against Rome and against the enthusiasts and Zwingli was actually one war. On either side, the *sola fide* was at stake, the proper distinction between Law and Gospel, on which the right understanding of God's Word depends and, hence, the preaching of the true Gospel and the existence of the Church. On either side, the question of the Sacrament was an issue of no lesser importance. For on both sides the Sacrament of the Altar was being destroyed. Rome, it is true, kept the Real Presence, though in the philosophical garment of transubstantiation. But, by making the Sacrament of Christ a sacrifice, the Roman church could not avoid placing the human priest side by side with the High Priest, Christ. Zwingli rejected the sacrificial character of the Lord's Supper. But, by rejecting also the Real Presence, he again made the Sacrament a human action, a feast of remembrance and a mere sign of grace. Thus, the two fights belong together.

It is impossible to accept Luther's attitude toward Rome and to reject his attitude toward Zwingli. The confessor of Worms is also the confessor of Marburg. In both cases he confessed the Gospel which comes to us in the Word and in the Sacrament. It is really true that the Sacrament is the Gospel, and the Gospel is the Sacrament. Even modern Christians that cannot understand the Sacrament will admit that at least for Luther it was so. They admit that for Luther the Real Presence meant that the Incarnation was more than a historical fact of the past. It was a reality. Here is God who became man; here is Christ in his divinity and humanity. Here is the true body and blood of the Lamb of God, given for you, present with you. Here forgiveness of sins is a reality — and, with it, life and salvation. This Sacrament is the Gospel.

This was the understanding of the Sacrament and the Real Presence for Luther and for the Lutheran Confessions. Can and will the church that calls itself Lutheran retain it — or, where it has been lost, try to regain it? This would be impossible if the doctrine of the Real Presence were only a human theory that has appeared time and again in various forms in the history of the church, perhaps in an especially-impressive form in the Lutheran Reformation. No human authority, no respect for a great Christian and doctor of the church, would be sufficient reason for accepting the Lutheran doctrine on the Sacrament. The only reason could be its strictly scriptural character. On the other hand, no objection that might be raised by our human reason against a doctrine of Scripture could justify its rejection. It is true, the doctrine of the Real Presence, of our eating and drinking the true body and blood of Christ, is still, more than any other doctrine of the church, 'unto the Jews a stumblingblock and unto the Greeks foolishness'. Luther was right when he maintained that Christ, though hidden (*occultus*) in all places where he reveals himself, is most hidden (*occultissimus*) in this Sacrament. And yet, thus far, no one has been able to remove the Real Presence from the New Testament.

We have tried on the preceding pages to show how deeply it is rooted in the Scriptures. All the great facts and thoughts connected with the Lord's Supper, such as remembrance, remission of sins, *sanctorum communio*, 'Come, Lord Jesus!', presuppose this Presence. The Words of Institution and Paul's commentary teach it clearly. Either Jesus meant what he said at the Last Supper, or he left to his disciples and to the church of all ages a puzzle which no one has ever been able, or ever will be able, to solve. Either we accept Paul's commentary or we reject it, and with it the authority of the New Testament. The acceptance or rejection of the Real Presence means, as Luther clearly saw, the acceptance or rejection of God's Word.

Just as the church stands or falls with the Gospel, so she stands or falls with the Sacrament of the Altar. For the Sacrament is the Gospel. This is the conviction, not only of Luther, but of the New Testament: 'For as often as ye **eat** this bread, and **drink** this cup, ye do **shew the Lord's death till he come**'.

APPENDIX I

What is the Sacrament of the Altar?

[This article was prepared for the first issue of the *Lutheran Theological Journal* (August 1967), the theological journal of the newly-formed Lutheran Church of Australia following the union of the ELCA and the UELCA on Reformation Day 1966.]

1

The Lutheran Church of Australia accepts unanimously and wholeheartedly the doctrine of the Lutheran Confessions on the Lord's Supper. It confesses unambiguously, in the sense in which Luther understood the words, concerning the Sacrament of the Altar:

> It is the true body and blood of our Lord Jesus Christ under the bread and wine, given to us Christians to eat and to drink, instituted by Christ Himself.

It is not conservatism and theological traditionalism which causes us to take this stand. We are fully aware of the problems, exegetical and historical, dogmatical and ecclesiastical, implied in such a confession in our time. We have learned this consensus not only as a great inheritance of our history, but as a gift of divine grace.

We are a small church, a minority within a small nation at the fringe of the vast world of the non-Christian nations of Asia. We have grown together out of many traditions. Our early fathers came from Prussia to find a country where they were able to live without the interference by the State, according to the dictates of their conscience, and to build up the Lutheran church. They were later joined by immigrants who were seeking a new home for different reasons, but who had a Lutheran background in Germany or Scandinavia. When our church had become English-speaking, Christians who came from other denominations joined us. Our first pastors came from Prussia. They were joined by men who had been trained at great mission centres such as Hermannsburg, Basle, and Neuendettelsau. Others came from America, partly after years of missionary service in India. The great conservative synods of the American Middle West also exercised a strong influence, such as Missouri, Iowa, and Ohio. This variety of backgrounds and theological traditions explains why deep theological differences have often divided us. These differences, however, have not destroyed our loyalty to the Lutheran doctrine of the Sacrament.

Luther's simple, and (as we believe) biblical, doctrine on the Sacrament of the Altar in the words of the *Small Catechism*, as our children learned them and as they even belonged to the act of confession with which many of our synods were opened, has proved to be one of the great unifying factors in our history, as also men who came from other ecclesiastical traditions (among them, Reformed pastors) have accepted it. The common understanding of the Sacrament and its meaning for the church has also been a strong bond of spiritual unity with our brethren in the faith abroad. In our long striving for true unity we have learnt to understand what the Seventh Article of the *Augsburg Confession* teaches about what is sufficient and necessary for the true unity of the church, namely, that

> the Gospel be preached with great unanimity in its purity and that the sacraments be administered in accordance with the divine word.[1]

If anywhere in the world this great doctrine has been tried out, then it was in Australia. It has proved to be the only means of establishing true unity among Christians and of preserving the Gospel and the sacraments of Christ.

2

Now we are facing the perturbing experience that we are more and more isolated from the rest of the Lutheran world, not on account of what we are doing or not doing, but by the fact that the Sacrament of the Altar, as it has been celebrated in our churches, is vanishing in many parts of the Lutheran world, and with it the unity of the Church which it has helped to preserve. The Lutheran sacrament is being replaced on the one hand by semi-Catholic masses or by ecumenical mystery-rites, which neither Rome nor the Christian East would recognize, and by Reformed communion rites on the other. There are Lutheran churches in America where the Sunday sermon is no longer fol-

---

[1]This is the correct translation of the German text, which was not fully understood by the translator in the *Book of Concord* (ed. Tappert), 32, who did not understand the word *einträchtiglich* which is rendered in the Latin text by *magno consensu.*

lowed (as is fitting), but replaced, by a High Church ceremony which is supposed to be the sacrament proper (as it is devised by the professional liturgiologists who watch over their laws like their predecessors, Matt. 23:5). While the Roman mass is today of an almost puritanical simplicity, the liturgical tinsel of ages past finds a place in Lutheran churches. But the clouds of incense which prevent us from seeing exactly what is going on at the altar cannot hide the fact that the nature of the Sacrament has changed. If we ask these people what the Sacrament of the Altar is, we no longer get the simple answer of Luther's *Catechism*, but a long discourse on the representation of the sacrifice of Christ and on our participation in this sacrifice as the true nature of this Sacrament. If we ask the question whether the bread is the body and the wine is the blood, we receive various answers. Some would say Yes; others would say 'Yes, *but*', which is the fashionable substitute for No, introduced by Karl Barth. In any case they would find the answer of the Catechism too simple, insufficient, and in need of a reinterpretation in the light of modern thought. For we are told even today by an over-enlightened Dutch Catholic professor of dogmatics: 'Every human statement, including that of a dogma, is time-conditioned. It is limited by the possibilities of language and style, by the subtleties that can or cannot be adequately expressed . . .'[2] That we have to use human language in theology is a truism; that human language should be unable to express objective truth would mean the end not only of theology, but of all science.

3

Like every great change in the history of the church, so also this one began slowly and almost imperceptibly. But now the results are conspicuous in the entire Lutheran world. When the Church of Sweden in 1922 accepted intercommunion with the Church of England, as it had been proposed by the Lambeth Conference of 1920, Söderblom had to defend this against what he called 'a narrow Lutheran institutionalism'. But the confessional protest ceased in the following years. When, some time ago, Sweden in the most solemn

———

[2]Quoted by Arnold Lunn in a letter concerning the Dutch Catechism with its ambiguous statement on the Virgin Birth. Lunn replies: 'The dogma of the virgin birth is either true or false. If true, it is as true today as when the gospels were written. It is a truth which is in no sense "time-conditioned" or "limited by the possibilities of style and language", still less by "subtleties that can or cannot be adequately expressed".' (*Herder Correspondence*, May 1967, 161).

way established intercommunion with the Church of Scotland, even Bishop Giertz, the leader of the *Kyrkliq Samlinq* had no objection. None of the Lutheran churches of Scandinavia seems to have been able and willing to maintain the basic requirements of the *Augsburg Confession* for altar- and church-fellowship. Consensus concerning the Gospel and the Sacraments is no longer required as a condition of church fellowship. The American Lutherans of Scandinavian background obviously had no objection to raise against the flagrant violation of the *Augsburg Confession* in their home churches. So the first pillar of the Lutheran church of the world collapsed. The other churches of Europe followed. The customary intercommunion between the Reformed (*Hervormde*) and the Lutheran Church in the Netherlands was justified in 1953 by an agreement which leaves the difference between the sacramental doctrines unresolved. The Lutherans 'ask' the Reformed whether they can maintain what is taught in Question 47 of the *Heidelberg Catechism* about Christ's human nature being in heaven and not on earth. The Reformed 'ask' the Lutherans whether 'an omnipresence (ubiquity) of the human nature of Christ does not actually mean an abolition of the Incarnation'. Obviously the Lutherans were not quite clear about their own doctrine, otherwise they would have answered that the 'ubiquity' is not a dogma of the Lutheran church, and that their doctrine that the body of Christ has more ways of being in one place than the local presence does not deny the reality of the Incarnation. But the level of this discussion obviously did not permit an intelligent investigation of the problems. The aim was not to solve the problem, but to have a document which could be used to justify what had been practised through ignorance for so long a time.

4

Much more serious was the attempt made in Germany in the so-called 'Arnoldshain Theses'. When in 1948 the new Evangelical Church in Germany (EKiD) was established (which comprises all territorial churches of Germany: Lutheran, Reformed, and United), the decisive hour of the churches of the Reformation in the world had struck. These are the Lutheran and the Reformed-Presbyterian churches; Anglicanism ceased to be a church of the Reformation when it *de facto* abolished the Articles of Religion, and the majority of the Protestant churches of America are only indirectly related to the Reformation or are the descendants of the Radical Reformation in Europe which could not develop in the Old World. It was German-speaking Europe, where Lutheranism and Calvinism had first met in that tragic encounter, which has proved so fateful for the history of the church.

It is understandable that, time and again, attempts have been made to overcome the great schism of the Reformation. But the theological means of the 16th and 17th centuries were insufficient for the settlement of the great controversy. And the 18th and 19th centuries could find nothing but political solutions, based on the ignorance of the churchmen and the indifference of the masses in these territorial churches. Nothing is more significant of the tragic situation than the fact that the unions which began in 1817 in Nassau, 1817 in Prussia, 1818 in the Palatinate, 1821 in Baden and Waldeck, and simultaneously, or soon after, in other territories, had a merely territorial character. Each of the newly-circumscribed States of Germany wanted to have its own church, its confessional character being merely based on the local conditions and not on a real theological consensus. Hence, in the middle of the 19th century, Germany had about seven different union churches with different theological bases, the largest being the Union Church of Prussia, which theoretically did not abolish the authority of the old confessions in the individual congregations, but *de facto* soon became the great unifying factor in Germany, especially since the majority of the universities and their theological Faculties was in the hands of the Prussian State. The Lutheran churches joined forces in 1868 by forming the General Evangelical Lutheran Conference, in close connection with Sweden and the General Council in the USA. In 1933 Hitler forced all territorial churches into the German Evangelical Church, which in 1948 transformed itself into the present EKiD after the last attempts of Lutherans in Germany to maintain their identity in a federation between a Lutheran, a Reformed, and a United church had been defeated. The new body with an ambiguous constitution (which could and can be interpreted as a federation or as a unified church) decided that a colloquy on the Lord's Supper should be held with the aim of bringing about a common statement on the Sacrament which would justify full intercommunion between all parts of the EKiD. Thus, the Arnoldshain Theses were written mainly by theologians of the United Faculties of Heidelberg and Bonn. Among them were outstanding representatives of Lutheranism within the Union, namely, Peter Brunner and Edmund Schlink (the latter, however, being more and more influenced by the ecumenical movement). Theologians from Lutheran churches, like W. Elert, declined the invitation because they knew nothing else but a formula of compromise could be the result. The author of this article refused to take part because he could not recognize the right of the EKiD to arrange an official colloquy on the Sacrament. E. Sommerlath accepted the invitation, but could not accept the result. However, for the majority of the German churches, their leaders, and their theologians, the Theses are the sufficient basis for establishing full intercommunion between all parts of the EKiD, which then would become the great union church of Germany. There is only one bishop who thus far has resisted the declaration of full intercommunion, though most of his pastors and laymen would desire it, and he himself personally would have no theological objections against it. Like all other Lutheran bishops of Germany, so also his future successor will certainly regard the Arnoldshain Theses as a sufficient basis for full intercommunion between Lutherans and Reformed, and that means the abolition of the present or former borderline between the Lutheran and the Reformed churches in one evangelical church.

5

What do the Theses of Arnoldshain teach? The main thesis which is meant to settle the old controversy is Thesis 4 which reads:

> The words which our Lord Jesus Christ speaks when He offers the bread and the cup tell us what He himself gives to all who come to this supper: He, the crucified and risen Lord, permits Himself to be taken in His body and blood given and shed for all, through His word of promise, with the bread and wine, and grants us participation, by virtue of the Holy Spirit, in the victory of His lordship, so that we, believing in His promise, may receive forgiveness of sins, life and salvation.[3]

This thesis must be read together with the rejection of certain erroneous views in Thesis 5:

> Therefore, what happens in the Lord's Supper is not adequately described,
>
> (a) when it is taught that, by means of the words of institution, bread and wine are changed into a supernatural substance, thus ceasing to be bread and wine;
>
> (b) when it is taught that a repetition of the act of salvation takes place in the Lord's Supper;
>
> (c) when it is taught that in the Lord's Supper either a natural or a supernatural 'matter' is distributed;

---

[3]We quote from the official English translation contained in *Lehrgespräch über das Heilige Abendmahl. Stimmen und Studien zu den Arnoldshainer Thesen der Kommission für das Abendmahlsgespräch der EKiD, herausgegeben von Gottfried Niemeier* (Munich, 1961), 332 ff.

(d) when it is taught that there are two parallel but separate processes, one an eating on the part of the body and the other an eating on the part of the soul;
(e) when it is taught that the eating on the part of the body as such saves us, or that participation in the body and blood of Christ is a purely mental process.

These theses contain a clear rejection of the Roman and the Zwinglian doctrines. But what about the doctrine of the Lutheran and of the Reformed churches? The Reformed have given up the idea of two parallel, but separate, processes of eating — a bodily and a spiritual one; they admit that what is given in the Lord's Supper is given **with** the bread and wine. The Lutherans have given up the doctrine that the consecrated bread **is** the body of Christ and the consecrated wine **is** the blood of Christ. The words 'through his word of promise' cannot hide the fact that the Lutheran doctrine of consecration has been abandoned. For even if by 'word of promise' the Words of Institution are meant, for Luther and the Lutheran church the Words of Institution are more than that. They are 'the Word and institution of our almighty God and Saviour, Jesus Christ, which always remain efficacious in Christendom' (*FC, Sol. Decl. VII,* 89), 'in virtue' of which (Luther in his last offer at Marburg — see below) the body and blood of Christ are present in the Sacrament. The strict denial of the gift of the Sacrament being either a natural or supernatural 'matter' shows how remote the new theory is from all previous doctrines of the Sacrament, Catholic, Lutheran, and Reformed. Even Calvin is nearer to Rome and Luther than to this new theory. If the body of Christ is not the body which was born of the Virgin Mary, which hung on the cross, was raised from the dead, and sits at the right hand of the Father, what, then, is meant by 'body' and 'blood'? In what sense are these words being used? Would it not be much more honest to replace them by other words? What is meant by the statement: Christ 'permits Himself to be taken in His body and blood . . . with the bread and wine' (German:. . . *lässt sich in seinem für uns alle in den Tod gegebenen Leib und seinem für alle vergossenen Blut durch sein verheissendes Wort mit Brot und Wein von uns nehmen* . . .)? What we receive is 'He', the person 'in His body and blood'. This is obviously a compromise between the view that the gift in the Lord's Supper is the body and blood of Christ, and the view that the gift is He Himself, His person. The Arnoldshain Theses belong together with many modern statements on the Lord's Supper which try to substitute the presence of the person for the presence of body and blood. Arnoldshain agrees substantially with the statement in the report of an American Faith and Order Conference of 1957 on 'The Table of the Lord' where we read:

> (2) Jesus Christ on the night in which he was betrayed chose bread and wine as the elements of the first Eucharist at the Last Supper. Rejecting any one-sided preoccupation with the elements in isolation, we agree that in the entire eucharist action the whole Christ is personally present as both subject and object, i.e. as the One who is at the same time the Giver and the Gift.
>
> (3) In view of our belief in Christ's active presence in the whole eucharistic action, we agree that this action is our participation in his risen life and the fulfilment of his promise to his church.
>
> (4) Christ's presence at his table follows from his promise and command. It is only in repentance and faith that the believer . . . receives the fruits of redemption, including the forgiveness of sins, justification, sanctification, newness of life and communion with his brethren . . . The Holy Communion is a means of placing us in the presence of Christ in a total way. In his Presence we are judged as well as forgiven (1 Cor. 11:17-34).[4]

If the American churches and sects which met at Oberlin had made such a statement, this might be understandable, because most of them have never taught the Real Presence of the body and blood of Christ — although it is neither understandable nor pardonable that the Anglicans and the Lutherans (American Lutheran Church, Augustana Lutheran Church, United Lutheran Church) failed to follow the example of the Quakers who did not take part in the negotiations of this Section, but later, in a statement added to the report, confessed their 'belief in the non-necessity of the outward elements of bread and wine to mediate the living presence of Christ to the believer in the act of communion with him'.[5]

But how is it to be explained that the German theologians with their thorough historical training do not understand the connection between the presence of body and blood of Christ and the presence of the whole divine-human person? Do they not know the Roman doctrine of the concomitance? Do they not know any longer the eucharistic hymns and prayers — the greatest of which are common to Catholic and Lutherans — in which the presence of body and blood is always understood as including the presence of the person? Does not at least Mozart's (since most of them are Barthians, Mozart must belong to their saints) *Ave Verum* ring in their ears: *Ave verum*

[4] *The Nature of the Unity We Seek.* Official Report of the North American Conference on Faith and Order, Sept. 1957, Oberlin, Ohio (ed. by P. S. Minear, 1958), 199, 205; the quotation from p 202.

[5] *Ibid.*, 205.

corpus natum / ex Maria Virgine / Vere passum, immolatum in cruce pro homine / . . . O Jesu dulcis / O Jesu pie / Fili Patris et Mariae? Or do we no longer remember the German version of Aquinas's *Lauda Sion salvatorem* which is to be found in every German hymnbook as *Schmücke dich, o liebe Seele*? The consequence of the Arnoldshain Theses, with their clear rejection of the old Reformed as well as of the Lutheran doctrine, would be that we should have to give up our Catechism. Wilhelm Niesel (*Lehrgespräch,* ed. Niemeier, 293) discusses the question whether the acceptance of the Theses with their rejection of the doctrine of Question 47 of the *Heidelberg Catechism* does not necessitate an alteration of this Catechism. The same has to be said concerning Luther's *Catechism*; its clear confession of the Real Presence of the true body and blood of Christ, its affirmation of the old 'Substantialism' in favour of a mere 'Personalism', its reaffirmation of the Lutheran *est* in the words 'It is the true body and blood of Christ' cannot be reconciled with Arnoldshain. Honesty would demand that we give up Luther's *Catechism*, but theologians have long ago learned to confess with the mouth what they do not believe with their heart.

What is the deepest reason for this new attempt to find a new doctrine of the Sacrament? It is not respect for the Word of God, for everybody knows that the literal understanding of 'This is my body' is the simplest way of doing justice to the text. It is not possible to deny that according to 1 Cor. 10:16, 17 the eating and drinking of bread and wine constitutes the participation of the body and blood of the Lord. It cannot be denied that 1 Cor. 11:27-29 has the same realistic meaning. One could argue: This is Paul's view, but what did Jesus mean? Can we really assume that Paul, who is so careful in rendering the genuine *paradōsis* (11:23, cf 15:1-3), should have smuggled in a different, 'Hellenistic' interpretation of the words of Jesus? Would none of his adversaries have noticed this, even if we could assume that Paul was capable of what amounts to a forgery? But Jesus as a Jew could not have meant that, we are told. Why not? In this most solemn moment he did not speak as a Jew only, but as the God-man. And if he really meant something different, what did he mean? Up to this very day no one has been able to give another explanation which would be acceptable to all New Testament scholars, to speak only of them. Even the men of Arnoldshain have not found a common explanation, for their Theses are differently understood even by their authors. As to the respect for the Word of God: Have we not in Holy

Scripture a Word of God which is not only the word of Jesus or the word of Paul or the word of another apostle, but **the** Word which may find its expression in different terminologies (1 Cor. 3:5ff; 4:1ff), but which is essentially one in the whole New Testament? But the scholars of Arnoldshain have obviously lost this Word. Let us be quite frank: behind this chaos of opinions there is not 'historical scholarship', but unbelief. In the discussion of the Theses it happened that some naive readers understood the words of Thesis 1 ('The Lord's Supper which we celebrate is based on its having been instituted and commanded by Jesus Christ') as referring to the institution at the Last Supper. They had to learn that the authors of the thesis were by no means agreed on this. Some find the roots of the Sacrament in previous meals; others regard it as instituted by the risen Lord in the earliest church. What kind of historical scholarship is this? In all churches of Christendom, in every mass, in every celebration of Holy Communion since the apostolic age, the words occur: *qui pridie quam pateretur*, 'in the night in which he was betrayed'. Must Christendom now stop saying this because German 'scholars' think that this Sacrament is an invention of the first church? But the churches will probably not be convinced that for almost 2,000 years, in the most solemn worship of the church, they have told a story which is not true, for this statement is the unanimous statement of the New Testament. This is not historical scholarship but a frivolous playing with the Word of God.

No one who knows German church life and German theology would have expected anything better. We know the tragedy of German Protestantism. There are faithful pastors; there are also professors who still take their churchly obligations seriously. There are some bishops whose eyes have not yet been blinded by the brilliant stars in their Faculties and by the fireworks of the ecumenical movement. And there are, above all, *die Stillen im Lande* who pray for the Church, and who sometimes cease to be silent and make a loud public confession. But how Luther's *Catechism* can again become the confession of the Christian people in Europe nobody can see.

6

Deeply saddened, though not surprised, by the development of the Lutheran churches of the Old World, we turn to America to experience our deepest disappointment. If we ask the great Lutheran churches of America: 'What is the Sacrament of the Altar?' we hear confused voices which are tantamount to the answer: We do not know exactly what it is, except that it is not quite what Luther believed and what our fathers have confessed it to be. We can no longer express the mystery of this Sacrament in the simple words of the *Catechism*: 'It is the true body and blood of our Lord Jesus Christ...' We have seen light, for we have revisited Marburg.

Marburg Revisited is the title of a book which appeared in 1966 at Minneapolis (Augsburg Publishing House), jointly edited by James I. McCord, President of Princeton Theological Seminary, and Paul C. Empie, Executive Director of the National Lutheran Council. It contains the official report (lectures and summary statements with some additional statements) on 'conversations between members of the Lutheran and the Reformed traditions' (tradition is the new term for what formerly was called confession) under the auspices of the 'North American Area of the World Alliance of Reformed Churches Holding the Presbyterian Order' and the USA National Committee of the Lutheran World Federation from 1962 to 1966. Churches outside these two ecumenical organizations, such as the Orthodox Presbyterian, the Christian Reformed Church, and the Lutheran Church-Missouri Synod, had been invited and took part. 'It was clear from the start that the individuals named to participate would speak for themselves, their conclusions neither necessarily representing nor binding the respective churches which appointed them' (Preface). 'During these four meetings we have examined carefully the major issues.' At some points it was 'discovered that our respective views of each other have been inherited caricatures, initially caused by misunderstanding or polemical zeal'. In other instances the differences are, in fact, complementary. Some difficulties remain, but 'we have recognized in each other's teachings a common understanding of the Gospel and have concluded that the issues which divided the two major branches of the Reformation can no longer be regarded as constituting obstacles to mutal understanding and fellowship'. This is then confirmed in the final Report to the Sponsoring Confessional Organizations (p 190) ' . . . we see no insuperable obstacles to pulpit and altar fellowship and, therefore, we recommend to our parent bodies that they encourage their constituent churches to enter into discussions looking forward to intercommunion and the fuller recognition of one another's ministries'.

Let it be understood from the outset that, whatever has to be said about this document, we regard the split between the two great churches of the Reformation as one of the major catastrophes of Christendom, in its consequences comparable only to the split between Rome and the East, and between the Orthodox and the Monophysitic churches in the Orient. For this split has been, and is still, the great obstacle which has prevented the message of the Reformation from penetrating the whole of Christendom. This split was especially fateful for America. One may well ask whether the absence of *one* great church of the Reformation has not made America the land of innumerable groups and sects in which the Gospel of Jesus Christ and the Sacraments of the New Testament were bound to be lost. And we must examine ourselves and ask whether this split has not made the Lutheran, as well as the Reformed churches in Europe and in America, the playground of an unbiblical, sectarian enthusiasm. What would Luther and Calvin say about the claim that the discussion in America has been a 'confrontation under the guidance of the Holy Spirit' and that God is praised 'for the evident working of his Spirit in our midst'? It is an unbiblical enthusiasm which speaks here, and not the Reformation, for to the Reformers the Holy Spirit was always an object of faith and not of observation. There may be, and there is, indeed, in the world an unrepentant, stubborn confessionalism. But we would not find it in a church which faithfully, and not only nominally, holds the confession of the Reformation, be it the Reformation of Wittenberg or that of Geneva, because these confessions know of the authority of the Word of God which judges us all and reveals to us all the merciful Saviour. The word 'Lutheran' does not appear in the *Book of Concord* except in a passage of the *Apology* where Melanchthon makes the complaint that the adversaries call the dear holy Gospel 'Lutheran'. The Church which we believe and confess is never our denomination, but the one Church of Christ, which is not identical with any individual denomination. Our Reformers died as excommunicated members of the Catholic church; they were not conscious of being members of a new church, although they had to organize their emergency churches. No one would deny the grave sins that have been committed in the polemics between the confessions. But it may well be asked whether they were greater than the sins which are today committed on behalf of ecumenicity: the destruction of the doctrinal substance of the Christian faith by our compromises, the misleading of Christian souls by allowing any kind of false teaching. What is worse: to fight against heresies, or to declare that there are no heresies, but only different 'traditions'?

One advantage the old Geneva had over the Geneva of today: the Fathers of the Reformed church knew the seriousness of the question: What is truth? The Lutheran Fathers were prepared to die for the doctrine they had confessed in the *Augsburg Confession*. Who would die for the Theses of Arnoldshain?

7

What we have to say by way of criticizing the new document is not directed against a serious discussion of the issues that divide our churches, nor against the attempt to find an agreement. The author of this article does not despair of the possibility of reaching unity between the separated churches of the Reformation. What we are criticizing is solely the method. In four sessions the committee was able to solve, or nearly solve, the problems of four centuries. In four sessions they covered all the issues that stood between our churches: Gospel, Confession and Scripture; Eucharist and Christology, and all the problems connected with this topic; Justification and Sanctification; Liturgy and Ethics; Law and Gospel; Creation and Redemption; the problem of the Two Kingdoms. As *donum superadditum*, we get in the last part a paper on 'Confessional Integrity and Ecumenical Dialogue' by Professor W.A. Quanbeck, who also wrote the opening chapter on 'Gospel, Confession and Scripture'. We take from this paper one example to illustrate our criticism of the method of these discussions. We read (p 186):

> . . . we can see clearly that the Nicene Creed uses the theological method and vocabulary of the fourth century to assert the truth about Jesus Christ and to reject misunderstandings of his person and mission which threatened the clarity and power of the Gospel. Those who drew up the Creed were compelled to use non-biblical language to assert the truth of the biblical message. The language of the creed is not biblical language, but that of fourth century philosophy.

This statement is crude dilettantism. The Creed of Nicaea was a liturgical formula consisting of biblical words (see 1 Cor. 8:6; Col. 1; Heb. 1; 1 Cor. 15). The Fathers of Nicaea added the famous *homōousios*, which is not a philosophical term. It was used to express the biblical idea that Jesus Christ is Lord and God. Bishop Alexander was no philosopher. His sole interest was to save the Church. For if Christ is not God, the entire Christian liturgy which treats him as such becomes a sin against the First Commandment. The *anathematismata* which were added to the Creed in its first form said nothing else. And they do not contain philosophy. Professor Quanbeck is obviously a victim of some obsolete books on the history of dogma. If the Nicene Creed uses concepts like *ousia*, substance, it uses words which were used already in the New Testament. Was the author of Hebrews a philosopher? Athanasius did not go from exile to exile because of a love for the word *homōousios*; in fact, he did not like it and used it sparingly (and never in his early writings), but it summarized briefly the biblical doctrine of the relationship between Father and Son. Quanbeck reveals the deepest reason for his criticism of the allegedly-unbiblical language of the Nicene Creed in the sentence:

> The problems of theology have a certain consistency from age to age, and yet the shift from substantialist, static thinking to developmental, dynamic categories means that every problem appears in a new light and from a different perspective (p 187).

This, then, is the attitude and philosophy of Professor Quanbeck. His developmental, dynamic categories replace what he regards as the substantialist, static thinking of the past. A new philosophy produces a new theology. Every problem appears in a new light and from a different perspective. This, then, applies also to the problem of the Lord's Supper. The old understanding is accused of resting on a substantialist, ontological philosophy. Now we apply the philosophy of our time, Personalism and Existentialism, to the doctrine of the Sacrament, in Arnoldshain, in Oberlin, and now in Princeton and Minneapolis. The gift of the Sacrament is not a 'substance', but the 'person'. A new philosophy has freed us from the *skandalon* which the words of our Lord, 'This is my body', must be to our human reason.

Space does not permit us to discuss the entire content of the book. We must be satisfied with the question: How does this theology understand the one and only question of Marburg 1529? The title *Marburg Revisited* is misleading insofar as the discussion covers the whole range of the issues between the Lutheran and the Reformed churches. Instead of travelling to Marburg and listening attentively to what was said there, these theologians have rather made a quick jet flight over the whole area between Wittenberg and Geneva, high up in the air. They have not seen very much of the issue of Marburg. Clouds seem to have sometimes obscured their sight. There are, of course, some good passages, especially in the Reformed contributions. But the articles could not exhaust so many subjects. The question which we have to ask is the question of Marburg: What did Jesus mean when he said, 'This is my body', and when he made the corresponding statement on his blood?

The answer is distressingly weak. Christ is present in the Word and in the Sacrament.

> The sacrament is a form of visible, enacted word, through which Christ and his saving benefits are effectively offered to men (p 104).
>
> The assurance of his presence is given in the self-witness of Christ in the instituting rite: This is my body; this is my blood. The realization of his presence in the Sacrament is effected by the Holy Spirit through the word.
>
> The significance of Christology in the Lord's Supper is that it provides assurance that it is the total Christ, the divine-human person who is present in the Sacrament, but does not explain how he is present.

This is the answer. The Lutherans who have accepted this document are no longer able to confess with a clear conscience concerning the Sacrament of the Altar: 'It is the true body and blood of Christ . . . ' Individual persons may believe that, but it is not essential for the Sacrament. It cannot, therefore, be the dogma of the church. All that the church can teach is the presence of the person of Christ. 'Christology' may give us the assurance that the Christ present is the total Christ. So we are left with the 'consolations of philosophy' and have no longer the firm foundation of the Word of the Lord himself. Luther never based his doctrine on philosophical-theological speculations, nor has the Lutheran church after him. The one and only basis of the Lutheran doctrine of the Real Presence of the body and blood of Christ has always been the words in which Christ himself once and for all gave the definition of this Sacrament: 'This is my body; this is my blood'.

Marburg Revisited with its papers and recommendations is now before the Lutheran churches in America. No church has so far committed itself to it, but only to its study. It will be put into the hands of all students of theology in the Lutheran and Reformed churches. It will be discussed on all levels of the churches. It will have far-reaching effects. As these discussions will coincide with the discussions which are now going on on a world-wide scale between Lutherans and Reformed, discussions in which the Lutheran churches in Europe have already surrendered the Lutheran doctrine of the Confessions, our brethren in America are facing a tremendous responsibility. It seems that the Lutheran World Federation and the Reformed World Alliance are — as far as their ecclesiastical and theological leadership is concerned — determined to carry out the great union in the spirit of modern ecumenism. So the hour of confession has come for the Lutherans in America — the hour of confession, and not of mere discussion.

No one wants to discourage a serious and thorough-going dialogue between the Lutheran and Reformed churches. On the contrary, we regard that as necessary. But this document cannot be the basis for such a dialogue. It can serve as an instrument to stir up churches and theologians, to help them to realize the great task that lies before them, but it cannot do more. It takes up too many problems, each of which needs a much more elaborate treatment than it could receive here. What we need for a real dialogue is, first of all, a clear statement on the issues to be discussed, a frank realization of the existing agreements and disagreements. What we need, further, is thorough research. It is not enough that two men each write a paper, and that these papers are then discussed and a few theses set up. The problems of sacramental theology must be more thoroughly studied in biblical, historical, and dogmatic research. The philosophical aspect, too, must be investigated much more thoroughly. What is the use of basing our discussions and their result on modern Existentialism, if, as every philosopher knows, existentialist philosophy is already on the way out? There are signs which indicate that the future will belong to a new metaphysics, and this would include a new ontology. Christian theology can make use of many different philosophical systems, using what truth is contained in each of them. But it should never be married to one system, which happens to be in fashion at the time.

Hence, it is our considered opinion that, though *Marburg Revisited* should be read for a start, there should not be a formal discussion of its findings, which have, by the way, no authority whatever. The participants were present as private theologians, and not as representatives of their churches. No one knows who is responsible for the results. There is a list of participants and consultants. But we do not know who was present when a certain 'summary statement' was accepted, nor whether it was accepted unanimously. In the list of the participants we find names of men from very conservative churches with deep dogmatic convictions. Did these men accept the results? If so, in what sense? I cannot imagine that any New Testament scholar is satisfied with the way in which the exegetical problem (which was, after all, the problem of Marburg) was brushed aside. Whoever may be responsible, documents of this nature have no validity in the church unless they are signed. This is a rule of the church of all ages. The creed and the canons of Nicaea had to be signed by all members of the Council. Everyone knows what the signatures under the confessions of the

Reformation have meant. Only in modern ecumenical conferences are resolutions adopted for which nobody is responsible.

8

What the Lutheran churches in America which were involved in these negotiations ought to do, in our opinion, is to bring the semi-official discussions out of the twilight of non-committal ecumenical conversation between private theologians into the daylight of responsible discussions and negotiations from church to church. We are not interested in what this or that professor or pastor thinks, but in the doctrine of their churches. Only then can we find out whether there is still a consensus on a basic doctrine such as the dogma *De coena Domini* among the Lutherans and the Reformed respectively. What we want to know is whether the Lutheran churches in America as churches still confess of the Sacrament of the Altar what our Catechism teaches, or whether the disintegration of the Lutheran doctrine in these churches has reached that degree which we find in European Lutheranism. We are very much concerned. A document published some years ago by the former United Lutheran Church was indicative of such disintegration. What we hear of the younger churches of Lutheran background is also alarming. It seems that the Lutherans in India in their negotiations with the United Church of India, a definitely Reformed body which is now being left even by thousands of Anglicans, the Lutheran *est* has been negotiated away. We ask our brethren in America to understand our deep concern. We refuse to believe that any of the Lutheran churches in America would endorse the results of *Marburg Revisited*, even if private persons accept them.

Why are we so concerned? It is our deep conviction that in defending the literal meaning of 'This is my body', Martin Luther did not defend a theological view of his own or of a theological school, but a basic dogma of the Christian Church. With this *est* the Incarnation stands or falls. And with the reality of the Incarnation stands or falls the Church of Jesus Christ. This is why we are concerned about the development in India. We do not want to make the people of India Lutherans. But we know that the highly-spiritualizing Indian soul needs the real Christ, not Christ as one of the *avatars*, a divine being that for a while descends to the earth later to return to the spiritual and divine world, but Christ Incarnate, the Son of God who accepted real human flesh and who never put aside what he once accepted, Christ who remains our brother in heaven.

This is why we are afraid to take away from India the real Sacrament with its full assurance of the Real Presence of the Incarnate One. We are confirmed in our concern when we read that a Lutheran professor in India has proposed to abolish Christian Baptism as a condition os membership in the Church.

A very similar concern causes us to insist on the *est* when we think of our Reformed brethren. We do not want to make them Lutherans, but to help them to regain what in the tragic history of the Reformation they have lost. The present doctrine of the United Presbyterian Church in the USA is contained in the 'Confession of 1967'.[6]

It is certainly nearer to Zwingli than to Calvin, and reveals, like all modern substitutes for the old confessions, the loss of the old dogmatic substance. We should ask ourselves whether the rise of unhealthy, unevangelical High Church movements, the 'Catholic' revivals in the once Reformed Church of England, but also in many other Protestant churches (including such as claim to be Reformed or Lutheran), is not the reaction to the loss of a Catholic truth. The Lutheran church has often been blamed for having retained in its doctrine of the Real Presence a 'popish remnant'. We should reply: What we have retained, or tried to preserve, is a truth which the Catholic churches in East and West have retained, for with them we are convinced that the Real Presence in the sense that the bread in the Supper is the body of Christ is the doctrine of the New Testament. Whether this is true or not was the issue under discussion at Marburg — the only issue. When Luther's sacramental realism met with Zwingli's spiritualizing, humanistic idealism, it was the realism of the Bible which met with a spiritualizing and rationalizing Christianity which had been a latent danger to the old Christian faith for centuries. This 'flight into reason (*fugere ad rationem*)' had come to the fore in the 11th century with Berengar. This spiritualizing

---

[6]Art. 4, 'The Lord's Supper': 'The Lord's Supper is a celebration of the reconciliation of men with God and with one another, in which they joyfully eat and drink together at the table of their Saviour. Jesus Christ gave his church this remembrance of his dying for sinful men so that by participating in it they have communion with him and with all who shall be gathered to him. *Partaking in him as they eat the bread and drink the wine* in accordance with Christ's appointment, they *receive from the risen and living Lord the benefits of his death and resurrection.* They rejoice in the foretaste of the kingdom which he will bring to consummation at his promised coming, and go out from the Lord's Table with courage and hope for the service to which he has called them.' *The Proposed Book of Confessions of the United Presbyterian Church in the USA* (Philadelphia, 1966), 186.

Christianity found its home later in the Lowlands, from where Cornelius Hoen passed on to Zwingli his doctrine of the merely significative character of the Sacrament. (It is strange to see how in the same country today Roman Catholic theologians try to replace the theory of 'transubstantiation' with their theory of 'transignification'.)

If our Reformed brethren tried to take into account for a moment the possibility that what happened at Marburg was the encounter of a realistic with an idealistic understanding of God's revelation in Christ, they would get a better understanding of Luther's stand at Marburg, even if they could not approve of it. It was perhaps the greatest moment in the tragic days of the colloquy, when the Lutherans, after the discussions had broken down, made their last offer. Since this offer corresponds exactly to what Luther had repeatedly declared to be his condition for a union in the question of the Sacrament, it may be assumed that also here he was the author of the formula. The proposal was that either side should declare:

> We confess that by virtue of the words, 'This is my body', 'This is my blood', the body and the blood are truly — *substantive et essentialiter, non autem quantitative vel qualitative vel localiter* — present and distributed in the Lord's Supper.

Neither at Marburg nor later on any other occasion did Luther demand that his theory on the 'ubiquity' (the term coined by his adversaries) which he had developed to refute those who denied any possibility of the Presence of Christ's body other than the local one, had to be accepted as dogma of the church. Even the *Formula of Concord* did not dogmatize it, but only the sentence

> that God has and knows more ways to be present at a certain place, not only . . . the one which the philosophers call local or spatial (*Sol. Decl. VII,* 97).

What he demanded as necessary was the affirmation that the true body of Christ (which means the body that was born of the Virgin, hung on the cross, and was raised from the grave) was present in virtue of the Words of Institution. This presence was to be understood not as a presence in 'quantity' or 'quality', and not in the sense of a local presence, as medieval theologians had already limited the 'in' and 'under'.[7] In other words, what Luther always demanded was that the words of Christ should be accepted in simple faith, while the *how* remained God's mystery. Oecolampadius was prepared to accept

---

[7]For details, see above, 214 ff.

the proposal. Zwingli could not agree because anything that was called 'substance' was unbearable for him — as for the Zwinglians at all times.

It is this last offer of Luther at Marburg which the Lutheran church has to repeat today in the negotiations and discussions with the Reformed churches. This does not mean that we need only repeat an old formula; we have first to regain the doctrine contained in it for ourselves. We shall never succeed in persuading anyone to accept it because it was Luther's doctrine, or by showing its profound philosophical presuppositions or consequences. The contention will be, as it was at Marburg, a contention about the meaning of the Sacrament in the New Testament.

One does not have to be a Lutheran to believe in the Real Presence. Many a thorough exegete has found in the New Testament the doctrine that bread and wine in the Lord's Supper are the body and blood of Christ. Even modern scholars who reject the doctrine for themselves admit that somewhere in the New Testament this view is present; some find it with Paul, others with John. But since they know only writings and strata of writings in the Bible, and no longer the New Testament as a whole, they do not draw the necessary conclusions from their observation. The day may not be far off when the crisis becomes manifest in which modern theology finds itself because it has lost the authority of the Bible as such. Much more promising than the discussions of our dogmaticians might be a thorough investigation of what the New Testament has to say about the Sacrament. The day when we shall have again a great theology of the New Testament may be nearer than many are inclined to think. And perhaps the time is not far away when Christendom can confess as an ecumenical article of faith concerning the Sacrament of the Altar:

> It is the true body and blood of our Lord Jesus Christ, under the bread and wine, given to us Christians to eat and to drink, instituted by Christ himself.

In fact, this is already the faith of the majority of all Christians on earth.

APPENDIX II

Sanctorum Communio

[This essay, written in German, first appeared in the book *Leuenberg-Konkordie Oder Diskordie?* (Berlin: Die Spur, 1974) in the section headed 'Systematic Theology'. It was first published in English translation (by H. P. Hamann) in the *Lutheran Theological Journal* VIII (August, 1974), 49-60.]

In the old World Conference on Faith and Order (not to be confused with the Commission of Faith and Order of the World Council of Churches), the sound rule obtained that all important documents should be published in Latin and Greek as well as in the three languages of the conference. As long as this rule was kept up, the lack of clarity which attaches to present-day ecumenical documents was avoided, as well as the deliberate ambiguity which is also, unfortunately, often present in them. How important it was for Christendom that the confessional statements of the 16th and 17th centuries right down to the Westminster Confession were available also in Latin, and that theologians of all denominations had the chance to engage in genuine dialogue with one another — a chance which they made very good use of.

It appears that English is becoming the church language of the Western world today; even the *Osservatore Romano* has to appear in an English edition. Now, it is true that English is one of the classic languages of Christendom — we need think only of the English Bible, Cranmer's liturgical texts, and the wonderful language of John Henry Newman. But modern English is too non-committal for dogmatic formulations. Added to this fact is the fatal tendency of modern theology to express its thoughts in continually-new terminology. The church, of course, has to find new terms, and theology may do so, when the old are no longer understood or are no longer adequate. Classic examples for this are the *homoousios* of the Nicene Creed and the struggle for suitable terminology for the trinitarian and christological dogmas (*ousia, hypostasis, essentia, substantia, prosōpon, persona, physis, natura,* and their equivalents in Syriac, Coptic, and Armenian, formed with such labour, and so often doubtful). But a new terminology is permissible only when it serves to clarify, and not to confuse ideas and becloud the truth. Otherwise, we run the risk that our theology becomes what Harnack called 'the systematic abuse of a terminology invented for that very purpose'. This danger is particularly great in the area of present-day ecumenical theology.

An unhappy case of this kind seems to lie behind the *Leuenberg Agreement,* which has no less an aim than to restore church fellowship among the Lutheran, Reformed, and Union churches of Europe. This is a Utopian undertaking in every respect. Such church fellowship is not only impossible; it is a logical absurdity. To search for a new and closer relation between these churches would be both thinkable and praiseworthy. But, however one might call such a relation, the expression 'church fellowship' for it is impossible, since this has a fixed meaning in the teaching and church law of the Lutheran church (and not only in that church), a meaning going back to the earliest church and one deeply rooted in the New Testament. It is the fellowship which, within the one, holy, catholic church, joins believing individuals and their local congregations to the unity of the body of Christ. It is fellowship of the church, not of the churches; unless one understands churches to be local congregations or dioceses, each of which is *the* church of Christ, *the* people of God, in the place concerned (for example, in Jerusalem, in Corinth, in Ephesus, in Rome).

The biblical word for this fellowship is *koinōnia, communio.* This *koinōnia* differs from other fellowships in that it is not of human origin, and in that it reaches beyond the sphere of the earthly and human. This fellowship is not formed by a decision of man's will, nor by a *contrat social*, nor is it an aspect of human religion, as Schleiermacher taught:

> The religious self-consciousness, like every essential element in human nature, leads necessarily in its development to fellowship or communion; a communion which, on the one hand, is variable and fluid, and, on the other hand, has definite limits, i.e., is a Church. (*The Christian Faith*, thesis of paragraph 6; cf paragraph 115, where it is said that 'the Church takes shape through the coming together of regenerate individuals'.)

It, rather, is produced by the divine means of grace, the Word of God and the Sacraments of Christ. 'That which we have seen and heard we proclaim also to you, so that you may have fellowship with us; and our fellowship is with the Father and with his Son Jesus Christ'

(1 John 1:3, see also 6, 7). The Greek word here is *koinōnia*. It is said of the first congregation in Jerusalem, directly after Pentecost and the baptism of the 3,000: 'They devoted themselves to the apostles' teaching and fellowship, to the breaking of bread and the prayers' (Acts 2:42). The fellowship is established by Baptism and finds its concrete expression in the Sacrament of the breaking of bread. This fits to a nicety the language of Paul: God called the believers 'into the fellowship of his Son, Jesus Christ' (1 Cor. 1:9); 'By one Spirit we were baptized into one body . . . and all were made to drink of one Spirit' (1 Cor. 12:13). The connection with the Lord's Supper is quite clear in 1 Cor. 10:16, 17; the *koinōnia* of the body and blood of Christ is one with the *koinōnia* of the church. We shall return to this passage later. That the fellowship of the church is at the same time fellowship with the Father, the Son, and the Holy Spirit is expressed by the apostolic benediction, 2 Cor. 13:14. The question has been asked whether the *koinōnia tou hagiou pneumatos* is a common participation in the Holy Ghost or the fellowship worked by the Holy Ghost. Naturally, it is both. That it is something produced by the Holy Ghost is made sure by 1 Cor. 12:13. The word is also used for the result or confirmation of this Spirit-worked fellowship. Accordingly, the collection which Paul gathered in his heathen-Christian congregations for the poor saints in Jerusalem is *koinōnia* (Rom. 15:26; 2 Cor. 9:13). So also in Heb. 13:16, *koinōnia* refers to the gifts of love within the congregation, while *eupoiia* points to the almsgiving that takes place also outside the congregation. When both are described as *thysia*, the solemn word for sacrifice, then we are reminded of Acts 2:42, where *koinōnia* probably means the offering of gifts in the divine service, so that in this passage we may find for the first time the four basic parts of Christian worship: proclamation of the apostolic Word, the breaking of bread, the offering of gifts or 'communion', and the prayers of the saints. Is this an accident?

The biblical thought of *koinōnia* found its deposit in the Third Article of the Western baptismal creed 'I believe in the Holy Spirit, the holy, catholic church, *sanctorum communionem*, the forgiveness of sins, the resurrection of the body, and the life everlasting'. The phrase, '*sanctorum communionem*', the last addition to the slowly-developing creed, has to be understood from the context. It is not an explicatory apposition to *sanctam ecclesiam catholicam*, as it was long held to be, and as Luther still understood it. It is not a sort of definition of the church. In contrast to the confessions of the East

('God of God, Light of Light, Very God of Very God'), the Roman creed has no explanatory repetitions, but every new concept describes a new reality. *Sanctorum communio* cannot be understood as the 'communion of saints'. In biblical Greek *communio* never means *congregation*. It describes a reality within the church, within the communion of saints. Within the holy Christian church there is a *communio sanctorum*. Now, *sanctorum* can be the genitive either of *sancti*, the holy persons, or of *sancta*, the sanctified or holy things. If an expression with a double meaning occurs in the *Credo*, it may be understood in a double sense, as is the case with a word of the Holy Scripture in a parallel case. So, if we think of the holy persons, it would be a matter of the *koinōnia* which, according to 1 John 1, exists among the members of the Church, just as, for example, the Catholic church understands its teaching concerning the fellowship existing in the three parts of the church: the church militant, the church triumphant, and the church in suffering in purgatory. As much as we Lutheran theologians must reject the teachings of purgatory and the invocation of the saints which Rome erects on its concept of the *sanctorum communio*, just so decidedly we must hold on to the biblical teaching of the *koinōnia* which exists among the members of the Church, as it is taught in 1 John 1 and as it reappears in the *sanctorum communio* of the Creed. Indeed, the use of *ecclēsia* in Heb. 12:23 for the city of the living God, the heavenly Jerusalem, permits us to go beyond the bounds of the earthly Church and, as the Fathers did, to understand all the saints and just men from the beginning of the world as belonging to the *ecclēsia*, and even to include in it the angels themselves and the *virtutes et potestates supernae*, as, for instance, Niceta of Remesiana does in his explanation of the Symbol.[1] He calls this church *sanctorum omnium congregatio,* the congregation of all saints.

> *In hac una ecclesia crede te communionem consecuturum esse sanctorum.* (In this one church believe that you will obtain the communion of the saints.)

The communion of saints is, accordingly, an eschatological possession which is to come the way of the members of the Church. This Church appears on earth in the form of the Catholic church, with which one must be in communion (*'cuius communionem debes firmiter retinere'*). There follows a warning against the pseudo-

---

[1] C.P.Caspari, *Kirchenhistorische Anekdota* I:356; cited by F. Kattenbusch, *Das apostolische Symbol* II:930; see also Werner Elert, *Eucharist and Church Fellowship in the First Four Centuries* (English translation of *Abendmahl und Kirchengemeinschaft*), 215 f.

churches of the heretics and schismatics, who do not belong any longer to that holy church, because under the influence of the demons they believe and live in a way different for the teaching of Christ and the tradition of the apostles.

This understanding of the *communio sanctorum*, based on the ecclesiology of Augustine, is, however, not the original, and therefore also not the only possible, meaning of the expression. There is much evidence that it originally meant the participation in the *sancta*, the consecrated elements in the Lord's Supper, which have become the body and blood of the Lord. This meaning of *sancta* goes back to the liturgies of the Eastern church, where the communion is introduced with *'ta hagia tois hagiois'*.[2] Although the personal understanding of *sanctorum* was dominant in the West, the old meaning was never quite forgotten. Hahn prints a text of the *Credo* in Old French which has our passage in the form: *'la communiun des saintes choses'*, and also refers to a late explanation of the *Credo* in German — it turned up in Ulm — which has the same understanding of *sanctorum communio*.[3]

If this understanding is the right one, then we actually have in the Creed a reference to the Sacrament of the Altar, the absence of which otherwise has often been missed. However, it is in any case contained in the 'communion of saints'. For the *koinōnia* which exists among the believers, the saints according to the New Testament, finds its clearest expression in the fellowship of those who receive the body and blood of the Lord as they assemble around his Table. 'The cup of blessing which we bless, is it not the *koinōnia tou haimatos tou Christou?'* (1 Cor. 10:16). The fellowship is not brought about by the actions of blessing and breaking, but by the content of the cup and the bread: 'For *one* bread (it is), *one* body we are, the many, for we all partake of *one* bread' (v17). The Greek for 'partake of' is *metechomen*, properly translated in the Vulgate as *participamus*, while for *koinōnia tou sōmatos tou Christou* we have *participatio corporis Domini,* and for *koinōnia* in v16 the translation is *communicatio*. The passage shows how closely the idea of the Church as the Body of Christ is tied up with the idea of the sacramental body in the Sacrament. It has rightly been assumed that Paul derived from the Supper the idea peculiar to him of the Church as the Body of Christ. At any rate, the passage 1 Cor. 10:16, 17 shows

---

[2]See References in Kattenbusch, 927 ff; Elert, 13 f; 209-218.

[3]Hahn, *Bibliothek der Symbole,* 3rd ed., 83.

that both meanings of *sanctorum communio* have their root in the phrase *koinōnia tou sōmatos Christou*. We shall have to investigate later how the relation between the *corpus Christi mysticum* and the *corpus sacramentale* is to be determined.

If these remarks are right, then one will no longer be able to say that the understanding of the Words of Institution does not belong to the articles of faith, as the Reformed have emphatically and tirelessly stated ever since Zwingli and Oecolampadius. From the start Luther protested against this to the men of Strasburg, and particularly to Bucer. Bucer continually defended the view that both Luther's and Zwingli's views of the Supper had legitimacy, and should be tolerated in the church. When, at the end of the Marburg Colloquy, Bucer admonished both parties to such toleration with moving and sincere emotion, he had to hear from Luther the fateful words: 'You have a different spirit'. For Luther, the teaching concerning the Lord's Supper was a binding dogma of the church, even though he did not find it expressed in the *Credo*. The Nicene Creed has no parallel to *'sanctorum communio'*, but it reckons Baptism among the articles of faith: *'confiteor unum baptisma in remissionem peccatorum'*. What must be believed and confessed is this: Baptism gives the forgiveness of sins. The question is suggested, by this fact, whether Baptism is not referred to in the Apostles' Creed in the phrase concerning the forgiveness of sins. It was often understood so. For instance, a formula in the Gallican church runs: *'per baptisma sanctum remissionem peccatorum'*;[4] a creedal formula in a manuscript of the 8th/9th century reads: *'remissionem peccatorum sive per baptismum, sive per poenitentiam'*.[5]

If we are to assess rightly these variations, and the uncertainty revealed behind them, then we must consider that the Third Article remained a problem also in the Eastern church. At Nicaea it was considered sufficient to have only: 'And in the Holy Spirit'. The old Nicene Creed is really a binitarian *Credo*. It was only as a result of the great debates concerning the *homōousion* that Athanasius came to the insight that the *homōousion* of the Son was not to be understood apart from the *homōousion* of the Holy Spirit. At the Synod of Alexandria in 362 agreement was reached with the Cappadocians and their teaching that Father, Son, and Holy Spirit were of the **same** essence (*homoios kat' ousian* = *homōousios*) not of **one** essence,

[4] Hahn, 77.
[5] Hahn, 99.

which is what *homoousios* meant originally. This represents a great concession by Athanasius: that one could use *homoousios* in both meanings. To the present day, the fine distinction remains between East and West in the church, that the former understands 'trinity' as 'three-oneness', the latter as 'three-foldness'. The result for the Third Article is to be found in the Constantinopolitan Creed (our Nicene Creed) of 381. Since the Council of Chalcedon accepted both texts, (i.e. the Apostolic and Nicene Creed) as of equal authority, and also recognized the Synod of 381 as an 'ecumenical' synod, it brought the formulation of the Confession to a close. But it still bears about it the character of incompleteness. It lacks, for instance, a clear confession of the *homoousion* of the Holy Spirit. This lack was remedied only by the West in the Athanasian Creed and by the addition of the *filioque*. In one form of the Creed, in the old Irish church, we read:

> *Credo in Spiritum sanctum, deum omnipotentem, habentem substantiam cum patre et filio; sanctam esse ecclesiam, abremissa peccatorum, sanctorum communionem . . .*[6]

It would take us too far to mention other references from the Middle Ages to show how *communio* and *remissio* were related to the Sacraments.

Where else but in the Third Article could a teaching concerning the Sacraments find a place? It is not only the teaching concerning the Church which suggests this position, but the article as a whole, for the Holy Spirit belongs to the 'Last Things'. The Holy Spirit, to be sure, is eternal God, from everlasting to everlasting. As such he has part in the creation and preservation of the world. To him belong both the kingdom of nature and the kingdom of grace. He gives man life (Job 33:4) and understanding (Job 32:8), joy (Ps. 51:13) and wisdom, and leads him on the right path (Ps. 143:10). The extraordinary powers of the warrior, the charismata of artist and ruler, and, above all, the gift of prophecy are his work. Above everything else, the perfection of the end time will bring a full measure of the Spirit for the whole people of God (Isa. 43:4; Joel 3:1, 2). The resurrection of the dead is the Spirit's work (Ezek. 37). With the resurrection of Christ as the firstborn from the dead, the resurrection of all the dead began (1 Cor. 15:21ff). Since then, it is the 'last hour' (1 John 2:18). Now, at the end of the world, the Son of God

---

[6] *abremissa*, late Latin for *abremissio* (cf *missa* for *missio; collecta* for *collectio*), is found also in other forms of the text. Notice the order: the Sacrament of Baptism precedes the Eucharist.

has appeared (Heb. 1:2). Now the prophecy of Joel concerning the outpouring of the Holy Spirit on all the people of God has been fulfilled. The Spirit no longer rests on some few men, on kings and prophets, but on the whole people of God, the whole Church. One can think of church in a general sense. Church is the whole people of God, all saints and believers from the beginning of the world. But the Church of Christ, Church in the proper sense, has existed only since Easter and Pentecost.

Church embraces also the Sacraments. To avoid that ambiguous and so often misused word of ecclesiastical Latin, we should say that Church embraces also Baptism, absolution, and the Lord's Supper. However one wants to name these things, whether one speaks of sacraments with the Latin church or of mysteries with the Eastern church, or whether one includes them with the Word in the collective term 'means of grace', one thing they all have in common: they have eschatological importance. The coming world is anticipated in them. They do not merely describe a divine, heavenly reality; they bestow right now a share in it. The forgiveness of sins, which we receive in Baptism and the absolution, is the anticipation of the acquittal in the Last Judgment. Our death and our resurrection to eternal life have begun already in our baptism (Rom 6:3-11). In the holy Supper Christ comes to us now and gives us a share in the 'messianic' heavenly feast. It would have been better to understand the Sacraments like this, as the anticipation of salvation at the end time, rather than to force them into the scheme or theory of signs. Augustine began this way of thinking. The dominant influence which he attained in the West bequeathed this scheme to all Western churches. Just to give one example, Augustine, in *De civitate Dei* 10,5, calls the visible sacrifice '*invisibilis sacrificii sacramentum, id est, sacrum signum* (the sacrament of the invisible sacrifice, that is, a sacred sign)'.[7] From that time on, medieval theology understood the Sacrament as a sign. Melanchthon still deals with the Sacraments under the title '*De signis*' in the first edition of his *Loci*. Johann Gerhard is the first to abandon treating the Sacrament '*in genere signi*' (Thomas: *Summa theologiae, III, Q. 60, Art. 1*), and to treat it instead '*in genere actionis*'. How dangerous the 'sign theory' is may be seen from Augustine's thought that sacraments belong to the essence of all religions, the true as well as the false. How much misery

[7] MPL (i.e. Migne's edition of the Latin Fathers) 41:282.

and unnecessary struggle, how many misunderstandings and false teachings Christendom would have been spared, if from the start the church had been satisfied to remain with what the Holy Scripture teaches concerning Baptism, absolution, and the Lord's Supper, instead of squeezing these sacred actions into the Procrustes bed of neo-Platonic philosophy.

However, no one was capable of such an action in the fourth century. For the Christian faith had by this entered the higher cultural levels of society, and had accordingly got into the hands of men whose thinking had been formed by the philosophy of late antiquity with its infusion of heathen religiosity. What Augustine said of his own conversion was true in one way or another of all the heathen who found their way to Christ: '*Sero amavi te*'. It was late, indeed, too late, when they came upon the Gospel. And so the great Alexandrines, including that biblical scholar Origen, read the Gospel with late Greek eyes. It is a proof for the indestructible vitality of the divine Word that it lived through this crisis as well. The East never developed a teaching of the Sacrament in the Augustinian-Western sense, partly because it did not have the word 'sacrament'. The Eastern church spoke instead of 'mysteries'. However, that 'sacrament' is the same as 'mystery' was never forgotten by the West. Hugo of St Victor, for instance, still wrote his dogmatic with the title '*De sacramentis*', and in accordance with that title spoke of the Sacrament of the Trinity, and so on. The original difference in meaning between the Latin and the Greek word consists in this, that *sacramentum* (derived from *sacer, sacrare*) points to the action of man, his prayers, sacrifices, etc., while *mystērion* designates the divine secret and what this secret means and conveys.[8] In the Latin of the Middle Ages these words were used promiscuously, probably under the influence of the Vulgate. German Catholics of the present day can still speak of 'receiving the holy secrets (*die heiligen Geheimnisse empfangen*)'.[9]

We have pointed to the linguistic problem because it throws such light on the history of the teachings concerning the Eucharist. The

[8] In late Latin *sacra* becomes a word to describe the cult. The governor of Carthage exhorts the martyrs of Scillium not to say anything derogatory *'de sacris nostris'*, i.e. concerning the heathen state cult (*Passio Scil. 5*). *Sacramentum* seems to have originally meant 'dedication', 'consecration', later the 'military oath' of the recruit, a meaning which was of importance to Zwingli.

[9] The best discussion of the linguistic problem is found in the commentary of the German Edition of Thomas, 30:380 ff.

uncertainty in theology and teaching is in part the result of ambiguity in terminology. However, there is no difference between East and West in the matter concerned. In 'sacrament' and in 'mystery' the reality involved in the body of Christ is the same. It is the body born of his mother Mary, which died on the cross, was buried, arose from the dead, ascended to heaven, and which sits at the right hand of the Father.[10]

This, and this alone, is the dogma of the church concerning the Lord's Supper. It lies behind the *'sanctorum communionem'*. There are two reasons why the dogma was not expressed in an unambiguous article of faith. For one thing, there was no church nor heresy which disputed it. Secondly, it stands in all the liturgies of Christian antiquity.

Now, there have been individual theologians who have doubted or have disputed this fact — but, then, what is there that theologians have not disputed? But there is no eucharistic liturgy which does not contain or presuppose this dogma. The NT itself contains the first traces of Christian eucharistic liturgy. For the four accounts of the institution of the Lord's Supper bear clear marks of liturgical texts. The most ancient fragment, and this goes back to the hoary Aramaic past of the church, is the *marana tha* of 1 Cor. 16:22. This is still found in its Aramaic form in the *Didachē* (ch. 10), while it appears in Greek dress at the end of the *Apocalypse* (22:20): *'erchou Kyrie Iēsou'* — Come, Lord Jesus! It could be that behind the sentence lies a Jewish petition for the coming of the Messiah. This thought is suggested by the custom still observed by Jews and Christians in the East, to leave a vacant seat 'for the Messiah' at festive meals. The fact that in the passages from Paul and John the '*charis*-formula' follows the petition for the coming of the Lord (cf *Didachē* 10), with which the Eucharist begins in the Eastern churches to the present day, could be an indication of such a context. In a very late form, behind which could well lie a Greek text, there is such a petition for the coming of Jesus to his Church as it celebrates the Eucharist. In the Mozarabic Liturgy, as the introduction to the eucharistic prayer, we have the words:

> *Adesto, adesto, Jesu, bone Pontifex, in medio nostri, sicut fuisti in medio discipulorum: sanctifica hanc oblationem: ut sanctificata sumamus per manus*

---

[10] Cf the medieval *'Gott sei gelobet und gebenedeiet'* (O Lord, we praise Thee, bless Thee, and adore Thee), the ideas of which appear in countless liturgies of the East and the West, and which is sung in many languages by the Lutheran church together with the two additional stanzas composed by Luther.

> *sancti angeli tui: Sancte Domine ac redemptor aeterne.* (Be present, be present, among us, Jesus, Thou good High Priest, as Thou wast among Thy disciples: sanctify this offering: as that which has been sanctified may we receive it back through the hands of thy servant, O holy Lord and eternal Redeemer.)[11]

Then follow the Words of Institution, and the *Postpridie*, which begins with the words:

> *Domine Jesu Christe, hanc hostiam vivam illustratione adventus sanctifica . . .* (Lord Jesus Christ, sanctify this living sacrifice by the light of Thy coming . . .).

So the Lord is asked to be among his congregation as he was among his disciples on the occasion of the Last Supper, and to do what he did then, namely sanctify the sacrificial gifts. This 'sanctifying' (*hagiazein, sanctificare*) is plainly more than the sanctifying of common food through the Word of God and prayer (see 1 Tim. 4:5). *Sanctificare* here means 'to consecrate' in our terminology.[12] As it is the Holy Spirit who, in the East, descends upon the sacrificial gifts in the *epiphoitēsis* and makes of them the body and the blood of the Lord, so, in the place just mentioned, Jesus is the Consecrator. He does just what he did at the institution of the Supper: he speaks the Words of Institution and so consecrates the elements. This is the meaning of this old liturgy.

So, then, what makes the Sacrament *sacramentum*, the Mystery *mystērion*, is that bread and wine become the body and blood of Christ. This, nothing else, is the dogma of the church concerning the Lord's Supper. The body and blood of Christ are the *sancta* which are given to the communicants, and which makes them *sancti*, and so binds them together in the unity and communion of the Body of Christ. It is this idea of unity which finds its complete expression in the Highpriestly Prayer of John 17. Hoskyns (*The Fourth Gospel*) rightly calls this prayer the 'prayer of consecration', in which Jesus consecrates himself as the sacrifice, and also offers his disciples and the church of all times to his Father: 'that they may all be one; even as thou, Father, art in me, and I in thee, that they also may be in us . . . I in them and thou in me, that they may become perfectly one' (John 17: 21, 23). Here we have the perfect communion of saints, *sanctorum communio* in the double sense of the words.

---

[11]MPL 85:116.

[12]Compare the prayer to the *sanctificator* which we find in the Roman Offertorium. It seems that the *'Veni sanctificator, omnipotens aeterne Deus, et bendic hoc sacrificium . . . '* is a remnant of an old *epiclesis* to the Spirit. Old Spanish and Gallic forms of the prayer add *Spiritus* or *Paraclite* to the words quoted. *Sanctificator* is a title of the Holy Spirit.

As, in John 17, the eyes of the praying Lord are directed from this world to the future world ('Father, I desire that they also, whom thou hast given me, may be with me where I am, to behold my glory . . .', v24), so the glance upwards to heaven belongs to the essence of the eucharistic liturgy. In most of the liturgies of East and West, the Son speaks the Words of Institution *'elevatis oculis',* with eyes uplifted to God, his almighty Father, just as in John 17:1 the upward glance to heaven introduces the great prayer. That heaven and earth, so to say, become one in the Eucharist, is one of the main thoughts in the great liturgical chapter, Rev.4. E. Peterson (*Das Buch von den Engeln*) has shown the parallel that exists down to details. So, too, the Sanctus belongs to the earthly service as it does to the heavenly. As Isaiah on the occasion of his call heard the Sanctus from the mouths of the seraphim surrounding the throne of God, so the same Sanctus is heard in Rev. 4:8 in its NT form ('. . . who was and is and is to come'). The Sanctus is the hymn of praise which the angels sing before God 'in never-silent theologies' (so the Greek liturgies). It is sung in the presence of God. Isaiah heard it in the temple of Jerusalem, where Yahweh's *kabod* (*doxa*, glory) dwelt. The triple Holy! is now referred to the Triune God. The Lord, whose praise is sung, is he who was and is and is to come. It was, according to John 12:41, Christ's glory which the prophet saw. How indissolubly faith in the Father Almighty and the confession of the full divinity of Christ belong together is seen in a passage like Rev. 5:13: 'To him who sits upon the throne and to the Lamb be blessing and honour and glory and might for ever and ever!', with which we must compare Rev. 4:11: 'Worthy art thou, our Lord and God . . .' and 5:12: 'Worthy is the Lamb who was slain . . .'

The Sanctus of Isaiah 6 begins to appear in the worship of the synagogue in the second Christian century, possibly as a result of Christian influence.[13] That it was used in the most ancient congregation at Rome, and that in connection with Dan. 7:10, is seen from 1 Clem. 34:6 f:

> Ten thousand times ten thousand stood ready before Him, and thousand times one thousand ministered to Him, and cried out: 'Holy, Holy, Holy is the Lord of hosts; the whole creation is replete with His splendour'. And so we, too, being dutifully assembled with one accord, should, as with one voice, cry out to

[13]The best discussion of the problem of the Jewish Kedushshah and its relation to the Sanctus of the church one will find in Jungmann, *The Mass of the Roman Rite. Missarum Sollemnia* II, 132 f. The Christian use in the liturgy seems to have been the model.

> Him earnestly, so that we may participate in His great and glorious promises. For it is said: 'Eye has not seen, and ear has not heard, and heart of man has not conceived, what He has prepared for those that await Him patiently'.[14]

That this use of the OT passage(s) is not yet part of the eucharistic liturgy is shown by the fact that there is no question here of an identification of the *Kyrios* with Jesus Christ, also from the fact that there is no hint of the coming of the Lord and no petition for that coming. There still remains the rift between heaven and earth; the Hosanna is still missing, with which the Church greets the One who is coming (Rev. 4:8). The text of 1 Clem. 34 is older than the great liturgical chapter of Rev. 4. Which is not to say that the earliest church at Rome did not know of the Real Presence. After all, the letter of St Ignatius to the Romans (7:3) contains one of those passages in which the bishop and martyr speaks of the flesh and blood of Christ, and this is plainly an allusion to John 6:53:

> Bread of God is what I desire; that is, the flesh of Jesus Christ, who was of the seed of David; and for my drink I desire His blood, that is, incorruptible love.[14]

Without this realistic understanding of the Sacrament, the standing Jewish and heathen reproach of ritual murder in the Christian *agapē* could hardly be understandable.

It would take us too far, if we were to pursue further the history of the eucharistic liturgy, in which the dogma of the Lord's Supper found its complete expression. One must experience the moving prayers of the Irish church, the doxologies in which the Church on earth becomes one with the Church in heaven, the solemn hymns in so many languages, in order to understand that it is in this Sacrament that the heart of the church beats. That this history was also the history of serious aberrations, even of an occasional return to heathenism — who would want to dispute this? Who would want to dispute the fact that reforms were necessary again and again, and that often enough a necessary reformation degenerated into an unnecessary revolution? That did not happen only in the 16th century; it happened in our own age, a time of the flowering of scientific and artistic study of the liturgy, when the Second Vatican Council carried through a reform of the Roman mass, at which no less a personage than St Zwingli seems to have acted as sponsor. But, taken as a whole, the history of the eucharistic liturgy is the very heart of church history.

---

[14]Translations by James A. Kleist, *The Epistles of St Clement of Rome and St Ignatius of Antioch* (Westminster, Maryland: The Newman Bookshop, 1946).

What does the church do anyway? is the question of men today as it was at all times in the past. It prays. The *ecclesia orans* is one of the recurring themes in the art of the early church. The church prays. It did this at the beginning. 'All these with one accord devoted themselves to prayer' (Acts 1:14) — this is the description of the first believers after the Ascension. 'And they devoted themselves to the apostles' teaching and fellowship, to the breaking of bread and the prayers' (Acts 2:42) are words referring to the Pentecost church. 'And day by day, attending the temple together and breaking bread in their homes, they partook of food . . . praising God and having favour with all the people' (Acts 2:46, 47). They founded no mission society, organized no inner mission venture, and wrote no books on 'dynamic evangelism'. Instead, they celebrated the Sacrament, and prayed without ceasing. 'And the Lord added to their number day by day those who were being saved' (Acts 2:47). And they kept on praying. The chief of the apostles was imprisoned, 'but earnest prayer for him was made to God by the church', till the chains fell from his hands and the door of the prison was opened (Acts 12:5 - 11). And so it went on. What does the church do? What could it do in those last years of Jerusalem to solve the problem of Palestine — when the politically-great powers had tried in vain for centuries to solve it? What could the church do to prevent the destruction of Rome and the priceless treasures of ancient culture? Instead of holding world conferences and engaging in endless debates over the questions of church and culture, it prayed without ceasing and sang the *Te Deum* on the ruins of a collapsing world. None of its prayers was in vain; they have mounted to heaven, even though their sound has faded away on earth. Only fragments have been preserved of the great liturgical books of the ancient churches in the languages of the West. Only odd remnants have come down to us, to be still used in the small sections of ancient Christendom which have survived the attack of Islam. The devotional literature of recent centuries pales in comparison with the fervency, the splendour, and the wonderful language of what is available to us of these treasures in Greek and Latin. There is no human concern, no matter how great or how small, that does not find moving expression in these prayers. These prayers always provide the frame for the same things: the altar where they are spoken, the *maranatha* or the petition for the coming of the Lord in the Sacrament as an anticipation of the *parousia*, the Sanctus and the Words of Institution. Perhaps the faith in the Real Presence can be fully understood only when these prayers are understood. Here God is present, God the Triune, Father, Son, and Holy Spirit. Here all philosophy is at an end. Here is what the ancient church called *theologia*, the praise of God, in the sense of John, whom the church named the 'theologian'. This is not a theology of mysteries in the sense of heathen or semi-heathen mysticism. It is certainly not a divine something that is present here, a supernatural reality which we label divine, and which is our own resemblance to God at bottom. Christ does not merely appear as a man like angels in the Old Testament or an Hindu *avatar*, like Krishna in the *Bhagavad-Gita*. He is no God in human form, a form which he later puts aside in order to return into the divine world of the Spirit. The resurrected and exalted One remains the incarnate One, as he remains the crucified One. '*Quod semel assumpsit, numquam deposuit* (What he once took on he never put aside)' — as we theologians say. This truth of a real incarnation finds its complete expression in the fact that he gives us his true body and true blood to eat and to drink, with the result that the *koinōnia*, the fellowship, which we have with him in the Sacrament is not merely something 'purely spiritual'. That the Lutheran church took over this teaching of the Greek Fathers is quite clear from the citations which the *Apology* for the 10th Article in the *Augsburg Confession* adduces:

> A little later he says, 'Therefore we must consider that Christ is in us, not only according to the habit which we understand as love, but also by a natural participation'.[15]

It is not possible to go further into the liturgy as the source of the dogma of the Lord's Supper. One point only needs a short consideration: the reception of the communion. The introductory prayers, the formula of distribution, and the answer of the communicants are an unambiguous attestation to the faith in the Real Presence. A few examples must suffice. At the communion of the clergy in the liturgy of St Mark, the priest says:

> Behold, it has been hallowed and perfected, and has become the body and blood of our Lord and God and Saviour, and the sacred things are distributed to the saints'.[16]

The formula of distribution has the very old wording: '*sōma Christou*

---

[15] *Die Bekenntnisschriften der evangelisch-lutherischen Kirche* (Gottingen: Vandenhoeck & Ruprecht), 248: 25 ff. The translation from Theodore G. Tappert, *The Book of Concord*, 179. See the whole passage and the citations from Theophylact and Cyril of Alexandria and other references.

[16] F. E. Brightman, *Liturgies Eastern and Western* (Oxford: Clarendon Press, 1896), 139.

(The body of Christ)'.[17] The liturgy of St Mark has the longer form: 'The holy body of our Lord and God and Saviour, Jesus Christ. The precious blood . . .' Under the influence of the East we find the same formula in the Latin liturgies. Augustine is our witness for Africa; the Mozarabic liturgy and that of Milan vary only slightly.[18] The answer of the communicant is regularly: 'Amen'. Ambrose explains (see note 18, the second reference) the seriousness of this Amen: 'That is true, this I believe'. In many liturgies of the East the Words of Institution spoken in a loud voice were originally confirmed by the Amen of the congregation.[19] The liturgy of St Chrysostom indicates to us how seriously the church took this Amen by the confession which precedes the reception of the elements. It is spoken by every individual, by the priest before he communes, then by the deacon when he receives the elements from the hands of the priest, and finally by all the communicants speaking together. It begins with the words: 'I believe and confess' and contains the sentence: 'I believe that just this is Thy immaculate body, just this is Thy precious blood'. A particularly weighty confession of this kind can be found in a text of the liturgy of the Coptic Jacobites:

> The body and blood of Emmanuel our God this is in truth. Amen. I believe, I believe, I believe and confess unto the last breath that this is the quickening flesh which Thine only-begotten Son our Lord and our God and our Saviour Jesus Christ took of the lady of us all the holy theotokos S. Mary: He made it one with His godhead without confusion and without mixture and without alteration. Having confessed the good confession before Pontius Pilate He gave it also for us on the holy tree of the cross by His own will, Himself for us all. I verily believe that His godhead was not severed from his manhood for ONE MOMENT nor for THE TWINKLING OF AN EYE. It is given for us to be salvation and forgiveness of sins and life everlasting to them that shall receive of it. I believe that this is so in truth. Amen.

Then the deacon says: 'Amen amen amen: I believe, I believe, I believe that this is so in truth. Amen.'[20]

This text from an old Monophysite church shows the anti-Chalcedonian direction of this church, but the dogma of the Lord's

---

[17] Hugo Duensing, *Der Aethiopische Text der Kirchenordnung des Hippolyt* (Gottingen: Vandenhoeck & Ruprecht, 1946) 61:14 ff; Edgar Hennecke, *Neutestamentliche Apokryphen*, 2nd ed., 580; *Apostolic Constitutions* VIII, 13.

[18] Brightman, 140; Ambrose, *De mysteriis*, 9:54; *De sacramentis*, IV, 5:25.

[19] It also happened that the first part of the *verba testamenti* was spoken softly while only the second part was spoken aloud. The Amen in that case followed the second part. See the fragment of an old liturgy from South Italy in C.A. Swainson, *The Greek Liturgies* (Cambridge: University Press, 1884).

[20] Brightman, 185.

Supper is unaffected by that fact. It is a noteworthy fact that Orthodox, Monophysites, and Nestorians show no difference in eucharistic teaching in their liturgies, however much they might have differed in other doctrines. The mass, as it was celebrated in the Nestorian churches of Persia, is the same as that of the Orthodox imperial church. How earnestly the Eastern Syriac church — the most widespread of all churches for centuries in the Middle Ages, extending to South India and China — how earnestly this church took the 'sanctifying' of the elements is shown by a recently-found instruction of Theodore of Mopsuestia, who was the great biblical scholar of the Syrian church:

> When the priest distributes, he says: 'The body of Christ . . . '; and therefore you say after him: 'Amen!' But as for you when you have received the body with your hands, you incline your head. . . With true and deep love you press that body to your eyes, kiss it, and address to it your prayers as to our Lord Jesus, who is near you.[21]

This, then, is the dogma of the ancient church concerning the Lord's Supper: Bread and wine in the Supper are, after the consecration, the body and blood of the Lord. Nothing more? No; nothing more. Naturally, there are questions to which we should like the answers. The one thing that the liturgy has to say besides is that the presence is worked through the petition for the Holy Ghost who descends upon the gifts and, in doing so, 'changes' them into the body and blood of the Lord. The technical expression of the Greek liturgy for this action is *metaballein*, in Latin *mutare*. The elements become, then, what they were not before. The ancient church, however, does not know of any definition of this change analogous to the Roman transubstantiation. The Eastern church took over this teaching under the influence of Rome, and called it *metousiōsis*. But this was only in the Middle Ages. It never became a binding dogma there. In any case, this would have been impossible, because a dogma is something that could be accepted only by the whole church as represented in an ecumenical council. None of the seven recognized councils did this, apart from an indirect decision of the Second Council of Nicaea in 787. This synod rejected a decision of an iconoclastic Synod of Constantinople (754), which had declared the consecrated elements to be the only permissible images (icons) in the church. This decision confirmed the explanation so often made by

[21] This Syrian text, published by A. Mingano (1933) has been translated and published in German, with an Introduction by H. Lietzmann in the *Sitzungsberichte der Berliner Akademie 1933*. The citation from p 13 (925).

the Greek Fathers, that bread and wine before the consecration could be regarded as a likeness (*typos, antitypos*) of the body and blood, but not the consecrated bread and wine, for these had become truly the body and blood of the Lord.[22]

The Fathers thought about this wonder just as much as theologians of all periods. They advanced theological theories about it, but the teaching of the church was unaffected by them. It is a serious mistake in our text-books of the History of Dogma that they hardly make a distinction any more between dogma and theological opinion (*theologoumenon*), between teaching which the church confesses *magno consensu* and theological theories which men (that is, more-or-less pious and more-or-less learned theologians) expound. Since Justin, and his pupil Irenaeus, the wonder of the Incarnation has been used to explain the miracle of the Supper. As the Logos assumed flesh, so bread and wine gain a divine quality by means of the eucharistic prayer (Justin, *Apology* I, 61) or of the *epiclēsis* (Irenaeus,*Adv. haer.* IV, 18:5), and so become bearers of the body and the blood of Christ. It is impossible to describe these individual thoughts as 'realistic' or 'symbolic', using these terms in their modern sense, since the original thoughts were clothed in the language and thought world of the mysteries. Wherever neo-Platonism determines theological thinking, as in the case of Augustine, there the symbolic-intellectual side becomes prominent; but one must beware of applying the categories of later centuries to the ancient church and its theology. We should also ponder the fact that the later christological schools all presuppose the same liturgy. The great theologian of the school of Antioch, Theodore of Mopsuestia, compares the occurrence of the coming of the Holy Spirit with the resurrection of Christ — the one is as real for him as the other. As there were different views concerning infant baptism in the ancient church, so there were different theological opinions about the understanding of the Eucharist. But, just as the baptismal liturgy was the same, whether an adult or an infant was baptized,[23] and as no one disputed the validity of infant baptism, so

[22] John of Damascus, *De fide orthodoxa* IV, 13: 'But if some have called the bread and wine likenesses of the body and blood of the Lord, like Basilius, they were speaking of these things not after the consecration, but before it. They used that designation also for the sacrificial gifts (i.e. what the congregation placed on the altar).' Cf Cyril of Jerusalem, *Cat. myst.*, 1:7; 5:6 — '*antitypa*' is even used in the *epiclesis* of the liturgy of St Basil. The use of the word involved no loss of the realistic understanding.

[23] The one exception is offered by the Nestorian Church, which possessed a special liturgy for the baptism of infants.

all received the Eucharist with the same formula of distribution: 'The body of Christ . . . the blood of Christ', and all pronounced with the church of all ages the Amen of faith.

Credo sanctorum communionem. Sancta sanctis, ta hagia tois hagiois! The whole secret of the biblical concept of *koinōnia* is contained in these sentences. They attest the inseparable connection between church and the Lord's Supper, between church fellowship and altar fellowship. The Lord's congregation gathers around his table, in order to become one with him through the reception of his true body and blood. Church fellowship is not established 'through the coming together of regenerate individuals to form a system of mutual interaction and co-operation', as Pietism held, and as Schleiermacher, that 'Moravian of a higher order (*Herrnhuter höherer Ordnung*)' formulated it.[24] Nor is it based on common philosophical convictions, as the enlightenment of all periods has held. As the Body of Christ, it is a fellowship *sui generis*, a unique fellowship, which cannot be made intelligible either in psychological or in sociological categories. From the point of view of the history of religion, it is also without parallel. The 'congregation', in which the convert to Buddhism seeks refuge, is not something that could be called the body of Buddha. The sacrifices, sacred meals, and other rites of the heathenism of Greece and Rome, the resemblance of which to the Christian Sacraments attracted the attention of ancient opponents of the church before it struck modern historians, explain at bottom nothing more than the truth that 'every dogma is as old as the world'. Church fellowship, again, is not what modern 'ecumenical' theology, including that of churches which should know better, reads in the 17th chapter of the Fourth Gospel or the 4th chapter of the Epistle to the Ephesians, in order to proclaim it as the saving Gospel of our day. I mean the wonderful organization which would come into being, if the hundreds of churches which belong to the World Council of Churches would embrace one another tomorrow with 'this kiss of the whole world'. This kiss would not be 'the holy kiss' with which the celebration of the Eucharist began in the New Testament church, but another kiss of which the New Testament also has something to say. It would be a riddle why so many earnest Christians of all confessions could have fallen victims of such an error, if we did not know of the serious and infectious

---

[24]*The Christian Faith,* paragraph 115.

spiritual disease of chiliasm. The unity of the church of which the Lord speaks in John 17, for which there are no earthly parallels and which is not to be defined in any theology, is the true *'ut omnes unum sint'* understood in accordance with the analogy of faith: that they may all be one; even as thou, Father, art in me, and I in thee, that they also may be in us, so that the world may believe that thou hast sent me' (v 21). The 'world' is obviously not the sum of all men who would just happen to be living on earth on the day of the final fulfilment of this wish. It means either the full number of those whom the Father has given the Son out of the world (17:2, 6), or it means the world at its end. In accordance with the New Testament, there can be no talk of a time in the course of world history when unbelief, and sin with it, have disappeared from the world of men. While the world lasts, the *una sancta* and the *communio sanctorum* remain articles of faith.

Topical Index

Index of Scripture Passages

ACTS

ROMANS

1 CORINTHIANS

2 CORINTHIANS

GALATIANS

Index of Modern Authors